MW01120570

Intimate Partner Violence in LGBTQ Lives

Routledge Research in Gender and Society

Intimate Partner Violence in LGBTQ Lives

Edited by Janice L. Ristock

Routledge
Taylor & Francis Group
New York   London

First published 2011
by Routledge
270 Madison Avenue, New York, NY 10016

Simultaneously published in the UK
by Routledge
2 Park Square, Milton Park, Abingdon, Oxon OX14 4RN

Routledge is an imprint of the Taylor & Francis Group, an informa business

Typeset in Sabon by IBT Global.
Printed and bound in the United States of America on acid-free paper by IBT Global.

Library of Congress Cataloging-in-Publication Data
Ristock, Janice Lynn
  Intimate partner violence in LGBTQ lives / edited by Janice L. Ristock.
    p. cm. — (Routledge research in gender and society ; 28)
  Includes bibliographical references and index.
  1. Intimate partner violence   2. Same-sex partner abuse   3. Lesbians   4. Bisexuals
5. Transgender people.   6. Gays. I. Ristock, Janice L. (Janice Lynn)
  HV6626.I5836 2011
  362'.8—dc22
  2010038730

ISBN13: 978-0-415-99879-6 (hbk)
ISBN13: 978-0-203-82897-7 (ebk)

Contents

1 Introduction

Intimate Partner Violence in LGBTQ Lives

Janice L. Ristock

A sensationalized headline about violence in same-sex relationships appeared in the Canadian national newspaper *The Globe and Mail*: "A skeleton that's still in the closet: Domestic violence is more widespread among same-sex couples than straights" (Anderssen 2008). There was a full two-page story in the newspaper that was based on the results of a Statistics Canada report on violence and victimization. On the one hand, relationship violence is a serious issue and it was powerful to read about the needs of a small population covered in a national newspaper, but on the other hand the headline reflected an underlying pathologizing discourse that represents lesbian/gay/bisexual/transgender/queer (LGBTQ) people as not just facing issues similar to those of straight people—but even *worse*. This kind of mainstreaming of LGBTQ issues serves more to exploit an already marginalized subpopulation than to integrate the issue of same-sex intimate partner violence into public discourse about relationships and family life, and offers little insight into the specific contexts of life for LGBTQ people.

It was, however, more than a sensationalized headline: the story was based on the results of a Statistics Canada survey on violence and victimization that for the first time asked respondents to identify their sexual orientation. With its large sample size of 23,766 randomly selected respondents, it seemed authoritative, although buried in the story was the figure that only 356 of those respondents identified as gay, lesbian or bisexual (they did not ask about transgendered identities). The survey asked about experiences of violence in relationships as well as violence and discrimination in public settings. They found, not surprisingly, that gays, lesbians, and bisexuals reported higher rates of violent victimization (sexual and physical assault and robbery) and discrimination than their heterosexual counterparts, which is consistent with other social science studies that report high rates of violence experienced by LGBTQ people. For example, survey research has found that 20% of women and 25% of men have experienced victimization based on their sexual orientation and another study found 60% of all transsexual/ transgender people have been victimized by hate violence (Ristock and Timbang 2005).

The headline news, though, was that Statistics Canada found that 15% of gay men and lesbians and 28% of bisexuals reported being abused by a partner in the last five years, in comparison to only 7% of heterosexuals. The message seemed clear: an impressively large Statistics Canada study had proven that LGBTQ relationships are much more violent than straight ones. The story suggested that the odds were one in six or seven of being victimized if one were in a same-sex relationship, but there are many problems with these truth claims.

First and foremost, they did not ask survey respondents if the abuse they were reporting actually took place within a same-sex relationship, or in an earlier, or current, straight one. So we have to ask: What do these statistics really tell us? In this study, higher rates of victimization were indeed reported by gay, lesbian, and bisexual people, but we cannot say that violence in same-sex relationships is more widespread because we do not know that the violence they reported in this survey occurred in a same-sex relationship.

Further, unlike other surveys, in this one there was no differentiation between types of violence (physical, emotional, sexual). Nor was there any attention to gender (differing experiences of gay men, lesbians, bisexual women, bisexual men). Buried in a footnote in the original report, and nowhere to be seen in the newspaper story, is the disclosure that LGB female respondents were combined with LGB male respondents in this huge study because there were not enough lesbians to meet the criteria (typically 25) for conducting statistically significant analysis.

Other large comparative survey studies that include lesbians, gays, and bisexuals have paid attention to differences. A report based on the U.S. National Violence Against Women Survey (Tjaden and Thoennes 2000) compared intimate partner victimization rates between same-sex and opposite sex couples. They conducted a telephone survey with a nationally representative sample of 8,000 women and 8,000 men about their experiences as victims of various forms of violence including intimate partner violence. They found that women living with female intimate partners experience less intimate partner violence than women living with male intimate partners. Nearly 25% of surveyed women said they were raped and/or physically assaulted by their male partner. Slightly more than 11% of the women who lived with a woman reported being raped, physically assaulted, and/or stalked by their female intimate partner. On the other hand, men living with male intimate partners reported more violence than men who lived with female intimate partners. Approximately 15% of the men who have lived with a male intimate partner reported being raped, physically assaulted, and/or stalked by a male partner while 7.7% of men who lived with women reported such violence by their female partner.

We know from other research that there are some specific abusive behaviors that reflect a larger context of homophobia, biphobia, transphobia, and heterosexism surrounding LGBTQ relationships. These behaviors include, for example, threats to reveal the sexual or gender identity of a partner to one's boss, landlord, or family member; threats to jeopardize custody of children because of a person's sexual or gender identity; threats to jeopardize immigration because of sexual orientation, and/or threats to reveal the HIV/AIDS status of a partner (Ristock and Timbang 2005). The impact of this larger context on LGBTQ lives cannot be underestimated.

The patterns and differences in experiences of violence in heterosexual and LGBTQ relationships need to be carefully examined (and the experiences of transgender persons need to be included) if our motive is to develop the best understandings, interventions, and prevention strategies. It has been my view, based on my research and community-based work on this issue, that all relationship violence is not the same, and that we can therefore not treat all cases of relationship violence as equivalent and interchangeable (Ristock 2002). While a few studies have reported that many LGBTQ peoples' perceptions are that violence in same sex relationships is the same as violence in heterosexual relationships (Distefano 2009: Hester and Donovan 2009) we have yet to research and fully interrogate the impact of differing levels of severity and types of abuse and the differing motivational factors for abusive behaviors. A recent study by Amanda Robinson and James Rowlands (2009) for example, exposes the differing risk profiles of gay male victimization and lesbian perpetration of violence that is currently not captured by generic models of risk assessment used in domestic violence agencies that assume homogeneity in experiences.

It is encouraging that several important studies have been conducted in a number of different countries that show the need to consider the specific contexts and spaces in which people experience relationship violence (see for example, Distefano 2009; Holmes 2009; Irwin 2008). Research has been exploring the impact of contexts such as one or both partners dealing with a stigmatized illness such as HIV/AIDS; the effects of alcohol and drug use; social isolation in rural communities; experiences of dislocation as recent immigrants; and experiences of the combined effects of racism, classism, and violence by intimate partners, by communities, and by the state. Although these differing contexts and spaces are not exhaustive and may overlap with one another, they reveal the ways that violence is connected to structural factors that create and sustain inequalities and disadvantages (Ristock and Timbang 2005).

Beth E. Richie (2005) reminds us of the importance of examining social, political, historical, and geographic contexts when she states:

> [I]s partner abuse different for lesbians when those relationships are not even recognized by the state? How does federalism leave Native women vulnerable to abuse on reservations in this country? What is the relationship between U.S.-sponsored war in developing countries and violence against women abroad as well as in the United States . . . By not even raising complex issues, we seriously threaten the authenticity,

the legitimacy and relevance of the anti-violence movement and the success we ascribe to it. (xvi)

This volume raises complex issues and brings together a collection of innovative research and community practice in the area of intimate partner violence (IPV) that is specific to the lives of LGBTQ people. While research on same-sex partner violence has been steadily increasing since the late 1980s, the majority of the literature focuses on lesbian couples, and mainly considers the experiences and needs of those who have been victimized, while very little work addresses trans experiences or those who engage in abusive behaviors. The field remains, at best, an "add on" to the field of heterosexual domestic violence, in part because the pattern of male violence against women remains so strong, but also because a focus on queer lives continues to be at the margins of most academic research. Attention to violence in LGBTQ relationships raises critical questions about the usefulness of the dominant gender paradigm used to understand heterosexual domestic violence, challenges binary categories of gender (male/female) and sexual identity (gay/straight) and raises many complexities about how to best categorize, understand, and respond to violence in peoples' relationships. These questions are addressed in differing ways by the authors in this collection.

This volume brings forward innovative, previously unpublished contributions that are organized around three central themes: framing and conceptualizing violence; exploring the lived experiences of violence; and responding to violence. It includes both conceptual and empirical work; a range of disciplinary and theoretical perspectives; and contributions from academics, practitioners, and activists.

Part I begins by exploring ways of framing the issue of intimate partner violence in LGBTQ lives. In looking at the historical conceptualizations of partner violence we have certainly moved a long way from the issue of "wife assault" as it was once called 35–40 years ago, but debates on how to best name and categorize experiences of violence remain. The terms "domestic violence" and "intimate partner violence" (IPV) are acknowledged as troublesome even though they are used throughout this volume. Both terms have been criticized for reinforcing a public/private dichotomy that makes visible certain types of violence (private, in the home, in certain types of relationships) while erasing other forms of violence (state violence, colonialism, racialized violence). Further, while naming relationship violence in LGBTQ lives as something different from heterosexual IPV can expose the normative assumptions built into the dominant paradigms of the field, using the unified category of "LGBTQ" partner violence can minimize the specificity of experiences of, for example, gay men of color, Aboriginal lesbians, and trans people. Of course the language of same-sex partner can be, as Durish states in her chapter "problematic at best and offensive at worst" given that the term conflates gender and sexual orientation.

Considering how best to frame and conceptualize intimate partner violence then, requires us to think critically about the assumptions embedded in our language and requires us to be more aware of the limitations of what we are able to see and know as a result of our framings.

The first chapter in this part, written by Kierrynn Davis and Nel Glass, takes up the "similarity versus differences" debate in which some research and community groups argue that the extent, nature, and consequences of violence in the lives of heterosexual and same-sex couples is the same while others are critical of this as an additive and homogenizing view that ignores key differences in experiences and socio-historical contexts that affect people's experiences. Using a postmodern intersectional framework, Davis and Glass argue for the need to move beyond heteronormative constructions of violence. Using three different women's stories of lesbian relationship violence, their analysis considers the intersection of both the micro and macro physics of power and control within the three relationships and within the responses from communities. What their analysis brings forward is the different dimensions of abuse that would have remained masked had a heteronormative gaze been maintained. The chapter by Diane Hiebert-Murphy, Janice Ristock and Douglas Brownridge critically interrogates the construct of being "at risk" for violence that is often used as a framework for understanding partner violence. Drawing on qualitative interviews where women in same sex relationships spoke about their perceptions of what it means to be "at risk" for violence, their chapter stresses the need to consider the differing social locations and the broader social context that might place women at risk for violence. An intersectionality framework that challenges us to move away from acknowledging only one pattern of IPV and from relying on either/or binary thinking is considered in relation to a framework of risk. The final chapter in Part I challenges the convenient use of an LGBTQ lens to show that we cannot homogenize queer lives when speaking about LGBTQ partner violence. Joshua Goldberg and Caroline White further trouble our understanding of both sexuality and gender in their critical reflections on their experiences as educators in the field of trans anti-violence. Their chapter raises provocative questions about how and where transgender lives fit in research, theorizing, and community practice in the field of IPV when we insist on relying on established binary categories of same-sex and heterosexual relationships.

The second part of the volume takes a closer look at the range and diversity of LGBTQ lives and experiences of violence. It brings forward cutting edge research (both qualitative and survey research) in Canada, the United States, the United Kingdom, and Australia. The authors of the chapters represent different disciplines (social work, nursing, psychology, policy studies) and community organizations. Some chapters demonstrate the need to understand the differing contexts in which violence occurs, while others pay attention to the impact of dominate discourses on relationship violence. The chapter by Catherine Donovan and Marianne Hester explores "discourses of love" that cut across gender and sexuality in their examination of abuse stories of heterosexual, gay, and lesbian relationships. They argue that to understand the dynamics of domestic violence it may be more necessary to see who is doing the "emotion work" and who is exploiting those feelings and practices of love in the relationship. Maurice Poon examines the dominant discourses and constructions of "victim and perpetrator" in the literature on gay male partner abuse. In particular he exposes the focus on individual pathology that permeates the area, making it difficult to fully understand a range of contextual factors that contribute to abusive behavior. Carroll Smith's chapter presents the narratives of twelve lesbians who had formerly abused their partners. Resisting overly simplistic binaries of good/bad, innocent/evil when analyzing their narratives, Smith provides an intimate portrayal of the women and conveys the complexities in each of their lives, reminding us that there is not one construct of an abusive person. Adding to this focus on how we understand perpetrators is the chapter by Nicola Brown who explores partner abuse in trans communities. In examining trans people as both victims and perpetrators of relationship violence, Brown's research, like Smith's and Poon's, disrupts the binaries of victim/abuser, powerless/powerful and calls for greater attention to the complexity of power relations in abusive relationships. What stands out is that some of her participants could not even conceptualize their trans partner's behavior as abusive because they saw him as socially oppressed and without power, and in the dominant gender-based paradigm it is only those in positions of power who are abusive. Interestingly, Jesmen Mendoza then examines the role of minority stress in gay men's experiences of relationship violence and reports on his survey research findings that internalized homophobia, discrimination, and stigma all seem to contribute to gay men's use of violence towards their partners. Finally, the chapter by David Pantalone, Keren Lehavot, Jane Simoni and Karina Walters reports on a qualitative study that examines relationship violence experienced by sexual minority men living with HIV. In exploring the "pathways" that led to their abuse experiences and to the vulnerability to HIV, the men's narratives reveal the impact of structural factors such as poverty and a context of trauma throughout their lives that included childhood instability, exposure to violence (in communities, in families, on the street), rejection due to their sexual or gender minority status, and mental health issues.

The final part, "Responding to Relationship Violence", addresses the ethical challenges of responding to the diverse range of experiences that are so clearly illuminated by the chapters in Part II. Here contributors write from differing locations as community educators, service providers, counselors, researchers, and activists. They bring forward many important initiatives that have been developed to respond to IPV while also being aware of the limitations of these efforts to address those at the margins of mainstream, urban LGBTQ communities. Cindy Holmes critically reflects on her work as an educator in an innovative community-based violence prevention program that delivered a healthy relationship curriculum for queer women. Her chapter examines how hegemonic norms, neo liberal discourses, and technologies of governance end up being relied upon and reinforced in same-sex/gender violence prevention discourses about what is healthy and unhealthy in relationships despite efforts to destabilize normalizing and exclusionary effects. Patricia Durish reflects on her work with the David Kelley Service Same-Sex Partner Abuse Project that operated in Toronto, Canada. Durish both documents and critically reflects on what was accomplished in the survey research, educational work, and advocacy that was undertaken over the three-year life of the project so that other activist initiatives might build on the lessons learned. Similarly, Kate Duffy reflects on the work of the Same Sex Domestic Violence Interagency in Sydney, Australia. Unlike the Toronto project that relied on time-limited funding, the interagency is comprised of representatives from several organizations throughout Sydney. Duffy describes several groundbreaking initiatives introduced by the interagency over the last ten years. Continuing with the approach of critical reflection, the chapter by Diane Dolan-Soto and Jesmen Mendoza describes two unique programs for batterers, one based in New York and one in Toronto. The authors describe their differing approaches to batterers programs and offer insightful recommendations for those who may wish to develop similar intervention programs. In the final chapter, Catherine Taylor and Janice Ristock examine the connections between partner violence in the lives of Aboriginal LGBTQ people and state violence against Aboriginal people in Canada. They argue that state violence is so deeply implicated in personal violence that responding to IPV ethically requires researchers to take action to oppose state violence. What we are reminded of by each of the chapters in this section is the call to action that is integral to doing this work. Whether providing services, educating, engaging in activism, or conducting research there is an underlying ethical obligation when working on the issue of violence in LGBTQ relationships. Responding to IPV requires taking a political stance so that our work remains linked to larger anti-oppressive and social justice efforts. To reduce personal violence, we have to reduce state violence.

The overarching aim of this volume is to provide new, more nuanced understandings of intimate partner violence in LGBTQ lives. The collection draws attention to both the material conditions (lived experiences, social contexts, intersectionality) and the discursive conditions (framings, binary categories, language) of violence. The collection will hopefully inspire others to engage in critical research and practice as there remains so much more work to be done. I always think about one young woman that I interviewed who talked to me about not being able to seek out any support services for relationship violence that she experienced. She said:

> "I feel like I can't talk about it, I mean how many therapists/social service providers are going to understand queer, s/m, abuse, intersexed,

interracial [all features of her abusive relationship]—It's too complicated, there is too much explaining that I'd have to do." (Ristock and Timbang 2005)

I think of her words because they so clearly remind me of the ways our knowledge is limited and partial, and how much we need to critically reflect on the understandings we produce in our research and mobilize in our practice. We need to keep asking the following questions:

Who benefits from the way we currently talk about relationship violence and what difference does that make?

Whose voices are heard and not heard when we use categories such as: domestic violence; same-sex domestic violence; victim/perpetrator, and so on.

Whose realities are blurred and/or erased when we focus on binary categories? Whose needs are not met as a result?

What if we mapped the range of experiences of violence in people's lives (partner, family, societal, state, colonial, etc)? How might that change our theorizing? How might that change our practice?

What if we imagined community responses to violence—what might those look like for research, for practice, and for action?

Questions like these underlie the work of each of the contributors to this volume, and our work is offered here to keep us moving forward in our efforts to end all forms of violence in peoples' lives.

REFERENCES

Anderssen, Erin. 2008. A skeleton that's still in the closet: Domestic violence is more widespread among same-sex couples than straights. *The Globe and Mail*, April 12, F1.

DiStefano, Anthony, S. (2009). Intimate partner violence among sexual minorities in Japan: Exploring perceptions and experiences. *Journal of Homosexuality* 56: 121–146.

Hester, Marianne and Catherine Donovan. 2009. Researching domestic violence in same-sex relationships: A feminist epistemological approach to survey development. *Journal of Lesbian Studies* 13: 161–173.

Holmes, Cindy. 2009. Destabilizing homonormativity and the public/private dichotomy in North American lesbian domestic violence discourses. *Gender, Place & Culture: A Journal of Feminist Geography* 16: 77–95.

Irwin, Jude. 2008. (Dis)counted stories: Domestic violence and lesbians. *Qualitative Social Work* 7: 199–215.

Richie, Beth. 2005. Foreword in *Domestic violence at the margins: Readings on race, class, gender and culture*, ed. Natalie J. Sokoloff and Christina Pratt, xv–xviii. Piscataway, NJ: Rutgers University Press.

Ristock, Janice L. 2002. *No more secrets: Violence in lesbian relationships*. New York: Routledge.

Ristock, Janice L. and Norma Timbang. 2005. Relationship violence in lesbian/ gay/bisexual/transgender/queer [LGBTQ] communities: Moving beyond a gender-based framework. Minnesota Centre against Violence and Abuse: Violence against Women Online Resources. Available at: http://www.mincava.umn.edu/documents/lgbtqviolence/lgbtqviolence.html [accessed November 2, 2010].

Robinson, Amanda and James Rowlands. 2009. Assessing and managing risk among different victims of domestic abuse: Limits of a generic model of risk assessment? *Security Journal* 22(3): 190–204.

Tjaden, Patricia and Nancy Thoennes. 2000. *Full report of the prevalence, incidence, and consequences of violence against women: Findings from the national violence against women survey.* Washington, DC: US Department of Justice.

Part I
Framings

2   Reframing the Heteronormative Constructions of Lesbian Partner Violence
An Australian Case Study

Kierrynn Davis and Nel Glass[1]

INTRODUCTION

The dominant voice that has formed the epistemic understanding of violence against women has been most clearly articulated within a heterosexual paradigm. As such, violence among women has been unable to claim epistemic space in a paradigm that predominately frames violence as heterosexual. While intimate partner violence has been recognized in the gay male culture, there have been minimal stories of lesbian partner violence (Eaton et. al 2008, 1), particularly in rural Australia. The literature has also merged Lesbian, Gay, Bisexual Transgender and Queer (LGBTQ) experiences. Therefore, there is still limited specific research on lesbian domestic violence and, as such, a comprehensive picture of lesbian domestic violence is not yet available. Furthermore, little has been clearly articulated on dyadic violence among self-acknowledged feminist lesbians and of equal importance, the disjunction between feminist rhetoric and the lived experience of lesbians. Our aim in this chapter is to explore, through a postmodern feminist intersectional lens, three stories of lesbians living with relationship violence in rural Australia. The following account will explore the research processes, relevant literature, theories that informed the analysis, and stories of lesbian relationship abuse, with concluding comments on the similarities and differences to heterosexual intimate partner violence and ways to reframe lesbian relationship violence.

ABOUT THIS RESEARCH

Women in a rural area in New South Wales, Australia were invited to be part of a study that examined the stories of informal support needs for rural women who have left relationships contextualized by intimate partner violence. Twenty-six women responded and twenty-three stories where analyzed and published (see Davis, Taylor and Furniss 2001). Three of the twenty-six women who participated told stories of leaving abusive lesbian relationships. The three lesbian stories were intentionally analyzed as a separate cohort and reported in a paper at the Twelfth International Conference of the Nursing Network on Violence Against Women in Adelaide, South Australia.

This chapter presents a secondary analysis of that conference paper. One story was related to violence between two non-intimate lesbians sharing a household. The other two narratives directly concerned lesbian intimate partner violence. In order to compete with heterosexual privilege, the stories of all three women are presented, because "stories have to be told if they are adequately to be answered" (Code 1998, 210). Moreover, presenting the three stories avoids the temptation to present a single lesbian voice of authority regarding marginal positionality within the discourse of lesbian violence, and increases understanding of the tensions that inter-lesbian violence creates for lesbian feminists. The inclusion of a story of non-intimate partner violence also allows the juxtaposition of intimate and non-intimate lesbian partner violence to reveal the continuities and discontinuities between intimate and non-intimate relationship violence. The telling of this story also extends the concept of domestic violence to include lesbian relationship violence, both intimate and non-intimate.

WHY TELL LESBIAN STORIES RATHER THAN WOMEN'S STORIES?

The discursively constructed voices presented in this chapter reveal stories that demand a de-centering of the dominant heterosexual voice. As such, they challenge the lesbian community to self-reflexively examine the way that the dominant epistemic voice has constructed an understanding and response to inter-lesbian violence. Furthermore, finding one's voice and being heard establishes a sense of self as embodied, geographically situated, and gendered (Code 1998, 205).

Russo argues that: "When lesbian activists against battering emphasize the similarities between lesbian and heterosexual relationships, we minimize the historical and social differences between us" (Russo 1999, 89). While this is so, it is not to ignore that some women do seek to control other women in the same way that men do, and should therefore be held accountable for their behavior. While the tactics of control may be consistent across sexual identity, taking account of the similarities and differences between lesbian and heterosexual battering means identifying the historical socio-political and legal contexts that impact on sexual identity and the resulting strategies of control.

TERMINOLOGY

A word about language is relevant at this point. The construction of inter-lesbian violence is problematic due to the diverse and inconsistent language that proliferates in scholarship, research studies, and everyday conversation within the LGBTQ community. The North American literature refers to lesbian domestic violence (Bornstein et al. 2006, 1; Osier 2001, 1), same-sex battering (Balsam and Szymanski 2005: 258), women-to-women battering (Girschick 2002, 14), lesbian battering (Kaschak 2001: 1), female same-sex intimate partner violence (FSSIPV) (Hassouneh and Glass 2008: 310), and lesbian relationship and interpersonal violence (Eaton et al. 2008: 1). Australian literature refers to partnership violence (Laing 2000: 2) and relationship violence (Dann et. al 1997: 179). These terms are advocated as more inclusive terms than the term "domestic violence," which has pre-dominately been associated with heterosexual relationship violence within the home (Ristock and Timbang 2005: 3). While recent research in Austra-lia refers to intimate partner abuse (Pitts et. al 2006: 51), a report entitled *Domestic Violence in Gay and Lesbian Relationships* indicates the persua-siveness of heterosexual conceptions of same sex violence (Chan 2005: 1). Much of the difficulty in determining the magnitude of same sex violence can be attributed to the plethora of terms and definitions. "Finding the language to get it right" will enhance understanding and the development of theoretical representations of the differentness of lesbian positionality within IPV (Hartsock 2006: 183).

PREVALENCE AND THE PROBLEMS OF DEFINING LESBIAN INTIMATE PARTNER VIOLENCE

In the United States, the rate of lesbian partner abuse is estimated to be anywhere from 11–73% (Renzetti 1998: 119). This is compared to Austra-lia where a more recent study by Bagshaw et al. (2000) indicated the rate of lesbian IPV was 22–46%, which is similar to the prevalence of male-female partnership violence as indicated by Girschick (2002:12).

Further Australian studies on the prevalence rates of lesbian IPV have been limited by the lack of sample size and by a dependence on service pro-viders' records that contain only that information that the client discloses, or the counselor thought important to record (Chan 2005: 2). However, in a survey study of 308 LGBT respondents at Sydney's New Mardi Gras Fair Day in 2006, 54.5% of participants identified as lesbians in abusive inti-mate relationships (ACON and SSDVI 2006: 7). In the largest study of Les-bian, Gay, Bisexual, Transgender and Intersex (LGBTI) health undertaken in Australia, 40.7% of women reported either being in, or previously expe-riencing an abusive intimate relationship (Pitts et. al 2006). While these results are very high the authors warn that it was difficult to determine if these women had been in same-sex relationships for every violent incident (Pitts et al. 2006: 51). Demonstrating the difficulty in establishing the true prevalence rate, Renzetti argues: "As long as homophobia forces lesbians to hide their identity from others, including researchers, a true prevalence study of lesbian partner abuse remains undoable" (1998: 119).

In the Australian context, Bird defined lesbian violence as "behavior by a woman adopted to control her victim, which results in physical, sexual and/or emotional damage, forced social isolation, economic deprivation, or behavior which leaves a women living in fear" (2004: x). Multiple scholars writing on same sex battering have referred to Barbara Hart's (1986) definition (see Ristock and Timbang 2005: 4; Russo 1999: 91), which is: "Lesbian battering is a pattern of violent and coercive behaviors whereby a lesbian seeks to control the thoughts, beliefs, conduct of her intimate partner or to punish the intimate for resisting the perpetrator's control over her" (1986: 173). The commonality in both Bird's and Hart's definitions is the control of one woman over another. Yet Hart's definition sets the socio-political context of that violence between intimate partners, while the scope of Kassa Bird's definition provides for the inclusion of any relationship structures.

HETERONORMATIVE DISCOURSE

Historically, heterosexual IPV was constructed as either a psychological problem or positioned within family systems discourse. The end result was that individual experiences were pathologized in such as way that women were blamed for the abuse (Sokoloff, 2004: 139). Feminists have constructed IPV as gender-based, with the inequality of women the major explanatory discourse; IPV was predominantly associated with male power and control. By highlighting abuse in lesbian relationships, our intention is not to negate the importance of the power and control model, rather it is to challenge the explanatory notions of power and control.

The Duluth Model historically and internationally has been the most pre-eminent explanatory model for domestic violence (Paymar and Barnes n.d.: 2). The violence of men against women is seen to be derived from socially reinforced notions of male entitlement. In other words men are violent because they believe they can be. In the words of Paymar and Barnes: " the Duluth curriculum's central focus is exploring and understanding power relationships and the effects of violence and controlling behavior on domestic partners"(n.d.:10). While this is so, in reaction to sustained criticism (see Dutton and Corvo in Paymar and Barnes n.d.: 7) the authors acknowledge that women are non-defensibly aggressive; however, men and women use violence in different ways (n.d.: 8). The power/control wheel has been the predominant visual model presented in most Australian pamphlets and information booklets seeking to educate women about domestic violence. However, as Price has noted (see Ristock 2002: 147), while originally the wheel was intended to be educative, it has become institutionalized in most women's services in North America, and this is also the case in Australia.

The use of heterosexual models to explain lesbian IPV ignores the diversity of experiences both within and between both groups. For instance, important considerations are the lack of traditional heterosexual behaviour within lesbian relationships such as mandated monogamy, "for-ever type relationships" (Russo 1999: 89), economic dependency, stigma associated with leaving relationships, or a lesbian-specific religious affiliation that supports partner abuse (ibid.). Furthermore, Renzetti, Elliot and Allen and Leventhal identified homophobia by heterosexuals and internalized homophobia on the part of lesbians as being a notable difference between heterosexual and lesbian IPV (Renzetti 1998: 119; see also Allen and Leventhal 1999: 75; Elliot 1996: 3). While all battered women suffer isolation, for lesbians, the threat of "outing" in small rural communities increases the sense of isolation and risk of social punishment and marginalization (Elliott 1996: 4). Further ignored are the ways in which race, colour, and class construct meaning and significance of the violence in lesbian relationships (Crane et al. 1999: 125). A notable difference for Elliott (1996: 4) is the construction of lesbian IPV as mutual abuse. Furthermore, Elliott believes that the myths that surround same sex violence are different from heterosexual violence. One such myth is that while battering may be part of male behavior, women cannot harm each other. Moreover, the perpetuation of a model that continually decontexualizes, downplays, and denies lesbian violence may encourage a discourse of invisibility thus blinding lesbians to their own and other women's violence.

It is only in recent years that gay and lesbian violence within relationships has been considered an important topic of research. While drawing on research that explains and describes violence against women, whether in lesbian or heterosexual relationships is helpful, it is also important to take account of the differences (Renzetti 1992: 23–24). Moreover, Elliott has argued that violence against women is about power and that sexism creates the opportunity for men to abuse women and "homophobia, a tool of sexism," provides the same opportunity for abuse within lesbian relationships (1996: 3). On the nature of power in intimate lesbian relationships, Kelly has argued that the sanctioned power men have within their intimate relations with women is different from, and can never be the same as, the unsanctioned power women have in lesbian relationships (in Websdale 1998: 70). There is a need to take account of identity as a women and the social oppression that results from identity as a lesbian. This is similar to the old lesbian feminist adage that lesbians are doubly oppressed as both a woman and a lesbian. These multiple spaces of oppression may not always be physically damaging, but rather, in the words of Maria Root they may be an "insidious trauma" that damages the spirit and soul (see Ristock 2002:

80). Arguably, there is a need to tell the stories "which explain the phenomena for every group that experiences it, not only the majority group" (Merrill 1996: 20).

INTERSECTIONALITY AND POSTMODERN FEMINISM

According to Eaton, et al. Lesbian IPV is complex and a single explanatory theory is unlikely to fully account for this complexity (2008: 7). Therefore the stories of lesbian IPV presented are informed by several theoretical positions, much like Foucault's notion of the "toolbox" (Lancombe 1996: 348). Rather than a single theory, ideas concerning intersectionality and postmodern feminism, and Foucault's work on the "microphysics" (Caluya 2009: 7) and "macrophysics" (Demirovic 2009: 9) of power, subjectivity, and agency/ resistance as strategies of power-knowledge (Lancombe 1996: 348), have framed the analysis.

Postmodern Feminism

Postmodern feminist approaches to theorizing inter-lesbian violence seek to de-center the dominant homogenizing grand narrative that accounts for all violence for all women in all situations. Postmodern feminism interrogates the binary constructions of victim/perpetrator and deconstructs discourses of power and control. It calls for ambiguous, partial, limited accounts, which are situated within space, time, social location and mobile subjectivities.

Postmodern feminism informed by Foucault's reframing of power has been met with varying levels of acceptance among feminists (MacLeod and Durrheim 2002: 41). On the other hand Foucault resisted labels and did not see himself as a postmodernist, rather as a scholar who called into question the Marxist notions of power as centralized in historically dominant institutions such as the state (MacLeod and Durrheim 2002: 44). Foucault, however, has much to offer a feminist analysis.

For Foucault, power implies a network of practices between individuals (Lancombe 1996: 342). Foucault refers to this network of power as the "microphysics" of power (Demirovic 2009: 9) or "micropower " (Lancombe 1996: 332). Micro does not refer to miniature; rather it refers to the practices of power in everyday relationships. Power is not held by one person, rather it moves and circulates through all aspects of our relationships with ourselves, others and the state. Therefore, in Crossley's view power emerges intersubjectivily (1996: 136). For Foucault, "micropower" is a strategy that produces control, the effects of which are not "unifying" or singular (Lancombe 1996: 332). Power as Foucault sees it is not confinement. Rather, "power is a mechanism that both constrains and enables action. In fact, resistance is at the heart of power" (Lancombe 1996: 342). As MacLeod and Durrheim (2002: 55) have suggested, for Foucault, power is not only repressive but also liberatory. In Foucault's words "this conception of power is not only inscribed in practices of normalization, but, most significantly, in practices of liberation (Foucault in Lancombe 1996: 334). What Foucault means by normalization is the cultural process by which an individual regulates his/ her behavior in order to conform to social rules (Shawyer 2006: 1).

Power is not necessarily linked to violence, although it can be in certain contexts. Crossley has argued that violence and power can "co-exist in the same sphere," but only in a context where "power acts upon action" (1996: 136–137). For Foucault, the central orientation of power relations is a lack of consensus or mutually agreed understandings. Therefore, power relations emerge within a structured pattern of conduct and this conduct governs other actions (ibid.). It is in this process of subjugation that subjectivity is created (Shawyer 2006: 1). Foucault talks about the technologies of self which "are the specific practices by which subjects constitute themselves as subjects within and through systems of power, and which often seem to be either 'natural' or imposed from above" (ibid.). The subject constituted in this way is the "docile self". Foucault also notes that "the subject is not the sole product of power relations" (Paton 2008: 1), however it is the ability of subjects to reflect critically on the formation and context of subjectivity that creates space for agency / resistance and the "active self" (ibid.; Eckermann 2002: 1).

Crossley, while arguing for the intersubjectivity of power, has identified five main features that sharpen Foucault's "use theory" of power (1996: 138), and provide an understanding of the technologies of power. Citing Foucault (1982: 223), Crossley first identifies the "system of differentiation," for example, an agreed language and/ or conduct associated with a certain social status (1996: 139), as a technology by which subjectivities form in systems of power. Second, power defines and delimits the actions and conduct of subjects who, in turn, re-create relations of power through their actions (ibid.: 140–141). Crossley also argues that power becomes stable within various social organizations and then emerges in a range of different power practices (ibid.: 142). Therefore, in Foucault's view, social institutions are "as much an effect of power as power is an effect of the institution" (ibid.: 142). Crossley's final point concerns Foucault's notion of "degrees of rationalization" (ibid.: 143), that is, the extent and manner in which forms of power adapt to the context in which power is practiced. As discussed earlier, Foucault also spoke about the "macrophysics" of power and inherent in this notion are the technologies of power practiced by social structures and institutions, which leads to a discussion of intersectionality.

Intersectionality

Cassidy and Jackson view intersectionality as both a theory and an analytical tool (2005: 448). An account that is intersectional considers the interplay of structural inequalities such as sexism, racism, classism, and heterosexism. Together with internalized and external homophobia, culture and social location are "'axes of power [that] cross each other'" to produce various forms of inter-related oppression (Mason as quoted in Hartsock 2006: 182; see also Sokoloff 2004: 139). The practices of power that produce the inequalities and oppression are what Foucault named the "macrophysics" of power (MacLeod and Durrheim 2002: 57). Such an approach resists the oversimplification of large social categories and labeling, thus resisting the essentialism of early feminist scholarship. Intersectionality also acknowledges the complexity, specificity and heterogeneity of intimate lesbian relationships and the forms of violence that occurs within multiple marginalized groups and contexts (Eaton, et al. 2008: 1; Ristock 2005: 10). Lesbian violence is viewed through multiple lenses allowing for a de-centering of a gendered construction of intimate partner violence while recognizing the inter-acting nature of multiple layers of oppression (Ristock 2005: 10). The process is dynamic and each layer is shaped, and in turn further shaped by another, creating a new dimension of oppression. Importantly, intersectionality is a way of overcoming the "incompatibilities in feminist theory on race, class, gender" (Davis 2008: 74). Thinking at the intersections is methodologically productive as it allows for the critical deconstruction of the victim/perpetrator binary (Ristock 2005: 10), and exemplifies the understanding of the lesbian experience of violence within an interacting "matrix of domination" (May and Ferri 2002: 132).

By highlighting abuse in lesbian relationships, our intention is not to negate the importance of the power and control model, rather it is to challenge the explanatory notions of power and control. Currently lesbian violence is blurred by a homogenizing discourse of power and control where lesbians fail to develop specific strategies that take account of the different ways power and control may be expressed in their relationships. While power and control may be features of abusive lesbian relationships, it is the contextualized "microphysics" of power relations for lesbians that is the focal point of this discussion (Ristock 2002: 128).

This notwithstanding, it is important to acknowledge the existing tension between dominant constructions of violence and that which seeks to explain violence within a marginalized context. Notably, while the discourse of "trauma talk" (Maracek in Ristock 2002: 113), that is, "the rhetoric of fear," and the victim/perpetrator talk of power and control may act to prevent a clear image of lesbian violence, it does not deny the reality of the violence experienced by lesbians (Ristock 2002: 113). In other words, in reality lesbians do suffer painful experiences of abuse regardless of how that abuse is framed. However, reframing the dominant explanations may offer lesbians new understandings and a new way to talk about the practices of power.

The microphysics of power, in the present research, refers to the relational, negotiated, and contextual operation of power in lesbian relationships.

This microphysics of power then operates within the complex social context of multiple spaces of oppression such as gender, race, class, religion, education, professionalism, and heteronormative assumptions which are the macrophysics of power (Caluya 2009: 7; Demirovic 2009: 9).

COLLECTING THE STORIES

Following institutional ethics approval, the researchers explained the research to the participants, each of whom signed a consent form. Each woman was interviewed initially for approximately one hour, to allow sufficient time for the recollection of memories of domestic violence. At the beginning of the interview, biographical data was collected relating to the woman's age, the date abuse started, and living arrangements. All three interviews were audio-taped.

DATA ANALYSIS

The audiotaped conversations were transcribed verbatim. In order to protect the participants each was represented by a pseudonym. While women who experience violence may be viewed through several competing "lenses" (Laing 2001: 3), the present analysis has been framed by intersectionality and informed by feminist postmodern conceptualization of power. This was done intentionally in an effort to understand and explain the interpersonal and social relationships within this feminist research on lesbian relationship violence. Paying attention to culturally situated dominant discourses within stories allowed vulnerability and exploitation, and power as agency and resistance, to co-exist within multiple levels of complexity and partiality rather than as binary constructs. The three stories that follow are rich and deeply revealing of the complexity of lesbian relationship violence.

THE WOMEN'S STORIES

The three women ranged in age from mid-thirties to fifties. One woman had been in two previous marriages with abusive male partners. All of the women were non-Indigenous, Australian born citizens with varying levels of education and class background. The types of abuse in their same- sex relationships were emotional/ mental, verbal, and physical.

The first story presented describes a non-intimate housing sub-tenancy arrangement where the abuse extended from the living situation with a shared kitchen into social abuse within the lesbian community. Two stories describe intimate lesbian domestic violence. All three identify that the abuse of women in lesbian relationships is more than an individual intrapersonal or interpersonal phenomena, but rather a social and community phenomenon. All participants stated that health professionals and other lesbians marginalized their experiences of violence. The stories begin with Kelly's experience of abuse in a co-tenancy relationship.

KELLY'S STORY

Kelly met with the researchers and discussed her thoughts concerning the paper, then provided the researchers with written comments. Her story was interspersed with the latter comments in order to avoid decontextualization of the story that can occur when the transcript is not presented verbatim from beginning to end. It is therefore a telling and re-telling of the story.

An exploration of Kelly's living arrangements revealed economic, emotional, and social exploitation that created levels of vulnerability which were further intersected by a series of complex life events. Kelly clarified the nature of her relationship with her co-tenant, described the exploitative and controlling aspects of the interactions, and then identified the effects this had on various aspects of her life.

Poverty and Social Vulnerability Intersecting with Classism and Professionalism

A second telling of Kelly's story revealed the dynamics of exploitative power and control within a context of poverty and social vulnerability related to ill health and isolation. Kelly stated:

> It was domestic only because [it] was about my "housing". She set the rules and I tried to follow them and as she changed them, I could not. It was an absence of "relationship" that meant I was vulnerable to her expectations to play, flirt and then later [she] became controlling with me. I would have left if there were any means to leave without financial disaster. I was a subtenant and had no legal power or rights at all. She was my landlady . . . [she had] the legal power to exploit my isolation, ill health, and poverty.

As Kelly told her story it became apparent that the use of psychopathological labels and categorization of victimhood by the co-tenant sought to minimize Kelly's power and control her behavior: "She told me I was 'phobic' . . . of knives . . . and it was my 'tough luck' . . . She accused me of having a victim mentality."

Unequal social positioning was a phenomenon in both Kelly and Marilyn's story (below). However, for Kelly the co-tenant chose to create an unequal power relationship that created disempowering interpersonal domestic interactions and revealed professional classism. Kelly stated: "It always is going to be fairly difficult when it's a person of high profile . . . then I know that telling some people the full detail . . . would be dangerous to me . . . because the person who was harassing me . . . was a person who should have known better." Furthermore, Kelly's need to tell her story resulted in an increased vulnerability due to her further marginalization because she challenged the stereotypes of those who abuse. She said:

> Revealing the nature of the domestic situation of abuse by high profile feminists [resulted in] skeptical reactions by counselors. Friends would scoff or their jaw would drop. I always seemed to be risking my integrity . . . my story meant that I was unbelievable, a perpetrator, a liar, a malicious dobber, or imaginative and crazy . . . My real story contains many details that are quite outside the usual stereotypes of who abuses and how. Professionals acting selfishly and deceptively [in order] to exploit the feminist lesbian privileges of their social power. I did not have social standing to threaten.

A tactic of control used by the co-tenant was to constantly change the rules, however, this abuse was extended into Kelly's social relationships by a trivialization of the abuse by others. Kelly described: "I presumed that when I went to seek support . . . that people would think it was just a 'cat-fight' between two women . . . and that I shouldn't have moved in if I couldn't keep the rules that she wanted to keep, rather than thinking that this woman is changing the rules repeatedly . . . And lots of people have had a bad flat-mate situation . . . and it would be hard to distinguish it as genuinely causing me . . . real health problems."

Power circulates through relationships. The co-tenant's talk brought into effect the dominant discourses of psychopathology as a tactic of control and classism and professionalism were macropower tactics that contained Kelly's conduct. The conduct of the co-tenant of constantly changing the rules and the normalization of power over relationships subjugated Kelly.

Agency and Resistance Intersecting Containment

Managing the violence was a continual feature of Kelly's life. Escaping and living a life outside of violence was not possible. Kelly employed several power tactics in order to contain the violence and to survive within the multiple levels of abuse she continued to experience. The ability to resist the exploitation and control was partial and involved the management, rather than the escape, from violence. In the re-telling of the story Kelly highlighted the tension between control and resistance: "I resisted intensely the whole time, offering resistance to her ego games [and] her bullying. I was powerless to physically escape so it was necessary to manage her instead. I could not react truthfully and empower myself in the situation but I was managing the real danger and control by preventing it [from] getting worse."

Externalizing the abuse through a writing strategy and telling others was a mechanism utilized as a reality check. Kelly wrote a complaint to the Australian Anti-Discrimination Board, thus alerting protective systems to her problem. However, initially Kelly could not name the violence: "But I don't think I ever actually told anybody . . . because I didn't identify it myself [as] 'domestic violence' . . . I just identified it as having a really difficult flat-mate."

Then writing and telling her story enabled Kelly to recognize the abuse:

"The process at least, of writing it down helped clarify to me that it really was abuse . . . And I couldn't actually *name* the situation to myself, until I'd left it. I would just keep comparing . . . if a man had waved a knife in my face in a kitchen, I would have been moving out within a week . . . But I stayed there for two or three months after that . . . the hardest thing to do, and the thing you need repeated support over, was naming it as abuse!"

Abuse Talk Intersecting Containment

Responses to Kelly's story, including responses by individual lesbians and groups of lesbians within the community, have acted to silence and control the "talk" about lesbian violence and to further marginalize her. Other lesbians and professionals in the community either knowingly or unknowingly responded in unpredictable and unsupportive ways: "People would be supportive for a few months and then they would get sick of you . . . And they would be a bit 'burnt-out' about wanting to support you . . . And they would sort of 'back off.' . . . Other people would be a bit unpredictable . . . and couldn't be very consistent about supporting you . . . people would be impatient . . . and . . . would want to sort of . . . solve the problem one way . . . [What] I wanted to hear . . . [was] that you just don't deserve it!" When Kelly sought to sustain herself within several overlapping contexts of violence, responses from other lesbians were minimizing of the abuse and socially normalizing.

All of the lesbian participants in this small rural community experienced defensive, attacking, impatient and fearful behavior from other lesbians. Lesbians would tire of providing support or attempt to solve the problem rather than "just listen." This response, coupled with the lack of recognition that the abused lesbian was actually in crisis, further compounded the situation. Kelly said: "[It was] very difficult to seek support over sexual harassment in the lesbian community . . . I was actually experiencing phobia of other lesbians. Because they might react [by saying] that I was attacking another lesbian, or another woman, by naming what she did . . . it's very hard for other lesbians to listen to you complain about lesbians without getting defensive about lesbians . . . Some people will attack you. Some people will ignore you. Some people will make excuses for the person." Kelly also related an implied idea of contagion. Those that helped, sometimes just by listening to an abused women, were somehow "tarred with the same brush," and seen to be part of the problem.

Distancing by adopting a professional or legalistic rather than a personal and humanistic response was compounded by counselors whose professional class identity was similar to the co-tenant in Kelly's story. For Kelly, small rural communities posed problems related to confidentiality, trust, loyalty and lack of experienced professionals to provide a forum for responding to ethical dilemmas. Moreover, the community saw speaking out about lesbian violence as aligning with other groups that have oppressed the lesbian community in the past. This resonates with Australian Indigenous people and their resistance to involving police in domestic violence (Davis and Taylor 2002: 80). Police are the oppressor. Failure by the lesbian community to recognize Kelly's crisis situation further contributed to the difficult journey to contain the violence, and Kelly continued to feel a lack of trust in lesbians in the community:

> I've had one friend for one area of support, and another friend for another area of support. I didn't have anybody for ALL areas of support . . . I was looking for a particular kind of lesbian confidential counseling support over the illegal [sex] issue . . . because I was actually trying to be ethical and make sure I didn't disadvantage her [the abuser] . . . It was a complete risk to tell people who weren't confidential. Under that veneer, you're in crisis, and they ought to notice as soon as you just jump from one subject to the other without it making any sense . . . and everybody expects . . . [you] . . . to have a black eye and be crying.

Loss of Social Networks and Isolation Intersecting Professionalism and Poverty

Later Kelly described her experience attempting to find someone "to empathize with [her] distress and be available to listen" as "a journey of continuous failures." Speaking about the abuse, and attempting to move on, resulted in the loss of friendship networks. The resulting sense of isolation was further enhanced by other marginalizing factors such as poverty and geographical isolation: "I have been able to maintain probably . . . one heterosexual friend and a few lesbian friends . . . two or three friendships that I might have lost." The loss of friendship was further compounded by professional responses to naming the violence with political, legal, and professional rhetoric that contributed to a sense of continued abuse resulting in despair, anger, and lack of trust:

> When you disclose to them that you feel you have been a victim of abuse . . . they . . . respond with their own subjectivity . . . or . . . they respond

as . . . professionals . . . they start talking . . . a bit like a pamphlet . . . like "You've got legal rights" . . . their understanding or ability to be listeners was a lot less, or that they would be triggered about their own stuff . . . I'd found, that as a single woman there wasn't any particular support . . . I remember ringing lots of support agencies and not being able to find any particular support . . . people were listening with a political response rather that listening with a personal response.

Kelly was asked what advice should be given to any health professional who wanted to understand her experience. Her story revealed a plea for a genuine caring, a need to describe the violence, for openness, for support groups, and for affirming friendships.

Power was a mechanism that was both constraining and enabling for Kelly. To some extent Kelly was able to resist the silencing tactics and "talk" about the violence. In the practice of care for the self, Kelly's reflection on the strategies of power from which the "docile self" emerges, enabled the emergence of the "active self" (Paton 2008: 1). As suggested earlier, resistance and liberation are at the heart of power and Kelly's writing and talking were empowering strategies of resistance. The tactics of macropower from which the discourse of contagion emerged added another layer that acted to contain Kelly's conduct.

MARILYN'S STORY

As suggested earlier, the central core of the Duluth Model of the cycle of violence differentiates abusive and non-abusive relationships on the basis of power and control versus equality (Paymar and Barnes n.d.: 5). Inherent in this conceptualization is the subjugation of self in an abusive relationship. The reclaiming of a sense of self within an equal relationship is defined by such features as value and respect for self and others, being non-judgmental, affirming, and understanding in our interactions with others (Glass and Davis 2004).

In a previous publication, we described the process of reclaiming self as a social as well as an intrapersonal process and a process that results in re-framing vulnerability as a healing process, therefore, empowering and liberatory (2004: 92). A postmodern feminist interactional framing of this process in the following two stories reveals three partialities, namely: the loss of self; the re-inscription of self intrapersonally; and a partial reconstruction of self in the broader social context.

Marilyn spoke of previously being in a heterosexual marriage and realizing her lesbianism through feminism. She had not been in a previous abusive lesbian relationship. Although she had left the present abusive relationship, the emotional and verbal abuse was ongoing. Marilyn had grown up in a violent family and she was aware that her ex-partner had been abusive in previous lesbian relationships. Her journey involved a partial reclaiming of self and a partial loss of self, re-inscription and reconstruction. The process of breaking free would have been more sustainable if the rural lesbian community had supported both women equally. Marilyn spoke about the abusive behaviors, not the abusive person being unacceptable, and how ostracizing the abusive partner only perpetuated the oppressive behaviors of heterosexual society. Here Marilyn has recognized the negative effects of the tactics of micro and macro power. She recognized the need to reconstruct the victim/perpetrator binary and create a space for the balance of power without violence.

Partial Loss of Self Intersecting Personal Sense of Unreality

Although Marilyn was aware that her partner had been abusive in previous relationships, the violence did not begin for her until she and her partner had been together just over a year. The onset was insidious and the intimate partner sought total control. Marilyn not only lost a sense of self but she was also unsure of what was "real" as the abuse was mental and emotional rather than physical.

Marilyn described her situation as follows: "Over that three year period of the abuse, I actually, slowly, without realizing it, slipped back into . . . victim behaviors . . . and undid all the counseling that I'd done for twenty years . . . I lost my sense of self and my sense of reality! I really needed my reality affirmed! The violence was non-physical and aimed at total control. It was . . . totally verbal, emotional and mental abuse. I'm not saying that . . . to minimize [it] by any means . . . I even think it's worse. I'd rather have been thumped I think because this way was so insidious." A friend validated Marilyn's sense of loss of self when she left the relationship, she said: "Congratulations! This is the best thing you have ever done! I'm looking forward to meeting the real you, that I haven't seen for a couple of years." The tactics of power in this context created the space of an emergence of the "docile self" at the same time encouraging the emergence of the "active self" (Paton 2008: 1).

Re-Inscribing Self Intersecting a Perception of Disloyalty

Voicing and naming the abuse to both her "straight" and lesbian friends and seeking counseling were the main strategies Marilyn utilized to partially reclaim the self that she knew before. She saw the lack of valuing of self by lesbians as a mechanism that prevented her from gaining their support. Furthermore, re-inscribing her self outside the relationship was hindered by a perception of disloyalty: "We set up counseling [together] . . . and at that stage I started to tell other people, both straight and lesbian. . . . [however], it's considered really disloyal in the lesbian community, to talk about it."

Resistance Intersecting Social Isolation

The reconstructed self was that of a compassionate woman who was attempting to reach out to friends yet there was a lack of close lesbian friends and an ex-partner whom she did not wish to totally reject. Nor did she wish the lesbian community to reject her ex-partner, and therefore remove support for her partner. She rejected the notion of constructing her partner in negative terms:

> I could go on staying with friends . . . as long as I didn't want to discuss "it" with them . . . So it's my choice now to say, "Do I want to stay friends with them?" . . . And I guess the choice I'm making is . . . No! I don't! I'd say I've lost a few more friends over it. How do you make a judgment about who is the victim and who is the perpetrator? . . . Even if you are supporting one, it doesn't mean that you see the other one as being wicked, evil and bad, and you're rejecting them. I still haven't mentioned [the domestic violence situation] in the lesbian community here . . . because, if I do that, then I cut off *her* support.

Marilyn resisted the discourse of victim/perpetrator, however the act of resistance also contained and silenced the "talk" about violence.

Micropower Intersecting with Macropower

Sustaining a non-violent life where her partner's abuse did not intrude on her everyday experiences was partial. Like Kelly, Marilyn believed that lesbians in the community were fearful of being included in the abuse cycle. The idea of contagion was also apparent in this story. There were a wide range of responses upon hearing of the abuse including no reaction; minimizing; a deliberate silencing of the talk; internalized homophobia of lesbians in the rural community; betrayal; and a lack of services. Marilyn described:

> I think that fear of violence is an enormous one. And I think that women are well conditioned to it . . . that is the biggest concern of other people! They just didn't want to be in it. They were frightened! We'd rather pretend . . . it's this lovely . . . rose colored [community] . . . rather than looking at any reality. [Marilyn asked] "Why didn't you tell me when you saw these things?" [They replied] "Well, you don't talk about that . . . you seemed ok . . . so we didn't say anything." [They said] "So, if you came here to stay, and your partner turned up to abuse [you] . . . then the neighbors might know . . . and they might find out at work I'm a lesbian." . . . So, homophobia came up! In a big way! . . . One of them said to me . . ."I'm frightened that your partner will turn up and . . . abuse us as well. Are we at risk?" They didn't want my partner to know

that they knew. So, I had to stay with them for a week . . . pretending
. . . [I felt] totally betrayed because I had nowhere . . . to talk about it.

Juxtaposed to Kelly's story, Marilyn's non-lesbian friends and health professionals offered the most sustainable form of support, a situation which
both surprised and disappointed Marilyn, as she would have preferred a
lesbian counselor. In terms of straight friends she reflected that a straight
friend "can sympathize but she can't empathize . . . because she doesn't
know. What has astounded me is that I couldn't find a lesbian to do that.
She's straight . . . and she's my support person. She's had no contact with
lesbians up until she met my partner and myself. [I] said 'If I need an escape
route, can I come to your house?' . . . 'Yep! Not a problem!' I didn't want
her to solve my problems for me."

Empowerment Intersecting with Disempowerment

When asked about further support Marilyn identified several aspects that
were helpful. She identified ongoing support as being important: "She took
on the responsibility of ringing me probably two or three times a week . . .
to see how I was. And that was really important because, then I could just
have this big blurt." Marilyn also emphasized the importance of listening not solving. With respect to lesbians in abusive relationships, she said
"listen to them. [Don't] problem solv[e] for them . . . that disempowers."
Marilyn also advocated the need for a reality check and to help find support
if it is needed. Lastly, Marilyn advocated the need to support both partners.
Some of Marilyn's friends said: "You are to tell your partner you have told
us. And tell her it doesn't affect our care for her . . . but that we expect her
to do something about her behaviors."

Classism Intersected by Feminist Discourse

Classism in the lesbian community and among professionals was disempowering. It contradicted the feminist philosophy that Marilyn had embraced
and further restricted her journey toward a life free of violence. Moreover,
Marilyn was also disillusioned with the feminist rhetoric:

> They *talk* about challenging their classism. . . . And they *talk* about
> challenging sexism, misogyny, and lesbophobia . . . But they talk about
> it at the political level. . . . But they don't *do* it at the personal level.
> Despite that they say that "the personal is the political" . . . they've
> actually separated their personal and political lives. And they don't
> do their personal work. The other thing that came up was the total
> "class" issue . . . My ex-partner is from a very well to do family . . .
> She is a very middle-class woman . . . I come from the working class
> . . . [laughs] when I went and spoke to lesbians "outside" . . . and said

"I want support" . . . classism came up again. That whole . . . middle class . . . sticks together.

Dismantling Victim/Perpetrator Discourses and the Tactics of Control

For Marilyn, a community that valued all of its members, where individual lesbians valued themselves and possessed a high level of interpersonal skills, would be an empowered community. The community would name behaviors rather than the individual as abusive. Marilyn noted:

> How do we teach women that they are valuable? And that they deserve love and respect. I think we can teach women assertion skills . . . and enough self esteem, such that they can stand up to violence without being violent themselves. Women don't have any skills to deal with [violence] . . . We are not trained to. We are trained to be submissive. We're trained to be "pacifiers," and "pleasers". We need to tell the perpetrator that . . . the behaviors [are] unacceptable. So it's not rejecting the person . . . It is totally rejecting behaviors. Support two women, then it is saying to the perpetrator "Your behaviors [are] unacceptable." . . . And it is saying to the victim "Yes, what happened to you was unacceptable." And . . ."How do you take responsibility for yourself so that you don't get yourself back into this situation again? How do you deal with *your* behaviors . . . alter your behaviors so that you don't repeat that?"
>
> I would want to deal with a lesbian. That would be, really a prerequisite if possible . . . I must say my counselor here is straight . . . There are no lesbian counselors. First of all, you have to, sometimes, educate these people [counselors] on lesbianism. And that's an enormous task! And even if [the counselor] is lesbian, what is her framework for understanding my domestic violence experience? . . . We have nothing because we have done nothing. We do the research. We write it and we have a framework . . . So that when this lesbian comes to this health care worker, who is preferably a lesbian or is lesbian-friendly [they have] done this training . . . we have a framework to understand lesbian DV.

Marilyn's story is rich both experientially and theoretically. She reflected on and deconstructed the dominant discourse of victim/perpetrator and actively sought to create the space for the "active self" to emerge. She also created the space for individuals to resist the subjugated "docile self" thus validating the technologies of self-care that resisted the macropower tactics of classism, feminist discourse, homophobia, and contagion as normalizing tactics.

JEAN'S STORY

Jean's two marriages to men were abusive. When compared with Marilyn's story, there were some similarities to as well as some differences from Jean's story. For Kelly, while the abuse relationship was with a co-tenant, there is some resonance with Jean's story.

Partial Loss of Self Intersecting Gender Identity

For Jean loss of self involved some difficulty in defining herself as a lesbian, with blurred boundaries around sexual orientation and a lack of understanding of *how* to be a lesbian: "I don't know . . . I've never . . . really had . . . lesbian tendencies . . . or anything . . . I don't call myself a lesbian at all." Jean's previous experiences in abusive relationships with men had led to struggles with power and feelings of powerlessness that resulted in a total loss of self, blurred boundaries between perpetrator and victim, self blame, and lack of self worth. Jean began her story:

> Early in my relationship . . . with a girl friend . . . we would have fights because . . . I had never been with the girls . . . before . . . and I wasn't used to the behavior that goes down. And she would flirt with all the girls when I was with her . . . and I would feel uncomfortable. None of them would focus on me . . . they were all just interested in her . . . And then I tried to explain to her why I was feeling the way I [was] . . . and she would tell me to get over it . . . and then I would get really violent. But the power was phenomenal. And then she would fight back, and she was more powerful than me . . . you know . . . She nearly killed me . . . she put a pillow over my face. I didn't have the strength to fight her off . . . [It was] very scary because she wasn't stopping honey, she was going all the way . . . I just thought "Oh well . . . what can you do? . . . Well, this is it then."
>
> For some unknown reason . . . there is a tendency to blame yourself immediately . . . Look what I have done now . . . Look what I have created . . . that person wouldn't have hit me if I hadn't have . . . yelled, or . . . whatever it is at the time and that is my experience . . . You aren't good enough. People have got to hit you.

Technologies of self created the subjugated "docile self" and this coexisted with conduct that controlled another.

Reinscribing Self Intersecting Self Silencing

Feminists that Jean met became supportive role models, and through observing and listening to women talk about their lives, along with choosing to " . . . [live] in ashramic-type communal lifestyle . . . [enabled] support."

Referring to the previous abusive relationship with a male partner, Jean described the influence of these women. At this time, however, she was unable to talk about her story of violence. Jean stated:

> I mean it's interesting and intriguing to me because there [were] some particular women in [the city] that . . . I was friendly with before I left . . . and . . . they were just stunning women . . . and they supported me . . . very heroically towards the end. They were very good to me when they saw that I was going under with [my previous partner] . . . They gave me a lot of guidance . . . they would all just talk to me about a spiritual level, where you know there is more to this existence . . . My intellect was constantly stimulated . . . I would listen to them and listen to their problems, and that would make me feel clearer about where I was going. But I never talked about myself.

For Marilyn feminist discourse was disempowering in the context of lesbian relationship abuse. For Jean, however, in the context of heterosexual relationship violence, feminist practices were empowering.

Reconstructing the Empowered Self Intersecting Normalization

For Jean, moving out of two abusive marriages, flirting with her attraction to women, and then pursuing this attraction more overtly, created a self that enjoyed life. She eventually claimed a lesbian identity and was feeling empowered: "[I] was very, very attracted to this woman and I couldn't control it . . . it was outrageous! I have never experienced it in my life before. I was becoming self-empowered." As suggested by the previous two stories women lead complex lives with many intersecting and overlapping contexts. Jean described the life with her female partner as abusive in that her partner had attempted to kill her, while her partner had no memory of this act of attempted suffocation. Jean described an abusive situation of physical aggression, attempted suffocation and throwing of furniture: "We got really drunk . . . she appeared to be flirting . . . and I didn't like it . . . so I told her . . . in the bedroom, I didn't do it in public, and she got really 'aggro' with me . . . and I just couldn't stand the attitude . . . so I wasn't going to tolerate it . . . and . . . we got into a real wrestle." Alcohol and drugs played a role in affecting the interactions and Jean's young son was present in the house at the time. For Jean the presence of drug and alcohol abuse produced a context in which abusive conduct was normalized (see Ristock 2002: 57). This behavior was further contextualised within her first lesbian relationship.

Mutual Empowerment Intersecting the Practices of Power

For Jean, a positive future meant rejecting the behavior but not the person and working through the problems together with one's partner. In

Jean's words, ending the violence resulted in empowerment, which was constructed as "staying together and talking . . . and sharing." Jean described: "After that I said to her 'that's it! It's over! Its finished! No more! I don't want to know! . . . But she didn't [go away] . . . she came back to try and understand me." Unlike Kelly and Marilyn, Jean did not seek help from other lesbians: "No . . . that's something private that went down . . . We were both in a bad state . . . so . . . these things happen . . . And it can be a 'once off.' But we both know what our potential is . . . so you work around that because we are both very powerful . . . We have worked out how to live . . . together . . . and [do] not have to compromise too much . . . A lot of respect . . . I couldn't live with anyone who wasn't trying to achieve that in their life." For Foucault, power in everyday life in part exists because of a non-consensual understanding or acceptance of communicative speech. Negotiated relationships are those in which attempts are made of reach a common understanding of the speech act. Jean has created a place for the circulation of power that is balanced and works positively rather than negatively.

CONCLUSION

Violence in lesbian relationships is the same as and yet different from heterosexual IPV. An exploration of the microphysics and macrophysics of power and control within lesbian relationships, and responses within the lesbian and non-lesbian community, have revealed that the interactive effects of multiple oppressive structures and social relations means that a new and different dimension is created. As with heterosexual IPV power and control were aspects of the dynamics of abusive lesbian relationships in this research, however this was not played out through one partner claiming a masculine identity or male privilege. Power circulated both within the personal relationships and was an effect of the social institutions. Both negative abusive and positive empowering power were evident. Macropower and control were related more to professional elitism, classism, internalized homophobia, and the socially containing notion of contagion as a normalizing and exclusionary tactic (Ristock 2002: 151). Paradoxically, the macropower tactic of social homophobia was not a feature of the participants' stories; if anything, heterosexual women where the participants' main support.

Disrupting the heteronormative constructions of IPV requires lesbians to create a space for non-oppressive power and empowerment for all lesbians. That new and different space requires the self-reflective challenging of the normative discourse of the victim/ perpetrator binary inherent in separate victim/ perpetrator services (Ristock 2002: 151). Creating opportunities for couples counseling would be a positive approach that would enable the space for the emergence of both lesbians as active empowered selves (Paton 2008: 1). Non-oppressive strategies by other lesbians and professionals would enable lesbians to deal with the self-abuse of internalized homophobia, thus positively interrupting the multiple layers of oppression. Creating a space to encourage caring feminist practices that are supportive, non-normalizing, and non -exclusionary would further disrupt the abuse cycle. Finally, the stories of rural lesbians present a particular geographical and social context that is intersected by personal contexts, such as first lesbian relationships and the associated marginalization. Therefore, there is a need to understand the unique factors, such as local geographies, that contextualize lesbian lives (Ristock 2002: 58).

Finally, the telling of these stories has been a positive and empowering strategy of self-care and has revealed the multiple interacting levels of violence that hinder the imaging and claiming of a non-violent intimate relationship within a broader anti-oppressive community.

NOTES

1. Acknowledgements: Southern Cross University for an internal research grant to conduct the research project.

REFERENCES

ACON (AIDS Council of NSW) and Same Sex Domestic Violence Interagency (SSDVI). 2006. *Fair's fair: A snapshot of violence and abuse in Sydney LGBT relationships.* Sydney: ACON.

Allen, C. and B. Leventhal. 1999. History, culture and identity: What makes GLBT Battering different. In *Same-sex domestic violence,* ed. B. Leventhal and S. Lundy, 73–81. Thousand Oaks, CA: Sage.

Bagshaw, D., D. Chung, M. Couch, S. Lilburn and B. Wadham. 2000. *Reshaping responses to domestic violence—final report.* Partnerships Against Domestic Violence, Department of Human Services, University of South Australia Adelaide.

Balsam, K. and D. Szymanski. 2005. Relationship quality and domestic violence in women's same-sex relationships: The role of minority stress. *Psychology of Women Quarterly* 29: 258–269.

Bird, K. 2004. Towards a feminist analysis of lesbian violence II. Paper presented at the Home Truths Conference, September 15–17, Southgate, Melbourne.

Bornstein, D. R., J. Fawcett, M. Sullivan, K. D. Senturia and S. Shiu-Thornton. 2006. Understanding the experiences of lesbian, bisexual and trans survivors of domestic violence: A Qualitative Study. *Journal of Homosexuality* 51(1): 159–181.

Caluya, G. 2009. Foucault and everyday security: Lessons from the panopticon. In *Foucault: 25 years on: On-line conference proceedings.* Adelaide: Centre for post-colonial and Globalisation Studies, University of South Australia. Available at: http://www.unisa.edu.au/hawkeinstitute/publications/foucault-25-years/caluya.pdf [accessed September, 24 2009].

Cassidy, W. and M. Jackson. 2005. The need for equality in education: An intersectionality examination of labelling and zero tolerance policies. *McGill Journal of Education* 40(3): 445–466.

Chan, C. 2005. Domestic violence in gay and lesbian relationships. Sydney: Australian Domestic & Family Violence Clearinghouse. Available at: http://www.adfvc.unsw.edu.au/RTF%20Files/Gay_Lesbian.rtf [accessed November 4, 2010].

Code, Lorraine. 1998. Voice and voicelessness: A modest proposal? In *Philosophy in a feminist voice: Critiques and reconstruction*, ed. Janet Kourany, 204–229. Princeton, NJ: Princeton University Press.

Crane, B., J. LaFrance, G. Leichtling, B. Nelson and E. Silver. 1999. Lesbians and bisexual women working cooperatively to end domestic violence. In *Same-sex domestic violence*, ed. B. Leventhal and S. Lundy, 125–134. Thousand Oaks, CA: Sage.

Crossley, N. 1996. *Intersubjectivity: The fabric of social becoming*. London: Sage.

Dann, S., M. Haertsch, A. Hartree and A. Delaflece. 1997. Lesbian domestic violence project: Looking out for each other; Workshop report. In *Health in difference: Proceedings of the 1st national, lesbian, gay, transgender and bisexual conference*, ed. J. Ritchers, R. Duffin, Janet

Gilmour, J. Irwin, R Richards and A. Smith, 178–179. Sydney: Australian Centre for Lesbian and Gay Research.

Davis, K. 2008. Intersectionality as buzzword: A sociology of science perspective on what makes a feminist theory successful. *Feminist Theory* 9(67): 67–86.

Davis, K. and B. Taylor. 2002. Voices from the margins Part 2: Narrative accounts of the support needs of Indigenous families experiencing violence. *Contemporary Nurse* 14(1): 76–85.

Davis K., B. Taylor and D. Furniss. 2001. Narrative accounts of tracking the rural domestic violence survivor's journey: A feminist approach, women and violence special issue, ed. A. Meleis, *Health Care for Women International Special Issue on Women & Violence* 22(4): 333–347.

Demirovic, A. 2009. Foucault, Gramsci and Critical Theory—Remarks on their Relationship. Paper presented 27 July 2009 at the Foucault and Critical Realism Seminar, Cultural Political Economy Research Centre (CPER), University of Lancaster. Available at: http://www.lancs.ac.uk/cperc/docs/CR-Demirovic-Foucault.pdf [accessed September, 24 2009].

Eaton, L., M. Kaufman, A. Fuhrel, D. Cain, C. Cherry, H. Pope and S. C. Kalichman. 2008. Examining factors co-existing with interpersonal violence in lesbian relationships. *Journal of Family Violence* 23(8): 697–705.

Eckermann, L. 2002. Foucault, embodiment and gendered subjectivities: The case of voluntary self-starvation. Academy for the Study of the Psychoanalytic Arts. Available at: http://www.academyanalyticarts.org/eckerman.htm [accessed September, 24 2009].

Elliott, P. 1996. Shattering illusions: Same-sex domestic violence. In *Violence in gay and lesbian domestic partnerships*, ed. C. Renzetti and C. Miley, 1–8. New York: Harrington Park Press.

Girschick, L. 2002. *Women-to-women sexual violence*. Boston: Northeastern University Press.

Glass, N. and K. Davis. 2004. Reconceptualizing vulnerability: Deconstruction and reconstruction as a postmodern feminist analytical research method. *Advances in Nursing Science* 27(2): 82–92.

Glass, N., Koziol-McLean, J., Campbell, J., and Block, C. R. (2004) Female-perpegrated femicide and attempted femicide. *Violence Against Women*, 10, 606–625.

Hart, B. 1986. Lesbian battering an examination. In *Naming the violence: Speaking out about lesbian battering*, ed. K. Lobel, 173–189. Seattle: Seal Press.

Hartsock, N. 2006. Experience, Embodiment, and Epistemologies. *Hypatia* 21(2): 178–184.

Hassouneh, D and N. Glass. 2008. The influence of gender role stereotyping on women's experiences of female same-sex intimate partner violence. *Violence Against Women* 14(3): 310–325.

Kaschak, E. 2001. Intimate betrayal: Domestic violence in lesbian relationships. *Women & Therapy* 23(3): 1–5.

Laing, L. 2000. Progress, trends and challenges in Australian responses to domestic violence. *Australian Domestic Violence & Family Violence Clearing House, Issues Paper* 1: 1–17.

Laing, L. 2001. Working with women: Exploring individual and group work approaches. *Australian Domestic Violence & Family Violence Clearing House, Issues Paper* 4: 1–18.

Lancombe, D. 1996. Reforming Foucault: A critique of the social control thesis. *British Journal of Sociology* 47: 332–352.

MacLeod, C and K. Durrheim. 2002. Foucauldian feminism: the implications of governmentality. *Journal for the Theory of Social Behaviour* 32: 41–60.

May, V. and B. Ferri. 2002. "I'm a wheelchair girl now": Abjection, intersectionality, and subjectivity in Atom Egoyan's *The Sweet Hereafter. Women's Studies Quarterly* 30: 131–150.

Merrill, G. 1996. Ruling the exception: Same-sex battering and domestic violence theory. In *Violence in Gay and Lesbian Domestic partnerships*, ed. C. Renzetti and C. Miley, 9–21. New York: Harrington Park Press.

Osier, M. 2001. Lesbian battering dynamics: A new approach. *Off Our Backs* 31(9): 36–39.

Paton, W. 2008. Foucault, power and subjectivity. Paper presented at the The Australasian Postgraduate Philosophy Conference, March 26–28, University of Sydney. Available at: http://conferences.arts.usyd.edu.au/viewpaper.php?id=809&print=1&cf=16 [accessed November 4, 2010].

Paymar, M. and G. Barnes. n.d. Counter confusion about the Duluth Model. Battered Women's Justice Project. Available at: http://www.bwjp.org/files/bwjp/files/Countering_Confusion_Duluth_Model.pdf [accessed September, 24 2009].

Pitts, M., A. Smith, A. Mitchel and S. Patel. 2006. *Private lives: A report on the health and wellbeing of GLBTI Australians.* Melbourne: Australian Research Centre in Sex, Health and Society, La Trobe University.

Renzetti, C. 1992. *Violent Betrayal.* Thousand Oaks, CA: Sage.

———. 1998. Violence and Abuse in lesbian relations: Theoretical and empirical issues. In *Issues in Intimate Violence*, ed. R Bergin, 117–127. Thousand Oaks, CA: Sage.

Ristock, Janice L. 2002. *No more secrets: violence in lesbian relationships.* New York: Routledge.

Ristock, Janice L. and Norma Timbang. 2005. Relationship violence in lesbian/gay/bisexual/transgender/queer [LGBTQ] communities: Moving beyond a gender-based framework. Minnesota Centre against Violence and Abuse: Violence against Women Online Resources. Available at: http://www.mincava.umn.edu/documents/lgbtqviolence/lgbtqviolence.html [accessed November 2, 2010).

Russo, A. 1999. Lesbian organizing lesbians against battering. In *same-sex domestic violence,* ed. B. Leventhal and S. Lundy, 83–96. Thousand Oaks, CA: Sage.

Shawyer L. 2006. *Dictionary for the study of the works of Michel Foucault.* Available at: http://cjas.dk/index.php/foucault-studies/article/viewFile/2483/2481 [accessed September, 24 2009].

Sokoloff. N. J. 2004. Domestic violence at the crossroads: Violence against poor women and women of colour. *Women's Studies Quarterly* 32: 1391–47.

Websdale, N. 1998. *Rural women battering and the justice system.* Thousand Oaks, CA: Sage.

3 The Meaning of "Risk" for Intimate Partner Violence Among Women in Same-Sex Relationships

Diane Hiebert-Murphy, Janice L. Ristock, and Douglas A. Brownridge

INTRODUCTION

Various approaches have been taken to further our understanding of the complex problem of intimate partner violence. One framework that has been developed builds on the concept of risk. This framework promotes the identification of factors associated with risk for intimate partner violence (e.g., Romans, Forte, Cohen, Du Mont and Hyman 2007). A different approach seeks to further our understanding of intimate partner violence by focusing on women's experiences of violence, including individual and social forces that influence the meaning women make of these experiences (e.g., Boonzaier and de la Rey 2003; Nash 2005; Sleutel 1998).

In this chapter we interrogate the construct of being "at risk" for intimate partner violence and what it means for considering violence in same-sex relationships. A risk framework is described including how it shapes our understanding of the nature and causes of violence. Both the strengths and the limitations of this framework for understanding violence among women in same-sex relationships are exposed. A risk framework is contrasted with the approach that focuses on women's experiences, with a particular emphasis on an intersectionality framework. Drawing from a larger project with women who have been identified as vulnerable to experience intimate partner violence, we discuss our research with women in same-sex relationships to illustrate these differing perspectives. We illustrate how our understanding of intimate partner violence in same-sex relationships is furthered by integrating multiple frameworks that together examine the probability of experiencing violence, risk factors associated with increased violence, women's perceptions of risk, and the social context in which the violence occurs.

CONCEPTUALIZING RISK

A Risk Framework

The term "risk" is used in a variety of ways within the field of intimate partner violence. A growing body of literature has focused on identifying factors that discriminate between individuals who will and will not be violent towards their partners. This research forms the basis of risk assessment tools used within criminal justice systems to inform their decision-making (see Dutton and Kropp 2000), an approach that is not without controversy (Hoyle 2008). While much focus has been on predictors of risk for perpetrating violence, more recently the concept of risk has also been utilized to understand victims of intimate partner abuse. Being identified as "at risk" means that, by virtue of belonging to a particular group or possessing a particular characteristic, an individual has an increased likelihood of experiencing intimate partner violence. *Risk factors* are those characteristics that are associated with increased violence, including, for example, demographic factors (e.g., gender, age, ethnicity, socioeconomic status, marital status) and/or personal characteristics (e.g., self-esteem) (e.g., Brownridge 2009; Papadakaki, Tzamalouka, Chatzifotiou, and Chliaoutakis 2009; Romans et al. 2007).

Central to this meaning of risk is the concept of probability. Although it is possible that any woman may experience intimate partner violence, not all women have this experience. Exploring risk involves identifying women who have an increased likelihood of experiencing violence and attempting to understand what accounts for this increased vulnerability. The construct of risk provides a framework for identifying factors that explain (and predict) why some women experience violence and others do not.

Studying risk as probability for violence relies on quantitative methodologies that survey large groups of women. Theory drives the selection of variables used to define risk groups as do social and political forces that define certain social categories. Understanding the probability of experiencing violence among different groups of women and isolating factors related to the occurrence of intimate partner violence identifies variables that must be accounted for in theories of causation. Research facilitates theory building by identifying these factors and uncovering how these factors operate in the prediction of violence. In terms of practice, determining risk factors leads to the identification of groups of women who are "at risk" and who may benefit from targeted intervention.

A number of studies illustrate the application of this framework for research. Using data from the 1999 Canadian General Social Survey, Romans et al. (2007) found that younger age, being divorced/separated or single, having children in the household, poor self-rated physical health, lower income, and being Aboriginal were risk factors for intimate partner abuse. Women who are separated from their partners have also been identified as a group who are particularly at risk for intimate partner violence. Research suggests that as many as 40% of Canadian women with a former partner experience violence by that partner during separation (Hotton 2001). Summarizing the findings from three national Canadian data sets, Brownridge (2009) identifies the following groups of women as among those who are vulnerable to experiencing intimate partner violence: women separated from their partners, Aboriginal women, divorced women, women in rental housing, women in stepfamilies, cohabitating women, immigrant women, and women with disabilities.

Although the risk framework has been very influential in guiding the study of intimate partner violence generally, it has not been widely used in the study of women in same-sex relationships. Limited research has attempted to identify factors associated with increased risk for violence among women in same-sex relationships. Renzetti (1988) found that abusers' dependency on their partners as well as perceived power imbalances were associated with violence in lesbian relationships. Building on this work, McClennen, Summers and Daley (2002) developed The Lesbian Partner Abuse Scale to measure the construct of power imbalance. The measure, comprised of six factors (communication and social skills, substance abuse, intergenerational transmission of violence, fakes illnesses, internalized homophobia, and status differentials), was able to differentiate between women in lesbian relationships who were abused from those women who were not abused. More recently, Eaton, Kaufman, Fuhrel, Cain, Cherry, Pope and Kalichman (2008) found that power imbalance and inequality when making sex-related decisions were associated with intimate violence for women in same-sex relationships.

There are a number of possible explanations for the limited application of a risk framework to research on women in same-sex relationships. On a practical level, the methodologies associated with this approach rely on large datasets. The challenges of obtaining large, representative samples of women in same-sex relationships have been well documented (Renzetti 1992, 1998). On an epistemological level, this approach is based on assumptions that are less congruent than qualitative methodologies with the views of many researchers and activists who have been at the forefront in bringing attention to the violence experienced by women in same-sex relationships. A focus on risk factors tends to individualize the issue of intimate partner violence in same-sex relationships thereby minimizing the role of structural factors in understanding the violence. While quantitative research has been used to document the incidence and prevalence of the problem, qualitative approaches that give a voice to women who experience violence in same-sex relationships have been seen as central to furthering an understanding of the context in which the violence occurs (Bornstein, Fawcett, Sullivan, Senturia and Shiu-Thornton 2006).

A Framework of Women's Experiences

In contrast to a risk framework is an approach to studying intimate partner violence that focuses on exploring women's experiences of violence including their perceptions of vulnerability (e.g., Bornstein et al. 2002; Giorgio 2002). This view is interested in the phenomenological experience of violence including how women perceive their vulnerability for experiencing violence and the complex interplay of personal and social factors that impact on those experiences. Within this framework, the subjective experiences of women are of interest; value is placed on uncovering the richness inherent in women's accounts of their experiences, including their insights about vulnerability for intimate partner violence.

The focus on women's experiences utilizes qualitative methodologies that provide an in-depth exploration of the lived experiences of women. These methodologies examine how women view various factors in their lives that play a role in the violence that they have experienced. Utilizing a variety of qualitative approaches including, for example, narrative analysis, discourse analysis, and participatory action research (e.g., Bornstein et al. 2006; Giorgio 2002; Irwin 2008), women are encouraged to share their experiences within broad parameters (e.g., using guided interviews). These methodologies embrace diversity and complexity while seeking to identify patterns or themes that promote a greater appreciation of women's experiences of violence.

Focusing on lived experiences of risk can both complement and complicate the analysis of risk based on probability. Exploring women's life experiences challenges the notion that risk can be categorized, a concept central to a quantitative approach to risk. Life experiences are not easily captured in discrete categories or by measurement tools. This approach exposes the limitations of a quantitative/probability framework, calling for a greater appreciation of the complexities of women's experiences and demanding that theory and practice embrace this complexity. Research on women's perceptions of vulnerability can inform theory by identifying aspects of women's lives that must be considered in models of risk. Furthermore, studying women's experiences of risk offers insights for intervention with women who experience partner violence. To be effective, intervention must address issues of importance to women and be offered in a way that is congruent with women's perceptions of vulnerability.

There is a growing body of research that has taken this approach to the study of women who experience partner abuse. Sleutel (1998) conducted a review of women's first person accounts of abuse and identified more than thirty studies that used qualitative approaches to understand women's experiences. More recent research has included a focus on the impact of the social context on women's experiences, paying particular attention to the importance of gender, race, and class (e.g., Boonzaier and de la Rey 2003; Nash 2005). More limited research has considered the experiences of partner violence among women in same-sex relationships. Ristock (2002), for example, conducted a qualitative study with 102 lesbian women who experienced relationship violence. She found a strong pattern of first lesbian relationships being violent. Often the abuser was older and had been "out" longer while the victim was younger and had not been in a prior same-sex relationship. Her research also identified several additional contexts of violence related to alcohol abuse, the negative effects of homophobia and racism, and living in isolated communities (e.g., rural communities, immigrant communities). Other research has also identified how a limited level of awareness of partner violence within their communities and the resulting isolation are significant in understanding the experience of women in same-sex relationships (Bornstein et al. 2006). Recent research has shown that gender role stereotyping shapes women's experiences of same-sex violence by influencing individual, family, community, and social responses to the problem (Hassouneh and Glass 2008).

Intersectionality and Women's Experiences

The construct of intersectionality appears to hold particular promise for advancing research on women's experiences. Intersectionality extends the understanding of experience by providing a lens through which the structural context and its relationship to individual experience can be explored. Based on the work of Crenshaw (1994), intersectionality proposes that we exist within complex social contexts that are created by intersections of various systems of power (e.g., race, class, gender, and sexual orientation). Intimate partner violence is one form of oppression and control that must be understood within this broader context. It is the intersections of these various systems of power that give meaning to the violence (Bograd 2005). Because not all violence is the same, we need to work to identify and uncover how the social context both structures and produces abuse dynamics differently for different people.

An intersectionality framework challenges us to move away from thinking about one pattern of violence. Intimate partner violence is not seen as a monolithic phenomenon (Bograd 2005). Although emerging from a feminist analysis, it suggests that there are limitations inherent in viewing violence through a simple gender lens that adheres to a power and control model in which men are the abusers and women the victims. Either/or, binary thinking that places people and experiences into discrete categories is replaced by an acceptance of greater fluidity and both/and thinking. For example, the concept of power as fixed and held by one person is replaced by a perspective which understands power as shifting and relational. While gender is not disregarded as an important source of oppression, within an intersectionality framework a gender-based analysis is not considered the only, or most important, perspective (Sokoloff and Dupont 2005). Gender is not privileged over other sources of oppression that include, for example, race, class, ability, and sexuality. Furthermore, these various systems do not simply add on to each other. As Bowleg (2008) illustrates, within an intersectionality framework it is the complex intersections of these various systems that define experience.

Applying an intersectionality framework to the study of intimate partner violence is distinct from a risk framework in a number of ways.

First of all, an intersectionality framework asserts that violence must be understood within the social context and cannot be reduced to a list of "objective" factors that can be defined and measured at the level of the individual. The social and structural implications of factors such as race and sexuality, for example, are not exposed if conceptualized as individual characteristics. From an intersectionality perspective, individual experience can only be understood by examining the structural context in which the violence occurs. Second, an intersectionality framework furthers knowledge by adding complexity to our understanding of intimate partner violence; the goal is not to reduce the experience of risk to a set of factors or to emphasize sameness across experiences of violence but to identify and account for differences between and among individuals. Third, this framework encourages an examination of the limits and assumptions of the language that we use to talk about violence and the categories that we use to define women's experiences. As such, it rejects the notion that experiences can be reduced to static constructs that can be operationally defined and reliably measured.

There is debate about whether intersectionality is a theory, concept, method, or heuristic (Lewis 2009). This discussion notwithstanding, employing an intersectionality framework requires a methodology that promotes situating intimate partner violence within the broader context of an individual's experience. Although it has been argued that intersectionality can be promoted by quantitative research (Cole 2009), an intersectionality framework more frequently relies on qualitative methods that encourage freedom in the telling of experiences of violence and the reporting of the subjective meaning of the violence. It looks at the meaning that women make of their experiences, while adding a level of analysis that looks beyond individual perceptions to the ways in which experiences of violence are structured and produced by the context. As Lewis (2009) explains, intersectionality involves thinking simultaneously at levels of structures, dynamics, and subjectivities. It joins what is learned from listening to the voices of individuals together with what an analysis of the discourse reveals about the ways in which social structures impact on the meaning of the violence. Particular attention is given to the intersections of systems of power and the limitations of language in capturing the richness of experience. Established categories and conceptualizations of risk are critically examined.

Given the focus on the structural context in which violence occurs, an intersectionality framework holds particular potential for enhancing our understanding of the experiences of women in same-sex relationships who by virtue of their location in society are likely to experience various forms of oppression simultaneously. This approach has, for example, been shown to be useful in the study of black, lesbian women (Bowleg 2008). As Bowleg discusses, social identities and inequality based on social location are not mutually exclusive (i.e., black + lesbian + woman) but are interdependent (i.e., black lesbian woman); one's identity is not the mere addition of various categories but a meaningful whole emerging out of these various parts. As will be discussed in the next section, our interest was in extending the use of this framework to the study of intimate partner violence among women in same-sex relationships.

STUDYING INTIMATE PARTNER VIOLENCE AMONG WOMEN IN SAME-SEX RELATIONSHIPS: HOW FRAMEWORKS INFLUENCE MEANING

It is tempting to adopt one of the preceding approaches to the study of intimate partner violence and privilege that framework over others. Our interest, however, was in exploring the possibility (including the tensions and potential benefits) of moving beyond an either/or view to one that regards each of these frameworks as contributing to an understanding of intimate partner violence. What follows is a discussion of our attempt to integrate these approaches in research with women who have experienced intimate partner violence in same-sex relationships.

Overview and Background

The specific goals of our research were to (a) examine existing Canadian national databases to determine if they can contribute to our understanding of the risk of violence among women in same-sex relationships, (b) explore women's perceptions of risk for violence in same-sex relationships, and (c) explore if an intersectionality analysis furthers our understanding of risk. In order to address these issues, quantitative and qualitative methods were integrated into the research design.

Findings: The Multiple Meanings of Risk

The Probability of Experiencing Risk

Three secondary data sets from Statistics Canada, including the 1993 Violence Against Women Survey (VAWS) and the 1999 and 2004 General Social Surveys (GSS), were examined to consider if they could be useful in understanding risk among women in same-sex relationships. These data sets are based on telephone surveys and are comprised of a randomly selected, representative sample of Canadians (over 12, 000 women in each). Preliminary examination of the datasets revealed the limitations of these databases to address our questions. With the VAWS, it was not possible to identify respondents in same-sex relationships because they did not ask about sexual orientation and assumed heterosexuality. Both the 1999 and 2004 GSS had small numbers of respondents who were in same-sex relationships, preventing more detailed analysis on violence. For example, in the entire 1999 GSS, only twelve women reported that they were living with a same-sex partner. None of these respondents reported having experienced violence in the twelve months or five years prior to the survey. Clearly women in same-sex relationships were underrepresented in the studies; it is possible that either some participants did not report being in same-sex relationships or that women in same-sex relationships were more likely to have refused to participate.

Even if the number of women in same-sex relationships in the samples was larger, it became increasingly clear that there were significant limitations imposed by the assessment of violence in these surveys. For example, only violence that occurred within the last year and the previous five years was assessed. A modified version of the Conflict Tactics Scale was used; the limitations of this measure are well-known (e.g., Dekeseredy and Schwartz 1998). Furthermore, respondents were asked questions about violence by current and ex-partners. The sex of ex-partners was not reported raising the possibility that violence by an ex-partner reported by women currently in a same-sex relationship may very well have been perpetrated by male partners.

The inability of these datasets to address violence among women in same-sex relationships was disappointing and demonstrates the need for additional large-scale, representative research that seeks to estimate the occurrence of violence experienced by this group of women. The small number of women in same-sex relationships in this "representative" sample suggests that greater consideration needs to be given to recruitment strategies and research protocols that identify and address barriers to participation of this group. It is also clear that careful attention must be given to the measurement of sexual orientation and relationship type (same-sex versus heterosexual). There must be an appreciation that sexual orientation is not necessarily static. Data about relationships (including both current and past) must clearly delineate the nature of the violence experienced, the type of relationship, and the time frame assessed. Findings based on the data must be interpreted with careful consideration of the limitations imposed by the measurement of the constructs.

Women's Experiences of Being at Risk

In our study, qualitative interviews were conducted to explore women's perceptions of being at risk for violence in same-sex relationships. Women were asked to talk about how they made sense of the violence, what they thought was important in understanding the violence, and factors that they thought put women at risk for violence. They were also asked to reflect on whether being in a same-sex relationship affected the pattern of violence in the relationship. For the purposes of this discussion, seven interviews in which the women identified having experienced violence in a same-sex relationship will be used to illustrate the meaning of risk that emerged. The women self-identified as lesbian (three women), bisexual (two women) and two women stated they were uncomfortable labeling their sexual orientation. Five of the women reported having disabilities. Five of the women were Aboriginal and two were white. Five of the women were unemployed or on disability pension and two of the women were working. This demographic information reveals the ways in which race, class, gender, sexuality, and disability intersect differently for each woman in the study.

Initially, the interviews were analyzed using a qualitative descriptive approach (Gilgun 2005). Interview data were coded and themes related to risk were identified using qualitative analysis procedures (Patton 2002). This analysis of the qualitative interviews suggested that the concept of "risk" had some value in helping women make sense of the meaning of intimate partner violence in their lives as well as for women in general. There was variability, however, in the extent to which the term "risk" fit with women's experiences. Some women could speak easily about risk factors for themselves and other women while other women required more probing. For a few, risk seemed to imply weakness or vulnerability that they did not accept. Other women, however, did seem to identify themselves as having been vulnerable to violence.

When asked about risk factors in their situations, all women identified characteristics related to themselves, to their partners, and, to a lesser extent, the situation. Individual factors such as lack of support or isolation, addictions, assertiveness (or lack thereof), poor self-esteem, personality factors, mental health issues, and fear of being alone were identified as associated with the abuse. A family history of abuse was also named as increasing risk because it made abuse "normal." Individual characteristics of their partners were also identified as increasing their risk. Their partners' jealousy, substance use, personality factors, isolation, a family history of abuse, and mental health issues were all seen as increasing the risk that their partners would be abusive. Less frequently, structural factors were reported as risk factors. Several women identified that circumstances related to poverty (i.e., being homeless, unemployed, and/or single parents) increased their vulnerability.

There were differences among women regarding the extent to which they perceived sexual orientation as a factor in the violence. One woman did not consider being in a same-sex relationship as a factor in the violence:

> Interviewer (I): Do you think that being . . . in a relationship with a woman affected the pattern of abuse in that relationship?
> Participant (P): No I think it's my pattern of intimate relationships in general. But it could, it could have been a kangaroo, I probably would have picked an abusive kangaroo, you know what I'm saying.

Another woman identified similarities between abuse in same-sex and heterosexual relationships: "I don't think there is a difference between the same-sex, no, you know and the conventional couple, as they put it. I don't. There's a really, any much of a difference if it's an abusive relationship. There's always the one person who takes the lead." Further, she did not see the need for separate services: "I don't think they should isolate, oh you're same-sex relationship people, you go to that house. Oh you're heterosexual, go on this house. What's the point of that? Everybody suffers from the same thing."

Other women, however, saw a distinction between abuse in same-sex relationships and heterosexual relationships. For example, one woman described how she felt more frightened in heterosexual relationships because of the difference in physical strength between a man and a woman: "So it was different. I didn't really feel like I was being abused in that relationship because I was fighting back. I more or less felt like we were on equal ground. It was in the [relationships with] men though, that's a whole different story, you know." Another woman identified the invisibility of abuse in same-sex relationships: "I don't know how common it is, but it's probably more common than what people think. . . . Abuse in general, but particularly in lesbian relationships. Most people wouldn't think that one woman would do that to another woman, being disabled or not. I guess cause women are seen as nurturers."

In addition to talking about risk for themselves, women were able to reflect on factors that put all women at risk for violence in intimate partner relationships. In many cases the factors that were identified for placing all women at risk were congruent with factors that they thought placed them at risk. For example, low self-esteem, lack of education about abuse, isolation, fear of being alone, power imbalance, dependency, substance use, and disability were identified as risk factors for women in general. Several participants identified specific groups of women that they felt were particularly at risk by virtue of their social location (e.g., sex trade workers, immigrant women).

Several women identified structural factors that increase women's risk. Poverty, for example, was identified as a risk factor for all women. As one woman stated: "When there's poverty, there's a lot harder life. There's more frustration, which makes people lash out, and money has a lot to do with a lot of people's stresses, which also poverty, there's more addiction. There's more crime. It's a harder life so people want to drown their sorrows. They want to do whatever they can and then they lash out. It's just the whole cycle." Overall, the concept of risk appeared relevant to how the women understand their experiences of violence and make meaning of the factors in themselves, their partners, and the situations that contribute to violence. The term "risk" was primarily associated with individual characteristics with some attention to situational factors. Although the influence of structural factors in their lives was clearly evident in their narratives, these structural factors entered into their understanding of risk in a limited way. That is, women's responses to questions about risk did not promote an in-depth examination of these structural themes in the data.

An Intersectionality Analysis of Risk

A second level of analysis shifted to examining the ways in which participants' narratives suggested ways in which their experiences had been produced by their social position, resulting in risk for violence. Attention was given to ways in which various sources of power intersected to produce their experience as well as ways in which language and discourses created dichotomies that fit/didn't fit with their experiences. This approach draws on feminist perspectives of discourse analysis and deconstruction which examine systems of oppositions that produce identities and meanings (Wilkinson and Kitzinger 1995) and is consistent with the data analysis approach in which experience is seen as a key source for action and empowerment and is also seen as a socially constructed text (Ristock 2003; Ristock and Pennell 1996).

Intersections of Power

When asked about their risk for abuse, some women made reference to factors clearly associated with poverty (e.g., housing, social assistance), although poverty was infrequently named as a risk factor. Even less frequently did explicit references to other structural factors such as ableism, homophobia, or racism appear. Asking women to explain what they perceived as placing them at risk did not elicit responses that illuminated the importance of these contexts. The absence of explicit reference to context was incongruent with their narratives that provided a powerful picture of their marginalization. This second level of analysis revealed that contexts of poverty, racism, homophobia, and ableism were important (to varying degrees) in the experiences of violence. Examining the stories the women told about their experiences of abuse demonstrated how these various contexts produced complexities in the women's lives and were integral to understanding their experiences of intimate partner violence.

The contexts of poverty and race and the social marginalization created by their intersection stood out and produced complicated stories of violence. For example, one Aboriginal woman talked about abuse that occurred with a partner that she had met while they were both in jail. Their histories included involvement with both the child welfare and criminal justice systems. Poverty was a clear factor in the abuse; the woman talked about how she stayed with her partner after the relationship ended because of a lack of housing. It was during this period that much of the abuse occurred: "We had broken up and we were still living in the same house and we were still sharing rent. . . . I didn't want her to leave because then I would be screwed for a place to live. So yeah, maybe I kept her around for that. But a lot of the, a lot of the abuse happened after we were not together anymore and it was during the separation, but we were still living in the same house." This woman had also experienced abuse in relationships with men and believed that race was a factor in the abuse she experienced in one heterosexual relationship:

"When I was in a relationship with a white guy, that was my first abuse and I swore that I'd never go out with any white guys ever again, unless I was a lot bigger than them and I could beat them up."

Living in a context of violence was also prominent in many of the women's stories. Reports of child abuse, abuse in other intimate partner relationships, and exposure to violence were commonplace in the narratives. For example, in addition to the intimate partner violence she had experienced in two relationships, one woman talked about a long history of exposure to violence—she saw her mother beaten by a boyfriend, knew of someone who was killed by her partner, had friends in abusive relationships, and saw intimate partner violence as a part of her neighborhood:

> I remember my mom, watching my mom getting beat up by her boy-friend . . . then I got to the age where I was trying to defend her and help her. . . .
>
> . . . My aunty told me like, and I'll never forget her when she said this. She said, when I was a little girl she said, when I was younger my cousin said to me, if he doesn't hit me, that means he doesn't love me. Until the day that he killed her, he loved her to death. . . .
>
> . . . Well my friend is in an abusive relationship and that's what she does, she isolates herself. . . .
>
> . . . And my cousin right now, is in an abusive lesbian relationship and she's having a hard time finding somewhere to go. . . .
>
> . . . I live right downtown, and you see women, you know, after they get their child tax [benefit], and by the time the weekend comes around, they have black and blue faces, you know. Then you know, you see women walking behind their men because they're afraid not any other reason. It's a sad thought but it happens every day, and like it's happening right now and there's nobody to do anything about it.

Disability also factored into the abuse of some women. One participant, for example, had left the country to be with her partner. She was financially dependent on her partner because of an inability to work due to a chronic health problem. She reported that the disability affected the pattern of abuse; when her physical disability was worse, she couldn't do as much for her partner, which her partner resented. She also talked about how she is impacted by negative attitudes towards disability: "I see people looking at me and at others, and just sort of, oh well you know, try and sit a little further away. It's hard and it's just hard to be accepted, I guess, as normal because you have a disability."

Whiteness, education, employment, and absence of disability reflected a buffer of privilege that gave access to resources and therefore an ability to leave abusive relationships, seek help, and reflect on what happened. One white woman who was employed as a professional talked about having more options than other women: "I went for counseling at [agency name] and I went for EAP counseling through my employee kind of thing, you know, I didn't feel a lack of services for that. I don't know that there's a lot of counseling options for people with very little income." These services provided her with support and helped her see that the relationship was abusive. She earned more money than her partner which addressed the financial challenges associated with leaving the relationship. Her experience stands in stark contrast to the experiences of other lesbian women who experienced greater marginalization. For example, one woman talked about the struggles associated with poverty. She held numerous low-paying jobs and also worked in the sex trade to supplement her income. Financial abuse was a prominent factor in her same-sex relationship and created barriers to her leaving the relationship.

Homophobia was not explicitly named, but seemed evident in some of the narratives. Several women reported that their abusive partners were not "out" and feared the consequences should their sexual orientation become known. They clearly did not want the relationship to be visible. One woman talked about the role of this fear of being revealed in the relationship:

> P: She [her partner] was afraid to be outed at work. She didn't know if she'd lose her job, small town and all.
> I: So do you think that played into the abuse?
> P: I think so cause she was upset with me for being so open. [*Pause.*] I guess because it would reflect back on her and it would be obvious.

Other stories showed the workings of heteronormativity. Some of the women experienced little support for their same-sex relationship, limiting the support that they could access to deal with the abuse.

> P: It was difficult not only just because of like to go somewhere safe, but to go tell my family cause they didn't know I was in a relationship like that, you know.
> I: In terms of being in a relationship with a woman?
> P: Yeah, and that's a really big issue.

Women also reported difficulties accessing formal services because the abuse occurred in a same-sex relationship. One woman was denied entry to a shelter because her abusive partner was a woman:

> When I was looking for help and I called a shelter and they said they didn't accept people who were in same-sex relationships . . . And I was like you know I need to get out of here, like me and my kid. Well what's his name? Well it's not a he, it's a her, and they said, well we don't really deal with that kind of thing. Like, what kind of thing? Well, how does that make it different? Yeah. So there isn't a lot of support for same sex relationships if there's violence.

Another woman talked about the difficulty obtaining a restraining order when your abusive partner is female and/or you are afraid of being outed:

> I don't know how easy it is to get a restraining order or not when you're in that situation, compared to men and women. You've got to prove you're being attacked or whatever. Then you get put down a lot because you're a woman looking for a restraining order against a woman. Again if you don't want to be outed, that's not a route you can go . . . I think that's a big step there, people worrying about being outed trying to get the resources they need.

Even if able to access services designed for women in heterosexual relationships, some women questioned if these services would be able to meet their needs. As one woman expressed: "Even as comfortable as I am with mine [sexual orientation], even I was, well, anxious in trying to figure out how to get the help I needed and being accepted. Like if I went to a support group for women being abused, odds are I'd be the only one there who was a woman being abused by another woman. Try to deal with that and how they're perceiving you while you try to get the help you need."

In summary, the women in same-sex relationships in our study experienced various forms of oppression that impacted their lives and their experiences of violence. In reviewing the women's narratives, it was clear that it was not possible to identify one system of power (or lack thereof) as more important than another (i.e., privilege one over another) in understanding their risk for violence. Understanding risk required a search for ways in which these various forces intersected within each woman's life, creating a context for intimate partner violence to take hold.

Limitations of Labels/Categories

In addition to expanding the understanding of the intersections of structural factors, this analysis also revealed the limitations associated with trying to label/categorize women's experiences. Women expressed difficulty with categories related to sexual orientation, cultural identity, separation, disability, violence, and victim/perpetrator roles.

Some women were comfortable labeling their sexual orientation while others rejected labels. For example, one woman was clearly not willing to label her sexuality:

> I: Okay. So the next few questions we'll talk about, we'll ask about the most recent abusive partner. So how would you describe your sexual orientation?
> P: I don't.

Some women reported a fluid sexual identity. Categorizing these women according to sexual orientation did not fit with their self-identity:

I mean how it is with my sexuality I guess, I don't know, um, I'm more physically attracted sexually, physically attracted to men. I'm more emotionally attracted to women, and I guess I have a conflict there. I guess I feel a conflict there, but I don't consider myself, I don't even really consider myself bi-sexual. I mean I just think it's what, a choice that you make in how to behave in a certain situation.

Cultural identity was also not always easy to categorize. One woman, when asked about her cultural identity replied:

> P: English, Scottish, and there's Aboriginal in there, Ojibway.
> I: So do you identify as Métis?
> P: Not really, sometimes. Depends.

Although her cultural identity was fluid, she was clear that racism was a factor in the abuse: "I was lower than her [her abusive partner] cause she was European, and I had Native in my blood, and she was this, what did she say now, this superior being. It was a little scary actually. She was talking about her nice white skin, even though my skin was whiter, like it really didn't make sense."

Categorizing the status of a relationship (i.e., separated or together) also proved to be difficult. It was not always easy to determine if the violence occurred while the couple was separated. For example one woman described that she perceived the relationship as ended but was still living with their partner.

> P: A lot of the abuse happened after we were not together anymore and it was during the separation, but we were still living in the same house.
> I: . . . So you said that the violence began while you were together or after you separated?
> P: I think it was more or less after we separated.

Defining disability was a challenge in the interview. This was particularly the case for women who experienced significant mental health issues. Many women reported mental health issues related to the abuse (e.g., depression). It was unclear if pre-existing mental health issues were risk factors for the violence or a consequence of the abuse or both. This was especially the case for women who experienced violence in multiple relationships. Defining their mental health problems as "disability" did not seem to fit for many women even if their functioning was significantly impacted by these difficulties. One woman talked about the difficulty defining disability for women who are dealing with the emotional effects of experiencing violence:

> Well it's not so much of a disability, it's now become a matter of having to mend so it's yeah, like where are the healings centers for to go

through this after this has occurred and it's over. It's not over. It's still there, so it's not so much as a disability, it's a caring process and so to be, I don't know, incapable sometimes of getting up, incapable of trying to look at something different than you have, so it's not so much a disability, it's just a matter of, you know, trying to go day to day, trying to say, look this is not gonna be this one of these days, it's gonna be a different day.

There were also clear limitations with trying to focus on one experience (or one form) of violence in a woman's life. Most of the women had experienced multiple forms of violence (e.g., child abuse, intimate partner violence, and sexual assault) and violence with multiple partners. It was difficult for many women to speak only about the violence experienced in their same-sex relationships. For example, when asked about the abuse in a same-sex relationship, one woman replied: "I'm trying to remember. I've been choked a lot. I'm trying to remember who's done what. It's sometimes hard." This speaks to the complexity of violence in women's lives. Each incident of violence can only be understood if viewed within the broader context of the woman's entire life history, including the many experiences of violence that she may have had.

Finally, it was also apparent that the distinction between being a victim and a perpetrator of violence is not always clear. Some women talked about fighting back in their relationships. While they were victims of violence, they also behaved violently with their partners: "I didn't really feel like I was being abused in that relationship because I was fighting back. I more or less felt like we were on equal ground."

CONCLUSIONS ABOUT THE STUDY OF RISK

Our examination suggests that there are both contributions and limitations associated with various conceptual frameworks. The risk framework facilitates the identification of factors associated with intimate partner violence as well as groups of women that are particularly vulnerable to this form of violence. This knowledge is useful for raising awareness of the factors that contribute to the occurrence of violence and for leveraging resources to address the needs of specific groups of women. The contributions of this framework for women in same-sex relationships have not been fully realized. Additional research is needed to understand the prevalence of violence among women in same-sex relationships and the factors associated with this violence.

As we found, however, the application of a risk framework to the study of women in same-sex relationships is not without its challenges. Obtaining large, representative samples of women in same-sex relationships is extremely difficult. Creativity and resources are needed to access women in same-sex relationships. Attention must be given to reducing the barriers to participation in this type of research. Further research in partnership with community agencies and activists is needed to advance our understanding of how best to engage women in same-sex relationships in research. In addition to sampling issues, greater attention must be given to the challenges of measuring key constructs such as sexual orientation, violence, relationship status, and disability. More work must be done to develop instruments that have acceptable reliability and validity for use with women in same-sex relationships. This area of research is extremely limited and hampers the application of a risk framework to the study of violence experienced in same-sex relationships.

The further application of a risk framework to research on violence experienced by women is same-sex relationships may advance our understanding of factors that are associated with risk. Identifying risk factors for intimate violence in same-sex relationships and examining how these factors operate in predicting intimate partner violence may lead to the development of complex causal models of risk for this group of women. There are, however, limitations inherent in this framework that will persist. As our study illustrates, many of the concepts of interest in intimate partner violence in same-sex relationships (e.g., violence, sexual orientation, relationship status), are multifaceted and fluid. Attempts to categorize these experiences will at best always be an approximation of the reality of women's lives.

Given the limitations of a risk framework, our research suggests that it is imperative to incorporate alternative frameworks in the study of violence experienced by women in same-sex relationships. Exploring women's perceptions of risk addresses some of the limitations of a risk framework by examining the complexity of women's lives and the processes by which they make meaning of these experiences. Our research suggests that the concept of risk is relevant to how women understand their experiences of violence and make meaning of the factors in themselves, their partners, and the situation that contribute to violence. As we have seen, an intersectionality framework has the potential to further expand our understanding of risk by promoting an analysis of the forces that create the social context in which the violence occurs and is experienced. The individual and relationship risk factors that women identify occur in complex contexts. Within the stories of the women that we interviewed, poverty, racism, homophobia, and ableism were evident and interacted in ways that added complexity to our understanding of risk. This analysis illustrates how women's experiences of partner violence are "messy," not the "classic" case to which one woman referred. The analysis exposed the limitations of categorizing women (based on sexual orientation or disability status), relationships (separated/together), and violence (including who is the victim and who is the perpetrator). This analysis draws attention to the contextual factors that must be integrated into both theory and intervention and exposes the limitations of approaches that attempt to reduce experience to categories. Intimate partner violence in same-sex relationships is complicated; efforts to intervene in the problem must appreciate and respond to this complexity.

An approach that focuses on women's experiences is not without limitations. For example, this framework does not answer questions about the prevalence of the problem and is limited in its conclusions about the generalizability of the findings to other women in same-sex relationships. Overall, understanding risk for intimate partner violence among women in same-sex relationships requires much further study. Our work suggests that expanding the range of frameworks used to conceptualize and study risk, integrating multiple frameworks within research programs, and critically examining the frameworks that are utilized, will enhance our understanding of the multiple meanings of risk for this group of women. While the integration of multiple approaches is not without conceptual and epistemological challenges, the embracing of a both/and approach to research holds promise for furthering our understanding of these complex experiences. The findings that will emerge from an integration of approaches will provide a stronger foundation for public education, policy development, service organization, and clinical practice. By expanding and challenging our understanding of risk, research can contribute to intervention efforts aimed at addressing violence among women in same-sex relationships.

REFERENCES

Bograd, M. 2005. Strengthening domestic violence theories: Intersections of race, class, sexual orientation, and gender. In *Domestic violence at the margins: Readings on race, class, gender, and culture*, ed. N. J. Sokoloff and C. Pratt, 25–38. Piscataway, NJ: Rutgers University Press.

Boonzaier, F. and C. de la Rey. 2003. "He's a man, and I'm a woman." *Violence Against Women* 9: 1003–1029.

Bowleg, L. 2008. When black + lesbian + woman ≠ black lesbian woman: The methodological challenges of qualitative and quantitative intersectionality research. *Sex Roles* 59: 312–325.

Bornstein, D. R., J. Fawcett, M. Sullivan, K. D. Senturia and S. Shiu-Thornton. 2006. Understanding the experiences of lesbian, bisexual and trans survivors of domestic violence: A qualitative study. In *Current issues in lesbian, gay, bisexual, and transgender health*, ed. J. Harcourt, 159–181. New York: Harrington Park Press.

Brownridge, D. A. 2009. *Violence against women: Vulnerable populations*. New York: Routledge.

Cole, E. R. 2009. Intersectionality and research in psychology. *American Psychologist* 64: 170–180.

Crenshaw, K. W. 1994. Mapping the margins: Intersectionality, identity politics, and violence against women of color. In *The public nature of private violence*, ed. M. A. Fineman and R. Mykitiuk, 93–118. New York: Routledge.

Dekeseredy, W. and M. Schwartz. 1998. Measuring the extent of woman abuse in intimate heterosexual relationships: A critique of the Conflict Tactics Scales.

In VAWnet, a project of the National Resource Center on Domestic Violence/Pennsylvania Coalition Against Domestic Violence. Available at: http://www.vawnet.org [accessed on March 2, 2009].

Dutton, D. G. and P. R. Kropp. 2000. A review of domestic violence risk instruments. *Trauma, Violence, & Abuse* 1: 171–181.

Eaton, L., M. Kaufman, A. Fuhrel, D. Cain, C. Cherry, H. Pope and S. C. Kalichman. 2008. Examining factors co-existing with interpersonal violence in lesbian relationships. *Journal of Family Violence* 23: 697–705.

Gilgun, J. 2005. Qualitative research and family psychology. *Journal of Family Psychology* 19: 40–50.

Giorgio, G. 2002. Speaking silence: Definitional dialogues in abusive lesbian relationships. *Violence Against Women* 8: 1233–1259.

Hassouneh, D. and N. Glass. 2008. The influence of gender role stereotyping on women's experiences of female same-sex intimate partner violence. *Violence Against Women* 14: 310–325.

Hotton, T. 2001. Spousal violence after separation [1999 data]. *Juristat* 21: 1–19.

Hoyle, C. 2008. Will she be safe? A critical analysis of risk assessment in domestic violence cases. *Children and Youth Services Review* 30: 323–337.

Irwin, J. 2008. (Dis)counted stories: Domestic violence and lesbians. *Qualitative Social Work* 7: 199–215.

Lewis, G. 2009. Celebrating intersectionality? Debates on a multi-faceted concept in gender studies: Themes from a conference. *European Journal of Women's Studies* 16: 203–210.

McClennen, J. C., A. B. Summers and J. G. Daley. 2002. The Lesbian Partner Abuse Scale. *Research on Social Work Practice* 12: 277–292.

Nash, S. T. 2005. Through Black eyes. *Violence Against Women* 11: 1420–1440.

Papadakaki, M., G. S. Tzamalouka, S. Chatzifotiou and J. Chliaoutakis. 2009. Seeking for risk factors of intimate partner violence (IPV) in a Greek national sample: The role of self-esteem. *Journal of Interpersonal Violence* 24: 732–750.

Patton, M. Q. 2002. *Qualitative research and evaluation methods.* 3rd ed. Thousand Oaks, CA: Sage Publications.

Renzetti, C. M. 1988. Violence in lesbian relationships: A preliminary analysis of causal factors. *Journal of Interpersonal Violence* 3: 381–399.

———. 1992. *Violent betrayal: Partner abuse in lesbian relationships.* Newbury Park, CA: Sage Publications.

Ristock, Janice. L. 2002. *No more secrets: Violence in lesbian relationships.* New York: Routledge Press.

———. 2003. Exploring dynamics of abusive lesbian relationships: Preliminary analysis of a multisite, qualitative study. *American Journal of Community Psychology* 31: 329–341.

Ristock, Janice L. and J. Pennell. 1996. *Community research as empowerment: Feminist links, postmodern interruptions.* Toronto: Oxford University Press.

Romans, S., T. Forte, M. M. Cohen, J. Du Mont and I. Hyman. 2007. Who is most at risk for intimate partner violence? A Canadian population-based study. *Journal of Interpersonal Violence* 22: 1495–1514.

Sleutel, M. R. 1998. Women's experiences of abuse: A review of qualitative research. *Issues in Mental Health Nursing* 19: 525–539.

Sokoloff, N. J. and I. Dupont. 2005. Domestic violence at the intersections of race, class, and gender. *Violence Against Women* 11: 38–64.

Wilkinson, S. and C. Kitzinger, eds. 1995. *Feminism and discourse: Psychological perspectives.* London: Sage Publications.

4 Reflections on Approaches to Trans Anti-Violence Education

Joshua Mira Goldberg and Caroline White

Influenced by both radical and socialist feminisms, a critical outcome of second wave dominant Western feminist anti-violence activism was to "name," "break the silence," and make "public" the widespread occurrence of certain kinds of male violence against women (namely, violence in intimate relationships as well as sexual assault by an acquaintance, stranger, or partner[1]). Women's consciousness-raising groups of the late 1960s and early 1970s were one of the few forums where some North American women felt "safe" to publicly disclose the male violence they experienced in their private lives. Increased public disclosure revealed the pervasive and ubiquitous nature of male violence against women and, through shared experiences, women began to build theoretical frameworks for why the violence occurred. Theories linking the source of male violence to the subjugated, second-class position of women were developed. As theories were built, so too were safe houses, shelters for battered women and rape crisis centers—spaces that aimed to offer women safety from male violence, support in healing, and a location for political organizing (Bannerji 1997; Fitzgerald, Guberman, and Wolfe 1982; hooks 1984; Hull, Bell-Scott and Smith 1982; Maracle 1993; Ross 1995; Timmins 1995).

In part because the dominant North American feminist movements of the 1960s and 1970s emphasized translating one's own personal experience into universal political theory, the anti-violence movement and its attending theories developed in that timeframe largely reflected the limited life experiences and at times racist, classist, heterosexist, and ableist values and visions of its leaders. What it meant to "name" the violence, "break the silence" or make it "public," as well as what constituted "safe space," were constructs defined by dominant Western feminism and yet assumed to have value and meaning to all women (hooks 1984). This was also true of the constructs of sex and gender that were positioned as the cornerstone of the movement and the key to understanding violence. Women of color and Indigenous women, working class and poor women, sex trade workers, lesbian and bisexual women, women with disabilities, immigrant and other women would all come to challenge the dominant analyses with varying degrees of success, but despite some shifts the core of the analyses remained fundamentally the same (Bannerji 1997; Fitzgerald et al. 1982; hooks 1984; Hull et al. 1982; Maracle 1993; Ross 1995; Timmins 1995).

While dominant North American feminism was shaping and strengthening its movement—and specifically its analysis of male violence against women—trans people were also immersed in a growing trans consciousness and activism in the late 1960s and 1970s. As with dominant feminism, trans activism often focused on immediate survival needs and included a broad range of issues such as access to employment, housing, health care, and social services. As in the feminist movement, gender and sex were the central analytic tools as was, to a lesser degree, sexuality. Gender and sex were not, however, perceived or understood as necessarily universal, binary, fixed, mutually dependent or ahistorical. Leadership was also critically different from the dominant feminist movement in that trans activism was led in large part by racialized working poor and working class sex trade workers and night club entertainers, many of whom identified as male-to-female (MTF) (Feinberg 1996; Members of the Gay and Lesbian Historical Society of Northern California 1998). As a consequence, the ways that "violence" and "safety" were tackled by trans activists were not limited in the same ways as dominant feminism; police violence, prison violence, violence against sex trade workers and people living on the street, violence in the psychiatric system, deaths resulting from refusal of emergency services, and other manifestations of systemic as well as interpersonal class-race-gender violence were high priorities for many early transgender organizers in urban areas throughout North America.

Predictably, as both dominant Western feminism and trans activism became more widespread and organized, they would eventually intersect and conflict, given their divergent views on gender and sex, their leadership, and the urgent need for trans people to access shelters and other emergency services organized on the basis of gender/sex. Also predictable was the space where the conflict would become most obvious, and consequently most contested—"women's spaces," including access to women's events, organizations, groups, and services. Some of the more sensationalized battles have revolved around access to cultural and political events such as the Michigan Womyn's Music Festival; however, in our experience, both MTF and female-to-male (FTM) trans people have generally been more immediately concerned about access to health and social services, and particularly residential services as these tend to be segregated on the basis of sex/gender.

DEVELOPMENT OF TRANS ANTI-VIOLENCE EDUCATION

Political Context

In the absence of *publicly* known and essential, basic services for trans survivors of violence, trans people have out of necessity tried a multiplicity of strategies, including: reliance on trusted friends, lovers, or family; creation of mutual support networks, housing collectives, and peer support groups; and advocating for improved accessibility of funded services. Given the historical tension between dominant Western feminism and trans activism, most early trans anti-violence work focused on making critical social services—specifically services for women who had experienced violence—accessible to trans people and, for the most part, trans *women*.

In Canada, the earliest records we could find of Canadian trans anti-violence work were in the early 1990s, when concerted efforts were made to raise awareness about trans women's needs for access to services for women who had experienced violence. In 1994, Mirha-Soleil Ross and Xanthra Phillippa distributed a questionnaire to twenty women's shelters in Toronto asking them whether they accepted transsexual women as clients and/or staff, whether they had requests for services from transsexual women, whether they knowingly provided services to transsexual women, and whether they had any policies regarding transsexual women's access to their organizations (Ross 1995). The YWCA of Metropolitan Toronto subsequently commissioned an extensive report on "whether services should be extended to pre-operative male-to-female transsexuals" (YWCA 1996: 1; see also Cowan and Lopes-Iraheta 1996). In 1999, Allison Cope and Julie Darke distributed a survey to all transition houses in Ontario, asking about transsexual women's access to their organizations and services, accompanying policies, and perceived barriers preventing organizations from becoming fully accessible (Cope and Darke 1999); the responses from this questionnaire were later developed into a manual called the *Trans Accessibility Project: Making Women's Shelters Accessible to Transgendered Women*. In addition to these and other public actions were the countless invisible and undocumented actions that transpired in and outside of women's spaces and organizations.

Although gaining access to services was the immediate focus, a number of individuals in North America have been writing more generally about violence and trans communities, including: personal testimony by survivors and advocates; research examining prevalence, trends, and needs for anti-violence services; and trans educational materials for anti-violence agencies (see for example: Bettcher 2007; Brown 2007; Cook-Daniels 2001; Courvant and Cook-Daniels 1998; Courvant 1997; Daley 2005; Devor 1994; Gehring and Knudson 2005; Kenagy 2005; Kenagy and Bostwick 2005; Koyama 2000a; Koyama 2000b; Lamble 2008; Lombardi et al. 2001; Moran and Sharpe 2004; Munson and Cook-Daniels 2003; Munson and Cook-Daniels 2005; Namaste 1996; Namaste 2000; Nixon 1997a; Nixon 1997b; Northwest Network 1997; Peek 2004; Sausa 2005; Shelley 2008; Stotzer 2008; Thomas 2004; Wharton 2007; White 2002; Wilchins 1997; Witten and Eyler 1999; Wyss 2004; Xavier et al. 2005). Although it is not a unified body of work, and to generalize findings would do a disservice to the range and complexity of the experiences of trans people and their loved ones, themes that have emerged from this writing include: the vulnerability to violence; the multiple barriers faced by survivors in accessing services; and the significance of not only transphobia but also racism, poverty and economic discrimination, sexism, and homophobia in experiences of violence.

Regional Context

In the area that we live and work in (occupied Coast Salish Territory, known colonially as the southwest region of "British Columbia"), some anti-violence organizations were motivated to develop trans accessibility policies and practices from a position of political commitment to inclusion, diversity, and equality. Additional and highly-compelling impetus for change also came from several high-profile human rights tribunal rulings that affirmed trans women's legal rights to access women's spaces, services, and organizations (*Sheridan v. Sanctuary Investments Ltd.*; *Mamela v. Vancouver Lesbian Connection*; *Nixon v. Vancouver Rape Relief Society*). A particularly prominent case was *Nixon v. Vancouver Rape Relief Society*. In 1995, Kimberly Nixon, a transsexual woman, filed a human rights complaint against Rape Relief after she was expelled from their volunteer peer counseling training program when a training facilitator determined that Nixon had "not been a woman since birth and had lived some portion of her life as a man" (*Nixon*, 7). In 2002, the BC Human Rights tribunal ruled in favor of Nixon. The decision was appealed by Rape Relief and overturned by the Supreme Court of British Columbia (*Vancouver Rape Relief Society v. Kimberly Nixon and British Columbia Human Rights Tribunal*). The reversal against Nixon was upheld by the BC Court of Appeal (*Vancouver Rape Relief Society v. Nixon*), and an appeal by Nixon was refused by the Supreme Court of Canada in 2007.[2]

Although the *Nixon v. Rape Relief* case was an important stimulus for collaboration between trans and non-trans feminists (by the time the final ruling was issued many women's anti-violence organizations had already declared their support for trans women's inclusion), the case was highly contentious and charged on both sides. In 2000, Trans/Action, a coalition of trans people and allies, received financial and political support from then BC Human Rights Commissioner Mary-Woo Sims to form the Women/Trans Dialogue Planning Committee (W/TDPC) to encourage and foster communication between women and trans communities. The W/TDPC, comprised of non-trans women and trans people of various genders, sponsored various educational initiatives, including the *Trans Inclusion Policy Manual for Women's Organizations* (Darke and Cope 2002). It was as part of this initiative context that we began to work together on trans anti-violence issues.

Personal Context

In order to better understand our position on trans anti-violence initiatives, it is important to outline the personal contexts which gave rise to and influenced our decisions to do trans anti-violence work. Joshua was born female and grew up in a secular Ashkenasi Jewish family and community committed to social justice. His involvement in anti-violence work started in the late 1980s in the form of activism against state violence, particularly in Indigenous solidarity, anti-militarism, and prison justice movements. His experience in an abusive relationship prior to his transition led him to become a client of a women's anti-violence agency in the early 1990s. Following transition in 1996, he worked for three years at a needle exchange (where he frequently acted as an advocate for survivors turned away by local anti-violence services) and volunteered at a crisis line while simultaneously helping establish local and province-wide trans community organizations to provide peer support, advocacy, and education regarding trans issues.

In 1991, Caroline began work at a sexual assault center (SAC) in Ontario as a service provider and educator. After several years and many talks, panels, and workshops on male violence against women, dating violence, child sexual assault, sexual harassment, dissociation, anti-racism, and oppression, Caroline became frustrated by the limitations of the analysis central to the SAC's work (limitations that started to sound more like convenient sound bites than an actual reflection of the complexities, and often, contradictions of the work). The working analysis of male violence against women became inadequate because it at times insisted on, while at other times defaulted to, binaries across gender (man/woman), sex (male/female), sexuality (heterosexual/homosexual), race (white/of color), and ability (able-bodied/with disability), among others, that did not, in and of themselves, exist. At the same time, there were specific instances when the analysis side-stepped the use of binaries altogether, such as the construction of the "universal" woman which in theory represented all women, but which in reality, only represented white, heterosexual, able-bodied, middle-class women successfully. The struggle with the constraints of the existing paradigms and analyses led Caroline to initiate trans-related policy and training at the SAC in 1994.

We met in 2000 when Joshua was hired by the Women/Trans Dialogue Planning Committee (of which Caroline was a member) to review the *Trans Inclusion Policy Manual for Women's Organizations* (Darke and Cope 2002). In partnership with the Justice Institute of BC, and the Trans Alliance Society, we again came together to write *Trans People in the Criminal Justice System: A Guide for Criminal Justice Personnel* (Goldberg 2003) and later *Making the Transition: Providing Service to Trans Survivors of Violence and Abuse* (Goldberg 2006).[3] Since then, together and alone, we have written several trans anti-violence publications (Goldberg and White 2004; Goldberg and White 2006; White 2002; White and Goldberg 2006a; White and Goldberg 2006b; White and Goldberg 2006c; White and Goldberg 2006d), as well as co-facilitated training workshops for anti-violence, health and other service providers based on the *Making the Transition* curriculum. In addition to our work together we have both been involved in multiple trans anti-violence initiatives with other colleagues, including the delivery of workshops for health and social service providers,[4] helping service providers and organizations develop best practice guidelines (Bockting , Knudson and Goldberg 2006; White Holman and Goldberg 2006a; White Holman and Goldberg 2006b) and consumer education materials (Gunn and Goldberg 2002; Simpson and Goldberg 2006), and performing a regional evaluation of trans community service needs that included assessment of need for anti-violence services (Goldberg 2003).

We have worked together as colleagues in anti-violence work for eight years. In this chapter we critically reflect on our combined years of trans anti-violence activism and education within women's anti-violence organizations, discuss the challenges of trans-specific and "LGBT" educational approaches, and explore directions for future work.

LIMITATIONS OF CONVENTIONAL ANTI-VIOLENCE FRAMEWORKS, PRACTICES, AND TOOLS

In seeking to advance feminist goals and raise awareness about intimate violence against women, dominant Western anti-violence services and movements have developed strong theoretical and political frameworks. Although originally rooted in the lived experiences of survivors, particular ways of defining, understanding and responding to violence are now becoming rigidly codified in training, institutional policy, and legislation. This entrenchment of theoretical and political anti-violence frameworks has had an enormous impact in shifting the discourse of violence against women and also public understanding of needed related services. For example, in British Columbia the "power and control wheel," a visual tool for analyzing and understanding sexist dynamics in abusive relationships created by feminist anti-violence organizers, forms part of the government policy regarding police approaches to calls concerning domestic violence. Further, transition houses, sexual assault centers, and violence prevention programs, while chronically underfunded, are sufficiently recognized to receive public funds and community support for fundraising efforts. At the same time, however, the efforts to entrench particular positions regarding violence have also created often narrow, oversimplified, and distorted understandings of the nature of violence and abuse, and have limited responses to the diverse and changing needs of individuals who fall outside of the evolving definition of what "survivor" constitutes (e.g., women of color, Indigenous women, women with mental health issues, sex trade workers, lesbians, immigrant women, men, trans people).

The Trouble with Conventional Gender

Ironically, despite differing views on how gender and sex are constituted, in much North American trans anti-violence work and analysis gender is, as in dominant Western feminist anti-violence discourse, the central component. Although some analyses have emphasized an intersectional approach, and particularly the racism, classism, and homophobia evident in the high rate of violence against transgender women of color living or working on the streets, violence against trans people is often portrayed as rooted in gender oppression, particularly *transphobia*, the hatred and suppression of gender variance.

As in feminism, in trans movements there are heated debates about whether gender is biologically innate or socially constructed, and conflict over what importance to place on physical manifestations of sex and gender in relation to identity. In arguing for access to anti-violence services, for example, some activists and educators have taken the position that trans women should be able to access women's services because trans women *are* women. Such an argument presupposes that there is such a category as "woman," whether that category is considered fixed and immutable wherever the line is drawn (e.g., whether an individual has had hormone treatment or genital surgery, or is living full-time as a woman), or a more fluid and shifting sense of self and the perception of others. This way of constructing gender and tying it to service delivery is problematic both in terms of the cultural specificity and the ethnocentrism inherent in assuming such definitions of gender are "natural" and hence universal, and also in terms of the inevitable attempt to police the boundary between "woman" and "other" with a consequent impact of excluding "others"—including crossdressers, Two Spirit people, genderqueers, people who identify as androgynous, people who are bi- or multi-gendered, people with shifting gender identity, non-trans men, and trans men—from accessing essential services.

As well, the emphasis on gender and particularly a binary approach to gender (male/female, or FTM/MTF) reproduces a conceptual framework where gender is either viewed in isolation from, or secondary to, other aspects of identity such as race, class, ability, or is conflated with other identities such as sexuality. It would seem that there is no easy language, no easy infrastructure, to understand identities which defy simplistic either/or categories.[5] The result is a hierarchy of inclusion where the degree to which the survivor matches the current dominant construction of woman or man within the traditional gender or sex and other societal classifications (white, middle-class, able bodied, heterosexual) indicates the degree they are likely to be included in discussions about violence and considered acceptable or "appropriate" to access anti-violence services. Women's organizations that base or have based access on trans women "passing" or having had sex reassignment surgery illustrate this point. It is credit to the work of trans anti-violence survivors, activists, and service providers that policies basing access on genitals or surgical status are now rare. However, the degree to which a survivor "passes" or "looks like women" continues to be a key predictor of the quality of service she will receive from women's organizations. Also challenging is the question of where trans people in the FTM spectrum and trans people who do not identify as MTF or FTM should access services, with some gender-based anti-violence organizations defining their client inclusion criteria on the basis of identity—more respectful than definitions based on body parts, but still not necessarily useful for FTMs who don't feel comfortable discussing experiences of abuse with non-trans men, or for people who do not identify as MTF or FTM.

On a practical level, this has been a challenge to us as educators in our workshops for anti-violence and as health and social service providers. Most of the people who attend our workshops have had little experience with trans issues and, for them, to even explore the definition of what it means to be a "woman" or a "man" often feels overwhelming and/or highly abstract. We have often used FTM/MTF as simplified shorthand for a spectrum of people with very different identities and experiences. We are aware, however, that by employing the MTF/FTM binary, even though we may be expanding the definition of what it means to be a "woman" or "man," we are at the same time reproducing and securing the dominant woman/man gender binary employed by Western feminist anti-violence discourse. As well, by failing to address how MTF and FTM identities are constituted through race, class and ability, for example, we only expand what it means to be a white, middle-class, able bodied MTF or FTM survivor. The overarching gender binary still exists, even though the definitions within the binary are no longer so discrete, stable or universal.

By adopting a MTF/FTM binary framework, we also risk adopting other elements of dominant feminist Western anti-violence rhetoric that may not fit the experiences of trans survivors. For example, although hate crimes are often thought of as being perpetrated by a stranger, in documentation of trans experiences of hate-motivated violence the perpetrator is frequently known to the victim. How "deception" and "betrayal" function in trans intimate partner violence are also complicated by questions of disclosure of gender identity or history (think here of what was commonly described as the "shock" scene in the *Crying Game* or the legitimization of violence based on "betrayal" in *Boys Don't Cry*). "Passing," transitioning, and the very language of violence (e.g., how "victims," "perpetrators," and "survivors" are defined; what constitutes rape and how body parts are described) are all further examples of how trans people's experiences of violence do not fit with and may differ from dominant understandings of violence against women.

As we have developed our educational materials together, we have been sharply critical of dominant Western feminist anti-violence frameworks and particularly the question of why gender and sex are the primary axes for designing anti-violence services. To question this is to challenge the foundation on which many anti-violence services are built (including ones we have worked in), and we have experienced tremendous and unexpected resistance to this type of discussion. Early in the development of the *Making the Transition* curriculum, for example, a proposed facilitated discussion of various models for anti-violence service delivery and reflections on the strengths and weaknesses of each model was nixed by reviewers on the premise that it would be too threatening to women's anti-violence organizations. The argument given was that trans issues were perceived by some women's organizations as divisive, manipulative attempts to delegitimize anti-violence service provision and women-only space; questioning whether gender-based service provision was an effective model for anti-violence services would only confirm the worst fears about trans people being a threat to feminism. One individual raised concerns that our materials could be used by government agencies to justify cuts in funding to women-only anti-violence services (an ironic concern, as the provincial government had recently made deep cuts to women's services, without using trans educational materials to justify its actions).

The imperative to follow a reformist gender agenda has been a challenge throughout our work, both with each other (as we have at times disagreed with each other about the ethics and politics of women-only service provision) and more broadly in our work with colleagues in the feminist, queer, trans, and anti-violence fields. While recognizing the sensitivity of the issues and respecting the need for women-only organizations to meet the needs of some survivors, it does not seem outrageous to suggest that no one model can do everything and that a diversity of models is the only practical way to meet diverse needs.

Although there is no question that many anti-violence services are financially and politically marginal and face significant struggles to survive, one of the dynamics that has been difficult to navigate in our education work is the resistance within some anti-violence organizations to acknowledging their power, and the associated portrayal of trans survivors as threatening, assaulting, and attacking women's anti-violence organizations (Lakeman 2006; Landsberg 2000). This response is so disproportionate to the reality that it is difficult to know how to respond. Although the power dynamics between trans people and non-trans people are complicated on an individual level not only by gender but also by racism, classism, ableism, heterosexism, and so on, it has been alarming that groups with significant community and institutional power have taken the position that they are being victimized by the trans community. While trans people have the power to seek state intervention (e.g., human rights complaints), within the trans community there is no institutional power to set policies that determine non-trans people's access to anti-violence services, as does exist in the women's anti-violence sector. Feminists have, through years of hard organizing, won significant battles and have a level of institutional power that must be acknowledged if the sector is to able to meaningfully shift and change to meet changing conditions over time. To make explicit this power structure does not minimize the significance of sexism in the lives of all women (especially those who are also racialized, poor, or otherwise marginalized on a base that is connected to gender). Rather, this discussion merely acknowledges that social service organizations tend to replicate dominant power structures, and this must be acknowledged if education is to be meaningfully transformative.

LGBT vs. Trans-Specific Approaches in Anti-Violence Education

In seeking to develop an awareness of trans issues, many trans activists and allies as well as service providers have adopted an "LGBT . . ." rubric as the theoretical and practical framework for their work.[6] Although the rationale for an LGBT approach varies widely, in our region the LGBT approach is rooted primarily in the efforts of queer-identified trans people trying to increase trans visibility within the queer community, promote trans inclusion, and create opportunities for education about the links between homophobia and transphobia. Others have taken a trans-specific approach that distinguishes between sexual orientation and gender identity in terms of personal identification, socioeconomic issues, and political organizing.

Although LGBT and trans-specific approaches are being advanced as a response to heterosexist and transphobic norms around intimate partner violence, in adopting these frameworks to try to broaden the understanding of experiences of intimate partner violence we risk making the same mistakes made by the dominant feminist movement in promoting a rigid framework, theory, and political agenda relating to violence. Becoming attached to a particular way of understanding violence not only marginalizes survivors whose experiences do not match the theory, but also perpetuates the misunderstanding that "LGBT" or "T" survivors have a homogenous experience and uniform needs in relation to anti-violence services. Of particular concern is the reinforcement of the stereotype that gender and sexuality are primary in understanding the needs of survivors of violence. In this section we describe our experiences with LGBT and trans-specific approaches in anti-violence education, and reflect on our struggles with the limitations of both frameworks.

The Trouble with "LGBT"

While addition of a "T" to "LGB" has increased visibility of trans issues and programs' accountability to trans people, too often LGBT is generalized as one homogenous group of people with identical experiences, needs, and concerns. There is little critical examination of why "L", "G", "B", and "T" came to be grouped together in the first place, and often very little understanding of the limits of that alliance and the distinct issues faced by lesbians, gay men, bisexual people of all genders, and trans people even in such obvious areas as differing physical anatomy leading to different needs in health care services, let alone more nuanced issues relating to the distinction between sexual behavior, sexual identity, and identification with a particular community. In our experience, this limited understanding of the complexities within LGBT has led to some significant challenges in our anti-violence education work.

For example, in approaching anti-violence organizations to discuss training on trans issues we were often told that the staff of such organizations was already familiar with trans issues because they recently attended an anti-homophobia workshop or a workshop on same-sex violence offered by a LGBT organization. Similarly, we have often been told that an organization is already able to meet the needs of trans people because they have policies and procedures to deal with homophobic harassment, and pamphlets on same-sex relationship abuse. Conversely, after taking our trans-specific workshop, participants not infrequently expressed appreciation for having a greater understanding of "gay" issues. Although great strides have been made in conceptually disentangling gender, sex, and sexuality the actual praxis remains challenging.

The same challenge is also prevalent within LGBT organizations. Because LGBT organizations tend to attract people who are strongly LGB- or queer-identified, and there have been fewer avenues for other trans people to make their voices heard, there is little awareness in LGB organizations (even among trans staff and clients) that many trans people do not identify as queer or as LGB and do not feel comfortable accessing LGBT organizations.[7] Among LGBT organizations that added the "T" after being pressured by queer-identified trans people to do so, there can be particular frustration at having the limits of their accessibility pointed out. One LGBT organization that we tried to engage with complained that "first we add the T because that's what we were told the trans community wanted, and now you tell us that's the wrong approach. We can't win no matter what we do." This positioning of a funded organization as the victim of a marginalized group of clients is, as we mentioned earlier, similar to responses from the anti-violence sector.

With anti-violence colleagues working within a LGBT framework, there has been little perceived value in critically examining the strengths and weaknesses of a LGBT approach to anti-violence education. LGBT organizations have, not surprisingly, tended to feel threatened and/or defensive by any discussion of the limits of an LGBT framework, particularly in reference to the inclusion of the "T." In one instance LGBT anti-violence educators declined our offer to work collaboratively to develop anti-violence resources, stating that "T" issues are already sufficiently and adequately covered by their organization and further, indicating any specific attention to the "T" would compete for already scarce funding and other resources (e.g., staff time, library purchases, workshop time).

In our region the "LGBT" is now so ubiquitous and familiar that considerable time is required to engage in any critical discussion and evaluation of its relevance and usefulness in policy, service provision, training, and educational tools. Unfortunately, time is not a commodity that service providers tend to have a lot of when producing policies or best practices or when delivering workshops—it is difficult to dissect the "LGBT" in a ninety minute or even three hour workshop, and even more difficult to take the discussion from theory to meaningful implementation as there are rarely opportunities to take material away, reflect, and then come back to discuss practical implications in day to day frontline work.

A larger question is whether the coupling of the "T" with the "LGB" even makes sense for anti-violence education. Why combine sexuality and gender into a single LGBT framework, for example, rather than dealing with violence from an anti-racist and anti-colonial perspective? Arguably, gender norms are as connected to racialization, class structures, societal standards regarding physical and mental ability, age, and other axes of oppression as to sexuality. The terms "LGBT" and "queer" essentialize multi-faceted identities into what has frequently come to mean white, middle-class, able-bodied gay and lesbian. Ruth Goldman refers to the absence of other identities as "constructed silences" and writes: "if queer theory is to truly challenge the 'normal,' it must provide a framework in which to challenge racist, misogynist and other oppressive discourses/norms, as well as those that are heterosexist and homophobic. We must not simply challenge heteronormativity but instead must question the very system that sustains heteronormativity" (1997: 174). Although Goldman addresses queer theory, heterosexism, and homophobia, it is easy enough to extend her thinking to include an LGBT framework, the "T" itself and transphobia.

Given the difficulties associated with the LGBT framework, which we have described above, one is compelled to ask: why use an LGBT framework in anti-violence education? It's an uneasy question that is most often met with either uneasy silences or passionate defense, rather than critical discussion. Questioning the LGBT framework is not unlike the challenging of dominant feminist theory and practice.

Although useful in challenging heterosexist norms around relationships and relationship violence, in terms of an analysis of violence our experience has been that an LGBT approach tends to result in little theory and/or practice that speaks to the specificity of trans experience(s). As a result, we, along with some colleagues have taken a trans-specific approach to anti-violence education.

A TRANS-SPECIFIC APPROACH: THE TROUBLE WITH "T"

In our education we talk specifically about trans people and loved ones, with a focus on intersections between trans issues and race, culture, class, disability, sexuality, and other parameters of personal and community identity, oppression, and resistance. Although we have used a trans-specific rather than an LGBT approach in our work, we have felt frustrated with its limitations. Similar to the production of a singular identity in the LGBT approach, the trans-specific approach is problematic as it fails, just as the

LGBT approach does, to account for the specific identities and experiences of survivors within the umbrella term of "trans." How trans identities and experiences are not only sexed and gendered but also racialized, classed, and otherwise constructed is too often lost. The "trans" umbrella is therefore not substantively different than any other categorization that conceals power differentials and falsely assumes shared identity and experience. As described by Koyama, this tendency to organize around an identity politic has important implications both in terms of political organizing and also anti-violence service provision:

> Within the movement against domestic violence . . . the pervasive notion of "women's shared experiences" and other feminist euphemisms hinder our ability to recognize our paternalism and to create structures that are truly survivor-driven. Worse, even when survivors' voices are centered, we frequently end up creating a similarly faulty notion of "survivors' shared experiences" which works to invisibilize specificities of each survivor's experiences within the complex matrix of social identities, roles and oppressions, usually to the detriment of women of color, poor women, immigrant women, and others marginalized and underrepresented within the domestic violence movement. (Koyama 2003: 14)

With regards to anti-violence work, homogenizing the T becomes extremely problematic if not dangerous when considering the dynamics of violence and services required across different gender identities. "Passing/not passing," for example, frequently places trans people in the MTF spectrum at greater risk than in the FTM spectrum while the issues for trans people in the FTM spectrum gaining access to anti-violence services are significantly different from those in the MTF spectrum.

Assuming a homogenous "trans" experience is not only misleading in terms of the diverse needs of individual trans survivors of violence, but also—like second wave feminism and the LGBT approaches—tends to reinforce the emphasis on gender and sex in analyzing why violence happens, and how we can stop it. In doing so, despite our best efforts to incorporate an intersectional analysis, by the very nature of the time spent answering trans questions in relation to gender, sex, and sexuality we mask the importance of colonialism, racism, militarization, class hierarchies, contempt for sex trade workers and injection drug users, ableism, religious bigotry, the prison-industrial complex, and other similar systemic influences on violence. In our experience, however, these same structural issues are most often key in trans peoples' lived experiences of violence.

The challenge for us as educators is how to teach about socially constructed concepts such as gender variance in a way that is respectful of the tremendous diversity in how gender identity, expression, and perception are understood within multiple, complex, and shifting systemic contexts. Although, for example, we separate out sex, gender, and sexuality, to try to disentangle "T" from LGB, we are also aware that for some individuals and in some cultures sex, gender, and sexuality are not separable aspects of identity, roles, or relationships. We situate our framework as a necessarily shifting construct rather than "truth," and encourage people to critically engage and counter it with cultural and other lenses that approach it in a different way. Still, the concern remains that the framework will be uncritically adopted as the new rigid framework and will inadvertently lead to service providers making a whole new set of culturally specific and other assumptions. It is difficult to let go of the desire to neatly categorize things as "this" or "that" and fix them in one's mind as being a particular way, rather than dealing with the complexities and paradoxes of life. This anxiety and tension, however, cannot be resolved by finding the "right" theory, language, category, or approach. If anything, our experience is that being effective in this work requires continuously becoming aware, and then letting go, of expectations so that we can interact in a fresh and genuine way with people as they are right in front of us, instead of attaching even more preconceptions based on our idea of what it means to be "trans" or "a survivor."

WHERE DO WE GO FROM HERE?

Given the political constraints of the time and place in which we have done our work, and our own limits and shortcomings as educators, the gains we have been able to make have been incremental, piecemeal, and at times contradictory. We have tried various strategies: adapting tools used by many anti-violence organizations (e.g., the "power and control wheel") to make them more relevant to work with trans survivors; facilitating development of trans accessibility policies and procedures, including systemic and institutional violence and abuse wherever possible; and trying to promote awareness about issues not typically included as "trans-specific" but in our view highly relevant to the trans people most vulnerable to violence such as sex trade workers, prisoners, and trans people with cognitive or mental disabilities. At times we have taken positions that we do not wholeheartedly believe in—arguing for trans women and trans men to be able to access women's services, for example—because on a practical level we want services to be available even if the form of delivery is not what we believe it should be. Throughout our work we have tried to adapt or add onto problematic frameworks because there have been limited opportunities to openly discuss, let alone meaningfully challenge, core problems within institutional anti-violence structures and creatively rethink these structures and services from the ground up. At the same time, we often feel that our training—as limited and flawed as it is—risks setting up frontline workers and their organizations because it introduces them to systemic structural and analytical issues but not with the depth required to substantively transform their agencies.

The systemic issues that we have discussed here are not likely to change in the near future. Our critique of the current structure's gender rigidity often leads people to think that we are suggesting that anti-violence services should no longer be organized based on gender; although this is an oversimplification of our vision for anti-violence services, and would not in and of itself be the kind of positive transformation we would like to see, it does pose the question of what it would take to create an anti-violence sector that was flexible enough to be responsive to the range of needs that exist. Unfortunately, anti-violence and LGBT agencies are not likely to have the financial resources or the confidence of political security required to engage in the kind of in-depth discussions necessary to meaningfully rethink an entire service sector. Institutional change is often slow and incremental at best, and within the anti-violence sector the deeply held political beliefs make it challenging to suggest changes. Given these constraints, which are not changeable by education alone, what can be done in terms of trans anti-violence education?

Our recommendations for education with anti-violence workers are based on our experience as two people working in a particular place at a particular time. Like all experiential knowledge, our knowledge and recommendations are limited and reflective of our biases, beliefs, relationships with the anti-violence sector and each other, our life history, and our politics. We make no claim that these recommendations are universal, but we hope that they are useful at least in stimulating discussion among people engaged in education within the anti-violence sector.

Although many of our criticisms of the anti-violence sector relate to a tendency to get stuck on a rigid way of understanding and responding to violence, we fear our tendencies to do the same. While intellectually we believe in popular education and critical pedagogy, in practice it can be challenging not to default to the "teacher" or "expert" role advancing a particular idea or framework. This has been particularly complicated for Josh, as non-trans people attending our workshops have tended to be reluctant to openly challenge his views as a trans person. Experiential knowledge can easily be confused—by both the participant and the facilitator—as some kind of essential "truth" rather than appreciating the limits of any one person's experience and understanding, and working on, together, developing a collective critical analysis. Participants have tended to be passive and quiet, in part perhaps because there has been so much fear about acknowledging that there are problems in the anti-violence sector or challenges to working in one's agency.

While Josh is often deemed "expert," he is also typically perceived as an outsider to anti-violence organizations despite his experience within them. Caroline, on the other hand, given her experience as a non-trans woman in anti-violence services, is mostly viewed as an insider and peer but sometimes as an outsider who does not fully/adequately understand women's politics and organizing. The insider/outsider duality has resulted in Caroline being more openly challenged about contentious points of view while at the same time more able to challenge workshop participants about dominant anti-violence frameworks.

In reflecting on the nature of our trans/non-trans working relationship, and the complexities of this and other power differentials between us, we have discussed the tendency in some anti-violence and LGBT organizations to select trans people to provide personal testimony as "education." Co-writing and co-facilitating as a trans and non-trans pair has been helpful in challenging the tendency for non-trans people to uncritically elevate/exoticize/otherwise mark trans people as "other," and has provided a model for principled solidarity that helps challenge the identity politics and binaries of "oppressor/victim," "insider/outsider" (either to trans or feminist anti-violence organizations), and "feminist/non-feminist" among others.

Working together has also been invaluable in providing peer support and accountability. This work can be very difficult and isolating and, as mentioned above, when unchecked can easily default into reproducing the very things of which we are critical. Our mutual respect has helped us to challenge each other, disagree with each other, and build a genuine commitment to continuous evaluation of our work. In the same vein, we have invited other anti-violence educators to meet periodically and attend each other's workshops in order to increase the critical engagement, integrity, and accountability between and within the various anti-violence sectors, but the response by the colleagues we initially approached was that it would feel like "policing" rather than support. One of the challenges then, is how to, as a network of anti-violence educators, transform this idea of policing into routine, reflexive engagement with one other, with survivors, with service providers and our communities in order to provide support and systems of accountability that will help us stay honest and keep the work fresh.

One of our concerns is that as we move farther away from the frontlines (as it has been some years for both of us since being clients or staff in anti-violence organizations), we will lose perspective on the current realities for clients and frontline staff. We have wondered if it might be more productive to shift from educating as outsiders to facilitating opportunities for people who are currently in the system to get support and advocacy assistance to challenge what is going on in their organizations and to redefine, at a ground level, what it means to really help survivors of violence. To transform practices, people who work together have to talk with and support each other; it cannot be done alone. As part of this process, staff and volunteers need the help of survivors who have recently been in the system and can be frank about how it worked or did not work well to meet their needs. Neutral advocacy resources that help clients of anti-violence services challenge unfair practices would go a long way to helping debunk the myth that anti-violence services are always right and good, a precondition to meaningful change within the sector. We close with comments by Emi Koyama, a groundbreaking activist/educator for whose work we are profoundly grateful:

> Like white anti-racists who must recognize the impossibility of purifying themselves of their racist white privilege, I came to realize the limitations of feminist conscience. I came to understand that we need structural changes, rather than better rules, staff, trainings or consciousness raisings, in order to make social interventions to domestic violence more accountable to the actual needs and demands of survivors. . . .
>
> . . . We need to challenge the notion of women's shared experiences and accept specificities of women's experiences in relation to the complex matrix of social institutions, not just the patriarchy. We need to challenge the notion that women do not have real power in this society, and address how all of us are capable of using our various powers and privileges lovingly or abusively. We need to acknowledge the limitation of our feminist consciousness and ethics, and pursue structural remedies to hold ourselves accountable to each other as women and as fellow human beings. (Koyama 2003: 5, 17)

NOTES

1. Second wave feminism's particular understanding of what constitutes "male violence against women" was and continues to be highly influential in shaping the structure of anti-violence services. For example, anti-violence services are not designed to address the violence of war, occupation, colonization, or slavery.
2. The Supreme Court of Canada (SCC) agrees to hear approximately 12% of all appeal applications submitted (Supreme Court of Canada 2009). The SCC does not make public its criteria for declining to hear any case.
3. Whereas "Trans 101" workshops (current terminology, definitions of gender, sex and sexuality, lack of access to essential services) are introductory in nature and often a vehicle for beginning to develop policy on accessibility within women's organizations, trans-specific anti-violence training and education such as the *Making the Transition* curriculum assume a basic level of accessibility (in the very least, accessibility to trans women). Similar to "Trans 101" workshops the *Making the Transition* curriculum was developed for non-trans service providers, and thus far has been delivered largely to women-serving agencies. The curriculum content is divided into four modules: (1) general information similar to "Trans 101" (meant to ensure that all participants have a similar language and context for the subsequent sections); (2) a macro introduction to interpersonal, institutional and systemic types of violence trans people may experience, as well as the limitations of conventional ways of thinking about violence (e.g., the power and control wheel); (3) more micro exploration of interpersonal/relationship violence including examination of specific ways different types of abuse—physical, sexual, emotional, economic, etc.—might manifest (e.g., assault on body

parts that signify notions of conventional gender, sexualized violence, hate crimes, barriers to leaving an abusive relationship, barriers to reporting, and case studies); and (4) identifying practices that create trans-positive environments and respond to common trans-specific service needs, including washroom and residential issues.

4. The Ending Violence Association of BC's Safe Choices program has been instrumental in supporting delivery of *Making the Transition* workshops for anti-violence organizations (predominantly social services and women's organizations) in the Vancouver/Lower Mainland area. Caroline and colleague Devon MacFarlane have conducted all of the Safe Choices workshops. The workshops facilitated by Joshua with other colleagues have been primarily for health and social service providers in mixed-gender organizations with a mandate to provide a broader range of services (but with survivors comprising a significant portion of the client base).

5. For discussion of race, bisexuality, and transgender, see Salvador (2001).

6. Locally, there are many variations on "LGBT" with the addition of other initials to attempt to be more inclusive of people who do not identify with the terms lesbian, gay, bisexual, or trans—e.g., in "LGBTT2SQQ", "TT" indicates transsexual and transgender, as in some regions those communities and terms are quite distinct; "2S" is intended to represent Two Spirit people, and "QQ" stands for Queer and Questioning (people who are questioning their sexual orientation and do not necessarily identify with any labels).

7. We thank Emi Koyama for helping us appreciate this dynamic through her constructive criticism of the way we were originally approaching intersex issues in our trans anti-violence training. For further discussion see Koyama's *Adding the 'I': Does Intersex Belong in the LGBT Movement?*

REFERENCES

Bannerji, H. 1997. Geography lessons: On being an insider/outsider to the Canadian nation. In *Dangerous territories: Struggles for difference and equality in education,* ed. L.G. Roman and L. Eyre, 23–41. New York: Routledge.

Bettcher, T. M. 2007. Evil deceivers and make-believers: On transphobic violence and the politics of illusion. *Hypatia* 22(3): 43–65.

Bockting, W. O., G. Knudson and J. M. Goldberg. 2006. Counseling and mental health care for transgender adults and loved ones. In *Guidelines for transgender care,* ed. W. O. Bockting and J. M. Goldberg, 35–82. Binghamton, NY: Haworth Press.

Brown, N. 2007. Stories from outside the frame: Intimate partner abuse in sexual-minority women's relationships with transsexual men. *Feminism & Psychology* 17(3): 373–393.

Cook-Daniels, L. 2001. SOFFA questions and answers. FORGE. Available at : http://www.forge-forward.org/handouts/SOFFA-QA.pdf [accessed November 30, 2009].

Cope, A and J. Darke. 1999. *Trans accessibility project: Making women's shelters accessible to transgendered women.* Kingston, ON: Violence Intervention and Education Workgroup.

Courvant, D. 1997. *Domestic violence and the sex- or gender-variant survivor.* Portland, OR: Survivor Project.

Courvant, D. and L. Cook-Daniels. 1998. Trans and intersex survivors of domestic violence: Defining terms, barriers & responsibilities. Survivor Project. Available at: http://www.survivorproject.org/defbarresp.html [accessed November 30, 2009].

Cowan, C. and R. Lopes-Iraheta. 1996. *Report of the YWCA committee on service to the transgendered and transsexual community.* Toronto: YWCA.

Daley, C. 2005. *Safety inside: Problems faced by transgender prisoners and common sense solutions to them—Testimony to National Prison Rape Elimination Commission.* San Francisco, CA: Transgender Law Center.

Darke, J. and A. Cope. 2002. *Trans inclusion policy manual for women's organizations.* Trans Alliance Society. Available at: http://www.transalliance society. org/education/ documents/02womenpolicy.pdf [accessed November 30, 2009].

Devor, H. 1994. Transsexualism, dissociation, and child abuse: An initial discussion based on nonclinical data. *Journal of Psychology & Human Sexuality* 6: 49–72.

Feinberg, L. 1996. *Transgender warriors: Making history from Joan of Arc to Ru Paul.* Boston: Beacon Press.

findlay, b. 2003. Real women: Kimberly Nixon v Vancouver Rape Relief. *UBC Law Review,* 36(1): 57–76.

———. Cases of note: Transgendered women lose human rights in court review of Human Rights Tribunal. Available at: http://www.barbarafindlay.com/ [accessed November 30, 2009].

findlay, b., S. LaFramboise, D. Brady, C. Burnham and S. (R.) Skolney-Elverson. 1996. *Finding our place: "Transgendered law reform project."* Vancouver: High Risk Project Society.

Fitzgerald, M., C. Guberman and M. Wolfe, ed. 1982. *Still ain't satisfied: Canadian feminism today.* Toronto: The Women's Press.

Gehring, D. and G. Knudson. 2005. Prevalence of childhood trauma in a clinical population of transsexual people. *International Journal of Transgenderism* 8(1): 23–30.

Goldberg, J. M. 2003. *Trans people in the criminal justice system: A guide for criminal justice personnel.* Vancouver: Justice Institute of BC and Trans Alliance Society.

———. 2006. *Making the transition: Providing services to trans survivors of violence and abuse.* Vancouver: Justice Institute of BC and Trans Alliance Society.

Goldberg, J. M. and C. White. 2004. Expanding our understanding of gendered violence: Violence against trans people. *Newsletter of the BC Institute Against Family Violence* 11(2): 21–25.

———. 2006. Anti-violence work in transition. In *Trans/forming feminisms,* ed. K. Scott-Dixon, 217–226. Toronto: Sumach Press.

Goldman, R. 1996. Who is that *queer* queer? Exploring norms around sexuality, race, and class in queer theory. In Queer Studies: A Lesbian, Gay, Bisexual, and Transgender Anthology, ed. B. Beemyn and M. Eliason, 169–182. New York: New York University Press.

Gunn, J. and J. M. Goldberg. 2002. In your house: Responding when you suspect relationship abuse. *Avoid Strange Men* 1(1): 21–29.

hooks, b. 1984. *Feminist theory: From margin to center.* Boston: South End Press.

Hull, G. T., P. Bell-Scott and B. Smith, eds. 1982. *All the women are white, all the blacks are men, but some of us are brave: Black women studies.* New York: The Feminist Press.

Kenagy, G. P. 2005. Transgender health: Findings from two needs assessment studies in Philadelphia. *Health & Social Work* 30(1): 19–26.

Kenagy, G. P. and W. B. Bostwick. 2005. Health and social service needs of transgender people in Chicago. *International Journal of Transgenderism* 8 (2/3): 57–66.

Koyama, E. 2000a. Whose feminism is it anyway? The unspoken racism of the trans inclusion debate. Available at: http://www.eminism.org/readings/index. html [accessed November 30, 2009].

———. 2000b. The transfeminist manifesto and other essays on transfeminism. Available at: http://www.eminism.org/readings /index.html [accessed November 30, 2009].

———. 2003. *Disloyal to feminism: Abuse of power and control within the domestic violence shelter system.* Portland, OR: Confluere Publications.

———. Adding the 'I': Does Intersex Belong in the LGBT Movement? Available at: http://www.ipdx.org/articles/lgbti.html [accessed November 30, 2009].

Lakeman, L. Sustaining our resistance to male violence: Attacks on women's organizing and Vancouver Rape Relief and Women's Shelter. *Canadian Woman Studies* 25(1/2): 129–132.

Lamble, S. 2008. Retelling racialized violence, remaking white innocence: The politics of interlocking oppressions in Transgender Day of Remembrance. *Sexuality Research & Social Policy: A Journal of the NSRC* 5(1): 24–42.

Landsberg, M. 2000. Rape crisis centre in B.C. endures assault. *Toronto Star,* December 23. Available at: http://www.rapereliefshelter.bc.ca/issues/Knoxonstar23.html.

Lombardi, E. L., R. A. Wilchins, D. Priesing and D. Malouf. 2001. Gender violence: Transgender experiences with violence and discrimination. *Journal of Homosexuality* 42(1): 89–101.

Mamela v. Vancouver Lesbian Connection [1999], BCHRT.

Maracle, L. 1993. Racism, sexism and patriarchy. In *Returning the gaze: Essays on racism, feminism and politics,* ed. H. Bannerji, 122–130. Toronto: Sister Vision Press.

Members of the Gay and Lesbian Historical Society of Northern California. 1998. MTF transgender activism in the Tenderloin and beyond, 1966–1975: Commentary and interview with Elliot Blackstone. *GLQ: A Journal of Lesbian and Gay Studies* 4(2): 159–187.

Moran, L. J. and A. N. Sharpe. 2004. Violence, identity and policing: The case of violence against transgender people. *Criminal Justice: International Journal of Policy and Practice* 4(4): 395 417.

Munson, M. and L. Cook-Daniels. 2003a. Transgender/SOFFA: Domestic Violence and Sexual Assault Resource Sheet. FORGE. Available at: http://www.forge-forward.org/handouts/TransDV-SA.pdf [accessed November 30, 2009].

———. 2003b. Transgender Sexual Violence Project: Final Review. FORGE. Available at: http://www.forge-forward.org/transviolence/docs/FINAL_ narrative_ implications.pdf [accessed November 30, 2009].

Namaste, V. K. 1996. Genderbashing: Sexuality, gender and the regulation of public space. Environment and Planning D: Society and Space 14: 221–240.

———. 2000. Invisible lives: The erasure of transsexual and transgendered people. Chicago: University of Chicago Press.

National Coalition of Anti-Violence Programs (NCAVP). 2008. *Lesbian, gay, bisexual and transgender domestic violence in the United States in 2007.* New York: NCAVP.

Nixon, K. 1997a. Statistics on violence suddenly alarming fact for M-F transsexuals. *Zenith Digest* 4(3): 17.

———. 1997b. *Violence against transgendered women in relationships.* Vancouver: K. Nixon.

Nixon v. Vancouver Rape Relief Society, [2002] BCHRT, No. 1.

Northwest Network. 1997. *Increasing accessibility/competence for trans survivors of domestic violence policy packet.* Seattle: Northwest Network.

Peek, C. 2004. Breaking out of the prison hierarchy: Transgender prisoners, rape and the Eighth Amendment. *Santa Clara Law Journal* 44: 1211–1248.

Ross, B. 1995. *The house that Jill built: A lesbian nation in formation.* Toronto: University of Toronto Press.

Ross, M-S. 1995. Investigating women's shelters. *Gendertrash* 3: 7–10.

Salvador, R. 2001. Challenging feminism's priorization of gender: Race, bisexuality, and transgender. Unpublished manuscript.

Sausa, L. A. 2005. Translating research into practice: Trans youth recommendations for improving school systems. *Journal of Gay & Lesbian Issues in Education* 3(1): 15–28.

Shelley, C. 2008. *Transpeople: Repudiation, trauma, healing.* Toronto: University of Toronto Press.

Sheridan v. Sanctuary Investments Ltd. [1999] B.C.H.R.T. No. 1.

Simpson, A. J. and J. Goldberg. 2006. *An advocacy guide for trans people and loved ones.* Vancouver: Vancouver Coastal Health, Transcend Transgender Support & Education Society, and Canadian Rainbow Health Coalition.

Stotzer, R. L. 2008. Gender identity and hate crimes: Violence against transgender people in Los Angeles county. *Sexuality Research & Social Policy: A Journal of the NSRC* 5(1): 43–52.

Supreme Court of Canada. 2009. Statistics 1998 to 2008: Bulletin of proceedings—special edition. Available at: http://www.scc-csc.gc.ca/stat/pdf/doc-eng.pdf [accessed November 30, 2009].

Thomas, S. P. 2004. Rising violence against transgendered individuals. *Issues in Mental Health Nursing* 25(6): 557–558.

Timmins, L., ed. 1995. *Listening to the thunder: Advocates talk about the battered women's movement.* Vancouver: Women's Research Centre.

Trans/Action. 1999. *Trans/Action presents Canada's first justice and equality summit for transgendered people.* Vancouver: Trans/Action.

Vancouver Rape Relief Society v. Kimberly Nixon and British Columbia Human Rights Tribunal, [2003] B.C.J. No. 2899, B.C.S.C. 1936.

Vancouver Rape Relief Society v. Nixon, [2005] B.C.J. No. 2647, B.C.C.A. 601.

Wharton, V. W. 2007. Gender variance and mental health: A national survey of transgender trauma history, posttraumatic stress, and disclosure in therapy. Master's thesis, Smith College School for Social Work.

White, C. 2002. Re/defining gender and sex: Educating for trans, transsexual, and intersex access and inclusion to sexual assault centres and transition houses. Master's thesis, University of British Columbia.

White, C. and J. M. Goldberg. 2006a. Expanding our understanding of gendered violence: Violence against trans people and their loved ones. *Canadian Woman Studies* 25(1/2): 124–128.

———. 2006b. Safety assessment and planning in abusive trans relationships. In *Aid to safety assessment and planning (ASAP) for women who experience violence in their relationships,* ed. G. Reid, 4.17–4.34. Vancouver, BC: BC Institute Against Family Violence Society.

———. 2006c. Supporting trans people and their loved ones in anti-violence services. ERA. Available at: http://erabc.ca/trans.pdf [accessed November 30, 2009].

———. 2006d. Understanding support for trans people and their loved ones. *Communique: The Newsletter of the BC/Yukon Society of Transition Houses* February: 36–38.

White Holman, C. and J. M. Goldberg. 2006a. Ethical, legal, and psychosocial issues in care of transgender adolescents. In *Guidelines for transgender care,* ed. W. O. Bockting and J. M. Goldberg, 95–110. Binghamton, NY: Haworth Press.

———. 2006b. Social and medical transgender case advocacy. In *Guidelines for transgender care,* ed. W. O. Bockting and J. M. Goldberg, 197–218. Binghamton, NY: Haworth Press.

Wilchins, R. A. 1997. Lines in the sand, cries of desire. In *Pomosexuals: Challenging assumptions about gender and sexuality,* ed. C. Queen and L. Schimel, 138–149. San Francisco, CA: Cleis Press.

Witten, T. M. and A. E. Eyler. 1999. Hate crimes and violence against the transgendered. *Peace Review* 11(3): 461–468.

Wyss, S. E. 2004. "This was my hell": The violence experienced by gender nonconforming youth in US high schools. *International Journal of Qualitative Studies in Education* 17: 709–730.

Xavier, J. M., M. Bobbin, B. Singer and E. Budd. 2005. A needs assessment of transgendered people of color living in Washington, DC. *International Journal of Transgenderism*, 8(2/3): 31–47.

YWCA. 1996. *YWCA discussion paper on serving transgendered individuals.* Toronto: YWCA.

Part II
LGBTQ Lives

5 Exploring Emotion Work in Domestically Abusive Relationships

Catherine Donovan and Marianne Hester

INTRODUCTION

Same sex domestic violence poses several challenges to both existing understandings of adult intimacy and domestic violence not least of which are, respectively, the extent to which understandings of love and intimacy are shaped by gender and/or sexuality and whether a feminist explanatory model is relevant to understanding domestic violence. Our research originated in a desire to resist a growing consensus among, mainly, North American writers on the issue to reject the feminist model as heterosexist and develop more individualized approaches to understanding the psychopathologies of perpetrators or the couple relationship dynamic (e.g., Island and Letellier 1991, and for UK context Taylor and Chandler 1995). Instead we decided to focus on what we assumed is the basis of most domestically violent relationships: that they originate in love and consent.

In this chapter we explore some of the findings from the interviews we conducted with women and men variously identifying as heterosexual and non-heterosexual to suggest that we are mistaken to only focus on gender and power as embodied in male and female bodies in our attempts to understand domestic violence. We found that what we call practices of love are often configured, constructed, imagined, expected and/or demonstrated through binary opposites that have been more generally associated with dominant understandings of masculinity and femininity. By exploring some of these practices of love, we argue that those who are willing to do the emotion work in a relationship—regardless of gender and sexuality—can be vulnerable to domestic violence. Victim/survivors indicate that abusers use relationships as a vehicle through which they can achieve their own needs/goals regardless of the cost to victim/survivors, and exploit the emotion work victim/survivors undertake in attempts to keep victim/survivors engaged in the relationship. Gender is important to understanding abusive relationships but so too are the differences in expectations of practices of love brought to relationships.

This chapter has five sections. In the first, we will briefly outline the critique of the feminist gendered analysis of domestic violence and rationale for our study. In the second section, we briefly outline some of the literature on adult heterosexual love and intimacy with some discussion of the relevance of this for understanding same sex intimacy and domestic violence. This will particularly focus on what has been called "emotion work." In the following section, we will explain the methodology for our study. Next, through use of three case studies from our study, we will explore how understandings of love and emotion work might be unhooked from gender in an attempt to understand domestically violent relationships. Finally, we will talk about some of the implications of our findings.

CRITIQUES OF THE FEMINIST APPROACH TO DOMESTIC VIOLENCE

The fundamental critique of the feminist explanatory model for domestic violence has been its focus on patriarchy with its unequal, gendered, hierarchical structures as the conceptual framework through which to interrogate the issues. This model, in which men as the dominant group and women as the subordinate group is believed to be reinforced, supported and often enacted either through violence or the threat of violence in both private and public spheres. Within the private sphere, the combined influences of dominant constructions of heterosexuality, masculinity and femininity are argued to create conditions of gender inequality that mean the operation of adult heterosexual intimacy can result in the abusive exertion of power and control by men over women.

One of the impacts on the domestic violence community of the reality of same sex domestic violence has been a fundamental questioning of this feminist analysis that has problematized masculinity and patriarchal values and centered gender as a crucial lens through which domestic violence has to be explored in order to be understood. This questioning has resulted in claims that the feminist approach is, at worst, heterosexist and at best of no relevance for understanding domestic violence in same sex relationships (e.g., Chandler and Taylor 1995, Island and Letellier 1991), and that alternative explanations should be explored (e.g., Elliot 1996; Renzetti 1998). Ristock (2002) has argued that feminism can be useful for understanding heterosexual domestic violence but that it cannot provide a universal explanatory model—or, as Renzetti (1998, 123) puts it, a "one model fits all"—and that such an approach has prevented a more inclusive one that recognizes heterogeneous experiences and allows for a diversity of response.

Our approach to exploring domestic violence in same sex relationships came from a belief that not enough is known about the issues to know whether apparent differences with heterosexual experiences of domestic violence are enough to warrant completely different explanations. In fact the evidence from North America suggests to us that there are many similarities both in the experiences of domestic violence in same sex and heterosexual relationships and the impacts on victim/survivors of that abuse (see for example, Bethea et al. 2000). Important differences do exist relating to the social context of same sex relationships, i.e. the heterosexism and homophobia that those in same sex relationships experience. It has been argued that this context may well contribute to the exercise of domestic violence because of internalized homophobia and, in the case of lesbians, internalized misogyny (Ristock 1991). It has also been demonstrated that homophobia and heterosexism (and/or the fear of these) reinforce the isolation of the victim/survivor who may be further controlled and wary of seeking help because of their sexuality (e.g., Bethea et al. 2000, Renzetti 1992, Ristock 2002).

Rather than focus on the differences between same sex and heterosexual relationship violence, however, we decided to focus on what might be similar: that domestically violent relationships are predominantly and initially, at least, based on notions of love and consent.[1] Several studies have pointed to the importance victim/survivors have placed on their love of their partner as the reason why they remain within the relationship (see Abrahams in Hester et al. 2007 and Hoff 1990 for work on heterosexual women; see Merril and Wolfe 2000 for work on gay men; see Renzetti 1992 for work on lesbians), yet there has been very little exploration of how and why love can provide such a rationale (see Wood 2001 for an exception).

LOVE AND INTIMACY

Many understandings exist about what love might be, but romantic love is generally understood to be a particularly dominant model in Western societies that rests on certain assumptions: that there is a Mr. or Ms. Right out there for everybody if they can only be found; that love is forever; that love is based on monogamy, fidelity, privacy, and loyalty; and that such love is essential to self-fulfillment. Smart (2007) has argued that sociological approaches to love have been of two kinds: disdain and translation. Many feminists exemplify the former approach as they have argued that romantic love has provided a trap for heterosexual women, institutionalizing gendered inequalities based on gendered differences in roles and responsibilities within the love relationship (e.g., de Beauvoir 1972, Douglas 1990, Evans 2003). Marriage and the family have been identified as twin parapets of an oppressive ideology of love with disproportionate consequences for women (and their children). Bauman (2003) and Beck and Beck-Gernsheim (1985), in different ways, each critique the ways in which the pursuit of love in late modern societies has reinforced the thrust of individualization and paradoxically been the source of deep dissatisfaction. Both these authors argue that the combined impact of a breakdown in traditional kinship rules and regulation of personal life and the structured prioritizing of individualized life agendas has undermined stable adult relationships and family life while simultaneously idealizing them. The result is, according to these authors, the constant dissatisfaction and isolation of people whose relationships fail and families break down and yet who continue to pursue the ideal. Evans (2003), who also takes a pessimistic approach, argues that it is by pursuing an understanding of love as irrational and ideological rather than a love that is rational and grounded in ideas of constraint or regulation that has resulted in widespread unhappiness in both personal and public life.

On the other hand, Smart (2007) identifies the work of Giddens (1992) on the transformation of intimacy as an exception to this trend, as Giddens more hopefully identifies lesbians as the pioneers of the pure relationship: living and loving outside heteronormative structures of intimacy, Giddens (1992) argues, have resulted in lesbians being able to pursue and organize democratic relationships of intimacy based on negotiation and contingency that exist for as long as each has their needs met. Giddens (1992) argues that romantic love, as the dominant model of love, is becoming less popular than what he calls confluent love. Confluent love in the pure relationship is understood to be predicated upon sharing emotional needs and desires, the mutual negotiation of the terms of the relationship and contingency: that adults stay together until they no longer feel their needs are being met. In other words, Giddens argues, because personal fulfillment within adult intimacy has become a central feature and expectation of intimate life, successful relationships are now contingent on each member of the relationship being able to negotiate and meet their needs. Gidden's (1992) argument continues that heterosexual relationships are changing in line with those of lesbians, with heterosexual women leading the way as their demands for the democratization of relationships gives them the agency to leave men who are unwilling or unable to join them in their quest for confluent love. Feminism, Giddens argues, has empowered women to have higher expectations of their intimate lives, and has encouraged women to push for an egalitarian negotiation of equals to fulfill their needs.

Many of those who have theorized about love have been critiqued for the lack of empirical substance for their arguments. Jamieson (1998, 1999) among others (e.g., Wight 1994) have critiqued Giddens' (1992) argument, pointing to the lack of empirical evidence for the pure relationship and highlighting the continuing material limits to contingency, negotiation, and egalitarianism—not least of which is the presence of children but also includes the inequalities around the distribution of resources that remain in many heterosexual relationships. Jamieson (1998) also argues that though "disclosing intimacy" may be aspired to as an ideal more so than in previous eras, it is more difficult to conclude that it is the most important aspect of intimacy. She argues that other aspects of intimacy may also be at least as important, for example, practical care and unconditional love.

In their work on families of choice, Weeks, Heaphy and Donovan (2001) found much empirical evidence of what they called the egalitarian ideal among same sex relationships—a reflexive commitment to finding ways of doing relationships that aspired to egalitarianism, coupled with an understanding from many that living outside the heterosexual assumption provided an opportunity to pursue this ideal in a way that was not as easy to achieve in heterosexual relationships because of gendered expectations about how relationships can be practiced. However, not all of the respondents had achieved the ideal and many were self-consciously aware that power dynamics existed in current relationships to which they had to attend and for which they had to compensate in their on-going negotiations of the egalitarian ideal (Heaphy, Donovan and Weeks 1999). Some also talked about previous domestically violent relationships in which the egalitarian ideal had not been possible at all.

Empirical work on love falls into Smart's (2007) second category of sociological work on love. Smart argues that often such work, instead of identifying new ways to conceptualize love, translates love into existing concepts—of emotion *work*, of *care*, or of *commitment* (that can be "measured" through statistics on divorce and marriage, for example). Instead, Smart champions: "The idea that love motivates action and association, it need not be an ideology with an underlying false promise" (2007, 78).

It is from a synthesis of the above academic work that we can begin to make some sense of how relationships based originally in love become understood and experienced differentially based on gender. For example, Cancian (1987) argues that love has been feminized such that its practice emphasizes the sharing of feelings, expressions of love and emotionally supportive talk—what Jamieson (1998) would call "disclosing intimacy"—which are all identified with the feminine role. Cancian goes on to argue that this feminized love has become intertwined with traditional gender roles; women are expected to find fulfillment from falling in love and a financially and emotionally dependent relationship with a man for whom she provides a domestic setting that nurtures him and their children. Often, it is in the lived experience of this ideal that many heterosexual women have found themselves deeply dissatisfied by the "problem with no name" (Friedan 1963).

The male role, on the other hand, is primarily focused on characteristics such as providing materially and financially for the family as practical aspects of care and on sexual fulfillment as an indicator of intimacy (Duncombe and Marsden 1995, Jamieson 1998). "Emotion work" as outlined above has not been given the same value, and has thus been identified as a key source of conflict and/or dissatisfaction in heterosexual relationships (Duncombe and Marsden 1995). In fact, Duncombe and Marsden argue that "asymmetry in intimacy and emotion work may be the last and most obstinate manifestation and frontier of gender inequality" (1995, 150). These authors go on to argue that heterosexual women often feel disappointed that their expectations of a shared emotional life fall far short in their relationships with the men they love. The men, for their part, are often baffled by and/or impatient of what they understand to be unreasonable, if not irrelevant, requests to emote. For example, initiating and engaging in sex is identified by many men as the moment in which they emotionally connect with their female partners. Talking and sharing worries and concerns and details of their day is of little interest to them (Duncombe and Marsden 1993, 1995). Duncombe and Marsden (1993, 1995) have argued that it is in the construction of dominant masculinities that men's emotionality and emotion work has been neglected and that this has resulted in an inequality in heterosexual relationships, leaving women with limited choices as to how they sustain those relationships. These authors have also highlighted how this gendered approach to intimacy of men and women often leave many women with the realization that their needs are secondary to the needs of their male partners. The relationship becomes the base from which men are able to go out and engage with the world, leaving women to tend to that base and be available, when men return home, to provide a relaxing space in which men can recharge their batteries with food, sleep, sex and care (see also, for example, Morris 1999, Vogler and Pahl 1999). In return, men understand their contribution is in providing materially for the home and family. In these terms, rather than the relationship being the joint project of the pure relationship, the relationship can become a vehicle through which some men can achieve their own goals.

On the other hand, as Jamieson has argued (1998, 1999), it may be that other practices of love such as practical care have been ignored in the emphasis on emotional support and disclosure. Thus, the kinds of practices of love that might be more associated with men are not included in the debates about how love is practiced. What is interesting to us is the ways in which certain practices of love have become gendered, with those pertaining to emoting being understood to be feminine, and those pertaining to practical expressions of love being understood to be masculine.

It is this gendered approach to love, intimacy and emotion work that we would like to explore in this paper. We suggest that what have become understood as gendered ways of thinking about and carrying out love, intimacy, and relationship practices are not necessarily or exclusively enacted by embodied women and men in heterosexual relationships. We wish to explore the idea that these behaviors can be enacted by individuals who are not heterosexual but who are living in same sex relationships. The desire and indeed (social) pressure experienced to seek out and find another person to be attached and commit to forever in a love relationship is neither inherently heteronormative nor gendered. The recent worldwide campaign for same sex marriage and partnership rights is evidence of this (Clarke, Finley and Wilkinson 2004). We are therefore interested in trying to unpack how what we call practices of love might operate to sustain domestically violent relationships regardless of gender and sexuality; and to begin a discussion about how we can make sense of this in relation to feminist arguments about gender and power in domestically violent relationships.

METHODOLOGY

The research on which this paper is based compared love and violence in same-sex and heterosexual relationships.[2] The study was multi-method, consisting of a survey of a national LGBTQ community sample, focus groups with self-identified lesbians, gay men, heterosexual women and men and interviews with sixty-seven self identified non-heterosexuals, including lesbians, gay men, homosexuals, bisexuals, "queers" and heterosexuals. This chapter focuses on the interview data. Of the interview sample, nineteen were lesbians, nineteen were gay men, fourteen were heterosexual women, nine were heterosexual men, three were bisexual women and three were queer women. We recruited most of our lesbians, gay male, queer, and bisexual respondents from the questionnaire, though in our attempt to include black and other minority ethnic respondents we also tried other avenues to recruit non-heterosexual volunteers. To recruit our heterosexual respondents we placed advertisements in local listings magazines and national interest group newsletters and circulated leaflets through domestic violence networks. Our attempts to recruit heterosexual women and men were not as successful as our recruitment of LGBT respondents, and we were very unsuccessful recruiting minority ethnic respondents with only two interviews with black lesbians being conducted. Most of the interviewees had experienced domestic violence: over three-quarters of the lesbians, bisexual, and queer women (when taken together as a group) and just over a half of the heterosexual women and gay men. In general, the profile of the sample was educated with incomes at or above the average (though men were more likely to have incomes between £21,000 and £30,000 and women were more likely to make £11,000 to £20,000 annually). Most participants were aged between twenty and fifty-nine years old, and only five identified as having a disability.

While we concentrate in this chapter on the parallels in experiences across gender and sexuality of those who undertake emotion work in their domestically violent relationships, there are also differences of experiences that seem to be influenced by gender. When looking at the interview sample as a whole, there were some gender differences that, while not necessarily statistically significant, provided what appeared to be some patterns of experience across gender and sexuality. Female victim/survivors were typically more likely to live with a violent partner and remain in a domestically violent relationship for longer than male victim/survivors. Male perpetrators were typically more physically violent and more physically coercive sexually while female perpetrators were typically more emotionally violent and more emotionally coercive sexually (patterns that *were* found to be statistically significant in our survey sample). Female victim/survivors were typically more likely to parent children than male victim/survivors which may partly explain why they were more likely to live with violent partners and/or remain in domestically violent relationships for longer.

Smart and Neale (1999) argue that love is perhaps the emotion most scripted as an essentialist set of magical, inexplicable, and/or possibly chemical characteristics by those who experience and investigate it. Yet as Jackson (1993) and others have argued, love is socially and culturally produced and experienced by many regardless of sexuality. Given its social and cultural production, we agreed with Hart (1986) and approached the study with the assumption that participants, regardless of sexuality or gender, have had access to and experiences of similar sources of knowledge production about love: families of origin, film, music, books, magazines, and so on. We wanted to explore whether and how participants enacted their understandings about how love could be in their abusive relationships. To this end, we explored with respondents accounts of their self-defined best and worst relationships. Individuals responded differently to this, with some providing a best and a worst relationship while others recounted a relationship that constituted their best *and* worst experience.

Smart (2007) discusses the ways in which in qualitative research on relationships participants may not ever refer explicitly to love or emotions as motivators of their relationship practices. However, in this study we explicitly asked respondents about love, whether they loved their partners and how they knew that they loved them, as well as whether their partners had loved them and how they knew that they were loved. In this way we kept notions of love central to the investigation so that we could explore how and in what ways practices of love might be implicated in domestically violent relationships.

We do not look to respondents' accounts to provide the definitive truth about "what happened" in these relationships (e.g., Heaphy, Donovan and Weeks 1998). Memory is an important influence here. All of the respondents talked about domestically violent relationships that had taken place in the past. In addition, in place of an exact account respondents focused on particular anecdotes as exemplars of the abusive partner. Such selectivity also draws on hindsight, another factor to take into consideration in making sense of their accounts. Previous studies on domestic violence in either heterosexual or lesbian relationships have highlighted the "cathartic" experience of interviews for participants talking about abuse for the first time and/or understanding it as abusive (Kelly 1988; Ristock 2002). These factors give a context to how respondents tell their stories, the influence of the questions asked and the context in which they tell them (Duncombe and Marsden 1996). However, as Ramazanoglu with Holland (2002) point out, respondents' accounts of their experiences are "a necessary element of knowledge of gendered lives and actual power relations" (2002: 127), and thus provide insights into the ways in which relationships can be understood.

Using Nvivo 7 to code and analyze respondents' accounts, we identified themes related to what in the literature are identified as being associated with emotion work. While undertaking the coding, it became clear that there were similarities in the accounts of victim/survivors, regardless of gender and sexuality, about their experiences of emotion work or practices of love (Morgan 1999), which included tending to the emotional care of partners and children, sharing relationship and individual worries and vulnerabilities, and giving and receiving emotional reassurances and support such as being told that one is loved or being held. In this chapter, we focus specifically on the following three practices of love: understanding the relationship as a joint project; making declarations of love; and performing emotional disclosures.   To illustrate these indicators of emotion work, we use a case study approach focusing on the accounts of a self-identified gay woman, a gay man, and a heterosexual woman. By concentrating on the accounts of three individuals we can convey the cumulative impact of the domestically violent partner on the respondent. This is especially important when the domestic violence has been primarily emotional as this resists attempts to deny or minimize its impact. Case studies also allow us to illustrate many of the similarities in experiences of domestic violence regardless of sexuality and gender, because they provide a consistency of comparison across each practice of love investigated. Using three case studies, we hope to convey some of the context of each relationship thereby providing a more holistic picture of each case study's experience. The three case study subjects are: Marie, a lesbian from another European country who was twenty-one when she came to Britain and began a twelve-year abusive relationship with a British woman seventeen years her senior who had three children from a previous marriage; Marcus, a gay man who was thirty-four when he began an abusive relationship that lasted for nearly two years with a man he did not live with; and Theresa, a heterosexual woman who began an eight-year abusive relationship when she was sixteen years old with a man who she married four years into the relationship and with whom she had two children.

RELATIONSHIP AS JOINT PROJECT

One of the ideals of a love relationship to which many aspire is that the relationship is a joint project in which both partners are considered and involved in mutually negotiating the terms of the relationship. This is sometimes expressed colloquially as "two becoming one," as it is assumed that the needs and goals of each become those of the couple. In the following excerpt from our interview with her, Marie explained how the terms of the relationship were set down by her partner:

> Marie (M): And she became, she became a Counselor . . . and then she did a degree in, Psychology while we were together as well. So, she was studying and things so I was really, at that point, running the house completely.
>
> Interviewer (I): So you did everything, did you?
>
> M: I did everything. Now if you want to know the percentage in this relationship, I did everything.
>
> I: For the twelve years?
>
> M: More or less, yeah. She never worked while I was with her and I mean, sometimes I would have about three jobs at the same time. Before I joined [current job], I used to work at night in a Petrol Station. I was going straight into a shop all day there, and then in the house, I did everything, DIY, cooking, tidying up, cleaning, the kids, the laundry, yeah, everything.

Marie was not alone in this experience of an abusive partner setting the terms for the relationship. This was echoed in every abusive relationship story we were told.

In gay male relationships, in which partners were less likely to live together, arrangements to spend time together were more obviously being made by the abusive partner. Marcus and his partner, for example, lived in different parts of the country and though they spent every weekend together, Marcus's partner generally determined the agenda:

> I: So how often did you get to see him?
>
> Marcus (M): Every weekend. And basically my whole life turned into George. . . .
>
> I: So when you saw each other did you sort of see each other equally here and down in [partner's town] or was it. . . .
>
> M: No, no. He, I, he kind of manipulated it more. . . . And he had this set up with [a gay men's social group] and . . . we'd always go walking . . . and it got really boring in the end. . . .
>
> I: So in terms of like decision making about what you might do or where you might be, was that mutual or was it mostly him making the decisions or . . . ?
>
> M: Him manipulating the situation really. He, er, it was him yeah, I would say he made the [decisions]—and I'm normally a very forthright kind of person . . . and people say "I can't believe that you went through this . . . you know, *you* Marcus," you know, and yet I did.

In heterosexual relationships however, the assumption that the relationship exists to service the man was most explicit, and often heterosexual women talked of their male partners' (usually husbands') total control over the terms of the relationship. Theresa illustrates this with her account. The violence she experienced started after a few weeks of dating the man she would later marry. Theresa explained about decision-making: "Right, no, he had all the power, all the control, there was no equality. Everything was his decision. His, y'know, I wasn't allowed any choices, over anything. Wasn't even allowed to choose what I wanted to watch on the telly. He totally chose where we went and who we seen and who was allowed in the house, and stuff like that." Theresa focused on the apparent minutia of television watching to indicate the degree to which the terms of her relationship were dictated by her violent husband.

More generally, the ways in which the relationship became a means by which the abuser could meet their own needs was not necessarily understood by survivors at the time, even though some might have experienced disquiet about being manipulated or may have realized that what was happening was "not right." This often depended on the degree to which the violence was covert and/or physical. The selfishness of the abuser that lies at the base of this approach to relationships was not explicitly referred to by any of the victim/survivors. Their accounts focus, not surprisingly, on the impact of the abuse on them. However, it is also startling how selfish the behaviors are and how removed they are from more dominant discourses of love or the pure relationship. There is little sense of mutuality or of shared goals. Far from it, in our interviews, participants related that the abuser would seek to establish their entitlements to live as they chose and expected support in that from their partner. The flip side of controlling and restricting the movements of their partner is that this freed abusers to live and do as they pleased.

DECLARATIONS OF LOVE

Emotion work is said to be undertaken in the main by women in heterosexual relationships. In this study, we found some evidence that abusers, regardless of gender, engaged in emotion work but only in so far as it achieved their ends. For example, Duncombe and Marsden (1993) argue that heterosexual men do not realize until their relationship has ended how much they have loved and emotionally need their partner. In this study we found that declarations of love were often made by abusers when victim/survivors were about to end the relationship. This was often a key time for abusers to engage in practices of love as a device to keep the victim/survivors engaged in the relationship. Most victim/survivors maintained that they had loved their abusive partner but more said that their abusive partner had loved them. The latter suggests that abusers' declarations of love were a powerful hold over victim/survivors, even in the face of few *demonstrations* of that love. In Marie's account, love was declared frequently by both partners, however, it is not clear how this was demonstrated in the relationship given the experiences of Marie outlined previously. Yet when Marie eventually tried to leave the relationship, her partner persuaded Marie to go to Relate (a marriage/partnership counseling organization) in an attempt to patch up their relationship problems. Marie said:

> I think she did love me. I mean she really didn't want me to leave towards the end, did everything, and when we went to Relate, you know, she was,—when I was able for the first time to actually say all the things that I wanted to say, she, she'd cry and she'd be unhappy and she would say, you know, "I can't believe I've behaved like that," and stuff like that. So she'd realize and apologize and things—in front of the Therapist anyway, yeah. [Laughing]. Well I think she, she loved me, she really didn't want me to go.

Leaving abusive relationships is a topic beyond the scope of this chapter, but it is worth mentioning here that, as with the experiences of heterosexual women, leaving relationships was often a catalyst to post-separation abuse in same sex abusive relationships (Donovan et al. 2006). This ranged from stalking and harassment of the victim/survivor, their family, friends and employers, to the use of the legal system to establish child contact or financial settlements. Another set of violent practices which result in the victim/survivor re-engaging with the abuser were threats that the abuser would end his or her own life if the relationship ended, or when the abuser made promises to change which were often accompanied with declarations of love. All of these relationship practices involved the abuser engaging in practices of love to convince the victim/survivor that their love was genuine and/or that the abuser needed them.

For Marcus, the fact that his abuser not only declared love for him but also claimed he wanted to be with Marcus forever, kept Marcus engaged with the relationship, even though Marcus had confronted the abuser several times with his abusive behaviors and finished or threatened to finish the relationship.

In the following excerpt, Marcus not only talked about this but also explained how his own practices of love were resisted by George, the abusive partner:

> M: and yet there was something in me that really kept me there, 'cause he said about the love stuff and, you know, how he wanted to be with me forever, er.
> I: So he continued saying that all the way through?
> M: Yeah he did really, yeah you know . . . [but] I started saying, you know, when we'd have rows I'd say "I feel like a glorified fuck buddy" to him. You know, "I don't feel there's any connection or any give to that," you know. He didn't really meet me and I know, you know, I'm hard work at times and bossy and all the rest of them, you know, but he

did, there was no real compassion there, do you know what I mean? He was a very hard and quite cold person and, and I just craved this kind of affection from him and, you know, er yeah. . . .

 I: And so what, when you tried to talk to him about that?

 M: He wouldn't, he wouldn't, he wouldn't talk.

 I: He couldn't get it?

 M: He, he just wouldn't talk, he said "I'm not talking about that."

Some respondents maintained that they had not loved their abusive partner but, for a variety of different reasons stayed in the relationship. Respondents stayed, for example, because: they cared about their partner and wanted to stay to see whether things could get better; they had been too young and inexperienced to know properly what love was about (see Donovan and Hester 2008); or they had entered the relationship as a result of circumstances other than being in love, usually due to conflict with family of origin (typically a reason given by heterosexual women). These reasons were not mutually exclusive and were often given alongside a key reason for staying with an abusive partner, which was that they believed the abusive partner loved and/or needed them. For example, Theresa said that she realized she did not love her abusive partner and had only *thought* she had at the time. She could not think of anything about him that she had loved apart from the fact that he was "handsome" and a "gifted musician." Theresa said that fear had been a factor that had kept her in the relationship, and that there had been an expectation from her family that what was expected of her was to meet a man, get married, and have children. However, when she was asked whether her abusive partner had loved her, Theresa explained:

 Theresa (T): I thought he did.

 I: Yeah? And what made you think that?

 T: Because like if I ever used to get upset and want to end it [the relationship] all, he used to be like, "oh but I'll kill meself [sic] and I love you," and which I know is like getting an emotional bloody thing that he used to play but *then* I didn't used to appreciate that so I used to be "oh well he must really love us."

Declarations of love were important in the armory of abusive practices. These acted as a glue to keep abusive relationships together. Victim/survivors believed that their partners loved them and sought ways to accommodate and explain the abusive behaviors they experienced as a result of this.

EMOTIONAL DISCLOSURE

As we have discussed, disclosing intimacy is an aspirational ideal in adult intimate relationships, but one more typically associated with women. In this, partners are expected to engage in sharing vulnerabilities, worries and

concerns in an atmosphere of trust so as to elicit support from their partners to overcome their histories and gain strength to achieve personal goals.
Again the emphasis is on the mutuality both of disclosure and support.
What we find in the accounts of our respondents is that a degree of disclosure did take place in abusive relationships but that the outcome and motive
for doing so was different depending on whether it was coming from the
abuser or from the survivor.

Appeals to Sympathy and/or Loyalty

Disclosure from the abuser resulted in survivors being willing to protect, defend and explain/excuse the abuser and the relationship. This was
usually a deliberate ploy on the part of the abuser that then provided a
rationale for abusive behavior. Marie said that she always defended her
partner from criticism because she had had an abusive childhood and had
come out of a very unhappy marriage. She explains: "I used to defend her
all the time, with her bad childhood and the way she was brought up and
everything, I used to just explain to people why she's like that. I'd defend
her to everybody."

Marcus found himself having to protect his relationship from friends
who disapproved. One friend in particular, Ryan, had treated George dis-
respectfully when they had been out together socially. George's response
had been to say that Ryan was jealous of their relationship and that Marcus
should not see him. He explains:

> [Ryan] kissed all my friends apart from George and then George, of
> course, played that off on me. You know, and I got loads of shit. You
> know, really, you know, he was fucking horrible, "Ryan's trying to
> split us up, I don't want you seeing him again," you know, rah rah rah.
> "He's really jealous of us" and rah rah. "Let him go." And Ryan, Ryan
> tried to do me a service, but it was to my disservice basically . . . and it
> isolated me even more. And then I, I couldn't go out with Ryan and Fe-
> lix because—you know with George—because they didn't get on now.

Marcus's frustration with Ryan's attempt to support him has to be balanced with his willingness to acquiesce to George's demands to protect
their relationship from the threat represented by Ryan's friendship. Marcus's decision to prioritize his relationship with George over Ryan was
intended to appease George and reassure him that their relationship
could not be threatened by Ryan thereby demonstrating his loyalty to the
relationship.

Theresa also protected her partner from criticism from her family who
did not particularly like him. She would also believe him when he made
appeals to her sympathy for him and promises to change. Having children
was an added factor that made her want to believe him.

‍‍‌‍‌‍‍‍

‍‍‍‍‌‌‍

‍‌‌‌‍

T: Yeah. Like when I used to say, "right, well that's the end of it," yeah, he definitely would say stuff like that. He'd make promises, it wouldn't happen again and that he was just very complex and I didn't understand him and neh, neh, neh. So yeah, it was always empty promises.

I: That you believed at the time?

T: That I believed at the time. And then when you've got two young children as well, you think, well, y'know, we've got two kids, he's gotta try hard for them, d'y'know what I mean?

Exploiting Vulnerabilities

While the emotional disclosures of abusive partners secured them some currency when victim/survivors were threatening to leave the relationship, the emotional disclosures of the victims/survivors become vulnerabilities to be exploited. For example, Marie admitted to her partner that she had had an affair while she had been on a very rare trip to her home country. This happened during their seventh year together. While for Marie this affair signaled the realization that she no longer loved her abusive partner, she stayed in the relationship another five years and submitted to being made to feel guilty for this betrayal. She explained:

M: And I came back and . . . [pause] . . . confessed to the affair and went through, oh, two or three weeks of just shouting and I think, I don't know, anybody would probably have just packed their bag and go, and I just didn't. I just took on what she had to say to me and, and just said erm, you know, "I was just a really bad person and I won't do it again," and, and stayed. And, erm, yeah, I dunno, it's like I got into erm, er—I don't know how to say it—I got into—I just stayed, and at that time, I knew I, I didn't love her anymore, definitely, because I really, I wanted to be back to what I had for a week with that person and. . . . But I didn't and we—yeah, five years I think, it took me, from that time on until I left, to leave her, to get the courage somehow to do it. . . .

I: But for those five years you realized that there was nothing and there was no love there for you?

M: Yeah. There was a lot of responsibility, a huge amount of guilt, because I thought, I thought I was the bad one, all the time, I had to apologize for my behavior, especially after having an affair. That was, I just, just guilt, constant guilt all the time and I, I would just do anything to make it up. I mean, she's even thrown me out before and I wouldn't go, when she'd go mad about me and I would just plead to stay. I can't explain it. I can't [laughs].

Marcus has already explained how his emotional needs were never attended to by his abusive partner even when Marcus attempted to engage George in talking about them. Marcus also talked about how George manipulated Marcus's insecurities about their sexual relationship and what impact this had on him. We have already heard that George's declarations of love and a commitment to "forever" were essential to Marcus's sense of connection to him. That their relationship would be monogamous was a crucial element of this that George used to exert control over Marcus. Marcus had ended the relationship for a short time because George had begun to charge him mileage when they went out in George's car. When they ended their relationship, George had gone on a holiday on which Marcus had been expected to accompany him. When George came back from the holiday, he turned up at Marcus's house and they reengaged in their relationship. Marcus explained what happened in the next few months, which included use of sexual coercion by George:

> And then he said a few months later that he'd met someone on holiday and he still kept that kind of thing going and I think it was some kind of lever to, kind of, like—bit of an insurance policy I suppose because we'd split up er. . . . [f]or the next year I was . . . I felt very insecure in the relationship, always worried about what he was up to and he'd, he'd say things like "oh if I haven't had sex with you in two weeks then, basically, I'm going to look elsewhere," kind of stuff, you know. It made me very insecure and I got very controlled by it and pushed in a corner and he was very domineering.

Thus, revelations of emotional need and declarations of love can be given by both partners in an abusive relationship. What differs from non-abusive relationships is the way that such revelations are used by one partner to further their own needs within a relationship.

In Theresa's account, it became clear that anything she might have indicated that she wanted to do was resisted or rejected by her partner. The fact that she might have desires or personal goals was not tolerable to her abuser who controlled almost every aspect of her life. She says: "I mean even then, thinking back like, I was actually quite controlled, quite miserable, I em, wasn't allowed to meet friends, em, like, I wasn't allowed to pursue learning to drive, he didn't like the fact that I worked, he, y'know, it was like the whole, everything, that went with it." Theresa also notes that "he wouldn't let me further meself with like going to college and stuff like that." Theresa's disclosures about her personal goals and dreams—to pass her driving test, to attend college—became part of her abusive partner's agenda for control. It seemed that anything Theresa identified as being something she would like to take part in or achieve immediately became activities that she was prevented from participating in. The accounts of Marie, Marcus, and Theresa illustrate how intimate disclosure on the part of the victim/survivor, rather than eliciting care and support, instead gave information to abusive partners that they used to increase the control they imposed.

DISCUSSION AND CONCLUSION

In this chapter we set out to explore the extent to which particular practices of love are gendered. The literature discussed at the beginning provides an argument that practices of love such as those captured by the notion of emotion work (intimate disclosure, sharing individual and relationship concerns and/or desires, and declarations of love) are associated with femininity embodied in women. Conversely, setting the terms of the relationship and having a sense of entitlement to pursue their own interests at the expense of those of their partner and as if they represent the interests of the relationship have been typically associated with masculinity embodied in men. By focusing on three case studies of domestic violence in a lesbian, gay male and heterosexual relationship (where the heterosexual woman is the victim/survivor), we have argued that those willing to engage in emotion work can be vulnerable to domestic violence. That most victim/survivors of domestic violence are heterosexual women may reflect the fact that emotion work is more typically enacted as a feminine trait in embodied women. However, Marcus illustrates how men are also able to engage in emotion work and Marie illustrates how some women, like her abusive partner, are willing to exploit the emotion work of their partners. In other words emotion work, while being typically associated with femininity, is not always or only enacted by women. Conversely, the traits more typically associated with masculinity in relation to emotion work are not only or always enacted by men.

It would be a mistake to conclude that same sex relationships are always or only gendered in the same ways as heterosexual relationships. Apart from the heterogeneity apparent in roles and behaviors among heterosexual relationships, the gendering of same sex relationships can be complicated further by the lack of structural constraints shaping and/or reinforcing gendered roles that are found in heterosexual relationships (Dunne 1998; Weeks et al. 2001). The unconscious and/or conscious performance or adoption of butch/femme roles within same sex relationships does not necessarily map across all relationship practices. For example, the woman who publically performs butch is not necessarily the one who organizes the finances or makes the decisions in the privacy of the relationship. In addition, the evidence—including from our own study—shows that appearances of butch and femme, whether in physical appearance or style, does not predict the perpetrator and the victim/survivor in same sex relationships (see also Renzetti 1988; Ristock 2002). However, our study suggests that with regard to those practices of love associated with emotion work, there is an enactment of what have come to be understood as gendered behaviors that are relational (Connel 2000), and that result in partners who are prepared to do emotion work being exploited by those who engage in practices of love only to the extent that it serves their own ends; this is regardless of gender and sexuality.

Arguments that push for an analysis of domestic violence in same-sex relationships that is particular and different from an analysis of domestic violence in heterosexual relationships do not focus on practices of love in domestically violent same sex relationship to build the case. For example, previous studies show how homophobia and heterosexism create a context in which victim/survivors are more isolated from potential help and support than heterosexual women. Authors also demonstrate the specific ways in which sexuality can be used to control and exert power within same-sex relationships. Further, previous studies have explored how internalized homophobia may provide an explanation for both the abusive behaviors of the violent partner and for the victim/survivor staying within the relationship. Authors also concentrate on the individual pathology of abusers, as well as on the inadequacy of a feminist analysis of heterosexual domestic violence focusing on patriarchy alone and on a gendered power lens as the core explanatory framework (see Chandler and Taylor 1995; Elliot 1996; Island and Letellier 1991; Renzetti 1998; Ristock 2002).

We agree that many of these particular experiences in same sex domestic violence are important in building an understanding of how domestic violence might be experienced differently in same sex relationships, and that an exclusive focus on gender as the key explanatory lens for domestic violence is limiting. However, we also argue that the feminist focus on domestic violence as a pattern of behaviors, the result of which is to exert power and control over a person in an intimate relationship, is essential to an understanding of how domestic violence can be identified and named regardless of gender and sexuality. In addition, in this chapter, we argue for a shift in the debates away from differences and individual pathology to an acknowledgement and interrogation of the social context in which most domestic violence occurs—within an adult relationship into which both partners have entered consensually and with positive feelings related to notions of love. By exploring expectations, understandings, and enacted practices of love and relationships, the focus can shift to identify how practices of love across gender and sexuality act to provide reasons to tolerate violence and sustain domestically violent relationships, and also to issues and situations of violence that apply to both heterosexual and same sex relationships. The impact on victim/survivors of experiencing declarations of love and intimate disclosure from abusers can be that domestic violence goes unidentified as such. However, for those in same sex relationships, the focus on gender and difference rather than love has also meant that recognition is possibly a bigger problem since the public story (within public and private heterosexual and LGBT communities) is that domestic violence is a heterosexual problem, that only men can be domestically violent and that only women can be victim/survivors (see Donovan and Hester 2010).

In conclusion, understanding the expectations about the love people bring to adult intimate relationships is a crucial aspect of understanding how violent behavior becomes "normalized" and "tolerated." Feeling and being in love with an abusive partner is a key reason why victim/survivors remain and/or return to domestically violent relationships regardless of gender and sexuality. We argue that in same sex and heterosexual relationships it is not necessarily gender roles or presentations of gender that are key to making sense of domestic violence, but identifying who is doing the emotion work and who is exploiting these practices of love regardless of identities of gender or sexuality. Having said this we also acknowledge that emotion work is characteristically feminine and understood to be part of the range of behaviors associated with being a woman. This means that we can begin to unpack the ways in which emotion work can be gendered or at least enacted in relational ways with intimate partners who resist or exploit the emotion work of their partners. By exploring people's expectations of love and the doing of relationships we can begin to identify those models of love/relationship that provide a context in which domestic violence may occur, and explain why many victim/survivors stay within or return to the relationship.

NOTES

1. The authors acknowledge that there are particular issues that arise as a result of what are called arranged and forced marriages, and that there is an important distinction between these (Home Office 2000). For further discussion of this see Chantler, Gangoli and Hester (2009).
2. The study was funded by the Economic and Social Research Council RES-000–23–0650.

REFERENCES

Bauman, Z. 2003. *Liquid Love*. Cambridge: Polity Press.
Beck, U. and Beck-Gernshim, E. 1995. *The Normal Chaos of Love*. Cambridge: Polity Press.
Bethea, A., K. Rexrode, A. Ruffo and S. Washington. 2000. Violence in lesbian relationships: A narrative analysis. *Electronic Journal of Behavioural and Social Sciences 3* (Fall). Available at: http://aabss.org.journal2000/f05Bethea.jmm.html [accessed October 2005].
Cancian, F. 1990. *Love in America*. Cambridge: Cambridge University Press.
Chantler, K., G. Gangoli and M. Hester. 2009. Forced marriage in the UK: religious, cultural, economic or state violence? *Critical Social Policy* 29(4): 587–612.
Connel, R. 2000. *The men and the boys*. Cambridge: Polity Press.
de Beauvoir, S. 1972. *The Second Sex*. Middlesex: Penguin Books, Ltd.
Donovan, C. and M. Hester. 2010. "I Hate the Word 'Victim'" An exploration of recognition of domestic violence in same sex relationships. *Social Policy and Society*. 9(2): 279–289.
———. 2008. "Because she was my first girlfriend, I didn't know any different": Making the case for mainstreaming same- sex sex/relationship education. *Sex Education* 8(3): 277–287.

100   Catherine Donovan and Marianne Hester

Donovan, C., M. Hester, J. Holmes and M. McCarry. 2006. *Comparing domestic abuse in same sex and heterosexual relationships*. Initial report from a study funded by the Economic & Social Research Council, Award No. RES-000-23-0650, November, University of Sunderland.

Douglas, C. A. 1990. *Love and politics: Radical and lesbian theories*. San Francisco: ISM Press.

Duncombe, J. and D. Marsden. 1993. Love and intimacy: The gender division of emotion and "emotion work"; a neglected aspect of sociological discussion of heterosexual relationships. *Sociology* 27: 221–241.

———.1995. '"Workaholics" and "whingeing women": Theorising intimacy and emotion work—the last frontier of gender equality? *Sociological Review* 43(1): 150–169.

———.1996. Can we research the private sphere? Methodological and ethical problems in the study of the role of intimate emotion in personal relationships, in *Gender relations in public and private: New research perspectives*, ed. L. Morris and E. S. Lyon, 141–155. London: Macmillan.

Dunne, G. 1998. "Pioneers behind our own front doors": Towards greater balance in the organisation of work in partnerships. *Work, Employment and Society* 12(2): 1–33.

Elliott, P. 1996. Shattering illusions: Same-sex domestic violence. *Journal of Gay and Lesbian Social Services* 4(1): 1–8.

Evans, M. 2003. Love: An unromantic discussion. Cambridge: Polity Press.

Giddens, A. 1992. *The transformation of intimacy: Sexuality, love and eroticism in modern societies*. Cambridge: Polity Press.

Hart, B. 1986. Lesbian battering: An examination. In *Naming the violence: Speaking out about lesbian battering*, ed. K. Lobel, 173–189. Seattle: Seal Press.

Heaphy, B., C. Donovan and J. Weeks. 1998. "That's like my life": Researching stories of non-heterosexual relationships. *Sexualities* 1(4): 453–470.

———.1999. Sex, money and the kitchen sink: Power in same sex relationships. In *Relating intimacies: Power and resistance*, ed. J. Seymour and P. Bagguley, 222–245. London: MacMillan Press.

Hester, M. and C. Donovan. 2009. Researching domestic violence in same sex relationships—a feminist epistemological approach to survey development. Special Issue, *Lesbian Studies* 13(2): 161–173.

Hester M., C. Pearson, and N. Harwin with H. Abrahams. 2007. *Making an impact: Children and domestic violence; A reader*. London: Jessica Kingsley Publishers.

Home Office. 2000. A Right by choice. *The report of the working group on forced marriage*. London Home Office Communications Directorate. Available at: http://www.fco.gov.uk [accessed October 2009].

Island, D. and P. Letellier. 1991. *Men who beat the men who love them*. New York: Harrington Park Press.

Jackson, S. 1993. Even sociologists fall in love: An exploration in the sociology of emotions. *Sociology* 23(2): 201–220.

Jamieson, L. 1998. *Intimacy and personal relationships in modern society*. Cambridge: Polity Press.

———. 1999. Intimacy transformed: A critical look at the "pure relationship." *Sociology* 33(3): 477–494.

Kelly, L. 1996. When does the speaking profit us?: Reflections on the challenges of developing feminist perspectives on abuse and violence by women. In *Women, violence and male power*, ed. M. Hester, L. Kelly and J. Radford, 3449. Milton Keynes: Open University Press, Milton Keynes.

McCarry, M, M. Hester and C. Donovan, 2008. Researching same sex domestic violence—constructing a comprehensive survey methodology. *Sociological*

Research Online 13(1/2). Available at: http://www.socresonline.org.uk/13/1/8. html [accessed March 2008].

Morgan, D. 1999. Risk and family practice: Accounting for change and fluidity in family life. In *The New Family?*, ed. E. Silva and C. Smart,13–30. London: Sage.

Ramazanoglu, Caroline and Janet Holland. 2002. *Feminist methodology: challenges and choices.* Thousand Oaks: Sage.

Renzetti, C. M. 1992. *Violent betrayal: Abuse in lesbian relationships.* London: Sage.

———. 1998. Violence and abuse in lesbian relationships: Theoretical and empirical issues. In *Issues in intimate violence*, ed. L. Berkowitz, 117– 127. Thousand Oaks, CA: Sage.

———. 1999. The challenge to feminism posed by women's use of violence in intimate relationships. In *New versions of victims: Feminists struggle with the concept*, ed. S. Lamb, 42–56. New York: New York University Press.

Ristock, J. L. 1991. Understanding violence in lesbian relationships: An examination of misogyny and homophobia. In *Women changing academe*, ed. S. Kirby, D. Daniels, K. McKenna, M. Pujol and M. Valiquette, 113–121. Winnipeg: Sororal Publishing.

———. 2002. *No more secrets: Violence in lesbian relationships.* London: Routledge.

Smart, C. 2007. *Personal life.* Cambridge: Polity Press

Smart, C. and B. Neale. 1999. *Family fragments?* Cambridge: Polity Press.

Taylor, J. and T. Chandler. 1995. *Lesbians talk violent relationships.* London: Scarlet Press.

Weeks, J., B. Heaphy and C. Donovan. 2001. *Same sex intimacies: Families of choice and other life experiments.* London: Routledge.

Wight, D. 1994. Boys' thoughts and talk about sex in a working class locality of Glasgow. *Sociological Review* 42: 702–737.

Wood, J. T. 2001. The normalization of violence in heterosexual romantic relationships: Women's narratives of love and violence. *Journal of Social and Personal Relationships* 18(2): 239–261.

6 Beyond Good and Evil
The Social Construction of Violence in Intimate Gay Relationships

Maurice Kwong-Lai Poon[1]

In recent years, there has been increasing concern about violence in intimate gay or same-sex relationships. Numerous articles and at least five books have been published to address this issue and discuss its policy and clinical implications (Daugherty 1992; Island and Letellier 1991; Leventhal and Lundy 1999; McClennen and Gunther 1999; Renzetti and Miley 1996). Many research studies have been initiated to illuminate our understanding of gay male partner abuse and explore the prevalence, patterns, frequency, and factors associated with violence; the experience of victims, which includes their reasons to stay in the relationship, help-seeking behaviors, decision making in reporting, attitudes towards law enforcement and courts; characteristics of perpetrators; the law enforcement officer's perceptions of same-sex domestic violence; and the validity of an abusiveness scale (Bryant and Demian 1994; Burke, Jordan and Owen 2002; Cruz 2000, 2003; Cruz and Firestone 1998; Cruz and Peralta 2001; Dutton et al. 2001; Farley 1996; Kuehnle and Sullivan 2003; Landolt and Dutton 1997; McClennen, Summers and Vaughn 2002; Merrill and Wolfe 2000; Nieves-Rosa, Carballo-Diéguez and Dolezal 2000; Peel 1999; Regan et al. 2002; Sarantakos 1996; Tjaden Thoennes and Allison 1999; Turell 1999, 2000; Waldner-Haugrud and Gratch 1997; Waldner-Haugrud, Gratch and Magruder 1997; Waterman, Dawson and Bologna 1989; Younglove, Kerr and Vitello 2002).

Indisputably, the recent proliferation of literature on this topic has many positive effects. It gives us a language to understand and articulate an experience that is otherwise overlooked. It provides us with some direction in dealing with this issue. However, it has also created a discourse system or, in Michel Foucault's words, "a regime of truth" that structures the way in which we understand gay male partner abuse. For Foucault, "Indeed, truth is no doubt a form of power" (1988a: 107). To further elaborate Foucault's thought, Stuart Hall explains: "Discourse . . . defines and produces the objects of our knowledge. It governs the way that a topic can be meaningfully talked about and reasoned about. It also influences how ideas are put into practice and used to regulate the conduct of others. Just as a discourse 'rules in' certain ways of talking about a topic, defining an acceptable and intelligible way to talk, write, or conduct oneself, so also, by definition, it 'rules out,' limits and restricts other ways of talking, of conducting ourselves in relation to the topic or constructing knowledge about it" (2001: 72). In other words, contemporary gay male partner abuse literature does not simply construct the way in which we understand this issue but also, and perhaps more importantly, it determines and limits, writes Janice Ristock, "what can be seen, heard, thought, known and done" about it (2002: 19).

In this chapter I examine the salient discourse on victims and perpetrators in contemporary gay male partner abuse literature. In particular, I explore how authors describe gay male victims and perpetrators of partner abuse and demonstrate how this construction—driven by the scientific and medical discourses—may have limited the way in which we understand and deal with the issue. It must be noted that the primary focus of my research is gay men. However, I have included texts that use the term "same-sex." Therefore the terms "same-sex" and "gay" are used interchangeably at times in this chapter, particularly when secondary sources are pointed to. It is important to keep in mind, however, that the points raised in the chapter do not necessarily apply in full to the lesbian communities that are commonly included in the term "same-sex."

THE NEED TO IDENTIFY THE "TRUE" VICTIM

Much of the literature can be seen as motivated by a need to distinguish between victims and perpetrators. According to the literature, gay men do not normally see themselves as victims of violence in intimate relationships. In fact, writes G. Bailey, "some gay men may need to be seriously physically hurt before they are able to associate their experience with being victimized" (1996: 2). In our culture, it is explained in the literature, the victims of violence are usually assumed to be female and the perpetrators male. This cultural assumption has led to a general perception that violence takes place only in heterosexual relationships. Consequently, violence in gay intimate relationships is often rendered invisible (see, for example, Bograd 1999; Carlson and Maciol 1997: Letellier 1994).

As argued in the literature, violence against men is also downplayed in our culture where men are commonly seen as powerful, dominant, and being in control. From this perspective, they cannot be victims. Mike Lew, for example, writes: "Our culture provides no room for a man as a victim. Men are simply not supposed to be victimized. A 'real man' is expected to be able to protect himself in any situation. He is supposed to be able to solve any problem and recover from any setback" (cited in Letellier 1994: 98). This cultural assumption of violence and gender, often based on a heterosexist standpoint, makes it difficult for gay men to identify themselves as victims of violence in intimate relationships (see, for example, Cruz 2000; Lev and Lev 1999; Smith and Mancoske 1999; Vickers 1996).

Furthermore, the cultural assumption of gender, as scholars and theorists of gay male partner abuse argue, leads to a general perception that violence in gay intimate relationships is a mutual abuse or combat. This misconception allows the perpetrator to blame the victim for his own violence and self-proclaim as the victim. Sandra Lundy, for example, in "Abuse that Dare not Speak its Name: Assisting Victims of Lesbian and Gay Domestic Violence in Massachusetts," reminds us: "In a variation on the myth of mutual abuse, the lesbian or gay batterer often claims to be the actual victim of abuse, thus seeking to exploit the fact that in same-sex relationships identifying the batterer is often more difficult than in heterosexual situations, particularly if the couple is about the same age, size, etc." (1993: 284; see also Dudley 2002; Walber 1988).

For these reasons, as purported in the literature, we cannot simply rely on gay men's perceptions of their own violent experience to determine which one is the victim and which the perpetrator. Emily Pitt and Diane Dolan-Soto, for example, write in "Clinical Considerations in Working with Victims of Same-Sex Domestic Violence": "The practitioner cannot necessarily assume that the patient is the partner who is the victim. If a patient identifies as a victim or abuser, it is important to recognize that her or his representation may not necessarily be accurate. This is not because of an intent to deceive, but because roles in same-sex relationships usually do not follow the same gender role behavior as heterosexual relationships" (2001: 166).

The role of victims and perpetrators in intimate gay violent relationships is so blurry that it makes it difficult for therapists, medical professionals, the police, and other service providers, to identify such violence. In their groundbreaking book *Men Who Beat the Men Who Love Them*, David Island and Patrick Letellier write: "With two men in a relationship . . . the roles of victim and batterer may appear blurry to an outsider. This apparent blurriness can make it difficult for counselors, therapists, medical personnel, police, or friends of the couple to determine which man is the victim and which the batterer" (1991: 87:, see also Bricker 1993; Potoczniak et al. 2003).

For these scholars and theorists, this blurriness has been a serious concern particularly because it may lead the police to arresting the victim "on a charge of 'mutual' combat and," writes Daphne McClellan, placing him "in a cell with the abuser" (1999: 252). On top of this, since the role of victim and perpetrator in gay male partner abuse is so unclear to many service providers, Richard Gelles argues, both the victim and perpetrator can "simultaneously seek services from the same shelter or agency," which may further put the victim's life in danger (1997: 121). This confusion about violence in intimate gay relationships, as claimed in the literature, has consequently prevented many of the victims from seeking assistance and has perpetuated the violence.

Hence, clinicians and therapists of gay male partner abuse insist that service providers (including medical professionals and the police) must educate themselves about the violence and develop screening processes to accurately identify the perpetrator and, in so doing, protect the victim. For example, Rachel Senseman, in "Screening for Intimate Partner Violence among Gay and Lesbian Patients in Primary Care," advocates for "universal screening for intimate partner violence in the primary care setting" (2002: 27). For Bailey: "Such screening is necessary to prevent victims from being further victimized by their partners. Without screening, the partner would have access to [the victim services or] the shelter . . ." (1996: 5). Unsurprisingly, one of the major tasks in this area is to develop screening tools that can accurately assess and identify the "true" victim and perpetrator. As Lisa Fox asserts, to prevent further marginalization of the victim, "the therapist must distinguish who the batterer actually is" (1999: 112).

This concern with sorting out who the perpetrator is and who the victim is has led to extensive attention in the literature to describing the characteristics of both victims and perpetrators.

THE PORTRAYAL OF VICTIMS AND PERPETRATORS

Although most scholars and researchers of violence in intimate gay relationships acknowledge that characteristics of victims and perpetrators vary from one person to the next, they point out that some common characteristics can be found in each of these two groups. For example, Sharon Daugherty, in her book *Closeted Screams: A Service-Provider Handbook for Same-Sex Domestic Violence Issues*, identifies ten behaviors commonly exhibited in the perpetrator, which she argues can be used "to spot an abusive partner" (1992: 50–51). Similarly, in *Love Between Men: Enhancing Intimacy and Keeping Your Relationship Alive*, Rik Isensee outlines ten characteristics to describe the victim and the perpetrator respectively (1990: 186–187). To help service providers differentiate the victim from the perpetrator, Josephine Sullivan and Lauren Laughlin, in "Identification and Treatment Modalities for Victims of Same-Sex Partner Abuse," provide a profile that contains eight personal traits frequently found in the victim and six in the perpetrator (1999: 96–97). Hence, a close examination of these literatures can help trace the inherent assumption of who are thought to be the victim and perpetrator in the field of violence in intimate gay relationships.

The Victim

Innocence

In the literature, violence is seen as a problem that commonly lies with the perpetrator, who is fully responsible for the violence in which he engages. In contrast, the victim is portrayed as naïve and innocent. He is not responsible for the violence. For example, Elizabeth Walber writes: "Survivors can no longer be blamed for the violence . . . Batterers/abusers must be accountable for their behavior and its impact on survivors and on the community" (1988: 253). Like Walber, Michael Cruz describes the victim as having "naiveté about violence," which keeps him in the abusive relationship (2003: 315).

From these authors' view, the victim is "fundamentally normal" and shows "no greater incidence of mental disorders, character flaws, organic dysfunction, or personality deviance than any other group of males" (Island and Letellier 1991: 105). He is a very trusting person and is manipulated into the abusive relationship. As Gregory Merrill writes in "Understanding Domestic Violence among Gay and Bisexual Men": "Some victims may have partnered with a batterer because they have difficulty detecting and responding appropriately to intrusive and controlling behavior. This may be . . . because they are simply very trusting and naïve or because they are desperate to be loved. Many other victims, however, have had healthy interpersonal relationships in the past and have become involved with a batterer because he skillfully emotionally manipulated them" (1998: 135). The victim chooses to stay in the abusive relationship not because he enjoys the violence or the pain caused by his partner's emotional and psychological abuse. Rather, it is love and the hope that his partner will change that keeps him in the relationship (see Cruz 2003; Merrill and Wolfe 2000; Walsh 1996).

However, as some authors point out, though in some extent affected by social factors, violence occurs at a personal level. "It is," write Island and Letellier, "always up to the victim to exit such a relationship" (1991: 40). "Unless a victim is saving money, plotting, planning, or in some other way actively working on a way to get out," Island and Letellier go on to write, "he is failing to accept the responsibility" (1991: 90). In other words, in our culture, the victim is seen as responsible for the abuse if he is not attempting or taking any action to leave the relationship.

Personality Characteristics

Though considered "fundamentally normal," as purported in the literature, victims may also "have tendencies or leanings and combinations of factors which may show some inclination toward victimization" (1991: 105). They tend to, write Island and Letellier, overestimate their capability of handling life problems, blame themselves for most interpersonal problems, mistrust their own judgment about people, "have unease with disagreement," "be pleasing to others," "submit to control and influence by others" and have the following characteristics: "Taking responsibility for others; a strong sense of independence; low self-worth or easily deflated self-esteem; a fatalistic world-view; tapping easily a considerable reservoir of guilt; liking people; trust and lack of suspicion; insecurity, such as a need or desire to trust in the 'comfort of control' by others; high ego strength; and trivializing or denying the negative or unpleasant" (1991: 105–106).

Like Island and Letellier, Ned Farley notes similar traits in victims. In "Same-Sex Domestic Violence," for example, Farley remarks that victims exhibit "inability to set limits, passive-aggressiveness, compulsivity, and utilization of emotional and psychological abuse as coping mechanisms within their relationships" (1992: 239). By the same token, in Sullivan and Laughlin's clinical view, victims "are not intrusive and do not assert boundaries," "internalize feelings" such as depression, "are overly focused on others," "assume too much responsibility for themselves and others," and "often feel inadequate within the relationship" as well (1999: 97).

Many victims, as these authors purport, have also shown some addictive behaviors. For example, Daugherty observes: "There is an addictive element in most significant relationships. Victims of battering and emotional abuse tend to remain in unhealthy relationships due to this addiction" (1992: 82). In other words, they are perceived to have co-dependency issues, enjoy being abused and seek out violent relationships. From this perspective, they are seen as pathological. Others claim that victims tend to have substance issues. For example, in "Domestic Abuse and HIV-Risk Behavior in Latin American Men Who Have Sex with Men in New York City," Luis Nieves-Rosa and colleagues found that there is "a strong association between the use of marihuana and cocaine/crack and being a victim of domestic violence" (2000: 86; statistical information omitted). Similarly, victims, as Merrill notes, "frequently use substance to reduce anxiety and to induce emotional numbing" (1998: 139; see also Cruz and Peralta 2001).

Low Self-Esteem

In the literature, victims are commonly described as having self-esteem issues. For example, Bailey writes: Victims "exhibit low self-esteem, guilt . . . helplessness, self-blame and chronic progressive isolation" (1996: 1). Like Bailey, Tod Burke and Stephen Owen remark: "Victims tend to share certain characteristics. . . . These may include self-blame, conflict avoidance, low trust in others, low self-esteem, depression, fear of abandonment, among others" (2006: 7; see also Farley 1992; Letellier 1996; Nieves-Rosa et al. 2000).

Although it is explained that the low self-esteem is a result of the violence or emotional and psychological abuse victims experience in intimate relationships, some authors point out that low self-esteem is also a contributing factor to violence. Gay men with low self-esteem are prone to being victims of partner abuse. For example, Island and Letellier observe that "prospective victims" tend to have "low self-worth or easily deflated self-esteem" that frequently result from societal oppression such as homophobia and heterosexism (1991: 106). For Farley, low self-esteem does not only make gay men vulnerable to abuse, but also causes them to fear that they will be unable to find a 'better' partner which often keeps them in the abusive relationship (1992: 239; see also Gillis and Diamond 2006;

Letellier 1994: Smith and Mancoske 1999). To put it more simply, the victim's low self-esteem is seen as facilitating the violence and leading to his own victimization.

Denial

According to the literature, the victim frequently denies and downplays the violence he experiences in the relationship. For example, Pitt and Dolan-Soto write: "[Victims] frequently tend to minimize the abuse or injuries they sustain and often second-guess their own feelings and perceptions . . . [Victims] will likely not identify abuse as the presenting problem, and in fact may not think of themselves as victims of abuse" (2001: 167). Similarly, Isensee notes that the victim "tends to deny that he has been abused" and minimize "the abuse he has experienced" (1990: 187). Thus, for these authors, the victim's view of his own victimization cannot fully reflect the seriousness of the violence and be trusted. Two main reasons, as they argue, contribute to this denial: (1) the social stigmatization attached to being a victim and (2) the social construction of violence and gender that does not allow men to see themselves as victims of abuse. The "inability or unwillingness of other people to accept their victimization as legitimate," writes Patrick Letellier in "Twin Epidemics: Domestic Violence and HIV Infection among Gay and Bisexual Men," also facilitates such denial (1996: 74).

Learned Helplessness

According to the literature, victims commonly exhibit learned helplessness, a condition that they develop when they lose their hope, feeling that they cannot escape from the violence. Coined by Lenore Walker, learned helplessness includes symptoms such as guilt, fear, anger, shame and feelings of losing control—features that are usually described in the literature to characterize the victim (see, for example, Bailey 1996; Daugherty 1992; Hanson and Maroney 1999; Island and Letellier 1991; Potroczniak et al. 2003; Sullivan and Laughlin 1999; Walsh 1996).

For example, Pitt and Dolan-Soto note that victims often "seem uncomfortable or anxious about the relationships" and "feel like [they are] walking on eggshells" (2001: 166). Similarly, Gregory Merrill describes: "Victims often blame themselves and express remorse for responsive and self-defensive behaviors" (1998: 132). They feel responsible for their own victimization and, writes Claire Renzetti in "Violence and Abuse among Same-Sex Couples," "express intense shame, particularly if they have defended themselves or fought back, but also because they are embarrassed by their victimization" (1997a: 76). Victims are often afraid of their partners and, as Daugherty purports, feel that they are "unable to protect themselves from irrational and often unpredictable outbursts" (1992: 56). Consequently, they numb their emotions and endure the violence.

Invariably, it is argued that such experiences have a dramatic effect and often lead to life-long suffering. For example, Merrill uses Lenore Walker's theory *Battered Woman's Syndrome* to argue that victims of gay male partner abuse show such symptoms. He writes: "Like women who have endured prolonged abuse, it is not uncommon for battered gay and bisexual men to exhibit *battered woman's syndrome*. This syndrome includes a cluster of anxiety-related symptoms, such as intrusive night-mares and flashbacks, depression, irritability, exaggerated startle response (being 'jumpy'), hypervigilance (never letting their guard down), emotional numbing, and difficulty sleeping, concentrating, and functioning normally" (1998: 135). Similarly, in "Gay Violence," Rochelle Klinger uses medical labels such as post-traumatic stress disorder to describe victims' experiences: "During the abuse and after leaving, victims may experience affective and anxiety disorders, particularly a post-traumatic stress disorder (PTSD). PTSD may occur immediately following the incident or much later" (1995: 121). Like Klinger, Lundy observes: "Victims of same-sex domestic violence, like other victims of domestic violence, often suffer from Post-Traumatic Stress Disorder, a condition common to people who have been involuntarily held captive and subjected to systematic, random violence" (1999: 49).

The Perpetrator

Power and Control

It is commonly portrayed in the literature on gay intimate violence that perpetrators engage in violence to control their partners. According to Pitt and Dolan-Soto: "What is marked about abusive relationships is the abusive partner's need to maintain control" (2001: 166). Perpetrators, writes José Toro-Alfonso in "Domestic Violence among Same-Sex Partners in Puerto Rico: Implication for HIV Intervention," tend to have issues with power, domination, and control, and they "are violent with those persons in relation to whom they feel they have 'power,' 'superiority,' 'more experience,' 'more capacity,' 'more possibilities of manipulation'"and from whom they can expect little reprisal" (1999: 72; see also Peterman and Dixon 2003; Tully 2001).

Invariably, the perpetrator is described as having most, if not all, of the power and control. For example, in "Domestic Violence in Gay and Lesbian Relationships," Emily Pitt writes: "In an abusive relationship, one person has most of the power and control" (2000: 195). Like Pitt, Island and Letellier remark: "The perpetrator ordinarily adopts the powerful role, whereas the victim ordinarily adopts the powerless role" (1991: 41). For these authors, power is one-dimensional in gay male partner abuse. To put it more simply, it is constructed that the perpetrator has power, the victim does not.

It is explained that the perpetrator tends to feel inadequacy and lack of control over his life and, to fill this void, seeks control over his partner.

Violence is used as a means to gain such control. For example, in "Childhood Sexual Abuse and Domestic Violence: A Support Group for Latino Gay Men and Lesbians," Michael de Vidas writes: "Batterers feel they have no control over any parts of their lives and therefore, seek control and power over their partners through physical abuse, economic control, sexual abuse, threats and intimidation, isolation and property destruction" (1999: 62). Similarly, in "Shattering Illusions: Same-Sex Domestic Violence," Pam Elliott claims: "A certain number of people, given the opportunity to get away with abusing their partners, will do so because they hunger for control over some part of their lives, lives over which they feel they have no control" (1996: 3). The severity of violence is largely determined, Merrill argues in "Ruling the Exceptions: Same-Sex Battering and Domestic Violence theory," by the perpetrator's capacity of "impulse control" (1996: 18).

Accordingly, violence is not only biological, but also frequently intentional. "Battering," writes Letellier, "is not a matter of losing control over one's behavior; rather, it is a systematic and deliberate pattern of abuse used to gain control over one's partner" (1996: 71). Similarly, Merrill observes: "Batterers tend to have little ability and willingness to control their violent and aggressive impulses and will go to extremes to get their way" (1998: 133). Likewise, in Island and Letellier's clinical view: "There is a pre-existing tendency in the abuser to desire and attempt to manipulate, control, and dominate others, especially the partner—and to succeed" (1991: 76; see also Allen and Leventhal 1999). From this perspective, perpetrators are predisposed to violent behavior.

History of Family Violence

In the literature, history of family violence is deemed as playing a key role in gay male partner abuse. For example, Rochelle Klinger and Terry Stein argue: "Individuals who witnessed or who were victims of family violence as children are more likely as adults to be violent toward partners or children" (1996: 811). Likewise, Farley (1996) notes in his clinical practice, that quite often perpetrators themselves have been victims of family violence or child abuse.

According to these authors, violence is a learned behavior. As they argue, children who grow up in a violent home learn that it is acceptable to express anger and resolve interpersonal conflicts through violence; these children frequently become violent in adulthood. Perpetrators learn such behaviors through witnessing violence at home. For example, Farley explains:

> Batterers come from homes where battering occurred. Such family histories are a major factor in domestic violence. Behaviors that are abusive become reinforced throughout childhood as an effective way

of dealing with any confrontive situation. When parents act out their anger in violent ways, children are taught that anger and violence are synonymous. Fear is also a natural part of family dynamics, and it is automatically assumed that in order not to be abused, you cannot be angry. Another prevalent factor in these family histories is the lack of ability to express feelings of almost any kind (other than anger). (1992: 233)

Like Farley, Joan McClennen writes in "Prevailing Theories Regarding Same-Gender Partner Abuse: Proposing the Feminist Social-Psychological Model": "Causation is most often based on social learning occurring in the family of origin" (1999b: 6; see also McClennen 1999a; Merrill 1996, 1998).

Interestingly, as some authors point out, many victims have also experienced family violence or abuse in childhood. What makes one become a perpetrator instead of a victim is largely determined by the type of abuse he experiences in childhood. As Farley points out: "Victims most often come from families that were psychologically abusive, whereas perpetrators usually come from families that were physically abusive" (1992: 238; see also Nieves-Rosa et al. 2000).

Manipulation

In the literature, perpetrators are usually portrayed as being very manipulative. They appear to be charming, gentle, attentive, and loving, and frequently use these public images to disguise their violent behavior and manipulate others into believing that they are innocent. For example, in "Domestic Violence between Same-Sex Partners: Implications for Counseling," Linda Peterman and Charlotte Dixon write: "To those outside the relationship, abusers usually appear to be decent human beings, attentive partners/lovers, and law-abiding citizens. Nevertheless, they usually have a dualistic personality referred to as a Dr. Jekyll/Mr. Hyde personality and are manipulative, unpredictable, possessive, jealous, unrealistic, and controlling" (2003: 43). Similarly, Letellier observes: "Perpetrators with AIDS will use their diagnosis, and their sickly appearance, to manipulate the police and the criminal justice system to their advantage" (1996: 75). Like Letellier, Ellen Meyers, in "Developing a Successful Community Outreach Program: A Look at Criminal Justice and the Lesbian and Gay Community," warns: "Even in controlled presentations to service providers and so on, do not assume that everyone there wishes to address the issue of domestic violence. It may be that an abuser 'among us' wishes to enhance his or her skills by attending the closed or targeted meeting for personal gain" (1999: 246). Lundy also purports: "The batterer is generally no less domineering and manipulative in the counseling and mediation sessions than he or she is at home" (1999: 44). To put it more simply, in these authors' view, perpetrators are scheming and not trustworthy.

Internalized Homophobia and Heterosexism

According to the literature, due to homophobia and heterosexism, perpetrators are frequently confused about their own masculinity. As a result, they internalize feelings of homophobia and self-hate that lead to low self-esteem. For example, in "Clinical Models for the Treatment for Gay Male Perpetrators of Domestic Violence," Dan Byrne observes that perpetrators have "internalized feelings of self-hate" and "have manifested a negative self-concept related to being homosexual, as well as negative feelings about who they are as a person" (1996: 109–110). Similarly, in "Domestic Violence: Gay Men and Lesbians," Bonnie Carlson and Katherine Maciol note that perpetrators are "confused about masculinity" and "lack healthy role models for intimate relationships in a context in which being gay is perceived as unmasculine" (1997: 108).

To resolve such confusion, writes Fran Walsh in "Partner Abuse," perpetrators equate masculinity with aggression and "seek to bolster up" their negative self-image "by having, and exerting, power over their partner" (1996: 193). Similarly, in "Pornography, Hypermasculinity, and Gay Male Identity: Implication for Male Rape and Gay Male Domestic Violence," Christopher Kendall writes: "Gay men who batter and abuse their partners have specific ideas about masculinity and what it means to be 'male.' This is, in part, a reaction to a complete lack of positive gay role models, a homophobic environment in which being gay means being 'nonmasculine,' and the internalization of social rejection and self-hate. Gay men, growing up in a world with little or no positive reinforcement, are inundated with a value system that equates masculinity (as the determiner of appropriate male behavior) with aggression, control, and frequently violence" (2006: 125; see also Cruz 2000; Gunther and Jennings 1999; Smith and Dale 1999). In other words, the perception is that perpetrators use violence to fill this void and increase their sense of masculinity and self-esteem.

Homophobia and heterosexism are also theorized as contributing to gay male partner abuse. According to the theory, they lead to social isolation that, in turn, leads to stress and high dependency needs between the couple. This stress and dependency increase pressure on the relationship and the risk of violence, particularly when one of the partners seeks relative autonomy and independence. As Christopher Alexander writes in "Violence in Gay and Lesbian Relationships": "If a gay or lesbian couple feels isolated, or if they do not have emotional support outside their relationships, it appears there is a risk for acting this out on one another" (2002: 97; see also Cruz and Firestone 1998; Merrill 1998; Renzetti 1997b).

No Remorse

According to the literature, perpetrators often deny responsibility and rarely express remorse for their abusive behaviors. For example, Renzetti writes: "Batterers . . . are quite vocal in legitimating their behavior. They are typically self-righteous and assert a claim to the label 'victim.' With indignation and undisguised anger, they will recite a litany of partner "transgressions" that justified their violence. They rarely express shame or even remorse, and while they may be willing to accept partial responsibility for the relationships, the abuse is never entirely their fault" (1997a: 76). Like Renzetti, Walsh writes: "Abusers will often deny responsibility, blaming their partner or the situation for the abuse. Sometimes they will deny point-blank that their behavior is, in fact, abusive" (1996: 192; see also Hanson and Maroney 1999; West 1998).

These authors argue that violence gives perpetrators a sense of power, control and satisfaction; thus, they will not change. For example, Island and Letellier argue: "Violence is a self-reinforcing act for the perpetrator. Its cessation is a release, a satisfier, a reinforcer" (1991: 43). Likewise, Sullivan and Laughlin claim: "Aggressors have no reason to change. They are in a relationship where they are able to vent their frustration and anger any way and at any time they want. There are no consequences to their actions. In fact, after they vent their feelings, in whatever violent manner they choose, they feel better. Ultimately, they are rewarded for abusing their partner" (1999: 99).

Those who write about violence in gay relationships also argue that perpetrators will not voluntarily seek assistance as they often ignore their abusive behaviors. For example, in "Hate Crimes, Domestic Violence, and the Lesbian and Gay Community," Carol Tully writes: "Regrettably, many gay and lesbian perpetrators of violence simply disregard any kind of social services, disengage from the current relationship, and move on to new relationships where the violence continues" (1999: 25–26). Like Tully, Walber claims: "Batterers typically ignore or deny their actions and simply move on to new relationships" (1988: 254).

Personal Disorders

It has been argued in the literature that diagnosable psychopathology in perpetrators is the primary factor that causes violence in intimate gay relationships. As Island and Letellier assert, "Abusers *intend* to harm their lovers. Therefore, domestic violence is an enormous mental health problem in America. A batterer cannot possibly be seen as a mentally healthy, well-functioning member of a domestic couple . . . batterers suffer from a diagnosable, progressive mental disorder in their domestic setting, with their partners as the targets of their unhealthy condition, manifested most clearly just before, during, and after one of their violent attacks" (1991: 2–3; authors' emphasis). "The most common psychiatric

diagnoses" among gay men who batter, writes Klinger, "include personality disorder (e.g., borderline, narcissistic, antisocial), substance abuse,
organic mental disorders, intermittent explosive disorder, anxiety and
affective disorders" (1995: 124). Farley found in his clinical practice:
"Addictive behaviors such as substance use, eating disorders, and sexual
compulsivity are common in perpetrators of domestic violence" (1992:
233, McClennen 1999b; Renzetti 1997b). The frequency and severity of
the violence, as these authors argue, is largely determined by the severity
of perpetrators' psychopathology. In other words, it is constructed that
the more frequent and severe the violence is, the more severe the perpetrator's psychopathology is.

Other therapists and clinicians found that perpetrators are pathological
and frequently have difficulty managing their own anger, frustration, and
impulses toward their partners. For example, Island and Letellier observe:
"Gay men's domestic violence involves at least one angry man, or, as more
likely the case, one very angry man . . . With domestic violence, however,
anger and intent to harm are typically present and are used by one man to
coerce, control, manipulate, or injure the other" (1991: 25; see also Farley
2003; Landolt and Dutton 1997; Sullivan and Laughlin 1999). Perpetrators
are often depicted as being extremely jealous and overly dependent on their
partner. As Klinger and Stein argue, these tendencies "pressur[e] the victim
to be more and more isolated from other contacts" (1996: 811). Likewise,
Pitt and Dolan-Soto claim: "Abusers tend to be jealous, accusative, and
blaming, and to present unpredictable mood swings regarding their attitude toward the victim" (2001: 167). In "Same-Sex Couples: Problem and
Prospects," Sotirios Sarantakos writes: "Jealousy and the wish of one partner to 'possess' the other are the most common causes of violence" (1996:
159; McClennen, Summers and Vaughn 2002).

Still some therapists and clinicians find perpetrators extremely self-
centered. They, write Pitt and Dolan-Soto, "generally are concerned about
their *own* rather than their partners' needs, and they tend to focus on getting these needs met" (2001: 167; authors' emphasis). Like Pitt and Dolan-
Soto, Merrill claims: "[Perpetrators] tend to be narcissistic and entitled in
the sense that they expect all of their needs and demands to be complied
with immediately, but they do tend to have a double standard because they
can be callous to their partners' needs. Developmentally, they are like the
2-year-old who has fierce tantrums when his needs are not satisfied to his
liking—except they are far more sophisticated, manipulative, and dangerous" (1998: 133). It is seen that perpetrators frequently lie and hold exceed-
ingly high expectations of themselves, their partners and the relationships;
that usually they are very suspicious and highly critical and judgmental of
others, extremely insecure about themselves and unable to trust others;
and that they have problems with substance abuse and are fascinated with
martial arts, weapons, injury, torture, and violence of all kinds (see Island
and Letellier 1991: 79).

DISCUSSION

The Focus of Individual Pathology: Why?

Individual pathology, as shown previously, is the central organizing theme in the literature of gay male partner abuse. It is claimed that the perpetrator's pathological personality characteristics are the primary factors that cause violence; in contrast, the victim's personality characteristics facilitate his own victimization and lead to long-term effects.

Interestingly, however, there is little, if any, evidence that supports the claim that personal disorders, psychological abnormalities, and/or substance use cause partner abuse. For example, in "Patterns and Correlates of Interpersonal Violence," Susan Miller and Charles Wellford write: "Individual-level explanations focus primarily on personality disorders and traits, mental illness, self-image problems with drugs or alcohol. Violence is seen as resulting from various psychological abnormalities, such as inadequate self-control, sadism, and psychopathology . . . To date, however, the available scientific evidence provides little, if any, support for these assertions. In addition, these theories are also unable to explain which abnormal personality traits are directly associated with violence, especially since only a very small proportion of mentally ill persons are violent" (1997: 22). Like Miller and Wellford, Renzetti notes: "Some of the most methodologically sound research has indicated that personality disorders are apparent in only a small percentage of heterosexual male batterers" (1997a: 88).

Similarly, the existing evidence does not entirely support the hypothesis that violence is a learned behavior and originates from the family. Although some studies found an association between history of family violence and violence against intimate partners, other studies fail to show such a link (see Makepeace 1997; Miller and Wellford 1997; Renzetti 1997a). This theory, as James Makepeace points out, also fails to explain why some perpetrators "do not come from violent homes or why there are so many nonviolent persons coming from violent homes" (1997: 40). Additionally, most of these studies include retrospective research that shows only the percentage of perpetrators who have a history of abuse or who witness violence in their family. They do not answer the question of what percentage of people who experience abuse in childhood or who witness family violence grow up to become perpetrators themselves (see Lamb 1996).

By the same token, some researchers challenge the claim that people who experience traumatic events such as rape and violence in intimate relationships must or will have life-long suffering, leading to PTSD. For example, in *The Trouble with Blame: Victims, Perpetrators and Responsibility*, Sharon Lamb writes: "Although many survivors have some of the symptoms, the rate of PTSD among survivors is not so high as to claim it as an inevitable reaction to abuse" (1996: 48). "Often," Lamb continues, "the mental illness-like qualities of women who have been beaten disappear in the years shortly after leaving the abusive man. And sexual abuse researchers have documented recently that the majority of sexual abuse victims do not show severe symptomatology" (1999: 111).

Then why do clinicians and therapists of violence in intimate gay relationships so "obsessively" focus on individual characteristics (particularly psycho-pathology) of the victim and perpetrator? To some extent, violence in intimate gay relationships is not a new area. Rather, it is an extended area of study in interpersonal violence that is heavily imbedded in positivist, modernist notions of science. Largely stemmed from the eighteen-century enlightenment philosophy, as Lindsay John purports, modernity is "characterized by the pursuit of a truth that has the character of absolute certainty" (1994: 51). It emphasizes rationality and external objectivity, and embraces, writes Jane Gorman, "a belief in the lawful nature of the universe and a desire to explain and control nature" (1993: 248). It is believed that, through science, we find knowledge or, in Foucault's words, "truth" that provides rational explanations about the world and solutions for social problems (1984: 43). As U. Kalpagam writes in "The Colonial State and Statistical Knowledge," modern science "seeks to provide 'explanations' in terms of deriving law-like generalizations about phenomena and of the cause-effect relationships that govern them" (2000: 45). Accordingly, it is believed, modernist views can lead to progress and freedom, liberating human beings from irrationality as well as immorality (see Chambon and Irving 1994; Damianakis 2001).

This modernist, deterministic view has driven the researchers and scholars to focus primarily on searching for the cause of and solution to violence. The "experts" (including researchers, theoreticians, scholars and clinicians in this area) draw relationships between different forms of violence (such as child abuse and family violence) and, writes Gillian Walker, "articulate them together to form generalized and universal theories" (1986: 19). As part of this process, individual variables such as anger and low self-esteem are identified and separated to determine their casual relationships to violence. Clinicians and scholars of gay male partner abuse have adopted this tradition, focusing heavily on identifying variables as well as finding the cause of such violence (Renzetti 1997b).

Additionally, there is a whole economy to support the pathologization of victims and perpetrators. Commonly assumed to be the cause of gay male partner abuse and suggestive of learned behaviors, the pathological personality characteristics of the perpetrator are depicted as correctable, capable of being unlearned through treatment such as counseling and anger management. For example, "Hamberger and Coleman advocated for counseling with the batterer to manage or correct pathological personality characteristics" (Turell 1999: 38). Similarly, in *When It's Time to Leave Your Lover: A Guide for Gay Men,* Neil Kaminsky asserts: "Violence does not get better without outside intervention. There is no way around this" (1999: 57). Like Kaminsky, Island and Letellier purport: "Batterers have learned to be violent, evidencing both a disorder which is correctable through treatment and behavior which is punishable by law" (1991: 3).

Therapy, as they argue, is the most important course of treatment both for the victim to end his victimization as well as for the perpetrator to correct his pathological personality characteristics. In "Intervention in Gay Male Intimate Violence Requires Coordinated Efforts on Multiple Levels," Kevin Hamberger writes: "Individual interventions are the first step in protecting and offering help to the victim and attempting to change the behavior of the batterer" (1996: 90). Like Hamberger, Island and Letellier assert: "One of the most helpful steps a victim of gay men's domestic violence can take for himself is to get into therapy. Whether or not he is currently being battered, has just left a violent partner (and may be ambivalent about staying away), or has been away from his abusive lover for quite some time, therapy is an appropriate and necessary tool for ending the victimization of a domestic violence survivor. Therapy can provide insight and understanding, education and support, all of which are invaluable to gay male victims" (1991: 201–202). They warn: "Batterers have a learned, progressive mental disorder and will continue to act out their illness until they obtain help for curing it and follow the treatment prescriptions . . . If untreated, the violence may progress such that the perpetrator may permanently injure or kill his partner" (1991: 45, 77).

For these authors, the perpetrator is mentally ill with symptoms of pathological personality characteristics; thus, "partner abuse" should be included in the Diagnostic and Statistic Manual for Mental Disorders (DSM) and, in so doing, be legitimated as a mental illness, which in turn justifies the perpetrator's need for mental health treatment services. Similarly, as Lamb argues, by treating the victim's reactions to the stress of violence as symptoms of PTSD, clinicians can legitimize such reactions as mental illness. In so doing, "victims can garner more support," though only from mainstream institutions. Of course, there is a great deal of money for mental healthcare services that are "tied into psychiatry (hospitals, research, medication, insurance) rather than, for example, neighborhood women's clinics" (1996: 49, 46).

Unsurprisingly, many authors and clinicians in this area strongly advocate for the inclusion of "partner abuse" in the DSM and label the victim's reactions to the stress of violence as PTSD symptoms. As Island and Letellier write: "Since so few batterers receive any treatment today, the psychological and psychiatric communities are petitioned . . . to develop new pathology nomenclature for abusive personality disorders for all batterers, in order to encourage entrepreneurial clinicians to treat more batterers, and get paid for it, and to increase the availability of treatment in general for batterers" (1991: 3–4). Similarly, Renzetti points out: "Mental health and hospital personnel will become more accepting of the problem of abuse and more perpetrators and victims will be treated by private practitioners because the DSM is used by insurers to determine diagnoses eligible for treatment reimbursement" (1997a: 88).

Pure Victims vs. Pure Villains

Based on dichotomous thinking or, in Foucault's words, "dividing practices" and "scientific classification" (1983: 208) that emphasize consistencies and orderly patterns, the discourse of victims and perpetrators in contemporary gay male partner abuse literature has created two opposite categories: one that is powerless and innocent; the other, powerful and evil. Indisputably, this discourse provides clinicians and gay men with a frame of reference to understand and make sense of their experiences, which are otherwise confusing and often incomprehensible. But what becomes problematic is when it polarizes these categories in order to seek certainty and truth—the rigid definition of victims and perpetrators (Berlin 1990; Kent 2002).

This discourse, associated with modernist traditions, obscures the complexities of violence necessary to fully understanding the issue while failing to account for a range of abusive experiences. As Nancy Hirschmann writes, using violence against women as her frame of reference: "When someone is labeled a 'battered women,' the social images the label conjures up, and the discourse that frames those images, transform the heterogeneity of lived experience into the homogeneity of social types" (2003: 125). To put it more simply, the discourse of victims and perpetrators in contemporary gay male partner abuse literature treats these categories as fixed, stable and autonomous identities. It ignores the multiple spaces that gay men can occupy, and prevents us from critically examining "the way someone can both be a victim and abuse systemic power" at the same time (Ristock 2002: 127).

In practice, few victims of gay male partner abuse are absolutely pure and few perpetrators, completely evil with no redeeming quality. However, to make the presumed storyline work, victims and perpetrators, writes Lamb, "would need to transform themselves into our view of them. And if they cannot change themselves to fit into our molds of purity and monstrosity, then we tend" to fit them into these roles (1996: 89). We justify it by saying that the victim denies and minimizes the abuse. For example, Donileen Loseke (2001) observes in her field work that when battered women's narratives fail to conform to the "wife abuse story," social workers and shelter workers often ask: "what is wrong with *women* who do not want to understand themselves as a character in the wife abuse story" (122; author's emphasis)? Similarly, we purport that the perpetrator is manipulative and never accepts any responsibility for the violence.

The portrayal of perpetrators as villains in contemporary gay male partner abuse literature does not allow other explanations except for those that see them as unremorseful, heartless, sick, and evil; whose motive for using violence is control. But, clearly, not all violence is the same. Meanings and motives underlying intimate violence vary among perpetrators in different racial and socio-economic groups (Bograd 1999; Renzetti 1999; 1997b). Not all abusers are "exercising power and control and causing fear and isolation in the victim . . . but in a context dominated by power and control discourse it is the only story allowed" (Ristock 2002: 177–178). This construction of the perpetrators removes the abuse from its context.

If the perpetrator behaves in a way that is not abusive, we dismiss this behavior by saying that the victim is trying to downplay the abuse. Or, we describe such behavior as a form of manipulation or, using Walker's cycle of violence theory, explain it as a honeymoon phase. For example, Daugherty claims: "After a threatening experience, the perpetrator displays kindness to the victim" (1992: 61). Likewise, Sullivan and Laughlin argue: "[The perpetrator] may choose to say they are sorry by bringing flowers home or taking their partner out for a nice dinner, but now that their negative feelings are vented, they can feel good about themselves as they enjoy being extra nice to their partner" (1999: 99; see also Merrill 1998). Rather than regarding the perpetrator's displays of kindness as a single aspect of a multi-faceted personality, we construct this "kindness" as manipulative and insincere.

No doubt, in many ways, these perpetrators are manipulative, but they can be loving and caring as well. This tension, often ignored by scholars of gay male partner abuse, has been acknowledged by some scholars of family violence. For example, Carol Ronai, in relating her experience as a victim of child abuse, writes: "In one moment of reflection I thought of my mother as 'vile,' while in others I thought she was the best mom a kid could have. She abused me physically and sexually, yet she often protected me from my father, who was far worse" (1999: 156). Likewise, Ristock describes one of her lesbian participants' experiences as follows: "She sees many sides to [the abuser] including being caring and fun, being depressed and in emotional pain, and being manipulative" (2002: 176). It is precisely these mixed emotions that make it difficult for the victim to leave the perpetrator, and complicate the situation. As Loseke writes in reference to women's experience of domestic abuse: "The lived experience of women can be one where love and hate, caring and violence are perceived as coexisting simultaneously, where the violence is difficult to classify given folks' understanding of 'normal' violence, where designating pure victims and pure villains ignores perceived relational cores of trouble" (2001: 120). In other words, the discourse of perpetrators as villains in contemporary gay male partner abuse literature reflects a particular construction (rather than the essential truth) of the perpetrator in our society.

Unwittingly, this discourse has other detrimental effects. It reduces perpetrators of gay male partner abuse into these "evils," who social workers and service providers alike frequently see as undeserving clients who cannot be helped. This negative attitude has been commonly found among service providers who work in the field of domestic violence. For example, Ristock observes: "Service providers are struggling with how best to offer services for lesbian victims, yet they are often unwilling to work with lesbian perpetrators. Some felt they were incapable of working with women who were abusive and others simply do not want to work with women who are abusive, seeing them as undeserving of services" (2002: 126). Like Ristock, Jeanne Marecek notes: "Men involved in abuse were branded as predators, scary, evil. Indeed, the ubiquitous term *abuser* shrinks a man's identity to a single dimension . . . Even though many respondents had no actual experience treating abusers, they believed that such clients could not be helped and did not want to change" (1999: 174; author's emphasis). This construction of partner abuse, rather than providing useful information in working with gay male perpetrators, undermines helping relationships.

Moreover, the discourse of perpetrators as villains in contemporary gay male partner abuse literature places full responsibility on these men for the violence, which in turn structures how treatment programs are being organized. These programs usually include two components: (1) education about violence in intimate relationships; and (2) learning interpersonal skills such as stress and anger management (see for example Bailey 1996; Byrne 1996; Carlson and Maciol 1997; Merrill 1998). The educational component frequently emphasizes teaching perpetrators to address their personal denial while accepting responsibility for their abusive behavior. Undeniably perpetrators should take responsibility for the abuse, however, such discourse, combined with the negative view of perpetrators as manipulative and unremorseful, can have unintended, but powerful effects on clinical practice with these men.

In his ethnographic study of treatment groups for male perpetrators of family violence in heterosexual relationships, John McKendy has demonstrated such effects. The discourse of full responsibility, as he observes, has limited what can or cannot be said in theses groups. The men "were only allowed to tell what happened by magnifying their own agency [and] reconstructing events as outcomes of decisions they had made" (1997: 148). It is thought that such discussions can help these men accept responsibility while simultaneously identifying the cause of their violent behavior. In contrast, they were not allowed to talk about their partner or give any context to the violence since this type of discussion was usually considered to be the men's attempt to blame the victim and remove their own responsibility for the abuse: "The men thought that certain things needed to be told for listeners to understand why they had acted as they did. The struggle to include information about the context was particularly contentious when this consisted of descriptions of the part their wives play in abusive incidents. Responding to such stories, the counselor worked conscientiously to discount the men's feelings of constraint and lack of full responsibility" (1992: 73). In so doing, the counselor silenced these men. Unsurprisingly, as McKendy notes, the men felt "puzzled, bored, shamed and angered; rarely were they engaged in the process of rebuilding their lives and transforming their selves" (1997: 148). Ironically, these men were seldom "pleased with themselves or . . . justified in what they had done. More often, they acknowledged that they had behaved badly" (1992: 73; see also Nurnberger and Robichaud-Smith 2004).

By the same token, the discourse of victims as pure in contemporary gay male partner abuse literature assumes a homogeneous experience and thus fails to account for the diverse experiences of victimhood. Clearly, meanings of violence vary among victims of gay male partner abuse in different racial and socio-economic groups; their experience is inevitably mediated through different forms of oppression such as racism, classism, and ableism within the relationships. Hence, there is no monolithic experience of abuse (Bograd 1999; McNair and Neville 1996; Ristock 2002).

Of course, victims deserve sympathy and support, but within this discourse, only gay men who conform to expectations are the victims. Those who fight back, those who feel in control, or those who do not feel powerless or helpless are somehow not seen as "real" victims or commonly labeled as being "in denial." Michele Bograd makes a similar point, though referring to women who experience domestic abuse: "Women who fight back are often judged as undeserving of protection because they violate social definitions of the helpless or passive victim" (1999: 280). Similarly, Lamb writes: "When a victim says she is 'over it' or that it was 'a long time ago,' she becomes suspect" (1999: 115). To put it more simply, the discourse of victims as innocent, passive and helpless in contemporary gay male partner abuse literature does not reflect the lived experience of these men, but a particular construction of victimhood.

Though unintentionally, this discourse has produced other effects. It reduces victims of gay male partner abuse to deficiencies. This image, as disempowering as it sounds, stands in stark contrast to the social construction of masculinity, in which men are depicted as being independent, self-reliant and emotionally in control. Those who are unable to protect themselves from being victimized or whose behaviors are seen as contradictory to the social ideal of masculinity are frequently associated with being weak and are thus ridiculed. For many men, to identify themselves as such is to admit personal weakness. They are not acting like "real" men. This image of victimization, rather than helping gay men identify themselves as the victims, makes it difficult for them to do so.

Moreover, within this discourse, victims of gay male partner abuse are perceived as passive agents who are waiting to be treated. This common assumption about victims, which does not account for agency, strength, and resiliency, has been challenged by some scholars in the recent literature of violence against women. For example, Bograd writes when referring to women's experience of family violence: "Even as there is a range of batterers, victims are coerced to varying degrees and have had varied opportunities to take action" (1999: 284). Like Bograd, Linda Alcoff and Laura Gray write as survivors of sexual violence: "All survivors face debilitating trauma, and no 'cure' exists that can take the pain away or remove all the effects of sexual violence, but we are not objects with attributes ('syndromes' or 'disorders'). We are fluid, constantly changing beings who can achieve great clarity and emotional insight even from within the depths of pain" (1993: 282). Instead of being passive agents, victims of gay male partner abuse, even in extremely difficult situations, possess agency, strength, and resiliency that enable them to actively resist while negotiating meaning from their experience.

The discourse of victims as life-long sufferers in contemporary gay male partner abuse literature often constructs these men solely with respect to their victimization. It rarely acknowledges that they can move beyond a violent experience that does not necessarily affect them so lastingly. Nor does it acknowledge any positive meaning that they may create out of their abusive experience. Simply, within this discourse, they are defined by their victimization and are forever victims. Their victimhood is static and fixed. This notion of victimhood, which makes it difficult to conceptualize these men's experience other than being victimized, has been challenged by some recent child abuse and HIV/AIDS literature. For example, Lamb writes when referring women's experience of violence: "Although rape, child sexual abuse, and wife battering are terrible experiences to have gone through, many people have 'survived' and moved beyond them, feeling as if their victimization is not something that has defined them or continues to affect them" (1996: 46). Similarly, Heather Dunbar and colleagues show that even people who face terminal illnesses such as AIDS can create positive meanings about their illness: "Some women have used the stress of HIV to transform their lives in positive and productive ways. . . . These personal accounts often depict the women actively using their HIV diagnosis as a stimulus to healthier and fuller lives" (1998: 145; see also Lewis 1999). In other words, the discourse of victims as life long-suffering in contemporary gay male partner abuse literature reflects only a particular version of victimhood in our society, rather than the reality of these men.

FINAL NOTE

If, as Foucault (1980) argues, knowledge is always and inevitably discursive, the construction of victims and perpetrators in contemporary gay male partner abuse literature is never value-neutral or pre-discursive. In fact, it is precisely this discourse that constructs the way in which we understand gay male victims and perpetrators of partner abuse. This construction limits our ways of thinking of these men and thus regulates our ways of working with them. As practitioners, we must be aware of such discursive effects and critically examine how they impose certain assumptions on us. We need to ask, for example, how our understanding of gay male partner abuse regulates and polices the way in which we understand the issue and interacts with these men in therapeutic settings or how the dominant discourse of violence in intimate gay relationships becomes a self-evident truth (knowledge) that imposes a uniform story on these men's lived experiences. In so doing, we liberate ourselves from the self-evidence of the dominant discourse (Foucault 1988b; Foote and Frank 1999).

Neither victims nor perpetrators of gay male partner abuse are simply "symptoms." The task for us, it is important to note, is not to seek "some final 'authentic' story" about them and, in fact, "any ideal of ever arriving at" such a story "must remain suspect." The point is, as Catherine Foote and Arthur Frank write, "not to invent a new story but to give the person the fullest choice among all potential stories" (1999: 179, 181). To put it more simply, instead of taking on an expert role to give diagnosis, our role as a therapist is to help these men search for meaning in past events that is relevant to *their* experience, regardless of whether this understanding necessarily fits into the normative discourse of gay male partner abuse (see Alcoff and Gray 1993; Nurnberger and Robichaud-Smith 2004).

At a conceptual level, to change the cultural assumptions of gay male victims and perpetrators in partner abuse, we also need a language that acknowledges multiple subjectivities of identity (i.e., one can hold multiple or even contradictory positions at one time or different positions at various moments) and, at the same time, theorizes how such subjectivities are constituted within a social context. We need "a language of power that allows us to map the multiple and interlocking nature of identity and systems of privilege and oppression that are part of the context of relationship violence" (Ristock 2002: 125). Power, as Foucault (1983) taught us, is never one-dimensional but rather circulated and multi-dimensional. When there is power, there is always resistance; therefore no one is completely powerful or powerless and power operates differently in various personal as well as social contexts.

Accordingly, to fully understand and explain how multiple subjectivities of identity are constituted in gay male partner abuse, rather than simply assuming that the victim is powerless and the perpetrator powerful and controlling, we must examine how power operates in particular personal and social contexts. In this way, we move away from abstract, but fixed notions of victims and perpetrators while allowing us to see multiple and sometimes contradictory aspects of their personality. It must be noted, however, that this conceptualization of power does not mean that power and control do not operate in violent relationships. Rather, it rejects the notion that power is fixed and rests simply with the perpetrator. It thus allows us to examine the complexity of these men's lives and "to scrutinize the power dynamics in [their] intimate relationships and in other areas of their lives" (Ristock 2002: 128).

Furthermore, with few exceptions, contemporary gay male partner abuse literature rarely addresses the effects of oppression other than homophobia and heterosexism; such as racism, classism, and ableism on these men (see Lev and Lev 1999; Méndez 1996; Poon 2000). This of course frequently reflects the socio-economic position of the authors: namely white middle-upper class gay men. In "Exploring Discursive Constructions of Lesbian Abuse: Looking Inside and Out," Cindy Holmes and Janice Ristock make a similar point, arguing that scholars often fail "to see how assumptions about private violence can re-centre a white, Eurocentric conceptualization of violence by ignoring the past and current effects of racism and the different experiences of private and public spaces" (2004: 99). To challenge the normative assumption of gay male partner abuse, we need to develop a language that accounts for the diverse experiences of abuse. We need to explore how the experience of violence is mediated, not only through homophobia and heterosexism, but also through privilege (whiteness) and other forms of oppression; how meanings of violence, power, control, agency, strength, and resiliency intersect with social dimensions such as race, gender, class, disability, and sexual orientation within relationships.

Language, as Ronald Adler and George Rodman remind us, does not simply "describe the world" but also, and perhaps more importantly, shapes "the way we look at the world and, in so doing," influences "the way we behave" (1991: 65). Changing our ways of talking will also and inevitably change the way we construct our social world. By changing the cultural assumption of gay male partner abuse, we change the way we construct this issue and thus the way we work with these men. As Tanya Lewis puts it, "changing assumptions based on normativity . . . allows for a reconception of the therapeutic process" (1999: 31). This change may better help us understand the complexity of gay male partner abuse and prepare us to work with these men more effectively.

NOTES

1. Acknowledgments: This chapter is a shorter and slightly different version of a chapter in my doctoral thesis. I would like to thank Suzanne Koso for her assistance with the literature.

REFERENCES

Alcoff, L. and L. Gray. 1993. Survivor discourse: Transgression or recuperation? *Signs* 18(2): 260–290.
Adler, R. B. and G. Rodman. 1991. *Understanding human communication.* 4th ed. Toronto: Holt, Rinehart and Winston, Inc.
Alexander, C. J. 2002. Violence in gay and lesbian relationships. *Journal of Gay and Lesbian Social Services* 14(1): 95–98.
Allen, C. and B. Leventhal. 1999. History, culture, and identity: What makes GLBT battering different. In *Same-sex domestic violence: Strategies for change,* ed. B. Leventhal and S. E. Lundy, 73–81. Thousand Oaks, CA: Sage.
Bailey, G. R. Jr. 1996. Treatment of domestic violence in gay and lesbian relationships. *Journal of Psychological Practice* 2(2): 1–8.
Berlin, S. B. 1990. Dichotomous and complex thinking. *Social Services Review* 64(1): 46–59.

Bograd, M. 1999. Strengthening domestic violence theories: Intersections of race, class, sexual orientation, and gender. *Journal of Marital and Family Therapy* 25(3): 275–289.

Bricker, D. 1993. Fatal defense: An analysis of battered woman's syndrome expert testimony for gay men and lesbians who kill abusive partners. *Brooklyn Law Review* 58: 1379–1437.

Bryant, A. S. and Demian. 1994. Relationship characteristics of American gay and lesbian couples: Findings from a national survey. *Journal of Gay and Lesbian Social Services* 1(2): 101–107.

Burke, T. W., M. L. Jordan and S. S. Owen. 2002. A cross-national comparison of gay and lesbian domestic violence. *Journal of Contemporary Criminal Justice* 18(3): 231–57.

Burke, T. W. and S. S. Owen. 2006. Same-sex domestic violence: Is anyone listening? *The Gay and Lesbian Review* 13(1): 6–7.

Byrne, D. 1996. Clinical models for the treatment for gay male perpetrators of domestic violence. *Journal of Gay and Lesbian Social Services* 4(1): 107–116.

Carlson, B. E. and K. Maciol. 1997. Domestic violence: Gay men and lesbians. In *Encyclopedia of social work*. 19th ed. 1997 supplement, ed. R. L. Edwards, 101–111. Washington, DC: NASW Press.

Chambon, A. S. and A. Irving, eds. 1994. *Essays on postmodernism and social work*. Toronto: Canadian Scholars' Press.

Cruz, J. M. 2000. Gay male domestic violence and the pursuit of masculinity. In *Gay masculinities,* ed. Peter Nardi, 66–82. Thousand Oaks, CA: Sage Publications.

———. 2003. "Why doesn't he just leave?" Gay male domestic violence and the reason victims stay. *The Journal of Men's Studies* 11(3): 309–323.

Cruz, J. M. and J. M. Firestone. 1998. Exploring violence and abuse in gay male relationships. *Violence and Victims* 13(2): 159–173.

Cruz, J. M. and R. L. Peralta. 2001. Family violence and substance use: The perceived effects of substance use within gay male relationships. *Violence and Victims* 16(2): 161–172.

Damianakis, T. 2001. Postmodernism, spirituality, and the creative writing process: Implications for social work practice. *Families in Society* 82(1): 23–34.

Daugherty, S. S. 1992. *Closeted screams: A service-provider handbook for same-sex domestic violence issues.* Denver, CO: Smith-Fliesher Soria Publishing.

de Vidas, M. 1999. Childhood sexual abuse and domestic violence: A support group for Latino gay men and lesbians. *Journal of Gay and Lesbian Social Services* 10(2): 51–68.

Dudley, R. G. Jr. 2002. Offering psychiatric opinion in legal proceedings when lesbian and gay sexual orientation is an issue. In *Mental health issues in lesbian, gay, bisexual, and transgender communities,* ed. B. E. Jones and M. J. Hill, 37–70. Washington, DC: American Psychiatric Publishing.

Dunbar, H. T., C. W. Mueller, C. Medina and T. Wolf. 1998. Psychological and spiritual growth in women living with HIV. *Social Work* 43(2): 144–154.

Dutton, D. G., M. A. Landolt, A. Starzomski and M. Bodnarchuk. 2001. Validation of the propensity for abusiveness scale in diverse male populations. *Journal of Family Violence* 16(1): 59–73.

Elliott, P. 1996. Shattering illusions: Same-sex domestic violence. *Journal of Gay and Lesbian Social Services* 4(1): 1–8.

Farley, N. 1992. Same-sex domestic violence. In *Counseling gay men and lesbians: Journey to the end of the rainbow,* ed. S. H. Dworkin and F. J. Gutiérrez, 231–242. Alexandria, VA: American Association for Counseling and Development.

———. 1996. A survey of factors contributing to gay and lesbian domestic violence. *Journal of Gay and Lesbian Social Services* 4(1): 35–42.

———. 2003. Same-sex domestic violence: A tool for batterers. In *The Therapist's notebook for lesbian, gay, and bisexual clients: Homework, handouts, and activities for use in psychotherapy,* ed. J. S. Whitman and C. J. Boyd, 234–237. New York: The Haworth Clinical Practice Press.

Foote, C. E. and A. W. Frank. 1999. Foucault and therapy: The disciplining of grief. In *Reading Foucault for social work,* ed. A. S. Chambon, A. Irving and L. Epstein, 157–187. New York: Columbia University Press.

Foucault, M. 1980. Two lectures. In *Power/knowledge: Selected interviews and other writings 1972–1977 by Michel Foucault,* ed. C. Gordon, 78–108. New York: Pantheon Books.

———. 1983. Afterword: The subject and power. In *Michel Foucault: Beyond and structuralism and hermeneutics.* 2nd ed., ed. H. L. Dreyfus and Paul Rabinow, 208–226. Chicago: University of Chicago Press.

———. 1984. What is enlightenment? In *The Foucault reader,* ed. P. Rabinow, 32–50. New York: Pantheon Books.

———. 1988a. On power. In *Michel Foucault: Politics, philosophy, culture—interviews and other writings 1977–1984,* ed. L. D. Kritzman, 96–109. New York: Routledge.

———. 1988b. Practicing criticism. In *Michel Foucault: Politics, philosophy, culture—interviews and other writings 1977–1984,* ed. L. D. Kritzman, 152–156. New York: Routledge.

Fox, L. J. 1999. Couples therapy for gay and lesbian couples with a history of domestic violence. In *A professional's guide to understanding gay and lesbian domestic violence: Understanding practice interventions,* ed. J. C. McClennen and J. Gunther, 107–126. Lewiston, NY: The Edwin Mellen Press.

Gelles, R. J. 1997. *Intimate violence in families.* 3rd ed. London: Sage.

Gillis, J. R. and S. Diamond. 2006. Same-sex partner abuse: Challenges to the existing paradigms of intimate violence theory. In *Cruel but not unusual: Violence in Canadian families,* ed. R. Alaggia and C. Vine, 127–144. Kitchener, ON: Wilfrid Laurier University Press.

Gorman, J. 1993. Postmodernism and the conduct of inquiry in social work. *Affilia* 8(3): 247–264.

Gunther, J. and M. A. Jennings. 1999. Cultural and institutional violence and their impact on same-gender partner abuse. In *A professional's guide to understanding gay and lesbian domestic violence: Understanding practice interventions,* ed. J. C. McClennen and J. Gunther, 29–34. Lewiston, NY: The Edwin Mellen Press.

Hall, S. 2001. Foucault: Power, knowledge and discourse. In *Discourse theory and practice: A reader,* ed. M. Wetherell, S. Taylor and S. J. Yates, 72–81. London: Sage.

Hamberger, L. K. 1996. Intervention in gay male intimate violence requires coordinated efforts on multiple levels. In *Violence in gay and lesbian domestic partnerships,* ed. C. M. Renzetti and C. H. Miley, 83–91. New York: Harrington Park Press.

Hanson, B. and T. Maroney. 1999. HIV and same-sex domestic violence. In *Same-sex domestic violence: Strategies for change,* ed. B. Leventhal and S. E. Lundy, 97–110. Thousand Oaks, CA: Sage.

Hirschmann, N. J. 2003. *The Subject of liberty: Toward a feminist theory of freedom.* Princeton, NJ: Princeton University Press.

Holmes, C. and J. L. Ristock. 2004. Exploring discursive constructions of lesbian abuse: Looking inside and out. In *Survivor rhetoric: Negotiations and narrativity in abused women's language,* ed. C. Shearer-Cremean and C. L. Winkelmann, 94–119. Toronto: University of Toronto Press.

Isensee, R. 1990. *Love between men: Enhancing intimacy and keeping your relationship alive.* New York: Prentice Hall Press.

Island, D. and P. Letellier. 1991. *Men who beat the men who love them.* New York: Harrington Park Press.

John, L. H. 1994. Borrowed knowledge in social work: An introduction to post-structuralism and postmodernity. In *Essays on postmodernism and social work,* ed. A. S. Chambon and A. Irving, 47–60. Toronto: Canadian Scholars' Press.

Kalpagam, U. (2000). The colonial state and statistical knowledge. *History of the Human Sciences* 13(2): 37–55.

Kaminsky, N. 1999. *When it's time to leave your lover: A guide for gay men.* New York: Harrington Park Press.

Kent, S. 1999. Egaliarianism, equality, and equitable power. In *Manifesting power: Gender and the interpretation of power in archaeology,* ed. T. L. Sweely, 30–48. New York: Routledge.

Kendall, C. 2006. Pornography, hypermasculinity, and gay male identity: Implications for male rape and gay male domestic violence. In *Gendered outcasts and sexual outlaws: Sexual oppression and gender hierarchies in queer men's lives,* ed. C. Kendall and W. Martino, 105–130. New York: Harrington Park Press.

Klinger, R. L. 1995. Gay violence. *Journal of Gay and Lesbian Psychotherapy* 2(3): 119–134.

Klinger, R. L. and T. S. Stein. 1996. Impact of violence, childhood sexual abuse, and domestic violence and abuse on lesbian, bisexuals, and gay men. In *Textbook of homosexuality and mental health,* ed. R. P. Cabaj and T. S. Stein, 801–818. Washington, DC: American Psychiatric Press.

Kuehnle, K. and A. Sullivan. 2003. Gay and lesbian victimization: Reporting factors in domestic violence and bias incidents. *Criminal Justice and Behavior* 30(1): 85–96.

Lamb, S. 1996. *The trouble with blame: Victims, perpetrators, and responsibility.* Cambridge, MA: Harvard University Press.

———. 1999. Constructing the victim: Popular images and lasting labels. In *New versions of victims: Feminists struggle with the concept,* ed. S. Lamb, 108–138. New York: New York University Press.

Landolt, M. A. and Dutton, D. 1997. Power and personality: An analysis of gay male intimate abuse. *Sex Roles* 37(5/6): 335–359.

Letellier, P. 1994. Gay and bisexual male domestic violence victimization: Challenges to feminist theory and responses to violence. *Violence and Victims* 9(2): 95–106.

———. 1996. Twin epidemics: Domestic violence and HIV infection among gay and bisexual men. *Journal of Gay and Lesbian Social Services* 4(1): 69–81.

Lev, A. I. and S. S. Lev. 1999. Sexual assault in the lesbian, gay, bisexual, and transgendered communities. In *A professional's guide to understanding gay and lesbian domestic violence: Understanding practice interventions,* ed. J. C. McClennen and J. Gunther, 35–61. Lewiston, NY: The Edwin Mellen Press.

Leventhal, B. and S. E. Lundy, eds. 1999. *Same-sex domestic violence: Strategies for change.* Thousand Oaks, CA: Sage.

Lewis, T. 1999. *Living beside: Performing normal after incest memories return.* Toronto: McGilligan Books.

Loseke, D. R. 2001. Lived realities and formula stories of "battered women." In *Institutional selves: Troubled identities in a postmodern world,* ed. J. F. Gubrium and J. A. Holstein, 107–126. New York: Oxford University Press.

Lundy, S. E. 1993. Abuse that dare not speak its name: Assisting victims of lesbian and gay domestic violence in Massachusetts. *New England Law Review* 28: 273–311.

———. 1999. Equal protection/equal safety: Representing victims of same-sex partner abuse in court. In *Same-sex domestic violence: Strategies for change,* ed. B. Leventhal and S. E. Lundy, 43–55. Thousand Oaks, CA: Sage Publication.

Marecek, J. 1999. Trauma talk in feminist clinical practice. In *New versions of victims: Feminists struggle with the concept,* ed. S. Lamb, 158–182. New York: New York University Press.

Makepeace, J. M. 1997. Courtship violence as process: A development theory. In *Violence between intimate partners: Patterns, causes, and effects,* ed. A. P. Cardarelli, 29–47. Toronto: Allyn & Bacon.

McClellen, D. 1999. Advocating on behalf of same-sex couples experiencing partner abuse. In *A professional's guide to understanding gay and lesbian domestic violence: Understanding practice interventions,* ed. J. C. McClennen and J. Gunther, 249–256. Lewiston, NY: The Edwin Mellen Press.

McClennen, J. C. 1999a. Future directions for practice interventions regarding same-gender partner abuse. In *A professional's guide to understanding gay and lesbian domestic violence: Understanding practice interventions,* ed. J. C. McClennen and J. Gunther, 297–312. Lewiston, NY: The Edwin Mellen Press.

———. 1999b. Prevailing theories regarding same-gender partner abuse: Proposing the feminist social-psychological model. In *A professional's guide to understanding gay and lesbian domestic violence: Understanding practice interventions,* ed. J. C. McClennen and J. Gunther, 311. Lewiston, NY: The Edwin Mellen Press.

McClennen, J. C. and J. Gunther, eds. 1999. *A professional's guide to understanding gay and lesbian domestic violence: Understanding practice interventions.* Lewiston, NY: The Edwin Mellen Press.

McClennen, J. C., A. B. Summers and C. Vaughan. 2002. Gay men's domestic violence: Dynamics, help-seeking behaviors, and correlates. *Journal of Gay and Lesbian Social Services* 14(1): 23–49.

McKendy, J. P. 1992. Ideological practices and the management of emotions: The case of "wife abusers." *Critical Sociology* 19(2): 61–80.

———. 1997. The class politics of domestic violence. *Journal of Sociology and Social Welfare* 24(3): 135–155.

McNair, L. D. and H. A. Neville. 1996. African American women survivors of sexual assault: The intersection of race and class. In *Classism and feminist therapy: Counting costs,* ed. M. Hill and E. Rothblum, 107–118. New York: Haworth.

Méndez, J. M. 1996. Serving gays and lesbians of color who are survivors of domestic violence. In *Violence in gay and lesbian domestic partnerships,* ed. C. M. Renzetti and C. Harvey Miley, 53–59. New York: Harrington Park Press.

Merrill, G. S. 1996. Ruling the exceptions: Same-sex battering and domestic violence theory. *Journal of Gay and Lesbian Social Services* 4(1): 9–21.

———. 1998. Understanding domestic violence among gay and bisexual men. In *Issues in intimate violence,* ed. R. Kennedy Bergen, 129–141. Thousand Oaks, CA: Sage.

Merrill, G. S. and V. A. Wolfe. 2000. Battered gay men: An exploration of abuse, help seeking, and why they stay. *Journal of Homosexuality* 39(2): 1–30.

Meyers, E. A. 1999. Developing a successful community outreach program: A look at criminal justice and the lesbian and gay community. In *A professional's guide to understanding gay and lesbian domestic violence: Understanding practice interventions,* ed. J. C. McClennen and J. Gunther, 239–247. Lewiston, NY: The Edwin Mellen Press.

Miller, S. L. and C. F. Wellford. 1997. Patterns and correlates of interpersonal violence. In *Violence between intimate partners: Patterns, causes, and effects,* ed. A. P. Cardarelli, 16–28. Toronto: Allyn & Bacon.

Nieves-Rosa, L. E., A. Carballo-Diéguez and C. Dolezal. 2000. Domestic abuse and HIV-risk behavior in Latin American men who have sex with men in New York City. *Journal of Gay and Lesbian Social Services* 11(1): 77–90.

Nurnberger, R. and D. Robichaud-Smith. 2004. A post-positive enquiry into men's relational motivations: Therapeutic construction and giving credence to men's stories about their use of abuse. *Canadian Social Work Review* 21(2): 169–188.

Peel, E. 1999. Violence against lesbians and gay men: Decision-making in reporting and not reporting crime. *Feminism and Psychology* 9(2): 161–167.

Peterman, L. M. and C. G. Dixon. 2003. Domestic violence between same-sex partners: Implications for counseling. *Journal of Counseling and Development* 81: 40–47.

Pitt, E. 2000. Domestic violence in gay and lesbian relationships. *Journal of the Gay and Lesbian Medical Association* 4(4): 195–196.

Pitt, E. and D. Dolan-Soto. 2001. Clinical considerations in working with victims of same-sex domestic violence. *Journal of the Gay and Lesbian Medical Association* 5(4): 163–169.

Poon, M. K. L. 2000. Inter-racial same-sex abuse: The vulnerability of gay men of Asian descent in relationships with Caucasian men. *Journal of Gay and Lesbian Social Services* 11(4): 39–67.

Potoczniak, M. J., J. E. Mourot, M. Crosbie-Burnett and D. J. Potoczniak. 2003. Legal and psychological perspectives on same-sex domestic violence: A multisystemic approach. *Journal of Family Psychology* 17(2): 252–259.

Regan, K. V., K. Bartholomew, D. Oram and M. A. Landolt. 2002. Measuring physical violence in male same-sex relationships: An item response theory analysis of the conflict tactics scales. *Journal of Interpersonal Violence* 17(3): 235–252.

Renzetti, C. M. 1997a. Violence and abuse among same-sex couples. In *Violence between intimate partners: Patterns, causes, and effects,* ed. A. P. Cardarelli, 70–89. Toronto: Allyn & Bacon.

———. 1997b. Violence in lesbian and gay relationships. In *Gender violence: Interdisciplinary perspectives,* ed. L. L. O'Toole and J. R. Schiffman, 285–293. New York: New York University Press.

———. 1999. The challenge to feminism posed by women's use of violence in intimate relationships. In *New versions of victims: Feminists struggle with the concept,* ed. S. Lamb, 42–56. New York: New York University Press.

Renzetti, C. M. and C. H. Miley, eds. 1996. *Violence in gay and lesbian domestic partnerships.* New York: Harrington Park Press.

Ristock, Janice L. 2002. *No more secrets: Violence in lesbian relationships.* New York: Routledge.

Ronai, C. R. 1999. In the line of sight at public eye: In search of a victim. In *New versions of victims: Feminists struggle with the concept,* ed. S. Lamb, 139–157. New York: New York University Press.

Sarantakos, S. 1996. Same-sex couples: Problems and prospects. *Journal of Family Studies* 2(2): 147–163.

Senseman, R. L. (2002). Screening for intimate partner violence among gay and lesbian patients in primary care. *Clinical Excellence for Nurse Practitioners* 6(4): 27–32.

Smith, D. and R. Mancoske. 1999. Contributing issues to violence among gay male couples In *A professional's guide to understanding gay and lesbian domestic violence: Understanding practice interventions,* ed. J. C. McClennen and J. Gunther, 63–75. Lewiston, NY: The Edwin Mellen Press.

Smith, R. and O. Dale. 1999. The evolution of social policy in gay/lesbian/bisexual domestic violence. In *A professional's guide to understanding gay and lesbian domestic violence: Understanding practice interventions,* ed. J. C. McClennen and J. Gunther, 257–273. Lewiston, NY: The Edwin Mellen Press.

Sullivan, J. S. and L. R. Laughlin. 1999. Identification and treatment modalities for victims of same-sex partner abuse. In *A professional's guide to understanding gay and lesbian domestic violence: Understanding practice interventions,* ed.

130   *Maurice Kwong-Lai Poon*

J. C. McClennen and J. Gunther, 95–106. Lewiston, NY: The Edwin Mellen Press.

Tjaden, P., N. Thoennes and C. J. Allison. 1999. Comparing violence over the life span in samples of same-sex and opposite-sex cohabitants. *Violence and Victims* 14(4): 413–425.

Toro-Alfonso, J. . 1999. Domestic violence among same sex partners in Puerto Rico: Implication for HIV intervention. *Journal of Gay and Lesbian Social Services* 9(1): 69–78.

Turell, S. C. 1999. Seeking help for same-sex relationship abuses. *Journal of Gay and Lesbian Social Services* 10(2): 35–49.

———. 2000. A descriptive analysis of same-sex relationship violence for a diverse sample. *Journal of Family Violence* 15(3): 281–293.

Tully, C. T. 1999. Hate crimes, domestic violence, and the lesbian and gay community. In *A professional's guide to understanding gay and lesbian domestic violence: Understanding practice interventions,* ed. J. C. McClennen and J. Gunther, 13–28. Lewiston, NY: The Edwin Mellen Press.

———. 2001. Domestic violence: The ultimate betrayal of human rights. *Journal of Gay and Lesbian Social Services* 13(1): 83–98.

Vickers, L. 1996. The second closed: Domestic violence in lesbian and gay relationships: A Western Australian perspective. *Murdoch University Electronic Journal of Law* 3(4). Available at: http://www.murdoch.edu.au/elaw/issues/v3n4/vickers.html#n19 [accessed July 1, 2001].

Walber, E. 1988. Behind closed doors: Battering and abuse in the lesbian and gay community. In *The sourcebook on lesbian/gay health care,* ed. M. Shernoff and W. A. Scott, 250–256. Washington, DC: National Lesbian/Gay Health Foundation.

Waldner-Haugrud, L. K. and L. V. Gratch. 1997. Sexual coercion in gay/lesbian relationships: Descriptives and gender differences. *Violence and Victims* 12(1): 87–98.

Waldner-Haugrud, L. K., L. V. Gratch and B. Magruder. 1997. Victimization and perpetration rates of violence in gay and lesbian relationships: Gender issues explored. *Violence and Victims* 12(2): 173–184.

Walsh, F. 1996. Partner abuse. In *Pink therapy: A guide for counsellors and therapists working with lesbian, gay and bisexual clients,* ed. D. Davies and C. Neal, 188–198. Philadelphia: Open University Press.

Walker, G. 1986. The standpoint of women and the dilemma of professionalism in action. *Resources for Feminist Research* 15(1): 18–20.

Waterman, C. K., L. J. Dawson and Michael J. Bologna. 1989. Sexual coercion in gay male and lesbian relationships: Predictors and implication for support services. *The Journal of Sex Research* 26(1): 118–124.

West, C. M. 1998. Leaving a second closet: Outing partner violence in same-sex couples. In *Partner violence: A comprehensive review of 20 years of research,* ed. J. L. Jasinski and L. M. Williams, 163–183. Thousand Oaks, CA: Sage.

Younglove, J. A., M. G. Kerr and C. J. Vitello. 2002. Law enforcement officers' perceptions of same sex domestic violence: Reason for cautious optimism. *Journal of Interpersonal Violence* 17(7): 760–772.

7 Women Who Abuse Their Female Intimate Partners

Carrol Smith[1]

Many research studies report on the victims of intimate partner violence (IPV). This trend began early in the domestic violence movement when female victims were seeking safe shelter from male abusers and heterosexual violence was ultimately constructed as a felony crime. Feminists who brought the focus to domestic violence in the 1970s viewed the victim as someone without blame, the problem as one of men abusing women, and the violence as a component of a patriarchal system (Berns 2004). As knowledge and constructs of IPV became more sophisticated, we realized that not all victims were women. Heterosexual male victims of IPV, although they may experience violence at a much lower rate than females, have little in the way of shelter or other support services and they do not often make it into the continuing dialogue about IPV. Additionally, we know that abuse also takes place in lesbian, gay, bisexual, and transgender (LGBT) relationships. These violent relationships are seldom reported although there is research literature about the victims of these same-sex abuses (Island and Letellier 1991; Lobel 1986; Renzetti 1992). Focusing on the victims seems natural; they have been harmed and may need medical, psychological, or social services to recover. However, a primary focus on the victim provides us with only a partial framework for examining the issues.

In looking at the other side of the coin, one encounters female perpetrators of abuse. We have recently begun to recognize that females, although fewer in number, are capable of abusing males and need services (Dutton, Nicholls and Spidel 2005; Seamans, Rubin and Stagg 2007). Heterosexual female abusers report reasons for their abuse as "self defense, provocation by their partners, poor emotional regulation, and retaliation for past abuse" (Stuart et al. 2006). The patriarchal culture that oppresses women is also a contributing factor. Lesbians who abuse their female partners are represented in the literature but to a lesser extent (Farley 1996; Glass, Koziol-McLain, Campbell, and Block 2004; Hansen 2001; Poorman and Seelau 2001; Smith, 2006). This chapter adds to this literature by reporting on a qualitative research study in which twelve women who had abused their female intimate partners were interviewed about the time(s) in their lives that they were abusive. I discuss commonalities such as abuse during childhood and other factors that may have put these participants at risk for battering their partners. I also examine how the lives of these women have been affected by North American culture as well as the intersection of multiple oppressive identities and what that means for the way we understand and respond to women who are abusive.

RESEARCH METHOD

The method used for this research study is Denzin's (2001) interpretive interactionism. Based on symbolic interactionism, this method emphasizes the interaction of two individuals (researcher and research participant) in producing thickly descriptive material or "deep, dense, detailed accounts of problematic experiences" (Denzin 2001: 98). Interpretive interactionism also calls into question the concept of the neutral or objective observer, given that the researcher reveals herself to the participant as well as the other way around. Interpretive interactionism is especially appropriate for this study in that the personal difficulties of participants are connected to larger public issues. In the case of female same-sex IPV, women play a generally unrecognized part, failing to fulfill the traditionally inscribed roles for women into which they do not fit, and defying sexual and gender norms which are becoming more and more fluid (Butler 1990).

Feminist and communitarian theories also underpin this research. Judith Butler (1990), Donna Haraway (1991), bell hooks (1995), and Patricia Hill Collins (1990) acknowledge the fluidity of gender and deconstruct cultural binaries regarding race, sex, and class. Collins, in particular, forces us to re-examine issues of race, particularly for black women, by placing black women and their own experiences of themselves-in-the-world at the center of the interlocking oppressions of race, gender, and class. In addition, I rely upon the literature of Gloria Anzaldúa (1987), a self-proclaimed mestiza (a person of mixed ancestry), who dwelt in the space between cultures/sexual orientations/races, and Patricia Ticineto Clough (1994) who discusses how feminists of color and queer theorists challenge us to examine colonialism, race, and gender. Anzaldúa and Clough were helpful when considering postmodern binaries such as white/other, able/differently-abled, butch/femme, and victim/perpetrator and when exploring the overlaps, disconnects, and some of the ways in which I blind myself because I assume either/or binaries.

Abusive lesbians break many of our cultural "rules." Very often they are not seen as "real women" nor do people believe they could be abusers in their intimate relationships. If they are particularly masculine looking, their abuse may be more believable. I see them as women straddling multiple worlds simultaneously. They do not stay in one place, but are part of many communities, merging and emerging their various selves. They make sure that I do not get stuck in simple binaries. My attempt is to see them as sexual minority women with identities in race/ethnicity, class, the criminal justice system, and for some, historical roots among colonized and enslaved people. My goal as a researcher is to interact with them in a just and non-hierarchical way as we co-construct the stories they tell me about their lived experiences.

My research also draws on communitarian frameworks (Clough 1994; Denzin and Lincoln 2000). Communitarians value "community over autonomy, solidarity, and care over justice, empowerment of all over hierarchies of power, subject as co-participant over subject as object, and morally involved observers over neutral observers" (Clough 1994: 275). This produces research in which a personally involved and politically committed researcher works with active participants to share and learn together.

RESEARCH DESIGN

A purposive sample of twelve women who self-identified as lesbians and had previously abused an intimate female partner were recruited for the study. They were all at least twenty-one years of age, spoke English, and were willing to discuss with the interviewer their experiences with IPV. They were recruited through notices on the Internet and advertisements in lesbian or lesbian-friendly publications. Women were excluded if they had abused anyone within the year prior to enrollment in the study or if they had ever abused a minor.

When a potential participant saw a notice for the study she was asked to call a protected, toll-free telephone number with voice mail where she could leave contact information and a time that a call could be returned when she would feel safe speaking to me. In the notice the women were also told to think of a pseudonym they could assume for the duration of the study. When returning each call I screened for eligibility, asked some demographic questions, learned the selected pseudonym, explained the study thoroughly, and set up a date for the primary interview. A total of eighteen women called the telephone line listed in the advertisement. The six who were ineligible were recent abusers, thought the study was for victims, or decided against participation once they learned more about the study. One woman agreed to participate who later called and cancelled.

Once the date and time for the primary interview were set, a site for the interview was secured. When participants lived in northern Illinois they were interviewed in a safe space in the College of Nursing at the University of Illinois at Chicago. In one case, the participant asked to be interviewed in her own neighborhood so a study room in a public library (her choice) was used. Most of the out-of-state interviews took place in public library studies or conference rooms. In one case, a hotel offered a free room in which to conduct the interview, and in another the interview took place in a partially empty restaurant at the participant's request. My goal was to hold the interviews in spaces where the participants felt safe to discuss their sensitive information and where we were free from interruption.

Face-to-face interviews were conducted using open-ended questions about the participants' experiences as abusers and were digitally recorded. The primary probe was: "Please think back to the time when you were in the relationship(s) in which you were abusive, and tell me the story about that time in your life." The women told me about their abuse, other relationships with men and women, their coming out stories, their families of origin, their work, their children, and many other interesting facets of their lives. Often they related this information with few or no additional probes. Toward the end of the study, each participant was given a summarized copy of her own story and asked to submit corrections if necessary. Several women corrected material in their individual stories. The group was also given a summary of the findings from the entire study to see if it was true to their own experiences. Each woman agreed that she could see herself in the summary and the study findings seemed accurate. All participants were also told that the material would be used to write and publish about the study, but with only the use of the pseudonyms. None of the participants objected to this. These member checks were an important part of establishing the truth-value of the information. Members of my dissertation committee provided expert crosschecking of my coding of the interview material as well as the subsequent analysis and interpretation. The next section will describe the findings.

SOCIODEMOGRAPHICS

The twelve eligible participants resided in seven different states within the continental United States; four lived in Illinois, three in Arizona, and one each in Oregon, Nevada, Florida, New York, and Connecticut. For each participant living outside the state of Illinois, I flew to her city and conducted the interview. The twelve participants each appeared on time for their interviews and seemed eager to talk. Afterward, many expressed that participation in the interview had been a significant decision for them. For some, the discussion was part of their recovery process from drug or alcohol misuse. Others stated that they experienced relief describing everything that had happened surrounding the abuse; they had not told anyone before. A few felt that participation in the research demonstrated their choice to do something positive to counteract the harm they had done by their abuse.

Each woman identified herself as a lesbian. Nine identified their gender identity as female and three identified as male. The women ranged in age from twenty-one to sixty-seven; the mean age was forty-four. Most of the participants were abusive during their twenties and thirties. One woman identified as Latina, three were African Americans, one was an African

American/Cherokee, one was a European American/Cherokee, and the remaining six were European Americans. There was a range of educational and work backgrounds. Three had never been to college, most of the remainder had at least some college, three had college degrees, one had an MSW, and one a PhD. One of the women who did not attend college *did* attended culinary school and was a chef. Six of the participants supported themselves through paid work. One was retired, two were on disability, one was homeless, one was supported by her partner, and one found work when she could, but was in arrears on many of her bills.

In answer to the question, "Do you have any disabilities?" seven women reported clinical depression, three of whom had been diagnosed with bipolar disorder and one who also had post-traumatic stress disorder. In addition, one reported gout, one Celiac-Sprue disease, four were obese, and one had lost an eye as a child. Additionally, one participant dealt with severe osteoarthritis, used a four-point cane to walk, and also had pseudotumor cerebrii (a condition of increased cerebral hypertension), and one was diagnosed with Arnold-Chiari malformation (a congenital malformation of part of the brain) for which she had had surgery. It is rare to achieve this much variability and complexity in such a small sample of women and certainly adds to the complexity of the analysis and interpretation of the stories.

Analysis of Findings

The following analysis involves all twelve women's stories rather than individual analyses of each. Even though each story was different, similarities do appear. The term "trajectory" is used as an organizing principle to describe the paths the women followed from childhood to their present life stage. Each woman described her own trajectory through time, in three dimensions, and through her own development. Because each woman had ceased abusing, I was also apprised of the stories of how they had stopped and of their lives afterwards.

The trajectories of the women's narratives included five major phases: Troubled Childhoods; Coming Out; Difficult Intimate Relationships; Abuse of Alcohol and Other Drugs; and Lived Experiences in the Present Moment. The phases did not always occur in this sequence and sometimes overlapped—they represent life as it really happened.

Troubled Childhoods

All participants grew up in households with two heterosexual parents and one or more siblings. This does not, however, imply they were all healthy families. Nine of the twelve participants were abused in their families of origin, some severely. Two of the nine were sexually abused. Some suffered racism and some were encouraged by their parents to bully others. For example, Kathy had encouragement to become the class bully:

> "First of all, I was a very small, petite, girl with an overbite and pigeon toes. My father always told me to go kick their butt because if you come home with your butt kicked, I'm gonna kick your butt. He told me always to go after the biggest one, so the other ones will leave you alone. So I became the class bully. When I was in junior high school, when you got sent to the principal, you'd have one index card (listing your misdemeanors). I had three index cards." The principal said, "Kath, you've got to quit fighting," and I said, "Well if you tell them to quit picking on me, I'd quit beatin' them up."

Also recalling an abusive childhood, Christine remembers: "My mom and I would smoke pot together. She didn't care what I did. When my mom died [she was murdered] I was in jail." These were everyday experiences for these women when they were young. Abuse by their parents was also a common occurrence.

Margaret and Topaz were both sexually abused by their fathers when they were young. Topaz described: " [I had] a father full of rage during the last few years before my mother divorced him: He threw things, kicked and beat the dog, and came after me several times but couldn't hold me down because of the rage in me. He was 6'4" and weighed about 280 lbs. At that point it was mostly verbal abuse, but there was some physical." Margaret remembers not only the sexual abuse but emotional violence: "I had a lot of emotional violence. My father screamed at me and cut me down and was contemptuous or ridiculing of me my whole life. He was full of rage. My mother was unable to stand up to him. I felt like most of my life I protected her. I have contempt for passivity in any form. I just feel like the red flag and the bull . . . I see people who are not willing to stand up and I just want to kill 'em." A favorite punishment for Christine by her foster mother was to put her head into the toilet.

If punishment was not meted out to these participants when they were children, they watched their mothers and siblings being abused by their fathers and stepfathers. Some of the most abusive parents were, at the same time, outstanding members of their churches, well-educated professionals, and community activists. I did not need to probe for this information. The women remembered the details and experienced the violence as deeply embedded parts of their lives.

Often, stories of addiction would surface in participants' narratives. For one of the participants, the misuse of alcohol and other drugs (AODs) began in childhood. Myer remembered clearly her first experience with marijuana: "The first thing I tried was pot when I was eleven years old. Where I used to go to grade school there was a latchkey program after school. One day during latchkey, one of the people who worked there got some dope and smoked it with us. I remember that very specifically. I loved it." By the time Topaz was age sixteen she was a heavy user of multiple drugs and alcohol. She stole money from her mother and from friends to support her habits.

Coming Out

These research participants were deeply affected by the revelation of their lesbian sexual orientation, their gender identities, and their varying gender expressions. Some described themselves as tomboys or as wishing to do the things that boys did when they were young. Others expressed an early and strong affectional pull toward women. Terry loved Tuffskins jeans, boys' gym shoes, and girls. Joan stated she knew she was different at age two-and-a-half or three, but could not articulate what that difference was.

Topaz said she knew she was a lesbian "day one . . . right out of the womb." At age eleven when she told her mother that she liked girls better than boys, her mother told her that it was a phase and that she would grow out of it. "All girls go through that," her mother said. Topaz heard this with great relief but she never outgrew it. Similarly, Kathy experienced her mother trying to make a sweet, little girl out of her: "I just became more and more of a tomboy and as the years went on I started liking girls. Boys just didn't seem to have it! When I was seven or eight years old I got a girlfriend. I didn't want a boyfriend, but I never let my mother know."

Although eight participants identified themselves as lesbians in their youth, four came out later in life: Val married briefly but disliked having sex with men; Margaret dated women only after dating men throughout her college years; Tiffany never married but had male partners—she decided to "try women" in her late twenties after her second son was born; and Phyllis remained in a heterosexual marriage until her last child left for college, at which point she divorced and went looking for female companionship. Responses from family members and others significant to these participants ranged from acceptance to total rejection. Terry's closest family member took her out on her twenty-first birthday to a famous department store and purchased her a beautiful man's suit, to which Terry expressed great delight. On the other hand, J. C.'s large, moneyed, African American family (she called them the black mafia) had a family caucus and voted her out of the family. She was turned out with no money at the age of seventeen and lived on the streets for the next three to four years. Joan's parents took her to a famous diagnostic clinic for a thorough workup. Her mother cried when the psychiatrist told them to "let Joan live her own life," as her parents had hoped for a cure. Some women never revealed their lesbian status to their families, and remained closeted for fear of disappointment and rejection.

Adult Intimate Relationships

As the research participants entered the next phase in their life trajectories, young adulthood, they formed new relationships. For many, these were their first intimate sexual relationships with women. Sometimes partners lived together, sometimes they did not. They met their partners in many of the same places heterosexual couples meet: bars, workplaces, or through friends. These early relationships were filled with the stresses of cultural stigma and marginalization as well as internalized homophobia (the fear and hatred of sexual minorities projected out by the culture and internalized by sexual minority individuals [Shidlo 1994]). If the women had not already begun misusing AODs, they often began as young adults. As seven out of the twelve participants had mental health issues, drugs were likely an important factor. In addition, it was primarily in these early relationships that the participants became abusive.

Every woman in this study abused an intimate partner in some way. Some only abused one time, while others abused many partners many times. The participants described employing physical abuse such as hitting; slapping; punching with fists; pushing; throwing objects at their partner; attempts to strangle; damaging clothes, furniture, and household items; hitting with objects (a cast iron skillet, a beer bottle, a hammer); the use of guns and knives; psychological abuse such as threats to a partner's life; overpowering anger or rage; controlling behavior; exertions of power over a partner; belittling behavior; verbal abuse such as shouting, yelling, screaming, hurling threats, using words that put the partner down, and telling the partner that she was worthless; and/or sexual abuse such as telling the partner that she was not as good sexually as former lovers, putting the partner's sexuality down, or withholding sexual activity.,

Margaret described that she abused her first lesbian partner in the following way:

> I was furious and contemptuous of all people at all times, so the woman I was with was insecure, not the sharpest tack in the box and I have no doubt I picked her for exactly those reasons, so that I could feel superior to her and so our relationship was more or less constantly me pointing out her stupidity. I was both in subtle ways and in quite overt ways cutting her down, denigrating her brains or ability, anything pretty much. That was also the relationship where I had my first and only attempt at physical violence against somebody else, which went like this: I got really drunk, she said something that annoyed me, and I took a swing at her. Within half a second, I was on the floor and she was sitting on top of me. So I stopped physical violence after that; clearly I was not suited for it and it does not speak to my strength. I mean, my strengths are a nasty and controlling mind and a real quick wit, and why bother with physical abuse when I can be so effective with emotional abuse.

Christine related the abuse she perpetrated after the death of her mother. When Christine's mother was murdered, all Christine had left were her mother's ashes. Christine was living with her partner who was twenty years older and had physically abused Christine for the first two years of their relationship. Christine described: "It was just the things she would say and do to me. One time she kicked my mother's ashes across the hall and I lost it. I mean, I beat the crap out of her. I mean, that was my mother. That was all I had of her. I picked her up and threw her out the window."

Kathy was in a relationship with Roxanne for eight years. She and Roxanne fought almost nightly, starting right after work. First would be verbal abuse that escalated into "arm tossing [and] fist fighting abuse." Jealousy played a large part in their relationship, as they each accused the other of being with other women. Kathy usually blacked out before the evening was over and remembered little of what had transpired. All of this was only a lead up to Kathy's final abusive act of shooting a woman who she perceived to be intruding on her relationship. Kathy was tried and convicted of second-degree assault with a deadly weapon (the woman she shot did not die), and spent four years in the state penitentiary as well as two additional years on probation. She suffered major financial losses while in prison and the court awarded the victim a large settlement in compensatory damages that Kathy has yet to pay. During her trial a court-ordered psychiatric examination led to a diagnosis of bipolar disorder and now Kathy also has post-traumatic stress disorder. Kathy and her physicians are still working to find the best combination of medications for her mental health disorders.

I elaborate on Kathy's story not to make her an example but to demonstrate how serious the consequences of lesbian IPV can be. There are those who dismiss lesbian IPV as "just a cat fight" between two women. Obviously, this type of violence may have serious consequences and can lead to death.

In addition to Kathy, three other participants had contact with what Belknap (2001) calls the "crime processing system." This contact occurred when police were called when participants became violent or when they were jailed briefly. Terry had some comments about police involvement: When two lesbians have a fight and someone calls the law, "once they get there and understand what's really happening and the relationship situation, they look at this as amusement . . . like a circus." She also said she had been taken in by the police more frequently than any of her partners because she looked like a male, "a bad tyrant or the bad wolf," while her partners looked like "damsels in distress."

The women related several reasons for their abuse. Six felt their violence was closely tied to their use of AODs. Other participants said they abused to keep the upper hand in the relationship, to maintain control over their partner, or to keep their partners in line. Two of the women who assumed male gender identities reported that it was part of their role to correct their partners' bad behavior and to remind them of their place in the relationship. One participant said she abused women because women liked it. She was also of the opinion that women are abused because they talk too much. Some participants alleged that their partners provoked them and once provoked they felt the only possible response was violence. The abusive action immediately followed the provocation and it was not the abuser's fault, but the fault of the provocateur.

Terry provided a graphic description of how she felt when she was violent: "Some part of the anger felt good inside. It was like a big ball on your shoulder, that when I grabbed my mate and I hit her or inflicted some pain on her, the ball was removed and the pressure was removed for that particular time. But then, sometimes, I did things because it felt good. I'm, not gonna lie. I don't know why, but just to bend their finger or, you know, like grab them up in a corner and slap them or somethin'" Like Terry, half the participants (six) described an overpowering rage that overtook them when they were angry and that usually ended in abuse. These same six participants had been the most severely abused in childhood and had also used AODs.

Alcohol and Other Drugs

Seven participants were heavy users of AODs in adulthood. They reported various combinations of cocaine, marijuana, methamphetamines, poppers, barbiturates, and benzodiazepines. In addition, one woman reported social drinking and one stated she "tried a few things" but never used regularly. At the time these women reported being violent and using AODs, the lesbian "bar culture" that had begun in the 1940s and 1950s in the US was still in strong evidence. Bars were places where lesbians could feel safe to be "out" and to meet new friends and perspective lovers (Kennedy and Davis 1993). Here also, besides alcohol, one could usually find drugs for sale.

Each of the seven eventually stopped using AODs. Four did this by attending twelve-step programs. It was during the time they were attending the twelve-step meetings that they realized they did not wish to be abusive any longer. I was not surprised to find so many of these participants having misused AODs. While substance misuse is not necessarily a cause of abusive behavior, studies have found it to be a strong correlate (Fortunata and Kohn 2003; Schilit, Lie and Montagne 1990). These participants all reported abusing substances during the same time period they were abusing their partners.

Lived Experience in the Present Moment

Renee, Margaret, Myer and Topaz each ceased using AODs through AA or Narcotics Anonymous (NA). They have each been free of alcohol and/or other drugs for between seventeen and twenty years. Subsequent to ceasing their substance use, they also stopped their violence toward others. All except Myer are working full time; she is on disability because of her health problems. Phyllis, who was only abusive one time, continues to live with her long-time partner and has not abused her physically again. Phyllis too is on permanent disability. Terry works full time and is completing her bachelor's degree. She has stopped abusing, but intimated that it would always be easy for her to abuse someone if she were provoked. Tiffany looks for work as a certified nursing assistant in home care and also earns money by providing "taxi" services for people in her community who need rides. She claimed to have lost her sex drive after menopause, so is not looking for a partner. At the time of her interview, Christine was trying to get a job, but her police record was making it difficult. She was homeless and, as a result, I was unable to conduct her follow-up telephone interview.

Kathy is now living in a different county in her state so she won't have to see familiar faces as she rehabilitates herself from her prison experience. She is currently on disability because of her mental health conditions. She has a caseworker and a therapist. She is not currently abusive and is trying to get into a program where she can learn how to repair and install computers.

Val is much happier now that she is working in a day center for mentally challenged adults. Her old job as a newspaper reporter was happily left behind. She has no current partner and has not recently been abusive. Joan has moved in with her partner, moving from the state where I conducted her interview to a place where she can be near her brothers and elderly father. She works full time and helps care for her father. She has learned through individual and group counseling how to control her anger and has not abused anyone for several years.

At the time of her interview, J. C. was trying to find a job as well as run the household for her partner and their four sons. She did not physically abuse her partner, but occasionally went into rages and sometimes damaged household items. J. C.'s therapist was adjusting her medication for her bipolar disorder but J. C. said she was not always compliant with taking her medications.

One can see from the examination of these interviews that although participants' lives differ from one another in many respects, there are several common factors among them. One of the most telling is that three-fourths of the women were abused physically, sexually, verbally and/or psychologically in their families of origin. Not only were they abused themselves, they observed family members being abused by other family members. At the same time, six of the nine who suffered childhood abuse also misused AODs. This combination of a history of violence in childhood, abuse of substances, and abuse of others in adulthood creates a major public health challenge. Though few in number, this combination of events also happens among heterosexual female abusers (Seamans et al. 2007). Women who suffer abuse in childhood are also at risk for a number of other health-related problems as adults, and the participants in this study revealed several of them, one of which is obesity (Kendall-Tackett 2002; Williamson et al. 2002). Obese women are at risk for diabetes (Lazar 2005), cardiac conditions (Wu et al. 2009), and osteoarthritis (Lohmander et al. 2008). One severely obese participant had already sustained crippling osteoarthritis.

Similarly, depression and PTSD are commonly occurring sequelae of childhood abuse (Nolan-Hoeksema 2001). Given that seven of the participants related diagnoses of depression, bipolar disorder, or PTSD it is possible that these are related to the childhood abuse. The women told me of these conditions but I did not probe deeply about them because that was not the purpose of this study.

Altogether, one can say that these study participants were at risk for many physical and emotional health conditions as they approached adulthood. Their tendency toward violence was only one among many problems they faced. I am reminded of a research study in which I participated with poor women who were at high risk for HIV infection ("The Vaccine Preparedness Study," 1995–1998). We the researchers were concerned with teaching them everything we knew about HIV and helping the women learn how to prevent it. They, however, were more concerned with getting food for their children, with how they could protect themselves and their children from their abusive partners, and with what they would do if someone got sick. HIV was only one among many issues the high-risk women faced, and not always the most important to them. In much the same way, we are concerned about childhood abuse and its long-term affects on women, how substance abuse correlates with abuse and how we are going to stop women from battering their female partners. The women who told me their stories, while vividly relating the episodes of violence, had many other life issues facing them at the same time such as homelessness, joblessness, poor or no family support, and mental illness. As such, their acts of abuse may not have been perceived as the most significant issue in their lives. In fact, being violent with a partner may have been one of the only times they felt in control of their situation.

INTERSECTIONALITY DEMONSTRATED IN A CASE STUDY

As lesbian abusers are seldom studied, an analysis would be incomplete without also including an examination of the intersections of race/ethnicity, gender, class or socioeconomic status, sexual orientation, and physical and mental health, as well as the ever-present patriarchal culture in which it takes place in North America. The patterns of oppression found when considering these constructs contribute to the overall context of behavior. As we now view intersectionality, these individual variables are not simply additive, but intersect with one another continuously. I use a single case from this research study to closely examine the issues.

The following is a summary of the transcript of Renee's two-hour interview. Renee is an overweight, African American/Cherokee woman (however, she refers to herself as black), of medium height, and is forty-four years of age. She has an MSW degree and works full time as a social worker. She lives by herself in an apartment in a mid-sized city in the Southwest. At this time, she has no intimate partner. She had been working the morning of the interview with a youth group supported by her social service agency.

She asked me to meet her in a hotel lobby in her city. She asked if we could conduct the interview in the hotel restaurant. I was concerned that being in a restaurant might inhibit her responses, but she assured me it would not. She asked the waitress to seat us in a back corner where we were relatively isolated and except for the waitress, we had that section of the restaurant entirely to ourselves for the two hours of the interview. Renee ate her lunch while she talked.

Childhood

Renee is the second daughter born to her mother and a father who abandoned his family when her mother was in labor with Renee. Renee always felt her mother was bitter about the man and his abandonment, and was also somewhat negative toward Renee and her older sister, also a child of the departed father. Subsequently, Renee's mother married and had three more children with Renee's stepfather.

Family life in the Midwest revolved around participation in their church where her mother was a missionary and an evangelist. Their vacations in the summer consisted of a week in a rented Airstream trailer travelling to big church gatherings. They also attended family reunions for both her mother and her stepfather's families. Her mother was active in civic events in their town and helped found a center for learning disabled students in the grammar school. Her mother also physically abused Renee and her older sister. When they disobeyed, she would tie them to the support posts in the basement of their home and circle them, whipping them with braided electrical cords. This abuse took place for many years. Renee had always felt that if her stepfather knew how her mother treated her, he would come to her rescue. She learned the sad reality the day her mother chased her and her sister through the house whipping them with electrical cords. Her stepfather was watching a football game in the same room and did not move to help the children. Shortly thereafter, Renee's grandmother reported her mother to a child welfare agency. There was a hearing to discuss her abuse of the children, and although her abuse was exposed, nothing negative happened to her mother. However, Renee states that she "had a good teacher when it came to being angry and being hostile and being abusive."

When Renee was eleven her parents moved from the city and built a new home on five acres of land in a small, rural town in the Midwest. Their family was the only black family in town. Renee's mother was a family friend of one of the United States senators from their state and apparently she called on him to smooth the way for the transition; he made phone calls to make sure people knew "the family was 'legit' and not a threat." Renee stated that her parents wanted the children to experience life in a small town, living where they could have a garden, with an acre of land eventually to go to each child. She described it, with irony, as their "Leave it to Beaver/Little House on the Prairie experience." Renee felt that she and all her siblings were affected negatively by the move. The extended family was not supportive of her parents moving the five children to the small, white town. They felt nothing good could come of it and they might be setting the children up for real danger. Renee described how each of the four school-aged children was in a different school building and that they each felt extremely isolated as the one black child in that school. Her stepfather continually repeated his "mantra," reminding the children that they had an equal right to be there. Her parents felt that the children had a better opportunity for a good education because it was an all white school. Renee's feeling is that the racism and cultural insensitivity far outweighed any opportunities there might have been.

Renee saw her share of racism in the new town, demonstrated specifically when a classmate who saw Renee undressing in gym class shouted, "Oh, my God, she's black all over." Another time two girls made racist remarks until Renee "bashed" them. She was close to her maternal grandmother by whom she felt totally accepted and she spent time with her grandmother every summer in a large Midwestern city. She was able to relax there, be around many people of color, and enjoy the respite from her mother's abuse and the racial tension at school.

Coming Out

Renee said she probably knew she was "different" in elementary school. She liked women and had crushes on her female teachers, but she had never heard the words "lesbian" or "dyke" until she was about twenty-three years of age. Her mother used them in reference to another woman they were discussing. Renee knew those words described herself. She states that as she grew older her family all knew she was a lesbian and "it was no big deal." She received a different message when none of the family came to her big wedding to her second partner. Renee noted: "when I started being *actively* lesbian and *publicly* lesbian, it was a big deal." When Renee's mother died suddenly about one week after the wedding, Renee brought her partner to the funeral. There were many difficult moments when the family tried to exclude her partner from activities. The mix of conservative church people, her mother's political friends, and Renee's gay and lesbian friends at the wake was more than her father could manage. He was quite outspoken about not wanting Renee's friends there. Ultimately, she excluded herself and her partner from all family activities. She told her family that she and her partner were a "package deal." She had no further communication with anyone in her family for two years after the funeral.

Adulthood and Intimate Relationships

Renee's first long-term relationship was abusive. Her partner had mental health problems and was not working for a period of time. Renee was a heavy alcohol abuser. Her partner's daughter lived with them. For the first two years their abuse was verbal. For the next three years, any time they fought they would ultimately become physically abusive with one another. Renee describes a lot of pushing, shoving, throwing things at one another, and continuing verbal abuse.

Eventually events escalated. She and her partner were fighting in the kitchen when Renee picked up a knife with intent to harm her partner. She stopped herself in time and realized that she needed to do something drastic. Renee finally realized she needed help for her alcohol abuse. That was the first time she went into treatment and that ended the relationship.

Renee's second long-term relationship occurred after she stopped using alcohol and other drugs. She married her partner in a lavish wedding with one-hundred-and-fifty guests. They raised the two biological sons of her partner, one an adolescent, the second a toddler at the time of the wedding. Renee became quite attached to the younger son. The relationship with this partner ended after eight years when the partner had an affair with another woman. Though they ended the relationship, Renee still co-parents the two boys (one now in his twenties, the other, ten years old).

Renee realized as the younger boy was growing up that she was becoming verbally abusive with him. One particular incident happened when they went fishing. Renee told him he would finally have to put his own worm on the hook. He demurred, as he was afraid of worms. Finally, Renee tried to force him to do it. As she saw herself behaving just like her mother, she quickly realized she did not wish to do this. Since that time she has had many talks with her son about more appropriate ways for her to behave in her relationship with him and she attempts to model that. When he becomes exasperated and wants to throw toys or behave destructively she works with him to show him he has many other choices of behavior.

Alcohol and Other Drugs

Renee continued drinking alcohol from the time she was eleven, when she first consumed an entire bottle of apricot brandy by mixing it with ice cream at a family reunion. She was able to secure alcohol easily in her small town by using her race to her advantage. Since the town was white except for her family, when she went into the liquor stores they thought she was someone just passing through town and sold her anything she wanted. She was known as a "partier" in high school. She participated in high school sports and community activities but was not much of a scholar and just barely graduated from high school. She was dismissed from her church-related college by December of her first year. Marijuana, speed, downers, and alcohol were all part of her life, and studying was not. She "kicked around" for a year or so, then decided she wanted to go back to college. She was able to start school at a new college on probation and she eventually graduated from that school with a criminal justice degree. She then worked for sixteen years as a probation officer. During some of that time she was drinking heavily and spending a lot of time in gay bars. She spent time in in-patient treatment centers, but did not stop using AODs until she began attending AA meetings. That was the beginning of her sobriety. Renee still attends three AA meetings per week and has been "clean" for twenty years. She defines her life as "pre-sobriety and post-sobriety." After "getting clean," she went back to school and obtained her MSW in 1993. She accomplished this with a certain amount of pride as her father had told her she would never amount to anything when she was first dismissed from college. She has worked full time as a social worker since 1993.

Life in the Present Moment

Since the time she left her partner two years ago, Renee has had some health problems. She has been hospitalized for severe headaches and other symptoms of Arnold-Chiari syndrome, a congenital brain malformation that required surgery. She has considered a move to a different state, as she doesn't think the climate where she currently lives is good for her. She remains sober and is actively involved with full-time social work. She also does volunteer work with groups of young people.

Naming and Interpreting the Intersections

The intersecting identities or social factors in Renee's life are race, ethnicity, class, gender, sexual orientation, age, religion, and ability. Renee described her racial background as African American and Cherokee. Her race and ethnicity intersect with absolutely every other marker of identity in her life. In the US, white people of European descent have dominated others since the earliest settlers colonized the continent (Roediger 2008). This leaves all persons of color, especially African Americans due to their heritage of slavery, in a subordinate position. Additionally, the indigenous Cherokee people experienced white domination as loss of lands and death at the hands of white settlers (Purdue and Green 2007). Renee experienced racism directly when her family moved to their new home in a small, rural town. She felt isolated in her school and by her classmates. She loved spending time with her maternal grandmother in a city that included many other people of color—others who looked like she did. The family returned twice each week to the city, one hour away, to services at their black church, but Renee disliked that as well. She may have felt constricted there as well, and going to her paternal grandmother's for fried chicken every Sunday after church was stifling.

Race and heterosexism may be closely entwined in Renee's case. Although most cultures/races/people are heterosexist, in her case, her family rejected her by refusing to come to her wedding to another woman. This was not only a refusal to acknowledge the importance of the relationship but a rejection of Renee's sexual orientation. The family continued to refuse to acknowledge her partner or their relationship at her mother's funeral. Renee's response was to withdraw from her family for a long period of time. She was happy in her relationship, she was sure of herself, and did not want a part in a family who rejected her. Renee experienced minority stress, a combination of stigma, prejudice and discrimination based on sexual minority status that can even lead to mental health problems (Myer 2003). This minority stress may also have been linked to her family and to heterosexism promulgated by African American churches (Douglas 2003).

Additionally, race and social class often intersect in Renee's narrative. From the clues given in her interview, Renee's family of origin was probably working class to middle class. Her mother seemed set upon upward mobility and liked "doing good" in her community. She was able to be a "stay-at-home mom" which allowed her time for community and political activities. She had close ties to a US Senator and exploited those ties. Her parents' desire to move to a small town and to acquire land may have been antithetical to middle class aspirations, but they also thought it would provide a better education for their children, a traditionally middle-class value. Renee's stepfather kept the garden and worked long hours at a working-class job. Renee had nothing but negative things to say about her life in the small town and obviously rebelled by drinking, using drugs, and partying in a way of which her mother did not approve. Renee told me the worst thing a child in her family could do was embarrass her mother and that child would surely feel maternal retribution. Renee experienced it. Her mother's abuse remained hidden until Renee's grandmother exposed it, but it intersected with her mother's ideas of upward mobility (class), her negative feelings toward her two older daughters (female daughters of the man who left her), her religion ("spare the rod and spoil the child"), and her status as a mother.

Gender also intersects with race and nearly every other construct. Being a female placed Renee firmly in a subordinate role within a patriarchal culture. There has been some movement toward equality of gender in the past forty years, but women still earn less money, have less political clout, have fewer positions of power, and have access to fewer types of resources.

The fact that Renee realized she was a lesbian and chose to live an "out" lifestyle intersected with her race, gender, and social class. Lesbians have a long history of being relegated to the outer edges of society. They do not conform to female gender or sexual stereotypes and they do not occupy the traditional spaces of women. Black women are especially dissuaded from coming out as lesbians both because of the influence of the church and because living as a sexual minority person is frowned upon by the black community (Greene 2000). Lesbians have typically been recognized in the lower social classes, but not in middle or upper classes (Rupp 1999). This may have been something that bothered Renee's mother; Renee interfered with her mother's image of herself as a middle-class, black mother, and thus, she refused to openly acknowledge Renee's wedding.

No one but Renee knew of her own violence except her first partner and perhaps some of their friends. Violence intersects with sexual orientation. Members of the lesbian community do not want to acknowledge the abuse that goes on between partners because it is one more mark against an already marginalized group. Members of the heterosexual community barely acknowledge lesbians, but when they do they frequently believe that lesbian relationships are utopian examples of equity and bliss. The lesbian community does not wish to consider that there could be violence within it (Ristock 2002). Lesbian abuse is little noted in many texts about intimate partner violence and it is only mentioned in passing in recent forensic nursing texts (Hammer, Moynihan and Pagliaro 2006; Olshaker, Jackson and Smock 2007). Violence among lesbians also intersects with gender. Women are not supposed to be violent, yet we know that women are violent in both lesbian and heterosexual relationships (Dutton, Nicholls and Spidel 2005).

Finally, violence intersects squarely with the use of AODs. More than half of the women in this qualitative study used AODs and many stated that they were using at the time they were violent. Sometimes their partners were using as well. We know that abuse is linked with the use of AODs in all types of intimate partner violence. Use of AODs may also intersect with race/ethnicity and social class, although a recent study of adolescent drinking patterns demonstrated that ethnicity was a much more powerful predictor of alcohol use than was class. In this study, European American adolescents drank the most, Latinos were next, and African Americans drank the least, with boys drinking more than girls (Stuart and Power 2003). Renee did not fit the norms of either social class or gender with her adolescent alcohol consumption. Her abuse of AODs may have been a reflection of the many stresses in her life.

The intersection of these many identities demonstrates that Renee dealt with several types of oppression. Through Denzin's theory of interpretive interactionism, one can see how Renee's personal difficulties connected to several larger public issues: heterosexism, racism, classism, gender inequities, cultural support of intimate partner violence, and extensive misuse of AODs in American culture. Unlike other forms of intimate partner violence the oppressions that are faced may be similar for lesbian women who abuse and for those who are victims. The lesbian abuser may have to create her own power over her female partner, as she is not constructed with that power. Both women in the partnership live on the border as Anzaldúa (1987) so aptly describes: "the Borderlands are physically present wherever two or more cultures edge each other, where people of different races occupy the same territory, were under, lower, middle and upper classes touch, where the space between two individuals shrinks with intimacy (Preface). They are women acting outside of acceptable sexual or gender roles, and they bear the stigma of unacceptable identities.

Renee was finally able to get out of the morass of substance use and is leading a more balanced life. Like the other women in the study, she is a survivor. Some may dislike my use of the term survivor because it is usually reserved for the victims of abuse. However, I view these twelve women who formerly abused their partners as having survived many negative, oppressive forces of their intersecting identities. They, too, are deserving of our attention and assistance.

Every participant in this study had intersecting issues like Renee's. In our interactions with lesbian abusers, we must remind ourselves of this fact. This has implications for future research with this population as well as for criminal justice and social service. We might also stop demonizing abusive lesbians, and this way, we can more effectively partner with them in research, intervention, and prevention projects.

Though the results of this study provide an intimate view of the lived experiences of twelve women who formerly abused their intimate partners, there are still many gaps in our knowledge base that need to be filled. For example, future research might answer the questions: Are there particular life events that put a lesbian woman at higher risk of becoming abusive? Do lesbian women who have been abusive have any insight into how their lives might have been different in order to prevent their abusive behavior? What more can they tell us specifically about the intersectionality of race/ethnicity, class, sexual orientation, use of AODs, religion or other variables that might lead us to further knowledge of minority stress underlying their abuse?

If the ultimate goal is primary prevention of lesbian IPV, my research provides some insight into how primary prevention interventions might be useful. It seems possible that a lesbian's ability to stop abusive behaviors may not occur until she is treated for or stops her abuse of substances. Thus, a part of any prevention program would include services for women who wish to stop their substance abuse. Substance abuse or experiencing violence during childhood may be key risk factors for the potential to abuse and one might wish to screen young women for these factors in order to anticipate those risks and properly target prevention information.

Another variable that could affect prevention programs is the young age (twenties and thirties) at which most of the lesbians in this study perpetrated abuse. Programs for young lesbians (high school through early twenties) may be the most effective in targeting prevention. This is especially important since some of the participants reported being in relationships with much older women who abused them. Older lesbians may seek partners over whom they can exert control through abuse; a young lesbian in her first relationship may not be aware of this dynamic until it is too late.

Lesbian abusers as a group are smaller in number when compared with some other abuser groups. This could be an advantage when researching interventions or primary prevention programs. Since some of the underlying risk factors are similar in all groups (misuse of substances, experiences of childhood abuse), prevention methods used with good effect with lesbians could have direct carry-over to prevention programs for other groups of abusers, women and men included.

Clearly, there is still much to explore with lesbians who abuse their female intimate partners. Finding funding for this research is not easy and will likely become more and more difficult to locate from federal agencies in the US. I strongly believe, however, that it is important research that could lead to prevention of abuse in this population. Given the high recidivism rates of current programs that have focused on remediating people's behavior after they have abused, we have much to gain by working from a different direction. My plan is to continue heading that way.

NOTES

1. I would like to acknowledge the following funding support for this study: National Research Service Award F31 NR008983, U.S. National Institutes of Health, National Institute for Nursing Research; Violence Against Women Research Award from the Center for Research on Women and Gender and Department of Gender and Women's Studies, University of Illinois at Chicago; Seth Rosen Research Award, University of Illinois at Chicago. I would also like to thank United Airlines and my son Michael Farrar for the many flights I made to complete the study. And finally, I thank all the women who contributed their time and stories to make the study possible.

REFERENCES

Anzaldúa, G. 1987. *Borderlands: The new mestiza-La frontera*. San Francisco: Spinsters/Aunt Lute.
Berns, N. 2004. *Framing the victim: Domestic violence, media, and social problems*. New York: Aldine de Gruyter.
Belknap, J. 2001. *The invisible woman: Gender, crime, and justice*. 2nd ed. Belmont, CA: Wadsworth.
Butler, J. 1990. *Gender trouble: Feminism and the subversion of identity*. New York: Routledge.
Clough, P. T. 1994. *Feminist thought : Desire, power, and academic discourse*. Cambridge, MA: Blackwell.
Collins, P. H. 2000. *Black feminist thought: Knowledge, consciousness, and the politics of empowerment,* 2nd ed. New York: Routledge.
Denzin, N. K. 2001. *Interpretive interactionism*. 2nd ed. Thousand Oaks, CA: Sage.
Denzin, N. K. and Lincoln, Y. 2000. *Handbook of qualitative research*. Thousand Oaks, CA: Sage.
Douglas, K. B. 2003. Homophobia and heterosexism in the black church and community. In *African American Religious Thought,* ed. C. West and E. S. Glaude Jr., 996–1018. Louisville, KY: Westminster John Knox Press.
Dutton, D. G., T. L. Nicholls and A. Spidel. 2005. Female perpetrators of intimate abuse. *Journal of Offender Rehabilitation* 41(4): 1–31.
Easton, C. J., S. Swan and R. Sinha. 2000. Prevalence of family violence in clients entering substance abuse treatment. *Journal of Substance Abuse Treatment* 18(1): 23–28.

Farley, N. 1996. A survey of factors contributing to gay and lesbian domestic violence. In *Violence in gay and lesbian domestic partnerships*, ed. C. M. Renzetti and C. H. Miley, 35–51. New York: Harrington Park Press.

Ford, H. 2006. *Women who sexually abuse children.* Chichester, England: John Wiley and Sons.

Fortunata, B. and C. S. Kohn. 2003. Demographic, psychosocial, and personality characteristics of lesbian batterers. *Violence and Victims* 18(5): 557–568.

Glass, N., J. Koziol-McLain, J. Campbell and C. Block. 2004. Female-perpetrated femicide and attempted femicide: A case series. *Violence Against Women* 10(6): 606–625.

Greene, B. 2000. African American lesbian and bisexual women. *Journal of Social Issues* 56(2): 239–249.

Hammer, R. M., B. Moynihan and E. M. Pagliaro. 2006. *Forensic nursing: A handbook for practice.* Boston: Jones & Bartlett.

Hansen, I. 2001. Lesbian relationship violence: A qualitative study of victims who became offenders. *Dissertation Abstracts International,* B 62/10, 4787, April 2002. (UMI No. 3029073).

Harraway, D. 1991. A cyborg manifesto: Science, technology, and socialist-feminism in the late twentieth century. In *Simians, cyborgs and women: The reinvention of nature*, ed. D. Harraway, 149–181. New York: Routledge.

hooks, b.1992. *Black looks: Race and representation.* Boston: South End Press.

Hughes, T. L., T. P. Johnson, S. C. Wilsnack and L. A. Szalacha. 2007. Childhood risk factors for alcohol abuse and psychological distress among adult lesbians. *Child Abuse & Neglect* 31(7): 769–789.

Island, D. and P. Letellier. 1991. *Men who beat the men who love them: Battered gay men and domestic violence.* New York: Harrington Park Press.

Kendall-Tackett, K. 2002. The health effects of childhood abuse: four pathways by which abuse can influence health. *Child Abuse & Neglect* 26(6–7): 715–729.

Kennedy, E. and M. Davis 1993. *Boots of leather, slippers of gold: The history of a lesbian community.* New York: Routledge.

Lazar, M. A. 2005. How obesity causes diabetes: Not a tall tale. *Science* 307(5708): 373–375.

Lobel, K., ed. 1986. *Naming the violence: Speaking out about lesbian battering.* Seattle, WA: Seal Press.

Lohmander, L. S., M. de Verdier, J. Rollof, P. M. Nilsson and G. Engstrom. 2009. Incidence of severe knee and hip osteoarthritis in relation to different measures of body mass: a population-based prospective cohort study. *Annals of the Rheumatic Diseases* 68: 490–496.

Meyer, I. 2003. Prejudice, social stress, and mental health in lesbian, gay, and bisexual populations: Conceptual issues and research evidence. *Psychological Bulletin* 29(5): 674–697.

National Institute of Health, National Institute for Allergy and Infectious Disease. 1995. *The vaccine preparedness study.* Chicago: University of Illinois at Chicago.

Nolan-Hoeksema, S. 2001. Gender differences in depression. *Current Directions in Psychological Science* 10(2): 173–176.

Olshaker, J. S., M. C. Jackson and W. S. Smock, eds. 2007. *Forensic emergency medicine* 2nd ed. Philadelphia: Lippincott, Williams & Wilkins.

Peter, T. 2008. Speaking about the unspeakable: Exploring the impact of mother-daughter sexual abuse. *Violence against Women* 14(4): 1033–1053.

Poorman, P. and S. Seelau. 2001. Lesbians who abuse their partners: Using the FIRO-B to assess interpersonal characteristics. In *Intimate betrayal: Domestic violence in lesbian relationships*, ed. E. Kaschak, 87–105. New York: The Haworth Press, Inc.

Perdue, T. and M. D. Green. 2007. *Cherokee nation and the trail of tears.* New York: Viking.

Renzetti, C. 1992. *Violent betrayal: Partner abuse in lesbian relationships.* Newbury Park, CA: Sage Publications.

Roediger, D. R. 2008. *How race survived U. S. history from settlement and slavery to the Obama phenomenon.* New York: Verso.

Rupp, L. J. 1999. *A desired past: a short history of same-sex love in America.* Chicago: University of Chicago Press.

Saradjian, J. and H. Hanks. 1996. *Women who sexually abuse children: Research to clinical practice.* New York: John Wiley and Sons.

Schilit, R., G. Lie and M. Montagne. 1990. Substance use as a correlate of violence in intimate lesbian relationships. *Journal of Homosexuality* 19(3): 51–65.

Seamans, C. L., L. J. Rubin and S. D. Stabb. 2007. *Women domestic violence offenders: Lessons of violence and survival.* Journal of Trauma Dissociation 8(2): 47–68.

Shidlo, A. 1994. Internalized homophobia: Conceptual and empirical issues in measurement. In *Lesbian and gay psychology: Theory, research and clinical application,* ed. B. Greene and G. M. Herek, 176–205. Thousand Oaks, CA: Sage Publications.

Smith, C. A. M. 2006. *Women who abuse their female intimate partners: a qualitative study.* PhD diss., University of Illinois at Chicago. Available at: http://proquest.umi.com.proxy.cc.uic.edu [accessed November 1, 2008].

Stewart, C. and T. Power. 2003. Ethnic, gender, and social class in adolescent drinking: Examining multiple aspects of consumption. *Journal of Adolescent Research* 18(6): 575–598.

Stuart, G. L., T. M. Moore, J. C. Hellmuth, S. E. Ramsey and C. W. Kahler. 2006. Reasons for intimate partner violence perpetration among arrested women. *Violence against Women* 12(7): 609–621.

VanNatta, M. 2005. Constructing the battered woman. Feminist Studies 31(2): 416–443.

Williamson, D. F., T. J. Thompson, R. F. Anda, W. H. Dietz and V. Felitti 2002. Body weight and obesity in adults and self-reported abuse in childhood. *International Journal of Obesity* 26(8): 1075–1082.

World Health Organization. 2006. Obesity Fact Sheet No. 311. World Health Organization. Available at: http://www.who.int/mediacentre/factsheets/fs311/en/index.html [accessed November 1, 2008].

Wu, A. H., K. A. Eagle, D. G. Montgomery, E. Kline-Rogers, Y. Hu and K. D. Aaronson. 2009. Relation of Body Mass Index to mortality after development of heart failure due to acute coronary syndrome. *The American Journal of Cardiology* 103(12): 1736–1740.

8 Holding Tensions of Victimization and Perpetration
Partner Abuse in Trans Communities

Nicola Brown[1]

I sat in a West Coast bar, finishing what I thought was a great interview with a dissertation research participant, a lesbian talking about her past relationship with a transsexual man. I asked my last question: "Is there anything you feel was central to your experience that we haven't talked about yet?" A pause. "Yes, but you have to turn off the tape." And thus began a second interview, one of emotional, financial, and physical abuse by the partner she had loved and championed, but finally left after an incident during which she thought she might die.

The abuse trajectory was very confusing to her—because she had greater race, gender identity, and financial privilege—yet she felt socially powerless within her immediate context. He was a high-profile, established activist—*who* in the community would believe her? And what could she possibly do to hold him accountable when she thought that he, a black trans man, would be crucified by the police they were protesting in their prisoner justice activism?

Her story haunted me, both for its complex intersections of power and identity and because I hadn't been looking for it in the research. We were both highly aware of trans people as already pathologized and the precarious political stakes of airing the proverbial "dirty laundry" that might contribute to their further marginalization. She was nonetheless courageous enough to tell her story and it became my noblesse oblige to find a way to tell it, and others like it, along with trans people's specific experiences of relationship violence.

This chapter continues to consider marginalized experiences of violence by examining trans people as both victims and perpetrators of relationship violence, and attempts to reconcile the different theoretical frameworks they engage. There is more focus on the less investigated experiences of partner abuse by trans people, not because it is more important, but because it compels us to ask some difficult questions about our anti-violence concepts and practices (Renzetti 1992; Ristock 2002). I will argue for the importance of attending not only to the relevance of the dominant culture, but also to the dominance of the relevant culture in our work, if it is to be inclusive and successful. An intersectional framework recognizes our multiple identities and these differing contexts, and may change both our understanding of, and responses to, violence. It is my hope that this model may be a bridge between the familiar domestic violence model and the less familiar examples where it seems to fail us.

TRANS PEOPLE AS VICTIMS OF RELATIONSHIP VIOLENCE

Prevalence Statistics

The literature suggests "the pervasive and everyday presence of violence and insecurity in the lives of trans people" (Moran and Sharpe 2004: 396). Recent studies using large community-based samples show that 25–43% of trans people reported being victims of violence and/or crime (Lombardi et al. 2001; Xavier 2000), and within that sample, trans women are repeatedly found to experience higher levels of violence (Tully, as cited in Namaste 2000).

Very little research has specifically addressed the issue of relationship violence in the lives of trans people. In the Transgender Community Health Project in San Francisco (Clements, Katz and Marx 1999), 8% of trans men (i.e., female-to-males, FTMs) and 16% of trans women (i.e., male-to-females, MTFs) reported physical abuse from a sexual or romantic partner in the last year, again suggesting that trans women are at elevated risk for intimate partner violence. Two studies examined experiences of life-time violence. Fifty percent of respondents[2] from the Gender, Violence, and Resource Access Survey reported experiences of rape or assault by a romantic partner in their lifetime, almost one-quarter of whom required medical attention for these injuries (Courvant and Cook-Daniels 1998). The Transgender Sexual Violence Project examined experiences of violence with identified perpetrators, where 20% of these perpetrators represented date rapists, and 29% intimate partners (FORGE 2005).

Vulnerabilities to Violence and Barriers to Care

Trans people are vulnerable to abuse in both individual and institutional ways. For example some of the HIV literature concludes that trans women who reported engaging in high-risk sexual activities with primary partners did so partly "in exchange for" the emotional fulfillment of their relationship (Nemoto et al. 2004: 730). This "exchange" was shaped by their perception that fewer men were interested in them as partners, as well as past transphobic experiences in which they had been rejected. Bockting, Robinson and Rosser (1998) also had some reports of shame, isolation, and loneliness contributing to trans people's vulnerability to high-risk sexual activity. These lowered expectations perhaps for themselves and their partners may offer some insight as to the psychological vulnerability faced by many trans people that may also increase their risk for partner abuse.

This psychological vulnerability occurs in the larger context of particular legal and institutional vulnerability and barriers in accessing social services, many of which are sex-based (Munson 2006; Namaste 2000; Ross 1995). For example, the shelter system has been a notoriously inaccessible and/or dangerous place for trans people (Mottet and Ohle 2003). Fundamental questions about definitions of womanhood, issues of access, and discourses of "safety" are clearly organized around non-transsexual women, leaving transsexual women further isolated (Namaste, 2000; also highlighted by the *Nixon v. Rape Relief* case—see Khan 2007). As an example, although the Toronto Shelter Standards state that city-funded shelters must accept clients according to their presenting gender (City of Toronto 2002), the policy lacks an implementation and accountability structure. Moreover, the policy does not extend to other domestic violence shelters and transition houses, which may or may not accept transsexuals, and which may or may not have clear policies (Ross 1995). These gaps introduce significant subjectivity left up to individual workers whereby entry depends on the degree of "passing" as the gender for which the service is designed (Namaste 2000). Low-income and poor people are necessarily discriminated against in this process, as they are rarely able to finance the means to transition (e.g., surgeries, electrolysis, make-up) that would facilitate their passing (Namaste 2000). Moreover, trans men face the difficult decision between risking potential violence in the men's shelter system and the degradation of hiding their identity as men to gain access to the women's system, where they are likely safer and the nature of services offered may better meet their needs (FTM Safer Shelter Project Research Team 2008; Strang and Forrester 2005).

Trans activism has highlighted serious problems in involving police with victimization experiences, including "lack of trust and confidence in policing, lack of police recognition, low detection rates, clear up rates and infrequent judicial determinations of guilt" (Moran and Sharpe 2004: 395). The pursuit of charges in which trans people's birth names might be used and made public through any legal process, thus exposing them to further discrimination, can also constitute a barrier to seeking help from partner abuse.

Despite the need for medical attention or exams following an assault, body dysphoria and fear of exposure are deterrents. Having to disrobe, having photographs taken and/or having to use, or having others use, different names for reclaimed body parts can be significantly re-traumatizing and compound any reluctance to present for treatment (Goldberg 2003). While all assaults are intrusive, there may be particularities in an assault that compound the humiliation experienced by a trans person. Examples of such factors include assaults involving body parts usually off-limits or dis-identified with, and trans men who are in early stages of hormone therapy having to consider the possibility of pregnancy. Very few health care providers have adequate knowledge and training to deliver effective and responsive care (Bauer et al. 2009).

While these constitute barriers to care and the ability to effectively leave abusive situations, the FTM Safer Shelter Project Research Team (2008) also notes that these barriers can themselves become pathways to relationship violence. Many of the FTMs they interviewed who were homeless or at risk of homelessness informally relied on their social network for places to stay (i.e., "couch-surfed") in order to avoid the lack of safety they feared in shelters. A minority of these participants described having unwanted sex and/or becoming entangled in manipulative relationships as part of this strategy to find "safe" places to stay the night. When much work remains to establish even basic human rights protections[3] for trans people, these vulnerabilities set the stage for abusive partners to exploit the institutional exclusion endemic to trans people's lives.

Abuse Tactics

Effective abuse tactics often exploit identity-based vulnerabilities (Munson and Cook-Daniels 2003; FORGE 2005; Goldberg 2003). Examples given by Munson and Cook-Daniels (2003) include deliberate attempts to undermine a trans person's identity, such as using wrong pronouns; ridiculing bodies or touching them in ways, or in places that have been set off-limits; and destroying tools trans people use to communicate their gender (e.g., hormone therapy, clothes, binders, wigs, make-up). Manipulating partner behavior by suggesting "this is what 'real' men/women do," or demeaning partners by suggesting they are not "real" men or women are additional identity-based abuse tactics.

Abusive non-trans partners may exploit trans people's fear of transphobia by threatening to "out" partners to friends, family, employers, or landlords or by undermining their confidence that they will be able to find other partners who will accept them. Perhaps most insidiously, abusive partners can also exploit the real consequences of transphobia, such as the isolation and lack of resources that may come from a poor social network, or the economic dependence on their partners because of employment discrimination. Given this discrimination, sex work is often a viable form of income generation for trans people in urban centers. I consulted with trans community leaders in Toronto as part of a group effort to develop resources regarding partner abuse (see David Kelley Services and the Coalition Against Same-Sex Partner Abuse 2008). In this consultation, threatening to report sex-working trans women to Social Assistance for undeclared earnings, and partners facilitating or encouraging drug use and dependence as a means of securing control over them were commonly reported abuse tactics among women using agency services for street-involved trans people. Alternately, abusive partners may explicitly incorporate the lack of safety in trans people's lives into the abuse tactics. Partners may heighten the trauma of abuse by referencing that police would be unlikely to protect or take their victimization seriously if they were to report it, or that they would be unlikely to find social services support if they were to leave the relationship. Goldberg (2003) also describes how people might use transphobia to rationalize control over their partner in seemingly loving or protective ways—for example, "it's not safe for you to leave the house without me" (31).

TRANS PEOPLE AS PERPETRATORS OF VIOLENCE

Prevalence

Discussions of abuse by trans people are largely absent in the literature, and in public discussions (Munson and Cook-Daniels 2003). It was in this collective absence that the reports of partner abuse by trans men in a Canadian-based study came as a surprise (Brown 2005).[4] Five of the twenty participants for my dissertation study of queer women partners of FTMs and their experiences of partner transition came forward with experiences of partner abuse, including emotional, physical, and financial abuse. These abuse experiences, including the sample, study method, and analysis are fully described in Brown (2007). That same year, a community-based organization For Ourselves: Reworking Gender Expression released the results of The Transgender Sexual Violence Project, designed to document how sexual violence affects trans communities in America's Midwestern states (FORGE 2005). The study included non-trans partners as part of the "community" and a significant minority of their respondents were so identified. It remains unclear from the data how many of these respondents wrote from the perspective of being a "secondary survivor" and how many were among the sample's 12% who reported being sexually assaulted by a transgender person. It is clear from the narrative data provided that at least some non-trans respondents were among the latter.

Because participants self-selected for the studies and because the studies did not use random sampling techniques, no conclusions about rates of prevalence per se can be drawn from this research (Ristock 2002). While the number of participants on which this chapter is drawn is small, the phenomenon of partner abuse in this context requires examination. I will highlight some of the unique sub-cultural aspects of these relationships that contribute to a context in which abuse can take place in the following sections.

Vulnerability to Violence and Barriers to Care

The few available quotes from The Transgender Sexual Violence Project suggest that the non-trans partner's "guilt around transphobia" (FORGE 2005: 11) facilitated the relationship abuse. An example of this included the non-trans person wanting to "protect" the trans person, seemingly on account of his or her marginalized status. Another example was the non-trans person coming to believe they de facto "owed" the trans person because of their greater social privilege.

Abuse in oppressed communities is a complex issue. Participants in Brown (2007) did not initially recognize their relationship as abusive in part because of the dominant feminist, gender-based (heterosexual) understandings of relationship violence in which the abusive person is the one with greater social power. In particular, the view that transsexual partners were "more oppressed" as a consequence of their transsexual (and sometimes other minority) status(es) interfered with and delayed the meaning-making process for participants. Sherisse remembers she thought of her partner as "so powerless in a societal sense that there would be no way he could have enough power to be abusive, so I didn't recognize it in a way that I would have otherwise . . . but I know that he used his various identities- trans included- to reinforce that myth for me."

Participants lacked available knowledge of a typical transsexual developmental trajectory. Additionally, that their partner was the only access point to other trans community, where participants might have found potential comparative experiences, disadvantaged them. Said Sherisse: "I felt like I had to learn a whole new set of rules that I learned later, were very specific to him . . . but because he was the first guy I was with and also because of the nature of it, he kind of spoke as though he defined trans experience." Similarly, Maria said although she could identify behaviors she thought were "unfair." "There was something about the fact that he was trans that let me think, 'Okay, maybe that's okay.'"

These narratives point to a potential vulnerability identified in Ristock's (2002) research on abuse in lesbian communities—the context of "first relationships." As outsiders to the community and in the absence of other community support, partners are "often dependent on their first lover for information" (Ristock 2002: 57). This is a useful analogy in understanding that some women in relationships with trans men expressed a particular uncertainty with respect to expectations of "normal" behavior. In states of confusion about what was "normal," participants often deferred to their trans partner who also normalized and dismissed violence.

In addition to the vulnerability of "first relationships," the social context of isolation due to transphobia may contribute to the risk of violence. Experiences with, and fears of fueling, transphobia serve to isolate partners of trans men from their pre-existing communities and make it difficult for them to identify abuse more publicly. Maria shared: "I can't tell [my family] the whole truth cause I'm busy convincing them that trans is okay [and that they don't need to be worried about me]. I needed them to understand and believe trans, and that was true of all of my friends. . . ." Because transphobia is systemic and pervasive, these political fears of backlash are well-founded and "create the conditions to make violence . . . into a secret or private issue" (Ristock 2002: 3).

Abuse Tactics

Lettelier (1996) found abusers "tailored" their abuse to specific partner vulnerabilities and this pattern appears to hold true in these cases as well. Munson and Cook-Daniels (2003) outlined numerous abuse tactics that trans people may use against their non-trans partners. Many of them, presumably anecdotal, appear to rely on the amplification of their "outsider" status for their power and persuasiveness. Examples include claims that hormones explained their abusive behavior and/or questions about transition expense or timing being met with accusations of non-support. The lack of cultural knowledge about trans people, and indeed, the "unknowable" quality of a marginalized life experience that one does not share, is exploited. In this way, trans people may make use of their *own* social vulnerabilities to perpetuate the abuse of others.

Similar findings of the use of trans status and/or political discourses against partners emerged in Brown (2007), where trans people used identity politics to explain their abusiveness, and manipulated participants' own investment in an identity characterized by progressive politics to have them care for, and not leave, them.

In numerous activist and/or political communities, one of the core principles is an opposition to oppression. A guiding assumption is that because of their direct and "insider" experience with oppression, the oppressed person has particular insight and expertise that the majority group does not. Because social privileges are not always visible to the privileged, majority members are encouraged to take direction from minority members on the minority issue. Sherisse experienced the exploitation of this dynamic: "I definitely felt like 'if I was going to be in the trans community that I should know [and do or not do] X, Y, and Z.'" Serena's partner would often deflect and invalidate her concerns about his behavior in this way: "'This is not about you, it's about me. *I'm* transitioning, not you.'" Similarly, Maria felt the political climate diminished the amount of social support she could seek and anticipate: "My impression is definitely that there is a lot of potential for hard times that nobody's willing to acknowledge because it's not P.C. [politically correct] to say, 'Actually the way you're treating me is like an *abusive* guy, not just a guy, right?'"

Trans partners exploited significant others' desires to support them by explaining abusive behavior as a function of transition or transphobia. When Serena confronted her partner, he said, "I realize . . . I'm not treating you well. I'm just really dealing with a lot or it [transition]'s bringing up these things for me," at which point she would revoke her threat to leave. Said Sherisse: "I always wanted to make things better for him, and so then he could do things and say, 'Well, it was because someone called me "she" today,' so like that sort of justifies him going off on me for two hours."

In communities where demonstrations of solidarity and being a "good ally" are highly valued, some partners unduly extended themselves. Warned

Serena, "I ended up compromising a lot in trying to be too understanding. I totally let my boundaries—about what's okay and what's not—[go] out the window." Other participants' values were explicitly manipulated by their partners. Sherisse remembered the emotional and physical exhaustion of working long hours to completely financially support her high-profile partner, who blackmailed her with the threat of "exposing" her to the community as "transphobic" if she did not: "I spent so much time paying for his blood work and his testosterone, which he needed and if I didn't pay for . . . I was a bad girlfriend, I wasn't supportive of him, and then I became 'anti-trans.'"

Adapting to and Explanations for the Abuse

Women's continuation of the relationship in Brown (2007) was in part sustained by a belief that the abusive behavior, when it became recognized as such, was only temporary. Clearly connected to the abusive tactics used by trans men, women themselves attributed their partner's violence to "deficient coping," "gender role," "minority stress" and/or "biology." The women also believed that increased effort and support on their part would assuage the violence.

A personal coping-based discourse utilized personality and personal problems as explanations for abuse. Collette identified her partner's own unresolved personal issues as contributing factors to his increasing anger. "He already *was* rageful . . . I thought the rage was his own fucked-up shit that he was going to have to take care of, no matter what. . . ." Amber thought transphobia was one aspect of the context, but not an explanation for abuse. "There were many compounded issues going on for [my partner]. Being trans doesn't happen in a bubble. I guess it just made things a lot harder." In this way, she also integrated personal history and responsibility: "It sounds selfish but I was scared the stresses he was about to face [with the disclosure of his transsexuality] would leak onto me. I already noticed a trend in his behavior—that is when he was hurt, he tended to shut down or be spiteful."

The gender-based discourse employed traditional gender role conceptualizations as accounting for abusive behavior. Participants alluded to the contributions of problematic cultural models of patriarchal masculinity. Cher's own observation from the trans men's community was that at times it encouraged competitiveness around machismo and created "peer pressure" to exhibit a stereotypical masculinity "especially when you want to pass." Maria wanted, but felt unable, to give her partner feedback about his behavior "especially if that's their idea of that's what guys do." The emphasis on gender roles produces a sympathetic view of trans men in a context of a desire for and pursuit of normalcy—that "fitting in" includes asserting a hegemonic masculinity[5] of establishing and having power.

The minority stress-based discourse explained abuse as a function of being an oppressed person. Minority stress is a popular psychological construct defined as "excess stress to which individuals from stigmatized social categories are exposed as a result of their social, often a minority, position" (Meyer 2003: 675). Minority stressors are characterized as unique, chronic, and socially-based. Despite describing acts of perpetration, sexual-minority women partners employ a discourse that functions to highlight the victimization of trans men. In one example of this, Maria drew on ideas about internalized transphobia: "In order to make himself feel okay, I had to feel so small all the time . . . I think he didn't feel satisfied with himself, so that anyone who loved him was going to feel that way . . . I think there's something about being really uncertain about your confidence and yourself and your identity that makes you try to control everything around you. . . ." Said Amber, "Li also was prone to making fun of stereotypical female behavior. He would call girls flippant or stupid or make remarks about women's bodies. He was suspicious of women: women were definitely something other than what he was. He constantly made distinctions between the 'way women act' and the way he acts." While open to multiple interpretations, this passage suggests a dis-identification process through devaluation. The construction is of a trans man distancing himself from, or rejecting, what is "female" to perhaps bolster his own sense of masculinity in a world that may undermine his identity. Maria and Amber both position the abuse primarily in the inequalities of the social world rather than with the individual partner.

The biologically-based discourse framed the troubling or abusive behavior as hormonal and developmental in nature through the use of trans-specific phases of transition. Drawing on biopsychosocial discourses of change not only minimized and excused the behavior, but indeed framed it in a manner that made it appear normal or "to be expected." For example, Cher[6] prefaced her own concerns with the idea that the problematic behavior was only temporary: "I think the *hormones are fighting inside his body* right now, so that's a bit hard, um and I'm assuming it will settle itself a little bit, in a couple of months, from what I've read and understood" (author's emphasis). She goes on to say that since starting testosterone, she and her partner have been having more sex than they have had in the past. Although she is unequivocally positive about this shift, she was at times uncomfortable with the nature of its expression: "I'm assuming again, that that will find its way *as his body copes with the surge of testosterone* because in a sense, *he's going through puberty*, right? Um, but there's a part of it that bugs me. It's not like, 'Wow I'm hot for you. I want to have sex with you,' it's like, 'I have this urge. I need to take care of it,' you know?" (author's emphasis). Cher employs the popular subcultural reference "he's going through puberty" as having developmental explanatory and normalizing power for her partner's behavior. Furthermore, she draws on the biological realm, in which "the hormones" are cast as a contributing force, a force the body is "fighting" and with which it is "cop[ing]." This active speech acknowledges the behavior as unusual (and by implication, something to be tamed) at the same time that it normalizes it. While not denying that hormones do affect the body's physicality, Cher's emphasis on the body also serves the function of positioning her partner's behavior as outside of his direct control. Collette also believed that apart from her partner's unresolved personal issues, the "[testosterone] made him more rageful . . . [the hormones] exacerbated [his own rage]."

Recognizing and Escaping Abusive Behavior

A top factor in recognizing abusive behavior, even if only retrospectively, for participants in Brown (2007) was meeting or knowing other trans men or other couples involving a trans man. Serena reported that meeting healthy people who had transitioned put her situation into perspective. Similarly, Sherisse later met more trans men and realized that there was no "one way" to be a trans man. "I spent some time after I broke up with him, learning to undo some of those 'rules,' sexually as well as politically." For Amber too, knowing another trans man, Sam, helped dispel the myth of Li's abusive behavior as being a normal part of the transition process: "Sam has, I feel, excelled at healing and transitioning at the same time. His disappointment, fear, anger and stress around being trans and the treatment of trans people in the society is handled with insight and self-love . . . Having Sam has helped me to see that anger and transitioning are not synonymous. I was in a relationship with an angry person."

Abuse is gradual in nature and sadly, another factor in identifying and leaving an abusive pattern was its escalation in severity. Amber's hopes that her partner's "angry spell would quiet in time" faded when he only "seemed to be taking it further and further." All participants described increasing violence from their partner, feeling fearful, and an ultimate incident or physical act that participants recognized as a personal "point of no return."

DISCUSSION AND IMPLICATIONS

The marginalized status of trans people is a central construct in the relationship abuse against them, as well as in the relationship abuse they perpetrate. Non-trans perpetrators are acutely aware of the individual and institutional vulnerabilities faced by trans people and these vulnerabilities feature explicitly in the abuse tactics and harm done. The vulnerabilities operate in the relationship as a "known quantity." Power is derived from this shared knowledge of, and exploitation of, the social context. An assumption I have, which may or may not be true, is that the majority of trans people in the survey studies were in heterosexual relationships. If so, we might understand these abusive relationships through "the relevance of the dominant culture" and in more traditional sociopolitical terms (Brown 2007:

387). Inequities facilitate abuse and the disproportionate victimization of trans women also fits a gendered lens.

Interestingly, on the one hand, trans perpetrators *also* make explicit their own vulnerabilities in explanations for the abuse against their non-trans partners (e.g., that of "minority stress"). On the other hand, while these vulnerabilities are made "known," they are often simultaneously presented as "unknowable." How might one fully appreciate a minority stress one is not exposed to, or challenge biological changes and developmental trajectories of which one has no direct knowledge? Power and authority are derived from this combination of the "known" social context and "unknowable" life experience. In a political sub-culture where the perspectives of those with less social status may be granted greater credibility,[7] we might understand these abusive relationships through the inverse of traditional terms; "the dominance of the relevant culture" (Brown 2007: 387).

Sadly, there are a number of texts in the transsexual literature that mirror the very explanations that some trans men and their partners provide for abusive behavior (Brown 2007). Aligning with the "minority stress" discourse, Rubin (2003) hypothesizes that the less secure a trans man's status as male, the more likely he is to "overcompensate with stereotypical forms of masculinity" in order to establish his legitimacy (167). Rubin's claim that under threat, trans men "will need to reiterate even the most offensive aspects of maleness" abdicates trans men of individual responsibility for their behavior (168), and serves as a potential justification for abuse. It is an argument that does not bear out in practice. If this were true, then trans men would reproduce less offensive behavior as their transition progressed, but participant reports show that the abuse and violence only escalate over time.

Participants' biologically-based arguments also appear in transsexual accounts and texts. Linking testosterone and aggression is a controversial and politically charged claim that has been both denied and supported in the existing literature. Some FTMs from interview-based studies and first-person accounts report a perceived increase in aggressiveness while others report the opposite effect of an increase in calm (Valerio 1998; Cameron 1996; Devor 1997; Rubin 2003). Cohen-Kettenis and Gooren's (1992) medical investigation concluded that androgens had no systematic effects on aggression and anger in trans men. Rubin (2003) suggests that trans men may depend on normative claims of male biology "to make themselves into recognizable, gendered subjects" (156). These claims, however, are not consistent with reports that trans men were often abusive only towards their female partners. While it may be that the traditional feminist literature fails to adequately capture the experiences of sexual-minority women partners of trans men, it is also true that available theory and accounts in the transsexual literature fail to offer a coherent explanation of abuse by a transsexual partner. These failures problematize the viability of singular explanations and underscore the need for context-based understandings of relationship violence.

Perpetrators perceiving and constructing themselves as victims, and having their partners join them in that construction, is a common tactic described in the violence against women literature and used to preserve an abusive relationship (Farley 1996; Jones and Schechter 1992). What is particularly persuasive about discourses of victimization in *marginalized* communities is that they are readily available and reinforced, and not *merely* a construction (Brown, 2007). Abusive partners use the context to shape the abuse by employing tactics based on the victim's commitments or attachments to issues of social justice, or that distort the victim's character with respect to these issues as a means of control (e.g., accusations of being "anti-trans"). Another dimension to the relationship's "hook" may in fact be guilt associated with the biological privilege she has that her partner does not. This was implied in participant ideas about the importance of being "understanding." When these aspects can be manipulated, partners "can be dominated by an abusive person with less actual power" (Merrill 1996: 19).

The fact that the criminal "justice" system involves disproportionate vulnerability and risk issues for trans partners (*Kavanagh v. Attorney General of Canada* 2001; Moran and Sharpe 2004) may be a significant disincentive to engage them. This dilemma speaks to the importance of the creation of community alternatives (e.g., Chen, Dulani and Lakshmi Piepzna-Samarasinha 2008), as well as working to improve knowledge and sensitivity in the "justice" system through anti-oppression trainings and increased liaisons with community.

Reducing trans people's vulnerability to violence requires pervasive social change to reduce their social vulnerability more generally. This vulnerability is fueled by processes of informational and institutional erasure where "trans bodies are not counted or recognized" (Bauer et al. 2009, 352). In much the same way that we might talk about heteronormativity as the expectation that all people are heterosexual, researchers have begun identifying "cisnormativity," "the expectation that all people are cissexual" as underlying this process of trans erasure (Bauer et al. 2009: 356). Cisnormative assumptions shape "policies and practices" as well as "the organization of the broader social world" in ways that have real and often devastating effects on trans people's lives, as described earlier (Bauer et al. 2009: 356).

While trans people are often victims of violence, this research reveals that they can also be perpetrators. This illustrates the need to understand power relations and violence in more complex ways than the oversimplified binaries of victim/powerless and abuser/powerful, which have traditionally been tied to gender (Ristock 2005). Vulnerability to abuse along lines of social privilege is a reality, but it is not the *only* reality. In this way, traditional feminist theory is not a sufficient explanation for vulnerability and resiliency to relationship violence.

CONCLUSION AND COMMUNITY-BASED IMPLICATIONS

This research shows the limitations of a traditional gender-based hetero-sexual model of relationship violence. While explaining many forms of violence, there are ways in which it also renders particular forms, such as those experienced in lesbian, gay, bisexual, and trans communities, incoherent and invisible, so much so that some participants could not *conceptualize* their trans partner's behavior as abusive because of his oppressed status. While the limitations of the popular model are not new, the existence of abuse in trans communities is not well documented. This suggests that concepts and violence prevention initiatives need to shift to be able to incorporate understanding of these phenomena if we are to fully appreciate the complexity of power relations and violence. More specifically, violence perpetrated by and against trans people should be part of community discussions and initiatives to raise awareness among members in order to better recognize and organize around it.

NOTES

1. Acknowledgments: This author would like to thank Dr. Mary Harvey, Dr. Sandra Pyke and Dr. Janice Ristock for their editorial comments at different stages of this work. An earlier version of this chapter appeared in *Feminism & Psychology*. This research was generously supported in part by a doctoral SSHRC grant.
2. This data, although heavily circulated and referenced in the existing literature on violence against trans people, should be interpreted with some caution. Contact with the secondary author suggests that the final data, including the number of participants, was never issued (L. Cook-Daniels, personal communication, March 31, 2004).
3. In Canada, this is true with the exception of Nunavut which was the first Canadian jurisdiction to pass explicit legislation in October 2002 (EGALE 2005). Ontario's Human Rights Commission passed a policy on discrimination and harassment based on gender identity in 2000, and at the time of writing, a private member's bill was set to be proposed during the fall sitting of the Legislature to add "gender identity" to the human rights code.
4. There is an unfortunate way in which the information I am able to report on may reinforce stereotypes of FTMs as abusers and MTFs as victims- both can be either. Abuse by or against trans people may happen in the context of same- or opposite-sex relationships, as trans people are represented in all categories of sexual orientation. Moreover, abuse may be present in relationships between trans people, although the chapter is written assuming a transgender-cisgender couple.
5. This contested term comes from the field of gender studies and suggests that there is a pattern of culturally normative practices which are thought to establish dominance in the gender hierarchy (e.g., "aggressiveness" facilitates men's dominance over women and some other men; see Connell and Messerschmidt 2005, for the concept's history and evolution).
6. Cher did not identify her relationship as abusive. She is not counted among the five participants but this questionable passage is included nonetheless.

166   *Nicola Brown*

7. Such standpoint theory principles are reflected in debates about who may make knowledge claims. Standpoint theory claims that one's position as an "insider" not only gives one "epistemic privilege" (i.e., a more rich and insightful understanding of other "insiders," as well as a superior and less distorted knowledge of that experience [Wolf 1996]), but that indeed, it "takes one to know one" (Wolf 1992, as cited in Kirsch 1999: 16).

REFERENCES

Bauer, G. R., R. Hammond, R. Travers, M. Kaay, K. M. Hohenadel and M.
Boyce. 2009. "I don't think this is theoretical; This is our lives": How erasure impacts health care for transgender people. *Journal of the Association of Nurses in AIDS Care* 20: 348–361.
Bockting, W. O., B. E. Robinson and B. S. R. Rosser. 1998. Transgender HIV prevention: A qualitative needs assessment. *AIDS Care* 10: 505–526.
Brown, N. 2007. Stories from outside the frame: Intimate partner abuse in sexual-minority women's relationships with transsexual men. *Feminism & Psychology* 17: 373–393.
Brown, N. 2005. Queer women partners of female-to-male transsexuals: Renegotiating self in relationship. PhD diss., York University.
Cameron, L. 1996. *Body alchemy: Transsexual portraits.* San Francisco, CA: Cleis Press.
Chen, C., Dulani, and L. Lakshmi Piepzna-Samarasinha. 2008. *The Revolution starts at home: Confronting partner abuse in activist communities.* Available at: http://www.incite-national.org/media/docs/0985_revolution-starts-at-home. pdf [accessed December 2, 2010]
City of Toronto: Shelter, Housing & Support. (2002). *Toronto Shelter Standards.* City of Toronto. Available at: http://www.toronto.ca/housing/pdf/shelter_standards.pdf [accessed December 2, 2010].
Clements, K., M. Katz,, and R. Marx. 1999. *The transgender community health project: Descriptive results.* San Francisco: Department of Public Health. Available at: http://hivinsite.ucsf.edu/InSite?page=cftg-02–02 [accessed December 2, 2010].
Cohen-Kattenis, P. T. and L. J. Gooren. 1992. The influence of hormone treatment on psychological functioning of transsexuals. *Journal of Psychology & Human Sexuality* 5: 55–67.
Connell, R. W., and J. W. Messerschmidt. 2005. Hegemonic masculinity: Rethinking the concept. *Gender & Society* 19: 829–859.
Courvant, D. and L. Cook-Daniels. 1998. Trans and intersex survivors of domestic violence: Defining terms, barriers, and responsibilities. Survivor Project. Available at : http://www.survivorproject.org/defbarresp.html [accessed December 2, 2010].
David Kelley Services and the Coalition Against Same-Sex Partner Abuse. 2008. Loves me, loves me not: A resource for trans people who may be wondering about their relationship. Available at: http://www.familyservicetoronto.org/programs/dks/AboutAbuseTrans.pdf [accessed December 2, 2010].
Devor, H. 1997. *FTM: Female-to-male transsexuals in society.* Bloomington: Indiana University Press.
EGALE. 2005. EGALE Canada supports bill to recognize human rights of trans people. EGALE Canada. Available at: http://www.egale.ca/index. asp?lang=E&menu= 20&item=1256.
Farley, N. 1996. A survey of factors contributing to gay and lesbian domestic violence. In *Violence in gay and lesbian domestic partnerships*, ed. C. Renzetti and C. H. Miley, 35– 42. New York: Harrington Park Press.

FORGE. 2005. Transgender Sexual Violence Project. FORGE. Available at : http://www.forge-forward.org/transviolence/docs/FINAL_Graphs.pdf [accessed December 2, 2010].

FTM Safer Shelter Project Research Team. 2008. Invisible men: FTMs and homelessness in Toronto. Wellesley Institute. Available at: http://wellesleyinstitute.com /files/ invisible- men.pdf [accessed December 2, 2010].

Goldberg, J. M. 2003. Trans people in the criminal justice system: A guide for criminal justice personnel. Justice Institute of BC and the Trans Alliance Society. Available at: http://www.jibc.bc.ca [accessed December 2, 2010].

Harvey, M. R. 1996. An ecological view of psychological trauma and trauma recovery. *Journal of Traumatic Stress* 9: 3–23.

———. 2007. Towards an ecological understanding of resilience in trauma survivors: Implications for theory, research and practice. *Journal of Aggression, Maltreatment and Trauma* 14: 9–32.

Jones, A. and S. Schechter. 1992. *When love goes wrong: What to do when you can't do anything right.* New York: Harper Collins Publishers.

Kavanagh v. Attorney General of Canada, [2001] C.H.R.D. No. 21. (Van H.R.T.). Available at: http://www.chrt-tcdp.gc.ca/ search/filest /505_2298de_08_31.pdf [accessed November 19, 2005].

Khan, U. 2007. Perpetuating the cycle of abuse: Feminist (mis)use of the public/private dichotomy in the case of Nixon v. Rape Relief. *Windsor Review of Legal and Social Issues* 23: 27–53.

Kirsch, G.E. 1999. *Ethical dilemmas in feminist research: The politics of location, interpretation, and publication.* New York: SUNY Press.

Lettelier, P. 1996. Twin epidemics: Domestic violence and HIV infection among gay and bisexual men. In *Violence in lesbian and gay domestic partnerships*, ed. C. Renzetti and C. Miley, 69–82. New York: Harrington Park Press.

Lombardi, E., R.A. Wilchins, D. Priesing and D. Malouf. 2001. Gender violence: Transgender experiences with violence and discrimination. *Journal of Homosexuality* 42: 89–101.

Merrill, G. 1996. Ruling the exceptions: Same-sex battering and domestic violence theory. In *Violence in gay and lesbian domestic partnerships*, ed. C. Renzetti and C. Miley, 9–22. New York: Harrington Park Press.

Meyer, I. H. 2003. Prejudice, social stress, and mental health in lesbian, gay, and bisexual populations: Conceptual issues and research evidence. *Psychological Bulletin* 129: 674–697.

Moran, L. J. and A. N. Sharpe. 2004. Violence, identity and policing: The case of violence against transgender people. *Criminal Justice* 4: 395–417.

Mottet, L., and J.M. Ohle. 2003. Transitioning our shelters: A guide to making homeless shelters safe for transgender people. National Gay and Lesbian Task Force Policy Institute and the National Coalition for the Homeless. Available at: http://www.thetaskforce.org [accessed December 2, 2010].

Munson, M. 2006. Practical tips for working with transgender survivors of sexual violence. Available at: http://www.forgeforward.org/handouts/Trans_survivor_tips.pdf [accessed December 2, 2010].

Munson, M. and L. Cook-Daniels. 2003. Transgender/SOFFA: Domestic violence/Sexual assault resource sheet. FORGE. Available at: http://www.forge-forward.org/handouts/TransDV-SA.pdf [accessed December 2, 2010].

Namaste, V. K. 2000. *Invisible lives: The erasure of transsexual and transgendered people.* Chicago: The University of Chicago Press.

Nemoto, T., D. Operario, J. Keatley, and D. Villegas. 2004. Social context of HIV risk among male-to-female transgenders in San Francisco. *AIDS Care* 16: 724–735.

Renzetti, C. M. 1992. *Violent betrayal: Partner abuse in lesbian relationships.* Newbury Park: Sage.

Ristock, Janice L. 2002. *No more secrets: Violence in lesbian relationships.* New York: Routledge.

Ristock, Janice L., and Norma Timbang. 2005. Relationship violence in lesbian/gay/bisexual/transgender/queer [LGBTQ] communities: Moving beyond a gender-based framework. Minnesota Centre against Violence and Abuse: Violence against Women Online Resources. Available at http://www.mincava.umn.edu/documents/lgbtqviolence/lgbtqviolence.html [accessed December 2, 2010].

Ross, M-S. 1995. Investigating women's shelters. *Gendertrash* 3: 7–10.

Rubin, H. 2003. *Self-made men: Identity and embodiment among transsexual men.* Nashville, Tennessee: Vanderbilt University Press.

Strang, C., and D. Forrester. 2005. Creating a space where we all are welcome: Improving access to the Toronto hostel system for transsexual and transgender people. Toronto, Fred Victor Centre. Available at: http://wellesley institute.com/files/a-2002-Creating-a-Space.pdf [accessed December 2, 2010].

Strauss, A. and J. Corbin. 1998. *Basics of qualitative research: Techniques and procedures for developing grounded theory.* 2nd ed. Thousand Oaks, CA: Sage.

Wolf, D. L. 1996. Situating feminist dilemmas in fieldwork. In *Feminist dilemmas in fieldwork,* ed. D. L. Wolf, 1–55. Boulder, CO: Westview Press.

Valerio, M. W. 1998. The joker is wild! Changing sex and other crimes of passion. *Counting past 2: Performance/film/video/spoken word with transsexual nerve!,* performance, curator M-S. Ross. Toronto, Canada.

Xavier, J. M. (2000). The Washington, DC Transgender Needs Assessment Survey: Final report for Phase Two. District of Columbia Government. Available at: http://www.gender.org/resources/dge/gea01011.pdf [accessed December 2, 2010].

9 The Impact of Minority Stress on Gay Male Partner Abuse

Jesmen Mendoza

The study of gay male partner abuse as a societal issue has occurred for less than two decades (Burke and Follingstad 1999; West 1998). Part of the research has been exploratory in nature. It is only recently that specific correlates of gay male partner abuse have been explored in lesbian and gay partner violence literature, much of which has been rooted in parallel research within the heterosexual partner abuse literature. Although this is important research, examining parallel factors in gay male partner abuse with other forms of intimate violence may imply that the experience of partner abuse does not differ across sexual orientation. Research is necessary to examine how specific factors for each community make the experience of partner abuse distinct. The experience of being a gay man may indeed be a factor in gay male partner abuse. How this impacts gay male partner abuse is the question that this chapter explores.

The latest research on gay male partner abuse has centered on investigating correlates found in heterosexual partner abuse literature. Among these correlates are witnessing parental partner abuse (Cruz and Firestone 1998; Farley 1996), child maltreatment (Bartholomew, Regan, Landolt and Oram 2008; Fortunata, and Kohn 2003; Lie, Schlitt, Bush, Montagne, and Reyes 1991; Mendoza 2007), and alcohol addiction (Cruz and Peralta 2001), to name a few.

As much as there are similarities among the correlates of gay male partner abuse and the other forms of intimate violence, the literature has also suggested that there may be unique factors in situations of gay male partner abuse such as internalized homophobia (Letellier 1994; Merrill 1996). In a qualitative study Cruz and Firestone (1998) discovered that internalized homophobia is associated with gay partner abuse, however, the relationship between the two is not entirely clear. Tigert (2001) theorized that lesbians perpetrating partner abuse were responding to the long-term impact and internalization over time of the trauma of heterosexism and homophobia on an individual. It may be possible that aggression towards one's partner can be an externalization of the self-loathing that is often experienced by gay men and lesbians. Bartholomew et. al (2008) argue in their quantitative study that there is an association between internalized homophobia and the perpetration of partner abuse. They agree with Tigert's (2001) interpretation of gay and lesbian partner abuse, and argue that internalized trauma associated with homophobia can cause partners to become violent.

Another interpretation as to why internalized homophobia might be related to partner abuse in gay male relationships posits that gay batterers, like other gay men, have been subject to external homophobia and heterosexism (i.e., hegemonic ideas and notions that uphold heterosexuality). This concept of external homophobia and heterosexism having an impact on gay male batterers specifically, and gay men in general, is a relatively new concept that has been termed "minority stress" (Lewis, Derlega, Griffin and Krowinski 2003; Meyer 1995; Meyer 2001). In general, minority stress has been defined as experiencing psychological and social stresses that arise from one's minority status (i.e., stigmatization), and the discrimination associated with it. Specifically, the identification and the level of status ascribed (usually negative) to a minority group can be considered to be stigmatization, a process in which the majority group engages. When members of the minority group believe this stigmatization or where this stigmatization goes unchallenged varying levels of internalized homophobia may result. The differential treatment that the majority group imposes upon the minority results in inequity and disparity, which is essentially discrimination.

Research on minority stress in gay men and lesbians has found that those who experience minority stress also experience adverse health effects. They often cope with their situations through maladaptive behaviors, such as concealing one's sexual identity (Lewis et al. 2003; Meyer 1995; Meyer 2001). Balsam (2001) theorized that lesbians who experience minority stress may try to cope with that stress by being abusive towards their partners. In a later study, Balsam and Szymanski (2005) analyzed minority stress in a community sample of two-hundred-and-seventy-two lesbian and bisexual women. Their study reveals that minority stress is correlated with the perpetration of domestic violence (Balsam and Szymanski 2005). These findings are echoed in a study of one-hundred-and-fifty-five gay and bisexual men carried out by Mendoza (2007), in which a correlation is also found between the perpetration of partner abuse and minority. Further investigation is needed to elucidate the mechanics of this relationship and exactly which parts of minority stress contribute to the perpetration of partner abuse.

Based on the preceding literature review, the study discussed in this chapter proposed to further test the relationship between gay male partner abuse and minority stress. Past research has shown that internalized homophobia and gay male partner abuse are related, and that minority stress is indeed correlated to gay male partner abuse (Mendoza 2007). However, it is unknown if discrimination and stigma, which are components of minority stress, have an impact on gay male partner abuse. Specifically, this study was more interested in how minority stress (the combination of internalized homophobia, discrimination and stigmatization) contributes to the perpetration of partner abuse. I hypothesized that all three factors of minority stress contribute to the perpetration of partner abuse in gay male relationships.

DESCRIBING THE RESEARCH METHOD

Participants

Prospective participants were recruited through advertisements posted at social service agencies that serve gay/bi/trans/queer (GBTQ) men, at Pride events in Southwestern Ontario, and over the world wide web on social networking websites (e.g., Craigslist). One hundred and fifty-five men who identified as being over the age of eighteen and as residents of North America were included in the study. The advertisement conveyed to participants that the research examined conflict in male same-sex intimate relationships. Participants were directed to the website address advertised to find further information about the study. The development of this website is discussed in further detail below.

Procedure

This study served as part of a larger study that examined a number of variables that were hypothesized to have an impact on gay male partner abuse (Mendoza 2007). Prospective participants were given a brief description of the entire study and its purpose (via the website) along with the researcher's contact information. Participants were informed that the questionnaire would take approximately twenty-five minutes to complete and that the information that that they revealed was anonymous, completed on a secured website where their information would not be shared with anyone outside of this study, and not associated with any email address. Further, participants were informed that Internet service providers were not checked, tracking of where they had accessed the Internet had not occurred, and that they could exit from the study at any time by choosing a link at the top of each web page they encountered. Participants were also informed that once all the data had been collected for the study it would be downloaded to a computer disc and the electronic version stored on the secured website erased. They were also informed that the data disc would be kept in a locked cabinet for five years following the publication of the aggregate data, after which time it would be destroyed.

After reading the description of the study and being given an explanation, informed consent was obtained from the participants that were willing to partake in the research. For participants to indicate their consent, they were required to choose the "yes" web button versus the "no" response. Those participants that chose the "yes" response were then directed to the online questionnaires. All participants (including those who withdrew early form the study) were directed to the debriefing page. Those participants who were excluded from the study (i.e., those who were under the age of eighteen and/or were not from North America) were directed to another web page before being directed to the debriefing page, thanking them for their participation.

Rationale for a Web-Based Study

Web-based studies have become a recent method of collecting data for researchers. The Internet as a research tool is helpful in that it can recruit prospective participants that might not otherwise participate in research. One reason that this method was used in this study was that its participants could fill out the survey anonymously. This was beneficial because as Turell (2000) points out, finding LGBTQ participants has traditionally been difficult because of their invisible minority status, and the external homophobia that oppresses their identification. Traditional methods would typically use recruitment methods such as recruiting at Pride events that could possibly encourage prospective participants to claim sexual identities (which could serve as a potential confound during the study). Additionally, the recruitment of prospective participants through the Internet also increases the catchment available to the researcher. Researching LGBTQ participants would not be limited to major city centers that have a sizable LGBTQ community. Instead the Internet-based recruitment strategies have the ability to reach more of the smaller LGBTQ communities. Finally, research has shown that there are no differences between Internet-based findings versus findings derived from traditional recruitment strategies (Gosling, Vazire, Srivastava and John 2004). Such advantages influenced the adoption of website recruitment and collection as the method for this study.

Despite the advantages, one major disadvantage existed with respect to a web-based approach to research. Traditional methods of collecting data from participants have the researcher typically onsite to handle questions about the study and/or address any unintended immediate affects that the research has on the participants (e.g., feeling upset or triggered by the survey). In web-based studies participants do not have the advantage of being able to receive immediate assistance from the researcher. To mitigate this potential risk to participants, I informed participants at the beginning of the process that the survey may trigger discomfort and that they could leave the study at any time by choosing a link at the upper-right of the page. Participants were also told that if they were in distress, they could choose another link and be immediately connected to a referral page where they could enter in their location and the nearest crisis center information line would be given.

Website Development of the Online Questionnaire

The website address advertised was developed by an online survey hosting service known as Surveymonkey. This site allows researchers to collect responses, summarize their results and provides online survey hosting services. Surveymonkey is confidential and assures the privacy of the data by physically securing their web servers (i.e., servers are kept in a locked cage, passcards are required to access the physical elements of the servers, and servers are carefully monitored by staff). The website also employs firewalls to ensure network security, and uses software security precautions. To further ensure the security of participants, all data transmitted over the web by Surveymonkey was encrypted and scrambled to ensure that any attempts to intercept information would fail—only the researcher would have access to the raw data. Finally, the Internet can be accessed anonymously, however, meta-data (e.g., browsing history) can be typically kept and stored on the computer that the participant used. To enhance a participant's anonymity and thus their security, participants were also given instructions on how to erase the meta-data that tracked their activity on the computer that they were using to complete the survey.

Instruments

The data collected in this study included demographic information, such as age, ethnocultural identity, education, occupation, and length of current or previous relationship. Further, all instruments were chosen based on their psychometric properties.

Conflict Tactics Scale, Revised Version—Short Form (CTS2-Short)

As described by Straus and Douglas (2004), this instrument consists of twenty items. Participants are asked to report the frequency with which a physically, psychologically, or sexually aggressive action was used to resolve a conflict in the last year on an eight point scale, where 0=this never happened, to 6= more than twenty times in the past year, with 7= not in the past year, but it did happen before (e.g., "My partner pushed, shoved, or slapped me," "I insulted or swore or shouted or yelled at my partner"). An annual prevalence score was used in this analysis and calculated using dichotomous scoring. A score of one was given to participants who endorsed a response of at least one act of violence (i.e., choosing one through six on any item). In contrast, those participants who chose either zero or seven received a score of zero. The CTS2-short is further composed of five subscales: Physical Assault; Psychological Aggression; Negotiation; Injury; and Sexual Coercion. The subscale that was used for this study was Physical Assault. Each subscale had four items where two items focused on perpetration of abuse while the other two items focused on the receipt of abuse. Items that focused on perpetration of abuse were used in this study. Again, dichotomous scoring was used as a way of transforming the variables involved in the study as a way of minimizing the skewed distribution that typically arises from violence research (Straus1999). With respect to how the CTS2-short has compared to the original CTS2, the concurrent validity ranged from .77 to .89 for those participants that indicated that they perpetrated behaviors on the scale and thus the CTS2-short is said to be a valid reflection of the original scale (Straus and Douglas 2004). Finally, it must be stated that the CTS2's limitation is that it does not incorporate forms of abuse that are specific and/or more prevalent in the gay male community (e.g., HIV-control) and that it is very specific in the forms of abuse it has investigated. However, despite this limitation, Burke and Follingstad (1999) suggested the use of the CTS2 to help standardize research in intimate partner violence in general and to add clarity to the discussion on making meaningful comparisons among different types of partner abuse, along with locating this discussion among the larger population.

Reactions to Homonegativity Scale, Short Version (RHS-S)

I relied on the RHS-S as described by Currie, Cunningham and Findlay (2004), which was a brief measure that consisted of twelve items and three subscales: Public Identification as Gay; Social Comfort With Gay Men; and Sexual Comfort With Gay Men. The RHS-S was derived from, and an improvement to, the Reaction to Homonegativity Scale developed by Ross and Rosser (1996). The RHS-S assessed covert forms of internalized homonegativity (i.e., the internalization of current attitudes towards homosexuality). Currie, Cunningham and Findley (2004) suggest that current views toward homosexuality have been more progressive than in decades past, and that gay men may have easily identified as being gay, but possess facets of internalized homonegativity that have been more covert than overt. Currie and his colleagues state that past measures of internalized homophobia/homonegativity were reflective of past societal attitudes toward homosexuality and thus may not account for more covert manifestations of internalized homonegativity. Hence, Currie and his colleagues developed and suggest the use of the RHS-S. Participants were asked to rate each item on a 7-point Likert scale from 1=strongly agree to 7=strongly disagree which yielded a total score on internalized homonegativity. Some of the examples of items from the RHS-S were "I am comfortable about people finding out that I am gay," "Most gay men prefer anonymous sexual encounters," and "Social situations with gay men make me feel uncomfortable." The RHS-S has had acceptable internal reliability with an alpha of .78, and its subscales around the .7 level, and the authors of the measure established external validity based on the sample it has used in the test development of the RHS-S (Currie, Cunningham and Findlany 2004).

Minority Stress Scales

Meyer (1995) originally defined minority stress as the effect of three factors for gay men: internalized homophobia; perceived stigmatization; and discrimination. Hence, measures were reflective of these effects. The RHS-S measures internalized homophobia and can be used as part of the calculations of the Minority Stress Scales. Perceived stigma was measured using a scale with eleven items that examined the belief that one might be rejected because of being gay. Examples of such items were "Most people believe that a gay man is just as trustworthy as the average citizen," or "Most people think less of a gay man," where participants rated their agreement with these statements on a six-point Likert scale from strongly agree to strongly disagree. Meyer (1995) reports the internal reliability of the Minority Stress Scale to be adequate at .79, and suggests that discrimination be measured by two questions: (1) In the past year, have you been the victim of antigay violence? That is, was an attempt made to harm you or were you harmed because you were gay?, and (2) In the past year, have you been discriminated against in any way because of being gay or because of fear of AIDS? Participants could answer either yes or no and scored one point if they answered yes to either of these questions.

RESULTS

Demographic information

One hundred and fifty-five participants partook in this study. Ages of participants ranged between eighteen and seventy-two years, with the average age of participants being 42.6 years of age and the mode being 44.0 years of age. The majority of the participants identified themselves as living in the United States (76.2%), with over half responding and identifying as being from the East Coast (30.8%) and the West Coast (24.3%) of the U.S. The remaining participants came from Canada (19.4%) with 80% of Canadian participants stating that they lived in Ontario. Four participants identified themselves as being from Australia, while one identified as being from New Zealand, however these participants were not included in the present study because of their geographic location. Additionally, 90.3% of participants had indicated that they came from an area with a population of more than 2,500.

Educational level of the participants was high. A professional/ Master's/ doctoral level degree was held by 40.6%, Bachelor's degree was the next highest group with 24.2%, while 21.7% of participants reported having some college or university experience. Additionally, 9.7% of participants noted having some postgraduate experience, while only 3.8% participants reported having a high school diploma or its equivalent. With respect to income, 50.5% of participants reported having a personal income in 2004 of more than $50,000, while 31.7% of participants reported having a personal income between $15,000 and $49,999. The remainder of the participants (17.8 %) reported having an income of less than $14,999. Ninety-five percent of the participants identified as being gay or homosexual, while the remaining 5% indicated that they were bisexual or queer. Further, all but three participants had indicated their gender identity to be male, while the remaining three participants identified as being transgender or being a "pink boy" (i.e., being "male with girlish qualities").

Approximately 72.4% of participants disclosed that they were currently single while 20.9% reported either being married or being in a common-law relationship. The remainder of the participants (6.7%) reported that they were divorced or separated. Additionally, 58.7% of participants also reported being in some type of intimate same-sex relationship. Of the participants currently in an intimate same-sex relationship, 19.7% reported that they have been in their current relationship with a man between six months to a year; 32% reported between two and five years, and 26% reported between six and ten years in their current relationship with a man. Further, 22.1% of participants reported being in a relationship with a man for more than eleven years or more, with respect to legal relationship status.

The participants were also surveyed with respect to the number of intimate relationships that they have had. Results revealed that 20.1% of participants disclosed that they had been in one intimate relationship (i.e., been with a significant, long-term partner, spouse or boyfriend). Approximately one-quarter of the participants reported having been in two intimate relationships, while 24.5% reported that they have had three intimate relationships. Further, 12.7% of participants noted that they had been in four intimate relationships. The remainder of the participants (42.7%) reported having been in five or more intimate relationships.

The participants were also asked to self-identify with respect to ethnicity. The overwhelming majority of the participants (80.5 %) reported being of Caucasian/European/White/Caucasian-North American descent. The next highest group of participants identified as being of Latino/Hispanic/Mexican-North American descent at 6.7%, followed by participants that identified as being of Asian- North American descent at 4.6%, and those that indicated that they had a Caribbean/African-North American background at 3.6%. Participants with a Native Middle Eastern/Jewish-North American background represented 2.5% of the sample, while roughly 1.5% of the population identified as being Native American or Aboriginal.

Multiple Regression Analysis

The data was analyzed using binary logistic regression because of the study's outcome variable, Physical Partner Abuse, being coded dichotomously.

Internalized homophobia, stigma and prejudice served as regressors in the analysis. Two models were tested. One model examined the impact of internalized homophobia on physical partner abuse. The second model examined the impact of internalized homophobia, stigma, and discrimination on physical partner abuse. The regressors were entered together and the results are summarized below in Table 9.1. The results from the first model demonstrate that as internalized homophobia increases, the perpetration of physical partner abuse becomes more likely. The coefficient of the internalized homophobia variable has a Wald statistic of 5.68, which is significant at the .02 level (critical value = 5.94, df = 1). The overall model is significant at .02 level according to the Chi-square statistic. The model predicts 84% of the responses correctly with the Nagelkerke R^2 at .064.

The results from the second model demonstrate that as internalized homophobia, stigma and discrimination increase and are considered as a whole, physical partner abuse also increases. The coefficients on internalized homophobia, stigma and discrimination variables have the following Wald statistics respectively, 6.62, 1.43, and 5.75. Of these coefficients, internalized homophobia and discrimination are significant at .01 and .017 levels. However, the coefficient for stigma has a p-value equivalent to .23 and is thus not significant. The overall model is significant at the 0.002 level according to the Chi-square statistics (critical value = 14.95, df = 3). The model predicts 85.1% of the responses correctly with the Nagelkerke at R^2 at .16. Further, according to the likelihood ratio test statistic, this model appears to be superior to the first in terms of overall model fit at .01 level of significance (critical value = 9.02, df = 2).

Table 9.1 Logistic Regression Results for the Dependent Variable Physical Partner Abuse

Variable	Model 1 Coefficient	Model 1 t-statistic	Model 2 Coefficient	Model 2 t-statistic
Constant	-4.00*		-5.64*	
		10.72		
Internalized Homophobia	.063*		.073	
		6.62		
Discrimination			-1.77*	
		5.75		
Stigma			.047	
		1.43		
Model Chi-Square (df)	5.94 (1)		14.95 (3)	
Block Chi-Square (df)			9.01 (2)	
% Correct Predictions	84%		85.1%	
McFadden's R2	.064		.16	

*Indicates that the coefficient is statistically significant.

DISCUSSION

Minority stress has been conceptualized as having three factors: internalized homophobia, perceived stigma, and discrimination. Past research has shown correlations between gay male partner abuse and internalized homophobia (Bartholomew, et al. 2008; Cruz and Firestone 1998). Past research has also demonstrated that there is a correlation between minority stress and the perpetration of gay male partner abuse (Mendoza 2007). However, how each factor contributes to the perpetration of gay male partner abuse is not known. The purpose of this study was to investigate this.

This study found that, indeed, the perpetration of physical abuse in gay male relationships is better predicted by the three factors that compose minority stress than by internalized homophobia alone. This study hypothesized that all three factors would have a significant impact upon the perpetration of physical partner abuse. However, the results suggest that stigma does not have the same impact that internalized homophobia and discrimination have on physical partner abuse. It would appear that having covert negative feelings about one's sexual orientation and feeling discriminated against somehow contribute to the likelihood of partner abuse in gay male relationships.

From these findings we can derive two conclusions. As Meyer (2001) has theorized, some LGBTQ people may use maladaptive behaviors as a way of coping with the minority stress that one faces. With respect to this study, physical violence in one's relationships may be a way of responding to the internal prejudice of being gay. The use of violence towards one's partner may be an attempt to resolve this internal conflict through externalization. Such externalization, albeit unhealthy and destructive, may be a means of gaining power for oneself, and a temporary way of dealing with internal struggles while in a relationship with a partner.

The second conclusion of these findings suggests that the mechanics of minority stress on gay male partner abuse may lie in being discriminated against. Discrimination creates external prejudice where a minority faces daily and systemic inequity. Such inequity can result in further stressors for the individual. For those gay men who use abuse in their intimate relationships, this sense of inequality may also be a way of entitling oneself to use violence in one's relationship. For example, the discrimination and subsequent disempowerment that this man receives in the workplace is countered by an attempt to regain power by exerting it over his partner when he arrives home.

Interestingly, stigma, the discrediting of one's position in society, was not found to be a significant contributor to the perpetration of physical partner abuse in gay male relationships. The fact that this does not play a more central role in physical partner abuse may be related to the idea that stigmatization is a process of attribution that contributes minimally to the stress of a gay man who perpetrates violence in his intimate relationships. Although society may ascribe negative stereotypes to gay men, it may be that the treatment of and discrimination against gay men is actually more stressful and thus more disempowering.

These findings also suggest that a separate analysis is needed to understand gay male partner abuse. The association of minority stress to gay men's use of violence in intimate relationship suggests that it is unique and possibly different from other forms of intimate partner violence. As Meyer (2003) suggests, minority stress is an added stressor that those without minority status do not have to contend with. A heterosexual man who engages in partner abuse does not have to cope with the systemic inequity that a gay male batterer faces, and may do so with different justifications and in different contexts than a heterosexual man. Some forms of abuse may be the same among the different forms of partner violence. However, the gay men who engage in abuse in their intimate relationships will have a different experience as compared to other forms of partner violence because of their unique experience of minority stress and social location within society. Theories of partner abuse in gay male relationships need to thus integrate minority status into their conceptualizations.

The findings in this study have important clinical implications with respect to examining the ways in which gay men entitle themselves to use abuse in their intimate relationships. Some gay men who engage in abuse toward their partner may rationalize their use of force as a way of dealing with their own internal struggles, or as a way to regain a sense of power when they have faced discrimination. Despite these rationalizations, there is no reason that ever justifies the use of abuse in an intimate relationship. Clinicians may want to develop interventions that challenge such erroneous beliefs. In my own clinical practice with gay male batterers, I have challenged men to consider how they replicate inequity in their intimate relationships vis-à-vis their justification of their own experience of inequity because of their minority status as gay men. For example, some men have recognized that the chronic stress of not being out at work has greatly contributed to their use of force or has given them permission to discriminate against other gay men, namely their partners. Such foci in my interventions have lead to more rich, authentic, and more personally relevant discussions in therapy.

Regardless of the findings of this study, there exist some limitations around its generalizability. The majority of participants were of Caucasian descent, highly educated and older. The sample collected should not be considered representative of the gay men's population in Canada and the United States. Hence, a selection bias may have existed. Another limitation lies in that the data collected relied on self-report. Participants may have attempted to present themselves and their responses in a more socially desirable manner. Finally, multiple regression analysis was used in this study and, although an advanced statistical technique, this analysis cannot assume causality in the relationships discussed. Such limitations caution the reader not to make broad generalizations.

The major finding in this study is promising in that it delineates how gay male partner abuse can be distinguished from heterosexual partner abuse and how the factors of internalized homophobia and discrimination are specific contributors to the perpetration of this abuse in gay male relationships. Such specific contributors imply that gay male partner abuse is distinct from other forms of partner abuse and that a different analysis is needed to understand it. Future research may want to investigate this by examining whether other variables might suppress the effect that stigma has on gay male partner abuse, and if other factors that are specific to the gay male community, such as attitudes regarding abuse, have an impact. Additionally, research on multiple minority stressors and their relationship to gay male partner abuse may prove to be another fruitful avenue for exploration. Recent research has supported the idea that black lesbians indeed experience "triple jeopardy" and are therefore qualitatively unique (Bowleg, Huang, Brooks, Black and Burkholder 2003). Thus, research on how partner abuse is impacted by the intersection of other minority identities, such as ethnicity, HIV-status and class, along with being a gay man, may also be useful. In summary, these future research directions can extend what has already begun in this study.

REFERENCES

Balsam, K. F. 2001. Nowhere to hide: Lesbian battering, homophobia, and minority stress. *Women and Therapy* 23(3): 25–37.

Balsam, K. F. and D. M. Szymanski. 2005. Relationship quality and domestic violence in women's same-sex relationships: The role of minority stress. *Psychology of Women Quarterly* 29(3): 258–269.

Bartholomew, K., M. A. Landolt and D. Oram. 1999. Abuse in male same-sex relationships: Prevalence, incidence, and injury. Paper presented at the annual meeting of the American Psychological Association, August 20–24, 1999. Boston, MA.

Bartholomew, K., K. V. Regan, M. A. Landolt, and D. Oram. 2008. Patterns of abuse in male same-sex relationship. *Violence and Victims*. 23(5): 617–636.

Bowleg, L., J. Huang, K. Brooks, A. Black, and G. Burkholder. 2003. Triple jeopardy and beyond: Multiple minority stress and resilience among Black lesbians. *Journal of Lesbian Studies* 7(4): 87–108.

Burke, L. K. and D. R. Follingstad. 1999. Violence in lesbian and gay relationships: Theory, prevalence, and correctional factors. *Clinical Psychology Review* 19(5): 487–512.

Cruz, J. M. and J. M. Firestone. 1998. Exploring violence and abuse in gay male relationships. *Violence and Victims* 13(2): 159–173.

Cruz, J. M. and R. L. Peralta. 2001. Family violence and substance use: The perceived effects of substance use within gay male relationships. *Violence and Victims* 16(2): 161–172.

Currie, M. R., E. G. Cunningham and B. M. Findlay. 2004. The Short Internalized Homonegativity Scale: Examination of the factorial structure of a new measure of internalized homophobia. *Educational and Psychological Measurement* 64(6): 1053–1067.

Farley, N. 1996. A Survey of factors contributing to gay and lesbian domestic violence. *Journal of Gay and Lesbian Social Services* 4(1): 35–42.

Fortunata, B. and C.S. Kohn. 2003. Psychosocial and personality characteristics of lesbian batterers. *Violence and Victims* 18: 557–568.

Gosling, S. D., S. Vazire, S. Srivastava O. P. John. 2004. Should we trust web-based studies: A comparative analysis of six preconceptions about internet questionnaires. *American Psychologist* 99(2): 93–104.

Letellier, P. 1994. Gay and bisexual domestic violence victimization: Challenges to feminist theory and responses to violence. *Violence and Victims* 9–(2): 95–106.

Lewis, R. J., V. J. Derlega, J. S. Griffin and A.C. Krowinski. 2003. Stressors for gay men and lesbians: Life stress, gay-related stress, stigma consciousness, and depressive symptoms. *Journal of Social and Clinical Psychology* 22(6): 716–729.

Lie, G., R. Schlitt, J. Bush, M. Montagne, and L. Reyes. 1991. Lesbians in currently aggressive relationships: How frequently do they report aggressive past relationships? *Violence and Victims* 6(2): 121–135.

Mendoza, J. 2007. Exploring a Multi-Integrated Model of Gay Male Partner Abuse. PhD diss., University of Toronto.

Merrill, G. S. 1996. "Ruling the Exceptions: Same-Sex Battering and Domestic Violence Theory." In *Violence in Gay and Lesbian Domestic Partnerships*, ed. C. M. Renzetti and C. H. Miley, 9–22. New York: Harrington Park Press.

Meyer, I. H. 1995. Minority stress and mental health in gay men. *Journal of Health and Social Behavior* 36: 38–56.

Meyer, I. H. 2001. Why lesbian, gay, bisexual, and transgender public health? *American Journal of Public Health* 91: 856–859.

Meyer, I. H. 2003. Prejudice, social stress, and mental health in lesbian, gay, and bisexual populations: Conceptual issues and research evidence. *Psychological Bulletin* 129(5): 674–697.

Ross, M. W. and B. R. Rosser. 1996. Measurement and correlates of internalized homophobia: a factor analytic study. *Journal of Clinical Psychology* 52(1): 15–21.

Straus, M. A. 1999. Child report and adult recall versions of the revised Conflict Tactics Scales. Available at: http://pubpages.unh.edu/~mas2 [accessed November 3, 2009].

Straus, M. A. and E. M. Douglas. 2004. A short form of the revised conflict tactics scales, and typologies for seventy and mutuality. *Violence and Victims* 19(5): 507–520.

Tigert, L. M. 2001. The power of shame: Lesbian battering as a manifestation of homophobia. *Women and Therapy* 23(3): 73–85.

Turell, S. C. 2000. A descriptive Analysis of Same-Sex Relationship Violence for a Diverse Sample. *Journal of Family Violence* 15(3): 281–293.

Waterman, C. K., L. J. Dawson, and M. J. Bologna. 1989. Sexual coercion in gay male and lesbian relationships: Predictors and implications for support services. *Journal of Sex Research* 26(1): 118–124.

West, C. M. 1998. Leaving a second closet: Outing partner violence in same- sex couples. In *Partner violence: A comprehensive review of 20 years of research*, ed. J. L. Jasinski and L. M. Williams, 163–183. London: Sage.

10 *I Ain't Never Been a Kid*

Early Violence Exposure and Other Pathways to Partner Violence For Sexual Minority Men with HIV

David W. Pantalone, Keren Lehavot, Jane M. Simoni and Karina L. Walters[1]

Historically, partner violence (PV) has been studied as only one aspect of violence against women, with heterosexist terminology and stereotypic views of men as perpetrators and women as victims of abuse (Kilpatrick 2004). However, one danger of this perspective is that it obscures the experiences of sexual minorities in general—and gay and bisexual men in particular—in terms of their vulnerability to PV, the extent of PV they experience, and its impact on their lives. Moreover, while there has been little PV research examining sexual minority men, even less work has considered gay and bisexual men who are HIV-positive. The twin public health epidemics of PV and HIV clearly overlap and their interrelation merits further attention for gay and bisexual men, especially sexual minority men of color.

Like PV, HIV/AIDS remains a contemporary public health concern. Interestingly, there are many overlapping risk factors for HIV and PV (e.g., early abuse, substance use) and, likely as a result, both PV and HIV disproportionately affect gay and bisexual men, particularly gay men of color. Since the introduction of powerful anti-HIV medications and increased access to medical care, the number of people living with HIV/AIDS has exploded (Center for Disease Control [CDC] 2007; Maman, Campbell, Sweat, and Gielen 2000). In the US, historically HIV has been a disease that disproportionately impacts men who have sex with men. Even today, 45% of current HIV infections are attributable to male-to-male sex (CDC 2004). Cumulatively, 65% of individuals infected are gay and bisexual men. Men who have Sex with Men (MSM) of color share a disproportionate burden in terms of morbidity and mortality from HIV, specifically, MSM of color are more likely to acquire and die from HIV than their white MSM counterparts (CDC 2007).

Compared to their HIV-negative counterparts, HIV-positive individuals appear to be at increased risk for PV—including physical, sexual, and psychological PV. With respect to *physical PV*, 29% of HIV-positive respondents in a nationally representative sample of gay and bisexual men reported physical PV in the past five years, a figure that was significantly higher than the 21% of HIV-negative respondents (Greenwood et al. 2002). Studies on *sexual PV* with HIV-positive gay and bisexual men have reported lifetime prevalence ranging from 12–22% (McDonnell, Gielen and O'Campo 2003; Nieves-Rosa, Carballo-Diéguez and Dolezal 2000). We were unable to locate a comparable lifetime statistic for HIV-negative gay and bisexual men, although one study that used a past five-year timeframe indicated that 5% of HIV-negative gay and bisexual men reported sexual PV (vs. 6% HIV-positive in the same sample; Greenwood et al., 2002). Alarmingly, in a study of HIV-positive gay and bisexual men participating in ongoing HIV clinical and behavioral studies, 73% (n = 51) reported past psychological PV (Craft and Serovich 2005).

Overall, the data suggest HIV-positive gay and bisexual men may be at heightened risk for PV. While the consequences of PV among HIV-negative individuals are well-documented, and include difficulties in a variety of physical and mental health areas (Campbell 2002; Resnick, Acierno and Kilpatrick 1997; Zierler, Witbeck and Meyer 1996), the extent to which research on HIV-negative individuals generalizes to HIV-positive individuals is unclear. Although there has been a call for continued study of the extent to which HIV-infected individuals in treatment experience their condition as a "reason" for the initiation or maintenance of the PV they face (Zierler et al. 2000), scant research exploring the details and dynamics of abusive relationships among HIV-positive individuals (Relf 2001; Relf, Huang, Campbell and Catania 2004) has been published. Given this gap in the literature and that gay and bisexual men are a high-risk group for both HIV and PV, we sought to explore these topics with this understudied group. Further, HIV-positive sexual minority men may be especially vulnerable to PV due to their multiple socially stigmatized identities. These individuals may have negative self-views or perceptions that there are fewer available partners who would accept them and, thus, may find themselves choosing to settle for abusive partners or remain in violent relationships despite a growing wish to leave.

The role of PV as a risk factor for, or a consequence of, HIV infection is an open, empirical question. For some men, one health-related consequence of PV may be the acquisition of HIV, either as an intentional attack (Letellier 1996) or as an indirect result of the power and control exerted by the perpetrator (Relf 2001). Indeed, there is a growing body of research looking at the ways in which PV is a risk factor for HIV infection among HIV-negative individuals (e.g., El-Bassel et al. 1998). Research in this area shows that the environmental context of poverty and substance use—as well as racism and homophobia—can drive the desperation that normalizes PV and makes alternative methods of coping with stress in romantic partnerships seem impossible (El-Bassel, Gilbert, Rajah, Foleno and Frye 2000; Seals 1996).

Structural, familial, contextual, and individual factors can lead to and maintain risk for PV and HIV. For example, among American Indian MSM, extreme childhood emotional neglect was associated with housing instability, and, housing instability was associated with unknown HIV status (Walters et al. 2008). With respect to poverty, a study among homeless and unstably housed HIV-positive adults found that prevalence of abuse exceeded that of general HIV-positive and homeless populations; moreover, risk factors associated with PV in this group included trading sex, depressive symptoms, and lifetime alcohol abuse (Henny, Kidder, Stall and Wolitski 2007). Indeed, substance use has been found to be consistently associated with PV among heterosexuals as well as gay and bisexual men (Bartholomew, Regan, Oram and White 2008; Houston and McKirnan 2007). Men may use alcohol and illegal drugs to cope with distress, and high levels of consumption may in turn be associated with remaining in high-risk relationships. Moreover, early abuse—including early forced-sex and gay-related harassment—is another contextual variable found to have been associated with both HIV infection and PV in adulthood in gay and bisexual men, especially men of color (Williams, Wyatt, Resell, Peterson and Asuan-O'Brien 2004; Friedman, Marshal, Stall, Cheong and Wright 2008; Fields, Malebranche and Feist-Price 2009).

For some individuals, PV may first occur at the diagnosis and disclosure of their HIV. For example, because of their physical illness, the individual may have a higher need for physical caretaking and emotional support from romantic partners as well as social support from friends and family. This need for support could be met with potential stigma for one's HIV disclosure from a romantic partner and family members and rejection of one's sexual and/or gender identity from family members, possibly putting the individual in a more vulnerable position. Moreover, PV could be potentially more devastating for HIV-positive than HIV-negative individuals, given their increased susceptibility to mental and physical health problems. Finally, an HIV-positive victim of PV may have fears of abandonment that are intensified through a negative self-image and hopeless view about obtaining a non-abusive relationship later (Relf 2001). All of these possible precipitating factors may be complicated by power differentials along multiple axes, including partnerships involving individuals from different racial, ethnic, cultural, or economic groups.

Another way that PV might impact HIV-positive individuals is by interfering with the ability to make health-promoting choices around their medical and psychosocial care. Critical issues for HIV-positive gay and bisexual men include stigma around HIV status disclosure and sexual identity disclosure; the need to make treatment decisions in the face of limited or conflicting data; continual adherence to complicated medication regimens with numerous side effects; and the high co-morbidity of anxiety and depression in this population (e.g., Remien and Rabkin 2001). Adding PV to this mix is likely to impede access to healthcare or complicate health management (Relf 2001), and the additional stress is likely to exacerbate mental health problems (Schnurr and Green 2004) and hasten disease progression (Kiecolt-Glaser and Newton 2001).

Clearly, PV and HIV status are related to one another in complex, multidimensional ways for gay and bisexual men. Scientific study of the intersections of these two major public health problems is essential to determine the scope of the problems as well as to ascertain potential intervention targets. Despite this need, there are no published qualitative investigations that explore the phenomenological experience of relationship violence among HIV-infected men. Thus, in this chapter, we report data from a qualitative analysis of twenty-four HIV-positive sexual minority men receiving care at an urban, public HIV clinic. The study initially aimed to describe factors that contribute to the initiation and maintenance of violent relationships. However, during the qualitative interviews about those topics—and without prompting by the interviewer—participants universally offered considerable detail about their previous life experiences which, they believe, have contributed to their vulnerability to acquiring HIV and experiencing PV. In this chapter, we describe main themes emerging from these stories, including childhood disruption and exposure to potentially traumatic events; mental health problems and substance abuse in self and family; structural factors; and abuse in adulthood by non-partners.

METHOD

Recruitment and Enrollment

Participants were recruited from an HIV/AIDS Clinic at a medical center affiliated with the University of Washington. The clinic serves an urban, medically underserved population of almost 2,000 patients including ethnic minorities (44%), women (18%), intravenous drug users (25%), and homeless individuals (9%). Approximately 77% of the clinic population is fully or partly funded by public sources and 46% report an income below the federal poverty level.

The enrollment period was December 2005 through March 2006. Based on an "opt in" database of research-related information about clinic patients, a research nurse recruiter was able to identify potential participants when they reported for clinic appointments. Eligible patients were biologically male (but could identify currently with any gender), over eighteen years old, English-speaking, currently receiving HIV-related care at the clinic, and had previously discussed experiences of same-sex PV with a healthcare provider.

Potential participants were formally screened for eligibility using the Abuse Assessment Screen (AAS), a brief violence assessment instrument comprising five face-valid questions about abuse shown empirically to compare favorably to longer research instruments (McFarlane, Parker, Soeken, and Bullock 1992). Patients whose AAS was positive for abuse were deemed eligible for the study. All screened patients met eligibility criteria, provided written informed consent, and were enrolled. Participants agreed to audio recording of the interview with the stipulation that any part of the conversation could be redacted later from the transcripts at the participant's request.

Interview Guide Development

The interview guide was developed based on a thorough review of the literature on HIV and PV. The research team first created an initial outline and list of basic and probing questions. The specific content, format, and order of the questions in the final guide were revised and approved by experts in qualitative methods, traumatic victimization, and HIV mental health.

Interviews

The interviews were conducted in a private clinic room and were digitally audio-recorded. Before the interview, participants were asked to fill out a paper-and-pencil demographics questionnaire. Qualitative interview questions posed to participants followed a structured outline format with individualized follow-up questions. Questions early in the interview were more general and, once rapport had been established, addressed more sensitive content. Each participant was asked to discuss the role of HIV in his life, give a brief overview of his romantic relationship history, and then describe the context and dynamics of one specific relationship in which PV occurred since having been diagnosed with HIV. Note that we did not specifically query about experiences that might have predisposed the participant to PV, however—as seen below—the participants were eager to share that information as well. At the close of each interview, participants were paid $25 in cash for their time and travel expenses, and given a list of free or low-cost resources related to housing, employment, and medical and mental health needs of people living with HIV.

Transcription

Audio recordings were initially transcribed verbatim by study staff. Each transcript was then reviewed for accuracy by a different research assistant and any discrepancies were noted. A third staff member reviewed and reconciled all discrepancies and finalized each transcript.

Data Analysis

Our qualitative analysis was guided by the theory and methods of content analysis (e.g., Krippendorf 2004), which is "a research method for the subjective interpretation of the content of text data through the systematic classification process of coding and identifying themes or patterns" (Hsieh and Shannon 2005: 1279). The goal of content analysis is to add to the collective understanding of a given phenomenon by classifying a large amount of relevant text into thematic categories that represent the central ideas present in the data. In this approach, the voices of the participants are placed at the center of the analysis, and it is the ideas and patterns generated through their comments that guide the analysis and eventual coding (Morgan and Krueger 1993). This methodology best fit this project because of the lack of description or theory in the literature concerning the experiences of PV in the relationships of queer men living with HIV (Morse and Field 1995).

The team began the analytic process by reading the transcripts to get a general sense of the topics in the data. To develop an initial template of categories (comprising multiple related codes), team members each read transcripts of three interviews to determine what content emerged as interesting or important. Each member generated a preliminary list of codes by highlighting relevant text from the transcript that captured key elements and assigning the code a descriptive label; codes could represent either explicit or inferred communication (Krippendorf 2004).

Then the iterative process of reading, coding, categorizing, discussing, and refining ideas began. The group met to review each of the first three transcripts line by line, discussing codes and potential categories for groups of codes. This process was repeated with two additional batches of three transcripts until a total of nine transcripts had been reviewed in this manner and we agreed on a coding scheme. The result was a list of codes and categories (e.g., relationship characteristics, HIV, abuse, disclosure) generated from the individual readings of independent coders as well as the culmination of multiple discussions together.

Finally, each transcript was reviewed and fully coded by two researchers. These coded transcripts were compared and any discrepancies were discussed and resolved through consensus (Hill, Thompson and Williams, 1997). During the data analysis process, research team meetings changed focus from a discussion of potential codes and categories to a discussion of themes (i.e., different ways of organizing the categories into conceptually meaningful groupings; see Morse and Field 1995) to address empirical questions about the PV experiences of HIV-positive sexual minority men.

The use of various forms of triangulation—multiple sources of data (i.e., participants), multiple readings, multiple coders, and the iterative process of consensual agreement—enhances the verification and validity of the analysis (Patton 2002). The most robust themes were identified and organized conceptually. Final codes, categories, and themes were entered into a computerized qualitative data analytic program ATLAS.ti (Muhr 2004) to maximize data organization. Exemplars from the text were identified to capture the meaning of each theme.

RESULTS

Participant Characteristics

Study participants (N = 24) had a mean age of forty-two years. There was considerable heterogeneity in terms of racial identity: 46% White (n = 11), 29% Black or African American (n = 7), 12% biracial or multiracial (n = 3), and 13% American Indian or Native American (n = 3). Eight percent (n = 2) of the total sample identified their ethnicity as Latino. Most participants (n = 21, 88%) labeled their sexual orientation as gay/homosexual and the remainder as bisexual. In terms of sexual behavior in the past year, the majority of the sample reported sex mostly or exclusively with men (n = 19, 79%). A large minority of the participants were in a relationship at the time of the interview (n = 11 or 46%); all partnered participants were involved with men or male-to-female transgender individuals. Despite 92% of the sample having a high school degree or more education (and 54% reported having at least some college), mean income was very low overall, with 63% living on $10,000 or less a year and 71% noting state or federal assistance as their major source of income.

Emergent Themes

Participants in this study were asked to discuss the abuse they faced in prior relationships and, additionally, to highlight the ways in which HIV played a role in their romantic relationships. However, during the course of the interviews the men were eager to share their thoughts on what "pathways" led to the abuse they experienced, and to their HIV positive status—despite not being asked specific questions about those data. Analysis of the resultant anecdotes revealed numerous themes, from which we surmise that many of the same factors predisposing them to HIV acquisition also made them vulnerable to victimization by a relationship partner.

The men's current situations appeared to result from a constellation of life experiences common among them, including chaotic childhoods filled with instability and violence, and a history of multiple abuse experiences as children and adults. Marginalization, based on their multiple minority statuses, as well as substance abuse and mental illness, provided the context in which they struggled to maintain their health and relationships. Participants also reported the need to negotiate multiple identities, including race, gender, and sexual identities and the oppressions flowing from them, including homophobia and racism. In some cases these stressors were reflected clearly in their partnerships, experiences that are linked to adverse psychosocial functioning and health risk behaviors (Walters et al. 2008). Despite the heterogeneity of the sample, the experience of multiple traumatic stressors was the norm. Taken together, these interrelated factors created a traumatic context in which the men were both more likely to acquire HIV and to enter into a cycle of violence. Four main themes and relevant sub-themes are described in the following sections.

I Ain't Never Been a Kid: Childhood Disruption and Trauma

Disruptive Early Environments and Unstable Relationships with Adults

Nearly all of the respondents reported significant childhood familial instability and stressors associated with living at or near poverty. Respondents reported complicated and chaotic family situations involving unstable familial relationships, including high levels of caregiver fluidity (e.g., multiple caregivers such as distant relatives over the course of their childhoods), exposure to institutional caregivers (e.g., foster care system), or single parent households that were economically stressed. All of these experiences predisposed the respondents to early adoption of "adult" roles:

> When I was a kid? I ain't never been a kid . . . I was grown, I've been, I guess, my mama . . . I've been going to bars since I was like five, six, seven years old. I'm nine years old going to bars, at the afterhours clubs with my mother. I started going to bars alone when I was thirteen.

Another participant reported:

> And, um, you know, and since I didn't got no schooling, I was really bad in school to begin with because my daddy used to beat us up all the time and I would skip school and I was, real bad grades. My dad sent me off one year, to um, Michigan to my Jehovah witness aunts, for, that was for a couple, for about two years. You know, and when I got shipped back home it was, it just got worse for me.

Some respondents identified abuse perpetrated by a parent on other children in the family, which contributed to the chaotic and unstable environment:

> They were pulling me out of class a lot because, at this point, they were investigating my dad for possible molestation of my sister. Apparently, when she was twelve, she had been molested by my father. Years ago, I remember my sister saying something about it, you know, when it happened, it was all hush-hushed real quickly, like within two, three days.

These contexts were not especially conducive to the development of a healthy sense of self or to the development of mutually beneficial relationships. One participant related:

Um, because I always felt, growing up and stuff, I was so . . . My mom was married five times and I was so responsible for everyone else's feelings and how they were gonna act—I just went through this the other day. This same freaking thing! . . . Of me being too concerned about what other people are gonna think, and carrying my burden and carrying my fear.

Parental instability, such as mental illness, substance use, and relationship problems, combined with inconsistent and poor caregiving, appear to be related to increased vulnerability to living on the streets as youth. Many respondents noted that parental problems and family instability motivated them to leave home early and strike out on their own. One participant stated:

I mean, I grew up on the street. I'm, I grew up on the street, like I told you. When I was like fourteen years old, I ran away from home and I started hitting the streets, Portland, Portland to Seattle.

Similarly, another participant noted:

I haven't had contact with my family since I was about fourteen. That's when, let's see, '86, that's when my twin brother got shot. That's what triggered all the messed up stuff in my head.

Others were thrown out of their homes before they were ready to live on their own. As in the case of the young man quoted below, it was often directly related to the participants' sexuality:

No, I mean, I was the, when I left, I don't know how my brothers and sisters fared. Because I was thrown out, you know? I saw them once in a while. I guess life got better for them, I don't know. I was discommunicated from the family. You know, they told me—they told me I should have been dead.

Some of the respondents reported witnessing violence perpetrated by one parent against the other and even becoming involved in the violence to protect a parent:

[The police] had been out to the house so many times, from domestic violence, and it was horrible. I had to lie so many times because her boyfriend would be stoned and she'd be drunk and—they just wouldn't believe that he beat her. They would . . . [pause] But I had to get her out of the house 'cause, I mean, he would just brutalize her. And I didn't have, I was, you know, actually it was while she was with him that I ended up gettin' big enough to, um, put a stop to it myself.

Another participant told a similar story:

> He came in drunk with—and like most drunks, he wound up whoopin'
> on her. And, at one point, she just wouldn't get whooped on no more.
> And she knocked him out with a skillet! And that's pretty much the
> last time we saw him. You ever heard the sound a head makes when it
> hits a skillet?

In some cases, respondents noted that violence was deemed to be acceptable
if it involved behavior that was perceived to be protective. For example,
one of the respondents reported witnessing his mother enduring domestic
beatings and not "fighting back" until the perpetrator turned his attention
to the participant:

> Yeah, I watched him beat my mom so many times and it killed me al-
> ways, 'cause, um, one day he hit me and my mom knocked him clean
> out! And I couldn't understand. It was so easy, too. I mean, it was
> one punch—and she straight knocked him out! But she would never
> defend herself.

This modeling about the kinds of violent behavior that are acceptable in a
relationship may have resulted in tolerance of different forms of violence in
the men's own romantic relationships.

Community Violence

In addition to violence in the home, some of the respondents experienced or witnessed violence in their neighborhood or local community.
Exposure to high levels of community violence in their youth placed
the respondents at a disproportionate risk for mental health problems in adulthood, particularly post-traumatic stress disorder (PTSD)
and depression:

> My brother and I were both in a gang . . . and he was all messed up on
> coke, and drugs . . . He died, like, right where the radiator is, in front
> of me. I couldn't—even today—I mean, it still messes with me. And it
> happened twenty years ago, nineteen years ago, exactly.

Violence and Trauma: Abuse from Adults

Nearly all of the respondents identified high levels of violence exposure
in childhood and adulthood; either through witnessing violence as noted
previously or directly experiencing physical beatings, sexual abuse, rape, or
public humiliation and degradation. Consistent with other studies among
MSM (Fields et al. 2008; Williams et al. 2004), many reported that they

experienced these assaults by caregivers, kin networks, adult caretakers, family friends and neighbors or community members known to them:

> The way I was raised, my dad used to beat me when I came home—for getting beat up at school. I don't let people beat me up anymore.

Some of the men identified maladaptive coping strategies in dealing with the aftermath of the violence exposure, such as blocking out the events, minimizing the salience of the event, or disregarding it altogether by normalizing the experiences. For some of the men, the cycle of abusive relationships began as early as adolescence. One participant even talked about violence that he experienced in what he considered to be a romantic relationship (although, given the age disparity, the incident was technically statutory rape by most accepted definitions). He related:

> Well, I'll start chronologically I guess. When I was about thirteen or fourteen, I was dating a twenty-seven year old ex-con who was out on, he was paroled or whatever. And, uh, he was what they called back then "manic depressive," which I believe is bipolar now. And he would just work himself up into an emotional tizzy-fit and then punch me in the mouth.

For a minority of the men, childhood abuse was quite severe and many were able to identify resulting relationship skills deficits that they carried into adulthood:

> But all my aunts and uncles and stuff, they were evil to me and they made my life a living hell . . . They did things to me—like send people over to kill my dogs on my birthday. Um, they were like, I—my family was very sick, and very much into control . . . For all intents and purposes, they raised me to be ignorant in several aspects of life that a healthy, well-adjusted person just isn't.

Rejection Tied to Sexual or Gender Minority Identity

For some respondents, having revealed a sexual minority identity created additional vulnerability to abuse and rejection. One participant told us:

> Um, I told my family, my mother . . . she was cool with it. And my father, before he passed, he was not. He was not down with it! He didn't, he didn't have no—he "didn't raise no gays," he said, you know?

Some of the rejection these respondents reported was based on misconceptions about non-heterosexual people held by family members or significant friends:

My family told me that I was going to molest children if I was gay, that gay people molested children. They had me convinced that I could not, I couldn't prevent it—that I couldn't *not* do it. That it was like, just, something every gay person did.

Clearly, with strongly held stereotypes such as these, many of the respondents failed to receive support or affirmation from their families. Rather, interactions with family and others created additional stressors. This rejection and ostracism by families of origin exacerbated the respondents' social isolation and loneliness they reported in adulthood. As a result of these strained family interactions, some men reported distancing themselves from relatives. Others were rejected outright and given a clear message of invalidation and ostracism.

Some respondents talked about being physically attacked for gender nonconforming behavior or for displays of their queer sexual identity. One participant related:

I had this one person who knew me almost a year. Found out I was gay, tried to beat my ass. A friend. Tried [emphasized] to beat my ass. Didn't happen. I had a pool cue in my hand. Not a good idea. I'm pretty bad, pretty good with a pool cue. And not just playing pool either.

Many of the respondents similarly contextualized the various survival strategies that they employed to negotiate homophobic or dangerous encounters, like learning to stick up for themselves when they were psychologically assaulted or physically endangered:

Maybe I'm getting more gutsy, maybe I'm, you know . . . this one black guy got in my face a couple months ago, I looked at him and said, "Nigga, I ain't afraid of you." I don't use that word, I don't believe in the n-word, but he just looked back at me—"I ain't afraid of you, I don't know who you fucking talking shit to." Come on. These things are great weapons [pointing to fi0ngernails]. And they're full length and they're acrylics, so, uh, they're, they will hurt you.

Fuck It Anyways, You Know? Like, Who Cares? Mental Health and Substance Abuse

Mental Health Problems in Self and Family

All of the respondents reflected on challenges and resilience related to their mental health. Many identified social and familial stressors that triggered PTSD, depressive or suicidal episodes. Many respondents referenced their own mental disorders or those of relatives or other adult caretakers.

Considering the life circumstances the men reported, especially the early abuse experiences, it is unsurprising that they faced their own significant mental health challenges in adulthood. Some of the respondents' comments indicate severe mental health problems with significant consequences, although this was not the typical presentation.

Respondents mentioned a range of mental illnesses, with mood disorders and posttraumatic stress disorder the most common—not surprising given the high levels of childhood and adult trauma exposure. One participant described:

> I just remember waking up at the residential center. I was handcuffed to the—I mean, with those leather straps—I was strapped to the bed. And they wouldn't tell me what I did, so I just went into a panic, and I busted my wrist. I ripped the pole out! And then they told me I had contracted PTSD from what I saw. The bipolar, I guess I already had, I was born with it. My mom and then her mom and then her mom, you know, going down the line. I guess I got the "mom genes."

It was unclear from the narratives the causal direction of the associations, however. For example, it is possible that the respondents' mental health problems and early sexuality or atypical gender presentation behaviors in childhood may have resulted in the young men being targeted for abuse or neglected by adult caretakers or peers (Burke and Follingstad 1999). Alternatively, there are significant data to suggest that mental health problems arise from child abuse (Campbell 2002). This was the case for the young man quoted below, who tied his childhood abuse directly to current low self-esteem and depressogenic thinking:

> Um . . . just low self esteem. I've, I've always, I mean, and that goes back to—not relationship abuse—but abuse growing up. If you're told you're shit your whole life, you basically, that's all you know . . . the old tapes, you know. I say, I've read enough self help books, too, growing up. It's those old tapes that run through your head, they're, it's, they're very hard to erase.

For some, depression manifested in a sense of giving up, or extreme apathy, and in some cases escalated into suicidal ideation. Apathy—and eventually social isolation—often resulted from mental health problems combined with social determinants that directly impacted the respondents' interpersonal relationships:

> Um, I was, I went through major, you know, again I've suffered from bipolar since I was a kid, and I had a very abusive childhood growing up. Um, so to me, I, I was sort of like, "Fuck it anyways," you know? Like, "who cares?"

Some of the abuse experiences led to the men's conceptions of themselves as "loners" which may, directly or indirectly, have contributed to the profound sense of social and psychological isolation that was commonly reported:

> I think that the fact that I was so, so tormented as a child . . . I mean, I jokingly say this but it's half kidding, half serious—the movie, "Carrie," with Sissy Spacek, was sort of based on my life. Just how she was so tormented and ostracized for, you know . . . So, you kind of learn to be on your own and be a loner and be okay with that, to a point. Um, and that carries on to this day, I'm very content just doing my own gig.

This severe social isolation further restricts potential sources of support and makes the men more vulnerable to controlling partners. Although social isolation may have been an important coping strategy to survive the teen years and being ostracized at school, this coping strategy may not be transferable to adult coping styles and adult relationship building. In fact, the loner strategy may place the men at greater risk for remaining with controlling or abusive partners.

The mental health issues also manifested as an overall sense of a foreshortened future. Having lives that involved so much structural violence, communal and familial abuse and chaotic conditions—coupled with few positive, longstanding relationships—seems to have resulted in many of the men, irrespective of their HIV-positive status, believing that they would not live long lives. This sense of the inevitability of an early demise was very common and may have influenced sexual and relationship choices made by the men. Expectations about a short life are likely a result of the stressful, violence-filled experiences of their childhood and continuing violence exposure in their adult lives. As one man told us:

> Um, you know I never thought I'd make it past twenty-eight. See, twenty-eight is the age—cause that's when Jim Morrison, Janis Joplin and Jimi Hendrix all died, at the same age—so I figure, okay, well, you know [laughs] . . . And, actually, I think Kurt Cobain too, I think he was twenty-eight. Um, so I, you know, I was like, "Who cares?"

Substance Abuse in Respondent and Family Members

Substance use and abuse were reportedly ubiquitous in the men's lives, and seemed almost inevitable, given their living situations and the context of their lives:

> The area we lived, you know, "cause the building I lived in, you know, downstairs they sold drugs. And in the back they sold drugs, of the house, you know. It was, like, crazy. Then the prostitutes just come over to get their drugs, too.

Although drinking and drugging were a constant, their form and function varied. For some, contact with alcohol and illegal drugs started in childhood, with substance-abusing parents. Given the lack of parental oversight and the early adoption of adult roles (discussed previously), it is unsurprising that experimentation with, or regular use of, drugs and alcohol began at an early age for this group. Although experimentation with alcohol is common in adolescence, in this sample, alcohol appeared to serve a function beyond fitting in socially and began the pathways for some to using alcohol and drugs as a way to cope or self medicate. One participant noted:

> I picked up a drink when I was seventeen. I said, 'This is what my body always needed!' I said, 'My goodness, I finally found it!' I finally found the answer.

For some of these men, substance use became a relatively effective short-term coping strategy, allowing them to occasionally check out of the reality of their lives or to help them cope with daily stressors:

> Uh, and you're always struggling for food, you're always struggling for this and that. Subsequently, it led me into a depressed, more depressed state where I was drinking so, just to ignore the problem.

Coping with mental health issues, especially mood disorders, was another catalyst for substance use mentioned by several men. One participant related:

> But, um, a lot of us who are bipolar, and have issues, we use. And I'm not saying this is an excuse to use drugs but, um, a lot of us do. So, like, you'll use it to medicate, just to get us on a base level—of feeling semi-decent. Granted, the aftereffects and the drama that goes with that are not fun, though.

Similarly, another participant told us:

> I keep a lot, I have drugs at my house. It keeps me nice and . . . stupefied, if I get those days. 'Cause there are days that I just want, it gets really bad, when I just want to walk out in front of that bus.

Some men specifically mentioned substance use as a means to cope with PV or physical pain more generally:

> No, and the drugs also helped numb that, so . . . I mean it's weird. It's like, you know it, like, drugs are bad, yes. But at the same point, it definitely buffered the whole thing . . . I was numb at the time.

Another noted:

> P (Participant): Well, like, when he hit me in the head with the laser printer, I used meth all day long the next day.
> I (Interviewer): Did it help?
> P: Umm, yeah, my head didn't hurt no more! [laughs] I don't remember it hurting and I stayed awake and had great sex.

Many participants noted that their substance use became more frequent over time and they became dependent on it. Patterns of use typically fluctuated depending on other ongoing events in the men's lives. One participant told us:

> Uh, me and Michael, as I said, living outside as long as we have—we were using alcohol for a release, you know? To, in order for me to go to sleep at night, I'd have to be pretty well intoxicated.

Another related:

> Cause what we did, it was nothing but drugs. Nothing but drugs and prostitutes, and it was just like, Wow!" So, it got really wild. . . .

One respondent highlighted the consequences of excessive substance use. While drug use (finding drugs, using drugs) can involve other people and be seen superficially as a social activity, he identified the idea that deep, meaningful connections are unlikely to result from a life of substance abuse, deepening the sense of marginalization and social isolation so many of the men talked about:

> Oh just, it makes you numb-er, it makes you more numb. [laughs] "Numb-er." I don't know if that's even a word. It makes you more numb and it's, it just is impossible to really connect on any level of authenticity, if you're numb or you're in, you know, an altered state.

A number of men noted a major turning point in their drug and/or alcohol use having to do with identity integration and self-acceptance, and often came at a time in their lives when they were attempting to leave their violent relationships. It appears that, for many men, violence, and substance use were highly intertwined—staying with one meant staying with the other, and leaving one behind meant leaving the other behind as well.

Structural factors

Many respondents also talked about structural factors that may have contributed to the acquisition of HIV and their experiences in violent partnerships. Like falling dominoes, one structural factor often led to the other. For example, for some, early poverty led to homelessness, which led to commercial sex work to earn money to secure stable housing, but which often led to legal problems. Other men did not mention their financial circumstances until discussing their diagnosis with HIV. Living in poverty exacerbated early responsibility burdens and adult role-taking as children:

> I don't know, I, I just been in—I've been independent or what is, independent or dependent? All my life, really, since I was fourteen. Always had to work and, 'cause my family ain't had a lot of money, my dad had to raise twelve kids, know what I mean? Yeah, I always had to work. I had to work at the Piggly Wiggly to buy my school clothes and which ... My dad bought some, don't get me wrong, but extra things like, like the boys with parents that was teaching school ... So, I had to go make that money myself, you know what I mean?

Marginal Housing and Experience with Street Life

For many men, poverty led directly to unstable housing situations, which they experienced intermittently throughout their lives. These situations ranged from temporary living arrangements with friends and acquaintances to being homeless and living on the street:

> Okay, I was homeless for basically ten years. When, now when I say homeless I wasn't, there wasn't one day that I slept under a bridge or outside. I either couch surfed with friends um, or had a boyfriend I would stay with.

Housing instability led to living on the street, involvement in drug culture, and developing friendships primarily or exclusively with other people living on the street, thus limiting social capital and social mobility. Respondents noted that this financial vulnerability contributed to their engagement in illegal behavior and involvement with drugs. Because they had lived on the street during their youth, there was high potential for the men to be exploited by older people. On the other hand, street capital gained as a youth may have translated into valuable street competencies and survival skills (Walters et al. 2008). Many of the men who engaged in survival sex did so after or during a bout of homelessness or housing instability which was typically precipitated by life crises such as escalating drug use, PV with a partner, or lack of shelter:

> I had run away from home. I was in Los Angeles. I needed a place to stay. Old Henry there is offering me a place and it's gonna be the park bench otherwise, so let's go to Henry's place and, you know, I'm obviously

gonna have to fool around with this man but hopefully I'll get a little cash out of it, or maybe some breakfast in the morning.

Commercial Sex Work

Some respondents confronting poverty and homelessness turned to prostitution. In fact, a large proportion of respondents reported that they had, at times, traded sex for money, shelter, or drugs. For some respondents, family and financial obligations were motivating their choice of part-time work in the sex industry. In addition, for some, this practice of "hustling" started early in their lives:

> No, not really because my lifestyle, being a prostitute all these years. I was surprised I didn't catch it before. I was turning tricks since the age of thirteen.

Similarly, another participant related:

> I was living with my paternal grandmother. She was recovering from surgery which amputated part of her leg, and I was her primary caretaker. I was a journalism and art history major, working at a newspaper during the day. And working as a male escort at night and on the weekends. And an unknowing alcoholic and drug addict. . . .

Ultimately, street competencies lead to a street career life where hustling became a pragmatic way of surviving for some, despite a desire to leave "the life." In the words of one participant:

> I was trying to stop turning tricks and I was trying to do more constructive things. Um, I think maybe at this point I actually had stopped turning tricks, but I'd done that for so long, that the pimp was still in the picture.

None of the men who reported commercial sex work indicated that they felt especially stigmatized by these experiences. Rather, in some cases, the men expressed great pride in it. Some men recounted the information nonchalantly which may suggest that sex work reflects attitudes about their accomplished street competencies and street capital, as opposed to an internalization of negative social attitudes toward prostitution. It is important to note that although such nonchalant attitudes existed, there were some who identified the social and emotional costs to sex work as noted previously. Many of the respondents were formerly homeless, and having achieved housing stability, they noted many street competencies translated into life competencies (Walters et al. 2008). Eventually, a number ended their street careers and leaving street life came at a point when they finally had "enough" or when they were ready to initiate a new stage in their life. As one participant said:

> Like I said, I had quit my job. I left my apartment and I slept underneath the bridge with that man for over 11 years—until finally I got up and says, "I can't take it no more!"

Other street competencies that translated into life competencies across a host of settings included adopting attitudes that included not caring what others think—potentially a form of psychological buffering against negative attitudes towards sexual minority individuals in non-street contexts (Walters et al. 2008).

Legal Involvement

Whether because of commercial sex work, drugs, or violence, multiple respondents reported involvement with the legal system. Many of the participants had been arrested and many had experience in the courts because of restraining orders they placed during their violent relationships. A number of the men reported having served time in jail or prison, environments notorious for sexual exploitation of sexual minority men:

> And then I got busted because I was downtown with some friends and, and I got busted with drugs. And then I went to, I went to this minimum camp they sent me to, to do two years for possession. And I went and did that and, while I was there at the camp they, I told them that I was HIV positive, and they prescribed the medication for me and stuff like that. And I was in there and then I was REALLY, really bummed out because—here I am, locked up in prison and I got HIV!

Abuse in Adulthood by Non-Partners

The early trauma and disruption, predisposing factors of mental illness and substance use, along with the structural disadvantages led directly to abuse in multiple relationships throughout the respondents' lives. All of the men interviewed had been in romantic relationships where they were victims (and some perpetrators as well) of PV. However, the men also reported being physically or sexually assaulted as adults by non-partners before their HIV seroconversions. In the following vignette, the victim was on a first date with a man whom he met on the Internet. This violent sexual assault happened before he had become HIV-positive. His story is as follows:

> It was, his, by the way he talked about things, and like I said, he had a soft demeanor. He was a nice guy and very attractive and, uh . . . it

was right after we laid down in my bed and we were watching TV, then he started doing some petting. Then when things started getting hot and heavy he turned me over on my stomach and—which I'm not used to—and uh, he tried doing it that way, but he didn't have any lube on. And, uh, but he did have a condom on, but no lube, and it hurt like hell, you know, with no lube! And, uh, so I asked him to put some lube on, which he did, "cause I had some there. And then he started doing his thing and, but, he wouldn't let me bend up so I could do my thing.

And then he suddenly pull, pulled himself out, and, uh, he tied me down with leather straps, top and bottom, where I couldn't move! And then, uh, he got out his, uh, sling that he had—that I didn't know he brought with him, "cause he went out to his car to get it—and he came back in and he put, uh, lube on the end of it and then he started shoving the pole of the sling—not the sling, but the whip, is what he had. Started shoving it, up, in . . . It hurt like hell! I was screaming at him, and then he took the whip and uh, started whipping my back with it, whipping my head.

And, uh, that's what I call physical abuse as well as mental abuse! Because he had told me at that time that uh, he didn't really care about me, he just wanted to get his rocks off. And that was enough for me to go through that, and uh, and not, not see him again.

And, uh, he was nice enough to take his rubber off and put it in the toilet. And I picked it up with a pair of scissors and looked at it to see if any, anything had broken. And nothing had broken, so I knew I was safe. But, uh, I had to get myself cleaned up, and then I just, I went to bed, and I cried myself to sleep.

Most telling in this incredibly graphic depiction of date rape is the respondent's comment, "And that was enough for me to go through that, and uh, and not, not see him again." Apparently, it occurred to him that someone (the interviewer, perhaps) might think that after being raped, there might be a second date. This comment, and others like it, point to the highly prevalent theme that violence is to some degree tolerable, normative, even acceptable.

Some respondents discussed the ways in which the relationships they have with their parents as adults were abusive as well. For one participant, his father's reaction at meeting his new romantic partner was an example of how psychological abuse continued into adulthood:

And, um, my dad looked him straight in the eyes and he goes, "What are you doing with my son? You know he's sick and diseased, don't you?" . . . That that was just my dad; he's a bastard like that. He used to go around saying what a bitch my mother was. After she died, he was the second person I called right after it happened. And he just said, "So, what do you want me to do about it?" I don't know, it's never been . . . that was kind of my last attempt at having anything to do with him.

CONCLUSION

These accounts from twenty-four gay and bisexual men with experiences of PV clearly elucidate common pathways to violence. Chaotic and violent childhood environments and unstable relationships with parental figures, often including physical, sexual, and emotional abuse from multiple adults, deprived the respondents of opportunities to be exposed to violence-free relationships. Moreover, being targeted because of their gay identities often exacerbated the abuse at the hands of rejecting family members. In concert and as a consequence of this early trauma and the structural factors impacting their early lives, many respondents developed mental health and substance use problems that predisposed them to situations and relationships that replicated their early chaotic upbringing.

Structural factors provided further barriers to loving and supportive social supports. Poverty, housing instability, and life on the streets, which often included sex work and brushes with the law, diminished the opportunities and abilities to identify partners who offer the potential for stable and healthy partnerships. For respondents who have yet to work through their traumatic history and to develop adaptive coping skills, re-victimization was common in adulthood. The cycle of violence is all too often linked to partner violence and adult decision-making in a context where violence is normative. Revictimized in adulthood, by non-partners and even family members, the respondents eventually experienced violence with their own partners, a seemingly inevitable conclusion based on their accumulated life experiences.

Although these were common pathways to PV in the stories of the respondents, they were by no means universal. While the majority of the interviews with the men were focused on the violence they had experienced, some men also talked about supportive family members, lifelong friends, and some academic and career success. Indeed, a few men who discussed their backgrounds noted that one of their first major life stressors was discovering their HIV-positive serostatus. Also, not all men were passive victims to their early trauma, predisposing pathology and substance use, and structural barriers. Signs of strengths and resilience were also noted. Further work should explore the exceptions to this type of narrative—highlighting unusual paths to violence and underscoring the strength of the men who had the fortitude to leave violent relationships and care for themselves, when precious few others ever had. This work will inform HIV prevention efforts targeting gay and bisexual men at risk for PV.

Meanwhile, interventions with this group must begin early, when trauma first appears. Co-occurring morbidities like mental illness and substance use should be considered, and health interventions should operate at multiple levels to address larger structural inequities that perpetuate violence and HIV risk in vulnerable men who are gay and bisexual, giving them opportunities and skills to stand up for themselves. Structural-level interventions as well as those aimed at increasing parenting skills may be useful for preventing the cycle of violence from recurring. Developing evidence-based support programs for gay and bisexual men to facilitate "coming out" may be helpful at increasing social support from a network of peers and instilling healthful group norms, e.g., minimizing risky sexual behavior or modeling alternatives to violence for solving problems. Presently, evidence-based behavioral and pharmacologic treatments exist for many of the mental health problems mentioned by the men, including depression, bipolar disorder, PTSD, and substance abuse. These treatments may need to be tailored to fit LGB individuals, and providers may need training in delivering them in a culturally-competent fashion. Another issue is dissemination; rather than just offering supportive counseling, LGB community centers and HIV clinics must provide state-of-the-art treatments to their clientele.

The qualitative narratives from these men reflect parental chaotic environments, emotional neglect, physical and sexual abuse and in some cases, outright abandonment and rejection from families of origin. Familial upheaval placed some of the men in highly developmentally inappropriate roles including primary caregiver (to self and other family members) at an early age. Future research will need to discern the relationship between caregiver instability and violence and caregiver support in supporting MSM health, wellness, and partnership decision-making and reduction in PV. Specifically, the narratives in which caregivers were supportive were qualitatively different than narratives related to caregivers who were not able to, for a variety of reasons (their own mental illness or substance abuse, for example) provide consistency in familial relationships or emotional caregiving. In fact, some literature on housing instability and MSM are showing that parental emotional neglect and abuse may play a large role in mental health and homelessness (Walters et al. 2008).

Overall, the narratives revealed high rates of lifetime traumatic stress exposure, elevated PTSD, depressive symptoms, and substance abuse. Taken together, trauma, alcohol and drug use, and poor mental health outcomes, including sexual risk behaviors—a triangle of risk—are associated with PV in adulthood (Simoni et al. 2004). Future research will need to examine the mediating effects of alcohol and drug use on sexual risk taking and exacerbation of PV-risk exposure. It is important to note that not all MSM who had high levels of trauma exposure held assumptions that violence is inevitable in adult relationships.

There are many other potential stress-buffering factors such as the role of identity, families of choice, self-acceptance, spirituality, and others that might cushion the effects of childhood abuse and caregiving instability on partnership decision-making, expectations, and PV exposure. Finally, it is

204   *David W. Pantalone, et al.*

important to note that although a number of the men accepted violence as a fact of life, their narratives also reflected themes of strength, generosity, and resilience. Moreover, interpretation of this data is problematic if analyzed outside of the larger context of institutional heterosexism, structural and economic violence, and prejudice in which the respondents live. In many ways, the normative sense of violence is understandable given the social conditions in which this violence is translated and perpetuated in family, peer, and social relations. It is critical to take into account the very real structural conditions under which sexual and gender minorities negotiate their everyday lives.

NOTES

1. This research was supported by an award from the National Institute of Mental Health (F31 MH71179) to David W. Panatolone. The authors wish to express sincere gratitude to the project participants, research assistants, and collaborators at the University of Washington and Suffolk University, and the staff and patients of the Madison HIV/AIDS Clinic at Harborview Medical Center. Correspondence should be addressed to David Pantalone, Department of Psychology, Suffolk University, 41 Temple Street, Boston, MA 02114. Phone: 617–573–8782. Fax: 617–367–2924. E-mail: dpantalone@suffolk.edu.

REFERENCES

Bartholomew, K., K. V. Regan, D. Oram and M. A.White. 2008. Correlates of partner abuse in male same-sex relationships. *Violence and Victims* 23: 344–360.
Burke, L. K. and D. R. Follingstad. 1999. Violence in lesbian and gay relationships: Theory, prevalence, and correlational factors. *Clinical Psychology Review* 19(5): 487–512.
Campbell, J. C. 2002. Violence against women II: Health consequences of intimate partner violence. *Lancet* 359: 1331–1336.
CDC. 2004. HIV/AIDS Surveillance Report: HIV Infection and AIDS in the United States, 2003. Vol. 15. Atlanta, GA: Division of HIV/AIDS Prevention, National Center for HIV, STD and TB Prevention, U.S. Centers for Disease Control and Prevention.
CDC. 2007. HIV/AIDS Surveillance Report: Cases of HIV infection and AIDS in the United States and Dependent Areas, 2007. Vol. 19. Atlanta, GA: Division of HIV/AIDS Prevention, National Center for HIV, STD and TB Prevention, U.S. Centers for Disease Control and Prevention.
El-Bassel, N., G. Gilbert, V. Rajah, A. Foleno and V. Frye. 2000. Fear and violence: Raising the HIV stakes. *AIDS Education and Prevention* 12(2): 154–170.
El-Bassel, N., L. Gilbert, S. Krishnan, R. Schilling, T. Gaeta, S. Purpura and S.S. Witte. 1998. Partner violence and sexual HIV-risk behaviors among women in an inner-city emergency department. *Violence and Victims* 13(4): 377–393.
Fields, S. D., D. Malebranche and S. Feist-Price. 2009. Childhood sexual abuse in Black men who have sex with men: Results from three qualitative studies. *Cultural Diversity and Ethnic Minority Psychology* 14(4): 385–390.

Friedman, M. S., M. P. Marshal, R. Stall, J. W. Cheong and E. R. Wright. 2008. Gay-related development, early abuse, and adult health outcomes among gay males. *AIDS and Behavior* 12: 891–902.

Greenwood, G. L., M.V. Relf, B. Huang, L. M. Pollack, J. A. Canchola and J. A. Catania. 2002. Battering victimization among a probability-based sample of men who have sex with men. *American Journal of Public Health* 92(12): 1964–1969.

Henny, K. D., D. P. Kidder, R. Stall and R. J. Wolitski. 2007. Physical and sexual abuse among homeless and unstably housed adults living with HIV: Prevalence and associated risks. *AIDS and Behavior* 11: 842–853.

Hill, C. E., B. J. Thompson and E. N. Williams. 1997. A guide to conducting consensual qualitative research. *The Counseling Psychologist* 25(4): 517–572.

Houston, E. and D. J. McKirnan. 2007. Intimate partner abuse among gay and bisexual men: Risk correlates and health outcomes. *Journal of Urban Health: Bulletin of the New York Academy of Medicine* 84: 681–690.

Hsieh, H. F. and S. E. Shannon. 2005. Three approaches to qualitative content analysis. *Qualitative Health Research* 15(9): 1277–1288.

Kiecolt-Glaser, J. K. and T. L Newton. 2001. Marriage and health: His and hers. *Psychological Bulletin* 127(4): 472–503.

Kilpatrick, D.G. 2004. What is violence against women: Defining and measuring the problem. *Journal of Interpersonal Violence* 19(11): 1209–1234.

Krippendorf, K. 2004. *Content analysis: An introduction to its methodology.* 2nd ed. Thousand Oaks, CA: Sage.

Letellier, P. 1996. Twin epidemics: Domestic violence and HIV infection among gay and bisexual men. In *Violence in gay and lesbian domestic partnerships,* ed. C.M. Renzetti and C. H. Miley, 69–81. New York: Harrington Park Press.

Maman, S., J. Campbell, M. D. Sweat and A.C. Gielen. 2000. The intersections of HIV and violence: Directions for future research and interventions. *Social Science and Medicine* 50(4): 459–478.

McDonnell, K. A., A. C. Gielen and P. O'Campo. 2003. Does HIV status make a difference in the experience of lifetime abuse? Descriptions of lifetime abuse and its context among low-income urban women. *Journal of Urban Health* 80(3): 494–509.

McFarlane, J., B. Parker, K. Soeken and L. Bullock. 1992. Assessing for abuse during pregnancy. *Journal of the American Medical Association* 267(23): 3176–3178.

Morgan, D.L. and A. Krueger. 1993. When to use focus groups and why. In *Successful focus groups: Advancing the state of the art,* ed. D. Morgan, 3–19. Thousand Oaks, CA: Sage Publications.

Morse, J. M. and P. A. Field. 1995. *Qualitative research methods for health professionals.* 2nd ed. Thousand Oaks, CA: Sage.

Muhr, T. 2004. *User's Manual for ATLAS.ti 5.0.* ATLAS.ti Scientific Software Development GmbH, Berlin, Germany.

Nieves-Rosa, L., A. Carballo-Diéguez and C. Dolezal. 2000. Domestic abuse and HIV-risk behavior in Latin American men who have sex with men in New York City. *The Journal of Lesbian and Gay Social Services: Issues on Practice, Policy and Research* 11: 77–90.

Patton, M. Q. 2002. *Qualitative research and evaluation methods.* 3rd ed. Thousand Oaks, CA: Sage.

Relf, M.V. 2001. Battering and HIV in men who have sex with men: A critique and synthesis of the literature. *Journal of the Association of Nurses in AIDS Care* 12(3): 41–48.

Relf, M. V., B. Huang, J. Campbell and J. Catania. 2004. Gay identity, interpersonal violence, and HIV risk behaviors: An empirical test of theoretical relationships among a probability-based sample of urban men who have sex with men. *Journal of the Association of Nurses in AIDS Care* 15(2): 14–26.

Remien, R. H. and J. G. Rabkin. 2001. Psychological aspects of living with HIV disease. *Western Journal of Medicine* 175: 332–335.

Resnick, H. S., R. Acierno and D. G. Kilpatrick. 1997. Health impact of interpersonal violence 2: Medical and mental health outcomes. *Behavioral Medicine* 23: 65–78.

Schnurr, P. P. and B. L. Green. 2004. *Trauma and health: Physical health consequences of exposure to extreme stress.* Washington, DC: American Psychological Association.

Seals, B. 1996. The overlapping epidemics of violence and HIV. *Journal of the Association of Nurses in AIDS Care* 7(5): 91–93.

Simoni, J. M., Sehgal, S. and Walters, K. L. 2004. Triangle of risk: Urban American Indian women's sexual trauma, injection drug use, and HIV sexual risk behaviors. *AIDS and Behavior* 8(1): 33–45.

Walters, K. L., D. H. Chae, A. T. Perry, A. Stately, R. Old Person and J. M. Simoni. 2008. "My body and my spirit took care of me:" Homelessness, violence, and resilience among American Indian Two-Spirit men. In *Health issues confronting minority men who have sex with men*, ed. S. Loue, 125–153. New York: Springer.

Williams, J. K., G. E. Wyatt, J. Resell, J. Peterson and A. Asuan-O'Brien. 2004. Psychosocial issues among gay and non-gay identifying HIV-seropositive African American and Latino MSM. *Cultural Diversity and Ethnic Minority Psychology* 10 (3): 268–286.

Zierler, S., W. E. Cunningham, R. Andersen, M. F. Shapiro et al. 2000. Violence victimization after HIV infection in a U.S. probability sample of adult patients in primary care. *American Journal of Public Health* 90(2): 208–215.

Zierler, S., B. Witbeck and K. Mayer. 1996. Sexual violence, women, and HIV infection. *American Journal of Preventive Medicine* 12: 304–310.

Part III

Responding to Relationship Violence
An Ethical Challenge

11 Troubling Normalcy
Examining 'Healthy Relationships' Discourses in Lesbian Domestic Violence Prevention

Cindy Holmes[1]

INTRODUCTION

In 2001 I had the opportunity to develop and coordinate a new feminist queer violence prevention initiative—the *Safe Choices Support and Education Program*. Aware of the limitations of hegemonic feminist anti-violence frameworks and the way they position white, middle-class, able-bodied, and/or heterosexual women's experiences as the norm, we were motivated to develop innovative anti-violence programming for queer women that would shift this framework. This chapter offers my critical reflections on some of the competing discourses in the "healthy relationships" workshop curriculum of this program, and some of the struggles facing us in the feminist and queer anti-violence movements.

The Safe Choices Support and Education program, located on Coast Salish Territories in the city known as Vancouver, British Columbia, a large socio-economically diverse Canadian city, is based in a non-profit, feminist, anti-violence, organization and funded by a health promotion program of the regional health authority. Each year, the program provides six service-provider training workshops about abuse in women's intimate same-sex/gender relationships and five healthy queer relationships workshops for lesbian, bisexual, queer, and Two-Spirit women. The healthy relationships workshops offer "information and opportunities to break isolation in order to improve the health of women who are currently, or have been, in abusive same-sex/gender relationships" (BCASVACP 2007, 5). Their goal is to empower women and strengthen queer communities to respond to the issue of abuse in same-sex/gender relationships·. Approximately seventy-five to one hundred women attend these free workshops annually.[2]

The curriculum manual includes five healthy relationships workshop modules: (1) After the Honeymoon: Healthy Communication and Problem-Solving; (2i) Knowing You-Knowing Me: Negotiating Separateness and Togetherness in Intimate Relationships; (3ii) Mind Your Own Business—Don't Air our Dirty Laundry: Talking About Relationship Concerns with Friends and Family; (4v) Sexuality, Intimacy and Desire; and (5) Keeping

Our Relationships Alive While Parenting. All workshops acknowledge they are open to all lesbian, bisexual, queer and Two-Spirit women (including those who identify as transgender) regardless of relationship status or the language they use to self-identify. They are not sequential and each is designed to be offered independently of the others. They follow a similar format, delivered over a three and a half hour period, and use a support and education model. They are not meant to function as a therapy or support group, but are intended to provide queer women with opportunities for connection, dialogue, exchange of information and resources, and skill building about healthy relationships.[3]

Over the years, participants have indicated through formal evaluations and informal feedback, that the workshops were innovative and helpful by offering support and information outside of traditional counseling services. Early in the program's history, the possibility of funding cuts prompted some participants to write to the health authority about the significance of the workshops in helping to combat the negative effects of homophobia on queer women's relationships. Many told us that participating in the workshops enabled them to make positive changes in their lives, including in some cases, ending abuse in relationships. Some said attending a workshop was a first step in breaking their isolation and connecting to other queer women. In several instances, facilitators ran into participants outside of the program hours (for example, on the street, in a coffee shop, the doctor's office or a community event) where women shared these stories about the positive effects of the workshops.

While it was clear that the workshops were offering a new and positive prevention strategy for many queer women, there were a few comments, as well as some unspoken and unwritten feedback revealed through some participants' body language and awkward silences, suggesting that the workshops may not have been meeting everyone's needs. While difficult to analyze this "feedback" without interview data or written evaluations, I had a growing sense that some of the discourses in the curriculum had normalizing and exclusionary effects. And as I will discuss, these issues were difficult to fully address in a neo-liberal context with excessive state monitoring and limited funding.

In creating the program, we shifted away from an earlier vision of providing on-going individual counseling and support groups, for two key reasons. First, we wanted to develop an innovative approach to queer violence prevention focused on creating healthy relationships. Second, we were compelled to work within the constraints of a limited budget and align the program more closely with the aims of the health promotion fund,[4] which centers on "cost-effective, innovative strategies for promoting and improving population health . . . build[ing] community capacities, skills and assets so communities can better identify and manage their own health needs" (Vancouver Coastal Health, 2008).

A "HEALTHY RELATIONSHIPS" APPROACH

Most LGBT anti-violence initiatives (primarily based in large urban centers) have traditionally focused on outreach, supportive counseling, and resources for victims and education for LGBT communities. Some have recently identified the need for innovative community-based approaches that concentrate on creating healthy queer relationships rather than focusing explicitly on domestic violence (BCASVACP 2007; Chung and Lee 2002; Northwest Network 2008; Ristock 2002; Ristock and Timbang 2005). Partly, this is in response to the challenges queer women face speaking about relationship violence, as our identity is already stigmatized through its association with pathology, deviance and violence. As well, many queer women do not name their experiences "domestic violence" or "abuse" as a result of the heteronormative framework of domestic violence. Further, our experience in the late 1990s in Vancouver (like that of other advocates in Toronto and Winnipeg) had shown that many survivors of abuse in lesbian relationships were not accessing lesbian abuse support groups for a variety of reasons. Some of those reasons included shame about publicly identifying themselves as being in an abusive lesbian relationship, concerns about confidentiality within small communities, and/or confusion about whether their experience would fall within the category of "abuse" (BCASVACP 2007; Chung and Lee 2002; Ristock 2002). Some advocates noted that more queer women were showing up for groups to learn about healthy relationships than to talk about their experiences of abuse (Ristock 2002: 165). At the same time, many of us supporting friends in abusive relationships spoke about feeling confused by complex dynamics we observed that could not be easily explained with the available feminist anti-violence frameworks. We often felt unconvinced that the traditional feminist power and control model and victim/perpetrator binary used in counseling practices were the most effective or accurate ways for understanding, intervening and supporting change in queer women's relationships.

This shift to a focus on "healthy relationships" was seen not only in queer anti-violence work, but also more broadly within the anti-violence movement in North America where an increasing number of programs began to develop healthy relationships curricula for (predominantly heterosexual) high school students. Interestingly, these efforts coincided with a differently motivated move taking place more broadly within the movement—that is, the increased alliance with the neo-liberal state.

Neo-liberalism is often used to describe the dominant economic, cultural, and political system that is driven by pro-corporate free-market priorities (Duggan 2002). Neo-liberal discourses support the development of economic and social policies that encourage the privatization of services. There is an emphasis on individual freedom and rights where "the role of government is to provide advice and assistance to enable self-governing subjects to become normal/responsible citizens, who voluntarily comply with the interests and needs of the state" (Richardson 2005: 516). In this chapter, I am concerned with the relationship between neo-liberal discourses, strategies of governance, and community-based anti-violence and health promotion initiatives.

Kristin Bumiller (2008) argues that over the past two decades, there has been a growing and problematic alliance between the neo-liberal state and the movement to end violence against women "where the feminist campaign was modified and integrated into state and quasi-state organizations and became part of the routine business of social service bureaucracies and crime control" (7). Alongside this, she argues, we can see how a growing anti-feminist backlash campaign contributed to a normalizing and mainstreaming of the movement focused on addressing violence by "situating it as part of programs to combat sexism in workplaces, build healthy relationships, and improve communication between men and women" (10). Interestingly, she makes the point that "the progressive ideals of this campaign deferred to the more pressing prerogatives of security, public health, preservation of the family, and other demands to maintain order" (7).

In the Safe Choices program, our attempts to shift the existing lesbian anti-violence framework proved to be very challenging in this neo-liberal context where our work in feminist anti-violence organizations was often highly constrained by the regulatory demands of state funding. The effects of neo-liberalism on the feminist anti-violence movement are complex and contradictory. While the move to neo-liberal principles of government has meant the divestment of state funding for public services in favor of privatization, it has also meant an increase in regulatory functions of the state and policies that enforce personal responsibility (Bumiller 2008; Richardson 2005). The feminist rationale for state funding of anti-violence services has become modified and transformed by the neo-liberal agenda. There is now a growing presence of the state within many feminist anti-violence organizations and these organizations often function as part of the regulatory apparatus (Bumiller 2008). As a result of these trends, many community-based anti-violence and health programs are burdened by funding requirements in conflict with their feminist philosophy that require an excessive amount of staff time to complete, such as guidelines for professional practice or "outcome measurements" expectations (Bumiller 2008). Ironically, the requirement to *measure* outcomes often comes without sufficient funding to *develop* strong and innovative programs in the first place. Importantly, those of us developing the healthy relationships workshops often spoke of the need for more time to critically reflect about the categories we were constructing, the gaps and limitations produced in the curriculum, and ways to disrupt white and middle-class lesbian norms in the healthy relationships workshops. However, the program was seriously under-funded and there was barely enough time to meet the "deliverables," let alone to reflect on, critique, and revise our work.

Despite our best efforts to disrupt these normative frameworks, I remained concerned that my own and other facilitators' white, and in some cases middle-class, privilege continued to influence the (re)production of hegemonic discourses and social practices in the program. Further, I had an underlying sense that the discourses embedded in the healthy relationships model we were building were homonormative and contributed to the making of the ideal "healthy citizen" of the neo-liberal, colonial nation-state. Like other feminist and queer scholars and activists, I worry that neo-liberal techniques of governance are presented as benign, necessary steps in creating healthy relationships and healthy societies, when in effect they may contribute to increased moral and social regulation. The workshops draw on a normalizing discourse of healthy relationships to counter homophobic constructions of queer relationships as violent and pathological, but in doing so may render white and middle-class queer subjects complicit with processes of nation building (drawing on Riggs 2006: 75).

This exploratory chapter is a response to these concerns and offers some preliminary theorizations of how hegemonic discourses of neo-liberalism, citizenship, homonormativity and whiteness operate through healthy queer relationships discourses.[5] I examine how healthy queer relationships workshops are implicated in processes of normalization and how these contribute to and/or resist forms of social marginalization.[6]

As I write this chapter, I am mindful of the current political context impacting the anti-violence movement in British Columbia, where the provincial government has announced further funding cuts to health and social services, including women's anti-violence services. Given this climate and the dearth of resources for queer and feminist anti-violence work, I am aware my critique could be misused to deny queer rights, eliminate designated services, fuel homo/bi/transphobia and anti-feminist backlash. I want to stress that my intention is not to deny or minimize the positive outcomes of this initiative and others like it. The Safe Choices program has been lauded for its innovative and unique programming, not only within Canada but recently in the UK where scholars and community-based advocates identified it as a "best practice" or "model" for other communities to adopt in their efforts to prevent and respond to same-sex domestic violence. I believe it has helped many women and offers crucially needed violence prevention tools. My interest is not to find fault but rather to examine some of the "pitfalls of well-meaning efforts" (Srivastava 2005: 29)—including my own—and the hegemonic tendencies within strategies deemed to be "health promoting," "innovative" or "anti-oppressive."

The concerns and issues I raise here are not specific to this program or to the anti-violence movement in Vancouver or Canada. They reflect common struggles that confront us, and a historical context of racialized and classed hierarchical power relations within the feminist anti-violence and queer movements in North America. The issues are embedded in a political context where there is a growing and problematic relationship between social movements and the neo-liberal state, contributing to normative conceptions of identity and citizenship that (re)produce social exclusions. I want to highlight the contradictions within normalizing discourses and interrogate my complicity and race and class privilege, with the hope that this investigation contributes to an on-going dialogue among anti-racist and queer feminist activists and scholars who are committed to a politics accountability. In doing this, I recognize the contradictions and dilemmas that come up in reflexive practice where declarations of white reflexivity can unwittingly draw on notions of moral goodness, and want to instead "trouble the possibilities for 'coming clean' in practices of researcher reflexivity" (Lather 2007: 17).

THEORETICAL FRAMEWORK: MAKING NORMAL, TROUBLING NORMAL

In this chapter, I trouble the taken-for-granted meanings and values attached to the category "normal." My analytical approach draws on the work of critical race, queer and feminist scholars influenced by the work of theorist Michel Foucault, who investigate and problematize the processes of normalization and their effects (Adams 1997; Butler 2004; Razack, 2002; Richardson 2005; Ristock 2002). This work examines relations of power and how social regulation and governance shape the making of normal.

According to Foucault (1978, 1984, 1991) power operates within and through the individual ensuring that bodies regulate themselves and one another in relation to a defined norm and through subtle practices of surveillance which produce two kinds of bodies: the normal and abnormal body (Adams 1997; Razack 2002). Foucault's (1991) concept of governmentality describes the way this normalizing power functions through techniques of governance that regulate and manage populations at a distance by relying upon people to govern themselves. Neo-liberalism has been described as a contemporary form of governmentality that deflects attention away from the socio-spatial, economic, and political conditions that produce violence or poor health, and emphasizes personal responsibility for preventing violence and illness through self-help discourses, expert knowledge and expert assistance (Bumiller 2008; Lupton 1999).

Recently a number of queer theorists have begun to critique the emergence of a new social category "the normal gay/lesbian" (Richardson 2005; Seidman 2001), and the homonormative discursive and socio-material practices articulated by gays and lesbians that support rather than resist heteronormative neo-liberal projects (Duggan 2003; Richardson 2005). These scholars are concerned with the way "normalizing social controls assign a moral status of normal and abnormal" to certain conceptions of family, intimate life, sexual acts and desires and subjectivities (Seidman 2001: 326; see also Puar 2007; Richardson 2005; Riggs 2006). As Diane

Richardson (2005) summarizes: "At the heart of neo-liberal responses to homosexuality there is frequently both a (continued) recognition and maintenance of difference and, at the same time, an attempt to disrupt this through the introduction of new policy measures that constitute lesbians and gay men as 'ordinary normal citizens'" (531). As well, homonormative neo-liberal discourses and political formations not only reproduce heteronorms of gender and kinship but national and racial norms as well (Thorpe 2005; Puar 2007; Riggs 2006). In the following analysis of the Safe Choices curriculum, I examine how some queer violence prevention discourses reproduce these troublesome normal/abnormal, irresponsible/degenerate binaries in ways that concurrently reproduce hegemonic forms of subjectivity.

Analysis of the Curriculum: A Discursive Mosaic

Discourses are shifting and unstable. As Foucault argues: "a discourse can be an instrument and an effect of power, but also a hindrance, a stumbling block, a point of resistance and a starting point for an opposing strategy" (Foucault 1978: 101). In my examination of the curriculum, I have identified a "discursive mosaic" (Kiely 2005) or an unstable discursive framework where contradictory discourses can be seen. This reflects both the curriculum writers' and facilitators' recognition of the limitations with existing discourses, as well as their investments in many of them. Various factors influence how discourses are taken up or resisted. Each facilitator brings a unique analysis and approach to the workshops, and their social locations and experiences of privilege and marginalization most probably come to bear on how facilitators' interpret the curriculum. Many women contributed to the workshop development, and the contradictions within may also reflect tensions and disagreements between them/us. It appears that despite falling back on certain normative frameworks that produce limitations and exclusions (which I discuss later), the curriculum is also a welcome departure from other educational materials on lesbian abuse which present a seemingly unified, coherent or universal narrative which does not fit with women's lived experiences (Holmes 2000; Holmes and Ristock 2004).

Feminist Anti-Oppression Philosophy

A "feminist anti-oppression" discourse is evident throughout the curriculum with references to "interlocking oppressions or identities," "multiple locations of oppression," "inclusion" and "diversity." While there are different meanings and effects of these terms, together they function as a discursive strand. The facilitator's manual begins with the philosophy of the Safe Choices program which outlines the program's feminist anti-oppression approach to same-sex/gender relationship abuse. It defines abuse and states that the social contexts of various forms of oppression interconnect and impact an abusive relationship in complex ways.

The curriculum reveals investments in a dominant feminist domestic violence discourse that can have what Foucault would refer to as a homogenizing effect of normalization (1984). For example, the curriculum relies on a power and control model emphasizing a power imbalance in all abusive relationships where the abuser has the power and the victim does not or where "abuse is abuse" (Ristock 2002). It also, however, complicates and challenges normative assumptions. The philosophy challenges hegemonic feminist discourses that take an additive approach to "difference" and argues instead that multiple systems of violence operate simultaneously and depend on one another. It foregrounds "the social context of structural inequality, systemic oppression and power imbalances based on gender, race, ethnicity, sexual orientation, gender identity, ability, age, immigration or refugee status, class and HIV status," as well as forms of abuse that are linked to "exploiting one's societal power by using norms of dominance such as racism, sexism, ableism, classism, anti-semitism and ageism" (BCASVACP 2007: 5). It states that the program "speak[s] out against harmful stereotypes and the scapegoating of communities such as people of colour, First Nations people, the bar crowd, the S/M community, femme/butch couples, transgender and bisexual communities"—groups often stigmatized as inherently "more violent" (6). In addition, by mentioning abusive dynamics that can feel confusing, abusers in one relationship who are also survivors of abuse in previous relationships, complexities of same-sex/gender abuse, and differences between abuse in heterosexual and same-sex/gender relationships, it offers another narrative: there is *not* one universal experience.

These examples show how the program attempts to shift hetero and homonormative feminist thinking about same-sex/gender abuse in new directions, specifically reflecting the influences of anti-racist critiques by feminists of color and Indigenous women over the past two decades (see Crenshaw 1991; Davis 1987; Kanuha 1990, 1996; Razack 1998, 2002; Smith 2004). Janice Ristock's (2002) research has also been influential in that her analysis about violence in lesbian relationships has been instrumental in highlighting problems with normative frameworks.

The philosophy is followed by a section that discusses how language is political and both shapes and reflects identity. It challenges notions of stable, static and universal knowledge and identities, and instead explains in non-academic terms how ideas, knowledge and identities are socially and historically constructed, fluid and changing. It stresses the importance of facilitators problematizing language and its implications for inclusion and exclusion:

The terms individuals and communities use to describe them/ourselves are informed by our age, gender, race, ethnicity, geography, etc. Language and meaning evolve as individuals, communities and social movements change. For example in recent years queer has been reclaimed from its oppressive origins and reclaimed as an expression of power and pride. However this does not mean that all members of the LGB and T communities will feel comfortable using or even identify with this term. Analyzing the language we use reveals the complexities of experience, history, politics and power that shape the meaning of the terms and concepts we use to think about identities and same-sex/gender relationships abuse. At Safe Choices we use same-sex AND same-gender to talk about relationships abuse because sometimes the two people in the relationship may NOT identify as the same gender, but identify as the same sex, or they may identify as the same gender but NOT the same sex. (BCASVACP 2007, Introduction: 7)

The example given is the use of gendered pronouns and the way they can impact bisexual women and transgender participants. It addresses a universalizing tendency within "LGBT" anti-violence models and approaches, where categories of gender and sexual orientation are often conflated which not only leads to confusion but also the erasure or marginalization of transgender experiences of violence (White and Goldberg 2006). This is a change from previous feminist educational discourses about lesbian abuse which have tended toward a rigidified analysis that relies on essentialist constructs (Holmes and Ristock 2004). Yet, there are contradictory discourses about identity within the curriculum where we see a reliance on many binary oppositions (male/female, lesbian/heterosexual, white lesbians/lesbians of color) all the while trying to foreground the multiplicity, fluidity and socially constructed nature of language and identity.

Through the language used, and in the examples of relationship scenarios, most of the workshops still privilege a non-trans lesbian identity. While the curriculum states that the healthy relationships workshops are inclusive of people who identify as transgender, this was a point of confusion for many workshop facilitators and transgender participants over the years. There were many times when trans-identified participants—specifically those who identified as gender queer, female-to-male (FTM) or neither male nor female—indicated they did not feel the workshops were inclusive or responsive to their identity and experiences. In a recent attempt to address this, the following was added to the philosophy statement: "we attempt to make our healthy relationships workshops trans inclusive. This means that women who are in relationship with a trans partner, trans couples, MTF (male-to-female) and FTM (female-to-male) trans people as well as people who identify as intersex are welcome" (BCASVACP 2007: 6–7). Examples, however, that address the very diverse experiences of these groups are on the whole, absent in the healthy relationships curriculum.[7]

Similarly, homogenizing and tokenistic inclusion strategies adopted by some facilitators in workshops to address bisexual women's experiences produced the very exclusionary effects they ostensibly set out to contest. Surprisingly, although the curriculum reminds facilitators that "our attempts to be inclusive [must] be reflected in practice as well as language, i.e. we want to avoid adding on other identities (such as trans) but not offering a curriculum that explores and addresses the unique issues trans folks face" (BCASVACP 2007, 8), this was mostly not the case because the content and examples are based primarily in non-trans lesbian experience. This example shows how an intellectual understanding about the problems with tokenistic inclusion strategies does not necessarily translate into an understanding of how to change practice. I now look at the way this anti-oppression philosophy addresses racial identities where similar issues surface.

Good Non-Racist Feminists

The discussion about language in the curriculum is followed by a section on the strengths and limitations of the program, which acknowledges shortcomings and encourages critical reflection for facilitators. It addresses how the program is innovative and the only program of its kind in Canada with on-going funding. It also notes that participants' feedback indicate that the program is meeting many community needs. It recognizes the combined efforts and knowledge of many queer women involved in the program's development, making special note of "the important contributions of women of colour and Aboriginal women" as advisory committee members, workshop participants and facilitators (BCASVACP 2007: 9). This is followed by the program's limitations where it states: "However, we also recognize that the majority of the workshops' curriculum has been produced and delivered by white middle-class non-disabled North American women working from within an anti-oppression lens and viewing the curriculum with an understanding of the intersectionality of all oppressions. More work is needed to increase the content to reflect the experiences and to honor the leadership of women of colour, Aboriginal women, low-income women, immigrant women and women with disabilities" (BCASVACP 2007: 9). A few pages later, there is a statement encouraging facilitators to expand the analysis, raise questions, and problematize ideas, emphasizing: "we are particularly interested in expanding the notes section in ways that reflect our commitment to provide inclusive, anti-oppressive workshops that reflect an understanding of the intersectionality of identities and the interlocking nature of oppressions" (9).

These statements could be seen as a "responsible" move to make whiteness, and other forms of dominance, visible—marking and destabilizing norms which are naturalized and made invisible. The emphasis is on the good intentions of the privileged subjects who "mean well." While different axes of identity are mentioned, I want to draw specific attention to racialized discourses and the way confessional narratives of good intentions, function in feminist discourses to recite and secure the dominance of white subjects. The program is represented as "meeting many needs" and yet anxieties about white racism—that there are women who are excluded, not having their needs met—appears in the narrative with the mention of women of color and Aboriginal women.

Anti-racist scholars argue that "whiteness gets produced through being declared" (Ahmed 2004: 12), and that these moves often mask other motivations, such as white feminist subjects' emotional attachments to innocence and to seeing ourselves as good non-racist feminists (Ahmed 2004; (Fellows and Razack 1998; Srivastava 2005). Discourses of benevolence and "good intentions" have been a historical foundation of whiteness (Riggs 2004; Srivastava 2005). While there is a recognition of gaps in curriculum content and related power imbalances in the production of knowledge, the declaration of explicitly naming the dominant subjects as "anti-oppressive" and "with a lens of intersectionality," works as a redemption discourse and further asserts our/their dominance—we cannot really be blamed for any exclusions or on-going oppression because our intentions were/are good. Here, as Sarah Ahmed (2004) explains in relation to whiteness, admitting racism or declaring whiteness does not represent evidence of anti-racist practice. Anti-oppression can become a matter of making dominant "anti-oppressive" subjects "feel better" about their dominance or the exclusions produced through it (33). Clearly, these declarations of privilege do not function merely as descriptions, but can also work as confessionals that recite the dominance of white, middle-class, able-bodied women. I argue that this example in the curriculum functions in this way despite its claims to do the opposite.

Intersectional Identities

Informed by feminist anti-oppression philosophy, efforts are made in the curriculum to contest and complicate universalist discourses that construct queer women's identity around race, class, age, and ability privilege, although to varying degrees and success. For example, a section on workshop planning offers guidelines for facilitators:

> Think about how race, immigration, ethnicity, class, ability, gender identity, sexuality, age, health, having children, homophobia and heterosexism, racism, colonization, sexism, ableism, ageism, classism, past or present substance use, and other factors impact our relationships as queer women and abuse. For example: fears of calling police because of the homophobia and racism of the legal system, or because you don't have your landed status yet; fears that no-one will believe you because your partner is a disability rights, feminist anti-violence or anti-racist activist, etc.; your partner's emotional abuse includes racist and ableist comments. (BCASVACP 2007)

There are also attempts to apply this analysis in a workshop on communication and conflict. In the workshop *After the Honeymoon: Healthy*

Communication and Problem-Solving, the narrative states that "styles and meaning of non-verbal communication vary tremendously across culture, class, gender, age, etc." and that health, extended family responsibilities, money, children, immigration and racism (among other factors) can impact a couple's communication (BCASVACP 2007). Likewise, the section on conflict instructs facilitators to "introduce this section by acknowledging that gender, class, race, culture, ability, family of origin, our own disposition and other factors such as stereotyping influence how we deal with and respond to conflict" (BCASVACP 2007). Yet importantly, there is no discussion of *how* these factors influence communication. The lack of language and theory about power differences based on class, race and ability in intimate lesbian relationships has made it very difficult to resolve conflicts and build healthy and just lesbian relationships (Kadi 1993). The curriculum reflects an awareness of this reality but the analysis is not fully integrated into the workshop content, which can inadvertently produce a universal subject whose life is not impacted by racism, classism, poverty, and ableism.

Thus, points of resistance and contestation to universalist discourses show up in the curriculum reflecting contradictions that produce a wider range of subjectivities than in the earlier educational discourses on lesbian abuse produced in the 1990s (Holmes 2009). I remain concerned, however, that a discourse of intersectionality or anti-oppression can mask a racist liberal "inclusion" or additive approach to addressing race/racism by white women, where issues of power are ignored (or discussed but not acted upon or changed) and where women of color are "needed" so as not to appear white. Often in these tokenizing "inclusion" efforts (perhaps now framed as "anti-oppression" efforts) queer women of color and Two-Spirit women are acknowledged without deconstructing the constructs that maintain white privilege and changing institutional norms and power relations.

As feminists, we must examine how feminist "anti-oppression" discourses are used by dominant subjects; are they mobilized to abdicate responsibility, as a way of "coming clean" and maintaining power, or do they help us address hierarchical power relations between women, create greater accountability and activate organizational change? We must examine the contemporary manifestations of historical constructions of racial innocence in feminist anti-violence organizing and be prepared to look at some of the problematic effects of well-meaning feminist anti-oppression efforts and make necessary changes (Srivastava 2005).

Expert Knowledge—Psychology and Health Promotion Discourses

In addition to feminist anti-oppression and anti-violence discourses, the workshops draw on psychology and health promotion discourses. These disciplines promote activities that can be identified as strategies of governmentality in the ways they construct and regulate the population through systems of knowledge (Foucault 1991), and produce health promotion and psychology experts who provide their knowledge "directed at improving individuals' health through self-regulation" (Lupton 1995: 10). Neo-liberal trends in responding to sexual and domestic violence emphasize a normative vision of professionalized service providers with specialized expertise to diagnose, treat and prevent sexual/domestic violence (Bumiller 2008). This has lead to defining the problem of violence through public health discourses of surveillance and expanded forms of expert psychological knowledge about, and programming for, women who have been victimized (Bumiller 2008).

The healthy relationships workshops begin by challenging this dominant neo-liberal discourse of expert knowledge that positions mental health, social service, criminal justice, and educational professionals as experts and in relations of power over "users" or "consumers" of services. The guide states: "Explain that you are not experts. Acknowledge that everyone in the room has experience and knowledge and that one of your goals is to make sure there are lots of opportunities for them to share some of it with one another. Add that you're there to facilitate and share some information and ideas about strengthening our relationships" (BCASVACP 2007). Further, the curriculum includes exercises that validate the participants' knowledge base, creating opportunities for collective knowledge production and problem solving. This was a deliberate move to contest professionalization and the resulting individualist models of many health and social service approaches that diminish the significance of collective self-help that has been a foundation of grassroots feminist anti-violence philosophy (Bumiller 2008).

Despite this, the discourses that inform and shape the facilitators' practice- social work, counseling psychology and education- position them hierarchically in relation to the participants. Deeply classed and raced psychological and social work discourses (including some that are "feminist") are extremely significant in the way in which one social group or class "comes to be responsible, often as professionals, for the moral regulation of the other" (Walkerdine 1996: 357). Individual facilitators may have different degrees of attachment to these expert discourses and questions remain as to what extent in practice they encourage participants to critically examine and challenge knowledge and taken-for-granted truth claims. Discourses of empowerment, critical pedagogy, and community development often mask the investments of "public health professionals in persuading groups to develop 'skills' and 'exercise control' over their lives" (Lupton 1995: 59–60). These so-called emancipatory discourses have been "absorbed into the complex bureaucratic network of public health" with increased focus on techniques of self-surveillance and control (76). Through government-funded health promotion programs the state functions as the facilitator shaping the health of the community, and in a neo-liberal context they ensure that citizens are healthy in order to promote productivity. Safe Choices is positioned in this way—emphasizing its role assisting queer women to develop skills to improve their health. While the program's feminist philosophy tries to contest these discourses, contradictions can be seen in the curriculum's narrative.

In the healthy relationships workshops, new information is offered after participants generate their own individual and collective knowledge. Nevertheless, information is presented from key texts written by psychologists-some of whom are lesbian and feminist- who are recognized as experts in the field. Although various feminist and queer/lesbian resources are recommended at the beginning of the curriculum, it is material from *No More Secrets: Violence in Lesbian Relationships* (Ristock 2002), *Lesbian Couples: A Guide to Creating Healthy Relationships* (Clunis and Green 2005), *The Seven Principles for Making Marriage Work* (Gottman and Silver 1999),[8] and material from psychologist Brent Atkinson (2003) that are most prevalent in the workshop content for two of the workshops on healthy communication and separateness and togetherness.[9] Most references to research in these modules refer to the work of Gottman and Atkinson.[10] Thus, while expert knowledge is seemingly eschewed by the curriculum, on closer examination, it is evident that the research of experts in psychology is privileged by the program.

Additionally, although beyond the scope of this chapter, my analysis of Gottman and Atkinson's work thus far reveals a de-gendered, de-raced, de-classed analysis of (predominantly) heterosexual couples, when this work is used in the curriculum, the diverse socio-cultural contexts of queer women's relationships recede or disappear with references to generic couples. I argue that by applying this material in this way, the unintended result was the reproduction of some of the hegemonic assumptions we were seeking to disrupt. As I show in the following section, this reliance on psychological, as well as health promotion, knowledge in the healthy queer relationships workshops is problematic in that it serves to reproduce normalcy.

Healthy Subjects = Normal Subjects?

The disciplines of psychology and health promotion play a role in governmentality through the (re)production of normalizing discourses that are racialized, classed, and heteronormatively gendered (Gleason 2003; Riggs and Augoustinos 2005; Walkerdine 1996). These discourses (re)produce binary oppositions between healthy/unhealthy or civilized/uncivilized subjects. We come to understand what constitutes a "healthy" (and/or "normal") self in part through comparisons between the self and "unhealthy" (and/or "abnormal") others (Lupton 1995). These disciplines rely on liberal individualist discourses that emphasize health as an individual and moral responsibility, which has a depoliticizing effect (George and Rail 2006). In addition, they are premised on a generic model of subjectivity, which constructs the subject as autonomous, rational, self-regulated, controlled, individualized, and civilized (Cermele, Daniels and Anderson 2001; Lupton 1995; Riggs 2007). The white able-bodied bourgeois heterosexual masculine body is valued as most closely conforming to this idea of the civilized body (Sibley 1995). Generic models of subjectivity rely on an additive approach to difference which misses how different axes of identity are connected and hierarchical. For example, these discourses position whiteness as an indicator of health (Cermele et al. 2001; George and Rail 2006; Riggs 2007).

In developing the Safe Choices curriculum we sought to disrupt generic and additive models of subjectivity and construct a queer subject whose experiences of abuse and health were shaped by many interconnected factors and social systems. Yet, many taken-for-granted "truths" show up in the curriculum, which do present a neo-liberal individualist discourse. In all of the healthy relationship workshops and in many of the handouts there are references to the importance of "self-care" and "taking responsibility for your own feelings and behaviour and needs" (BCASVACP 2007). In Foucauldian terms these could be described as psychological "technologies of the self" such as self-esteem, self-knowledge, and self-discipline. Most (heterosexual) relationship self-help manuals are based on the "notion of social obligation in that technologies of the self such as self-discipline and self-knowledge are the 'right', or ethical, thing to take on, not only for the sake of the self, but for one's partner and for the wider society. By prescribing what is emotionally 'right' or 'healthy' for the individual they also provide a picture of how healthy relationships between individuals should be conducted, and the healthy society that would result" (Hazelden 2003: 425). These neo-liberal individualist discourses produce effective healthy citizens who are self-regulating and who can take care of themselves, rather than subjects that are interdependent and relational (Hazelden 2003; Kiely 2005).

Similarly, neo-liberal approaches to violence against women promote individualistic strategies of problem solving rather than those that rely on more complex understandings of the multiple forms of domination and violence in women's private and public lives (Bumiller 2008). In social work and public health literature this discourse focuses on how "women need to be trained to make better choices" so that they can have a "normal, non-violent family" (84).

Once again, the Safe Choices healthy relationships curriculum is contradictory in its up take and resistance to these discourses. References to self-care and taking responsibility for one's self, feelings and needs are consistently combined with discourses of relationality, accountability, mutuality, community, interdependency, and a social context of hierarchical power relations. All of the workshops emphasize the importance of the individual's connectedness to community and a number of them address the complex role and significance of extended family in queer women's lives, including responsibilities to and/or loss of extended family and "chosen family" in the context of a heteronormative, homophobic and racist culture.

One example of a discourse of community connection and accountability is the workshop *Mind Your Own Business, Don't Air Our Dirty Laundry: Talking About Relationship Concerns with Friends and Family*. The workshop speaks to the silence about partner abuse in many queer communities, and the reality that many queer women who have been in abusive same-sex/gender relationships are more likely to talk with a friend or family member about the abuse, than anti-violence, health care or social service providers (Ristock 2002). As a departure from neo-liberal discourses of self-help or expert knowledge, the workshop seeks to increase the capacity of friends and queer communities to strategize and problem solve together about relationship violence. The workshop examines how "community values" play a role in supporting, condoning, or preventing abuse and sustaining healthy queer relationships. It encourages critical thinking about discourses of shame, privacy, and accountability and promotes collective dialogue about ways queer women can support values that foster safe, strong, healthy, accountable, and non-violent relationships and communities.

This discourse clearly challenges neo-liberal individualist discourses by emphasizing interdependency, collective power, social and communal responsibility, and accountability. The regulatory power of the state-funded health promotion model, however, and the neo-liberal techniques of governance it produces, may limit and constrain the potential of this discussion to move in more radical or transformative ways. As well, even when there is attention to interdependency and relationality, neo-liberal technologies of the self (self-esteem, self-care, and self-improvement) can still function to privatize and individualize socio-economic and political issues (such as poverty, racism, and violence). I also wonder how, as a technology of governance, the workshop may unwittingly encourage queer subjects to monitor and regulate one another.

Neo-liberal discourses also "promote a narrow kind of sexual subjectivity which obscures sexual pleasure and desire" (Kiely 2005: 254). Heteronormative neo-liberal discourses pathologize queer sexuality and promote heterosexual sex within the confines of marriage only, while homonormative ones desexualize queer identity in order to promote a responsiblized, respectable homosexual citizen (Richardson 2005; Seidman 2002). As well, normative discourses about lesbians erase the possibility of sexual assault within lesbian relationships.

Interestingly, Safe Choices' *Sexuality, Intimacy and Desire* workshop offers a counter-hegemonic discourse that troubles these normative narratives. The goals are to help women develop a language to talk about sex, intimacy, and desire in queer women's relationships, to identify the socio-cultural "messages we receive about our sexuality" from "dominant society and lesbian/queer communities," to understand some of the barriers to talking about sex, these issues and strengthen communication skills when talking about sexuality (BCASVACP 2007). This workshop also addresses the topics of consent and boundaries and provides information and discussion about sexual assault in women's same-sex/gender relationships.

Evident here are deconstructive strategies that provide opportunities to examine discourses influencing our sexuality and desires. The narrative disrupts neo-liberal normalizing techniques that assign a moral status of normal and abnormal to queer sexual acts and desires (Seidman 2001), with discussion of a wide range of issues such as polyamorous and non-monogamous relationships; butch/femme; transgender and bisexual experiences; sexual practices such as masturbation, S/M, and the use of sex toys; erotica/porn; and social factors such as racism, aging, health issues, and disability. A queer feminist discourse of desire is combined with a discourse of relationality, ethics, and accountability to self and one's sexual partner(s). These non-normative sexual discourses, however, fade in some of the other workshops in the curriculum. Given that the workshops are not offered sequentially and that women do not necessarily attend them all, these non-normative discourses of sexuality and desire remain marginal which could have the effect of promoting a desexualized queer subject in the rest of the curriculum.

CONCLUSION

In this chapter, my concern has been to examine the extent to which the Safe Choices healthy queer relationships workshops rely on and reinforce normative frameworks and neo-liberal discourses and technologies of governance. My examination reveals many contradictions within the curriculum's discursive framework. The workshops both resist and reproduce some of the neo-liberal discourses of professionalization, expert knowledge, individualism, and narrow approaches to responding to violence. Neo-liberal self-help discourses are evident in the workshops but integrated with relational, communitarian, and social discourses to varying degrees. As well, the curriculum destabilizes narrow neo-liberal models of subjectivity that desexualize queer women. A discourse of intersectionality and anti-oppression challenges universalism, however it functions in complex and contradictory ways—to complicate generic models of subjectivity and relationship violence in some cases, but also to reinscribe them most often through white feminist moves of dominance. The presence of discourses of benevolence and racial innocence ("being good nonracist feminists") position white queer women not only as the norm but also as "benevolent helpers" to racialized others.

This exploration raises a number of areas for future research, education and organizing work. Clearly there are different levels of engagement with neo-liberal agendas (Richardson 2005), and the contradictions in the Safe Choices program reveal this. These discourses and techniques of governance, however, are insidious and their normalizing power is often secured through common-sense language.

The limited funds and excessive state monitoring of the program greatly impacted our capacity to invest resources in curriculum development, facilitator training, mentoring and grassroots community organizing. While queer anti-violence initiatives need stable financial resources to accomplish their work, I am also mindful of how a reliance on state funding can create increased surveillance of social movements, thus constraining our ability to challenge racist, classist and (hetero)sexist state policies and practices. My analysis is similar to the critique of the Non-Profit Industrial Complex by Incite! Women of Colour Against Violence Against Women (2007; Russo and Spatz, 2007) which highlights the regulatory state structures and systems that non-profit organizations must follow and that regulate and constrain our social justice work. I do not see simple or easy answers to the dilemmas and questions raised about the impacts of state funding and neo-liberal ideologies on the LGBT and anti-violence movements. But as anti-violence and queer activists, we must engage with one another in a critical dialogue about some of these paradoxes and pitfalls with our reliance on state funding and explore creative strategies for transformation of social movements that resist processes of bureaucratization. This also requires looking at the role of the state in perpetrating violence and the forms of state violence in queer women's lives.

We need to exercise caution about the development of "best practice models" given the growing alliance between feminist anti-violence and LGBTQ organizations and the neo-liberal state. While developing these tools can be helpful in sharing knowledge and encouraging consistency, neo-liberal trends suggest that best practice models and educational tools can become techniques of governance and contribute to rigidified and universalist analyses that perpetuate normative constructions and exclusions. Similarly, we must continue to resist the professionalization of social movements, instead encouraging collective peer resource and community mobilizing strategies as well as on-going dialogue and critically reflexive dialogue about the values guiding our choices and how these expert and professional discourses shape our violence and health prevention efforts within non-profit organizations. As well we need to examine the way these discourses produce us as dominant normative queer and feminist subjects and ask how we are accountable to marginalized communities struggling for social justice. In these collective and self-reflexive efforts we need to move away from a moral and regulating stance and keep focused instead on an ethical stance (Ristock 2002: 170). A strength in the Safe Choices curriculum is the frequency with which the narrative reminds facilitators to think critically about the inclusions and exclusions produced through language, how it foregrounds the social construction of knowledge and is grounded in popular education philosophy. But the "critical" language we use can lend itself to the same techniques of governance that we critique (Ahmed 2004: 9), and as programs become more established, often popular education strategies and philosophy fade as facilitators fall back on more familiar and state-supported social service models. For dominant feminist and queer subjects, this stresses the importance of staying implicated in what we critique, attending to our responsibility and accountability, while at the same time, moving away from a focus on ourselves as hegemonic (white, middle-class, able-bodied) subjects (59).

Queer anti-violence strategies need to place the experiences of women of color, Indigenous women and low-income women at the centre, rather than focusing on increased accessibility or specific multicultural programs (Smith 2004). This requires addressing institutional power and hierarchical relations within feminist and LGBT organizations and widening the circle of power and opportunity. It also means working on grassroots political issues that are not typically defined by white and middle-class queers and feminists as "queer anti-violence issues". For example, community organizing with queer women around issues such as welfare cuts, racist immigration policies, on-going struggles for Indigenous sovereignty, police violence, or the structural violence imbedded in the live-in caregiver program in Canada. Similarly, queer anti-violence prevention initiatives could focus resources on strengthening relationships and alliances with grassroots groups working on these issues. The Safe Choices program did participate in events surrounding many of these issues, however the requirement to meet the programs' "deliverables and outcomes" often meant there was little space to expand in new ways and the focus became service delivery (workshops) despite a desire to work from a social justice and community-organizing framework.

My analysis of the healthy queer relationship curriculum suggests that we bring greater attention to how "health" as a category is never neutral, universal or inherently good, and the way healthy relationships are constructed through various normalizing discourses. This requires greater understanding of which models of "health" and "family" are sanctioned by the neo-liberal and colonial state and whether our anti-violence prevention and health promotion efforts destabilize or prop up white and middle-class nationalist agendas. It means resisting trends towards white middle-class homonormative relationship models and (re)envisioning the many ways queer women *can* and *do* form non-violent and ethical intimate relationships. We can focus on promoting ideas about subjectivity, health and citizenship that are not only relational, but that further stress the interconnections of the socio-economic and political contexts of queer women's lives and the way these contexts shape our understandings of queer women's health, relationships and violence through normalizing frames.

NOTES

1. Acknowledgments: I would like to thank Anne Fleming, David Jefferess, Deborah McPhail, Janice Ristock and Caroline White for helpful feedback. Thanks also to those at Safe Choices, including but not limited to

228   *Cindy Holmes*

Christina Antoniuk, Susan Armstrong, Norine Braun, Cheyene Dyer, Lydia Kwa, Donna Lee, Tracy Porteous, Deborah Prieur, Sally Shamai and Caroline White. Appreciation to Christina Antoniuk, Sarah Leavitt and Angela McDougall for their early vision and efforts to secure funding. I would also like to acknowledge the Vancouver Coastal Health Authority for their funding commitment to Safe Choices and to the Social Science and Humanities Research Council of Canada (SSHRC) and the SVR Research Team (Sexual and Gender Diversity: Vulnerability and Resiliency) funded by the Canadian Institute for Health Research (CIHR) for supporting my work.

2. Safe Choices: Support and Education Program is a program of The Ending Violence Association of BC which was formerly known as the BC Association of Specialized Victim Assistance and Counselling Programs. This program is funded by the Vancouver Coastal Health Authority. In addition to service provider training and healthy relationships workshops, it provides referrals, consultation, resource development, and facilitator training.
3. The program was developed in 2002 and expanded over six years. In 2008 a facilitator's manual was produced.
4. Referrals to counseling services are offered to women wanting additional support, however there are few appropriate affordable services. As a result, capacity building and training for existing service providers is an important component of the program. Using a co-facilitation model, the workshop activities include information sharing, self-reflection exercises, and large and small group discussions. Unlike most anti-violence groups, these workshops do not include an intake process to assess dynamics of abuse or victim/perpetrator roles.
5. My focus is not the curriculum writers and facilitators themselves, but rather the discourses and the way they constitute us as subjects. That being said, I do not view subjects as passive or un-implicated in the statements we produce through discourse.
6. While I view systems of oppression as interlocking, this chapter focuses primarily on sexuality, gender, and race with a limited discussion of class. My analysis about normative frameworks and their exclusions could also be applied to (dis)ability and age.
7. The only exception is the workshop on *Sexuality, Intimacy and Desire* which integrates an analysis of trans experiences within same-sex/gender relationships more than the other workshops, reflecting the analysis of a specific facilitator and curriculum developer—Caroline White—who is also active as an ally in the trans movement.
8. Gottman's work is used widely by family and marriage therapists and he is currently conducting a research project on Creating Healthy Relationships funded by the U.S. government (Gottman 2009).
9. These workshops were offered more often than others based on requests by participants.
10. The exception is the Sexuality workshop which includes references to research on lesbian sex as background resources for facilitators.

REFERENCES

Adams, M. L. 1997. *The trouble with normal: Postwar youth and the making of heterosexuality.* Toronto: University of Toronto Press.
Ahmed, S. 2004. Declarations of whiteness: The non-performativity of anti-racism. *Borderlands e-journal* 3(2). Available at: http://www.borderlands.net.au/vol3no2_2004/ahmed_declarations.htm [accessed November 6, 2010].

Atkinson, B. 2008. Core differences in ways of maintaining emotional stability. The Couples Clinic. Available at: http://www.thecouplesclinic.com/resources [accessed November 26, 2010].

BCASVACP. 2007. *Safe choices: Support and education program healthy relationships curriculum.* Vancouver: BC Association of Specialized Victim Assistance and Counselling Programs.

Bumiller, K. 2008. *In an abusive state: How neo-liberalism appropriated the feminist movement against sexual violence.* Durham: Duke University Press.

Butler, J. 2002. *Undoing gender.* New York: Routledge.

Cermele, C., S. Daniels and K. Anderson. 2001. Defining normal: Constructions of race and gender in the DSM-IV casebook. *Feminism & Psychology* 112): 229–247.

Chung, C. and S. Lee. 2002. *Raising our voices: Queer Asian women's response to relationship violence.* San Francisco: Family Violence Prevention Fund.

Clunis, M. D. and D. G. Green. 2005. *Lesbian couples: A guide to creating healthy relationships.* Emeryville, CA: Seal Press.

Crenshaw, K. 1991. Mapping the margins: Intersectionality, identity politics, and violence against women of color. *Stanford Law Review* 43(6): 1241–1299.

Davis, A. 1987. *Violence against women and the ongoing challenge to racism.* Latham, NY: Kitchen Table Women of Color Press.

Dua, E. 2003. Towards theorizing the connections between governmentality, imperialism, race and citizenship: Indian migrants and racialisation of Canadian citizenship. In *Making normal: Social regulation in Canada*, ed. D. Brock, 4062. Scarborough: Nelson Thomson.

Duggan, L. 2002. The new homonormativity: The sexual politics of neo-liberalism. In *Materializing democracy: Toward a revitalized cultural politics*, ed. R. Castonovo and D. Nelsonds, 175–194. Durham: Duke University Press.

Fellows, M.L. and S. Razack. 1998. The race to innocence: Confronting hierarchical relations among women. *Journal of Gender, Race and Justice* 1(2): 335–352.

Foucault, M. 1978. *The history of sexuality.* New York: Random House.

———. 1984. *The Foucault reader.* Ed. P. Rabinow. New York: Pantheon Books.

———. 1991. Governmentality. In *The Foucault effect: Studies in governmentality*, ed. G. Burchell, C. Gordon and P. Miller, 87–104. London: Harvester Wheatsheaf.

George, T. and G. Rail. 2006. Barbie meets the bindi: Discursive constructions of health among young south-Asian Canadian women. *Journal of Women's Health & Urban Life* 4(2): 45–67.

Gleason, M. 2003. Constructing Normal: Psychology and the Canadian Family, 1945–1960. In *Making Normal: Social Regulation In Canada.* Ed. D. Brock, 104–120. Toronto: Thomson Nelson Publishing.

Goldberg, D. T. 2009. The threat of race: Reflections on racial neo-liberalism. Malden, MA: Wiley-Blackwell.

Gottman, J. 2009. Healthy Relationships Research Project. Available at: http://www.gottman.com/research/projects/ [accessed November 12, 2010].

Gottman, J. and N. Silver. 1999. *The seven principles for making marriage work.* New York: Three Rivers Press.

Hazelden, R. 2003. Love yourself: The relationship of the self with itself in popular self-help manuals. *Journal of Sociology* 39: 413–428.

Holmes, C. and J. L. Ristock. 2004. Exploring discursive constructions of lesbian abuse: Looking inside and out. In *Survivor rhetoric: Negotiations and narrativity in abused women's language,* ed. C. Shearer-Cremean and Carol L. Winklemann, 94–119. Toronto: University of Toronto Press.

Holmes, C. 2009. Destabilizing homonormativity and the public/private divide in lesbian domestic violence discourses. *Gender, Place and Culture* 16(1): 77–96.

Incite! Women of color against violence, ed. 2006. *Color of violence: The incite! anthology.* Cambridge, MA: South End Press.

Kadi, J. 1993. Love, space aliens and politics. In *Sister/stranger: Lesbians loving across the lines*, ed. J. Hardy, 93–106. Pittsburgh: Sidewalk Revolution Press.

Kanuha, V. 1990. Compounding the triple jeopardy: Battering in lesbian of colour relationships. In *Confronting lesbian battering: A manual for the battered women's movement*, ed. P. Elliot, 142–157. St. Paul: Minnesota Coalition for Battered Women.

———. 1996. Domestic violence, racism and the battered women's movement in the United States. In *Future interventions with battered women and their families*, ed. J. Edleson and Z. C. Eisikovits, 34–50. Thousand Oaks, CA: Sage Publications.

Kiely, E. 2005. Where is the discourse of desire? Deconstructing the Irish Relationships and Sexuality Education (RSE) resource materials. *Irish Educational Studies* 24(2–3): 253–266.

Kinsman, G. 1996. *The regulation of desire.* Montreal: Black Rose Books.

———. 2003. National security as moral regulation: Making the normal and the deviant in security campaigns against gay men and lesbians. In *Making normal: Social regulation in Canada*, ed. D. Brock, 121–145. Scarborough: Nelson Thomson.

Lather, P. 2007. *Getting lost: Feminist efforts toward a double(d) science.* New York: SUNY Press.

Lupton, D. 1995. *The imperative of health: Public health and the regulated body.* London: Sage.

Northwest Network. 2008. Relationships skills class. Seattle Northwest Network. Available at: http://www.nwnetworkweb.org/news.php [accessed November 1, 2008].

Puar, J. K. 2007. *Terrorist assemblages: Homonationalism in queer times.* Durham: Duke University Press.

Razack, S. 1998. *Looking white people in the eye: Gender, race, and culture in courtrooms and classrooms.* Toronto: University of Toronto Press.

———. 2002. When place becomes race. In *Race, space and the law: Unmapping a white settler society*, ed. S. Razack, 1–20. Toronto: Between the Lines Press.

Richardson, D. 2005. Desiring sameness? The rise of a neo-liberal politics of normalization. *Antipode* 37(3): 515–535.

Riggs, D. W. 2004. Benevolence and the management of stake: On being "good white people." *Philament: A Journal of the Arts and Culture* 4. Available at: http://www.arts.usyd.edu/publications/philament/issue4_Critique_htm. [accessed November 26, 2010].

———. 2006. *Priscilla, (white) queen of the desert: Queer rights/race privilege.* New York: Peter Lang.

———. 2007. Queer theory and its future in psychology: Exploring issues of race privilege. *Social and Personality Psychology Compass* 1: 1–14.

Riggs, D. W. and M. Augoustinos. 2005. The psychic life of colonial power: Racialised subjectivities, bodies and methods. *Journal of Community and Applied Social Psychology* 16: 445–467.

Ristock, Janice L. 2002. *No more secrets: Violence in lesbian relationships.* New York: Routledge.

Ristock, Janice L. and Norma Timbang. 2005. Relationship violence in lesbian/gay/bisexual/transgender/queer [LGBTQ] communities: Moving beyond a gender-based framework. Minnesota Center against Violence and Abuse: Violence against Women Online Resources. Available at: http://www.mincava.umn.edu/documents/lgbtqviolence/lgbtqviolence.html [accessed November 1, 2008].

Seidman, S. 2001. From identity to queer politics: Shifts in normative heterosexuality and the meaning of citizenship. *Citizenship Studies* 5(3): 321–328.

————. 2002. *Beyond the closet: The transformation of gay and lesbian life.* Routledge: New York.

Smith, A. 2004. Beyond the politics of inclusion: Violence against women of colour and human rights. *Meridians: feminism, race and transnationalism* 4(2): 120–124.

Srivastava, S. 2005. You're calling me a racist? The moral and emotional regulation of anti-racism and feminism. *Signs: Journal of women and culture in society* 31(1): 29–62.

Thobani, S. 2007. *Exalted subjects: Studies in the making of race and nation in Canada.* Toronto: University of Toronto Press.

Thorpe, J. 2003. Redrawing national boundaries: Gender, race, class and same-sex marriage discourse in Canada. *Canadian Woman Studies* 24(2/3): 15–21.

US Department of Health and Human Services. 2009. Benefits of healthy marriages. Washington: Administration for Children and Families. Available at: http://www.healthymarriageinfo.org/docs/ACFGuideto09.pdf [accessed November 10, 2010].

Vancouver Coastal Health Authority 2008. The smart approach to healthcare. http://www.smartfund.ca/docs/smart_approach.pdf. [accessed November 26, 2008].

Walkerdine, V. 1996. Subjectivity and social class: New directions for feminist psychology. *Feminism and psychology* 6(3): 355–360.

White, C. and J. Goldberg. 2006. Expanding our understanding of gendered violence: Violence against trans people and their loved ones. *Canadian Women's Studies* 25(1/2): 124–127.

Yakush, J. H. 2008. *Legalized discrimination: The rise of the marriage- promotion industry and how federally funded programs discriminate against lesbian, gay, bisexual, and transgender youth and families.* New York: SEICUS (Sexuality Information and Education Council of the United States) Public Policy Office.

12 Documenting the Same Sex Abuse Project, Toronto, Canada

Patricia Durish

Over the past two decades, there has been a great deal of organizing around the issue of Same Sex Partner Abuse in Toronto. The focus of this activism has been on raising public awareness within the LGBTQ community and beyond, as well as on improving service providers' understanding of, and response to, this issue. Unfortunately, as with many issues pertaining to marginalized communities, the paucity of funding has meant that for every grant won to study and organize around same sex partner abuse, there follows a few fallow years. As a result, each new project tends, necessarily, to replicate rather than build on the knowledge gained by the project that went before. For example, the majority of projects that I am aware of, both past and present, have been primarily concerned with producing public education resources, brochures and posters. Funds are rarely available to go beyond this initial stage to focus on research, documenting clinical interventions, and so on. Every few years, subsequent funding is made available for the further production of public education resources. Much of the first year at the David Kelley Services (DKS) project was spent developing a set of brochures to replace the brochure and posters that had been produced during two prior rounds of funding.[1] In my experience, this appears to be a result of a complex set of influences including funding constraints, a lack of vision on the part of administrators, and the absence of a network connecting activists across geographical distance. The project that this chapter describes received the longest sustained funding grant ever dedicated to the issue of same sex partner abuse in Toronto and was the product of more than a decade of writing and activism by LGBTQ community members and service providers. What follows is an attempt to document the results of this project name the David Kelley Services—Same Sex Partner Abuse (DKS-SSPA) project, so that those who come after—and there will be others—can build on what was accomplished over the three years of the project's life span, rather than being forced to engage in the Sisyphean task of re-charting the same terrain.

This chapter is meant as a study in activism, specifically activism undertaken within a marginalized population around an issue that is poorly understood and is widely considered threatening to people both within, and outside, of the LGBTQ community (Poorman 2001; Seelau, Seelau and Poorman 2003; Wise and Bowman 1997). Although the project involved a wide range of activities, the following discussion is a report of the knowledge gained through project-related activities such as clinical practice, research, reading, conferencing, educating, and talking endlessly with individuals and service providers about their experiences of LGBTQ intimate partner violence. The final pages of the chapter will focus on the challenges of incorporating this knowledge into various initiatives that reflect the diverse needs and experiences of the community, as well as on outlining lessons learned and making recommendations for future work on the issue.

The original loose coalition of activists and service providers who wrote the start-up grant application for the DKS-SSPA used the term same sex partner abuse (SSPA). Once the project got off the ground it quickly became clear to those of us working on the project that the terminology of DKS-SSPA was inadequate considering the diversity of the LGBTQ community. The inclusion of trans and bi individuals within the scope of the project rendered the language of same sex partner abuse (SSPA) inaccurate at best, and offensive at worst, because it excluded a large segment of the LGBTQ community that suffered a similar degree of marginalization due to their queer identities, but did not identify their partnerships as being same sex. The term SSPA also does not clearly reflect the distinction between sex, as a biological category, and gender, as a social category; a distinction that is essential to queer politics and identities.[2] The issue of language was never resolved for project participants. The project continued to refer to the phenomena of abuse in queer relationships as same sex partner abuse by default. I have taken to referring to the phenomenon of abuse in LGBTQ relationships as LGBTQ intimate partner violence (LGBTQ-IPV), however, as I feel this respects the diversity of the community and side-steps some of the gender-based assumptions attributed to the mainstream domestic violence movement. There is much debate within the mainstream domestic violence community over the use of IPV and its failure to clearly designate the gendered nature of domestic violence.[3] In the end, I feel that the terminology shift reflects a deep personal commitment to respecting diversity and hence I have chosen, for the purpose of this chapter, to use the term LGBTQ-IPV to refer to abuse in LGBTQ relationships, while retaining the designation SSPA when referring to the project itself.

As this chapter concerns the challenge that diversity poses for projects involving advocacy and education within marginalized communities, it is important that I, as the author, position myself within the narrative. I am a white, lesbian-identified, clinical social worker, working in the area of domestic violence, and teaching critical race and feminist theory at the University of Toronto. Although this chapter is not meant primarily as a scholarly discussion of LGBTQ-IPV, my analysis of the issue will reflect my knowledge of current writing and research in the field of equity and anti-oppression politics.

THE DKS-SSPA PROJECT

The Same Sex Partner Abuse Project received three years of funding from the Ontario Ministry of the Attorney General beginning in 2005 and ending in 2008. The project was part of the David Kelley LGBTQ-HIV/AIDS Services, one of the many programs offered by Family Service Toronto. The initial plan was to focus on supporting and building up the Coalition Against Same Sex Partner Abuse (CASSPA) a loose organization of service providers and community members who had been working in the area of SSPA for over a decade and whose work had resulted in funding for the project. As with many volunteer organizations, membership in CASSPA had ebbed and flowed over the years due to it being dependent upon non-renewable, project specific grants and subject to the time and energy limitations of the revolving membership. As with a number of other volunteer run groups in the LGBTQ community, CASSPA members were primarily white, professional gays and lesbians. Therefore, the original funding application emphasized the need for the project staff to do outreach within those groups who were chronically under-represented by CASSPA, in particular communities of color, ethno-cultural and First Nations communities, as well as trans and bi individuals.

For a variety of reasons not covered in this chapter, it proved difficult to maintain the project's commitment to CASSPA. In particular, recruitment and retention of new members was unsuccessful, and internal politics made it challenging and time-consuming to undertake collaborative work.[4] One key initiative that was accomplished through the joint efforts of CASSPA members, project staff, and additional community members, however, was the creation of a set of four educational pamphlets that addressed abuse in gay, lesbian, bi, and trans relationships.[5] For a number of reasons, many of which are attributable to the act of introducing funding to a group that has functioned as a loose coalition of volunteers, the membership in CASSPA dwindled over the life of the project.

Additional project initiatives include providing dedicated clinical services to individuals and couples, conducting research to determine service provider's current levels of knowledge and practice regarding LGBTQ-IPV, developing a training program for service providers, reviewing the existing clinical literature on LGBTQ-IPV, developing resources for individual survivors and agencies and organizing a public awareness campaign. As with many projects, the original funding application was extremely ambitious. Although many of these activities were initiated, the difficulties associated with administering and coordinating funded projects, including staff recruitment and retention and under staffing, meant that many initiatives could not be completed within the fixed timeframe given the project. Several aspects of the project are continuing on a voluntary basis, or have been picked up by other departments within the home agency, Family Service Toronto (FST).

LGBTQ-IPV: A DISCUSSION

The following is a discussion of the knowledge gained through undertaking the various initiatives that comprised the DKS-SSPA project. I have incorporated things that were learned from a variety of different activities and used this knowledge to frame my discussion of the research findings. The formal research activities of the project consisted of developing and disseminating a series of on-line surveys to poll the current understanding, clinical practices, and training needs of community service providers in the Greater Toronto Area (GTA). The first, and most widely circulated, survey consisted of thirty-four questions organized into three categories. This survey was aimed at service providers and asked questions about a range of issues including information about the respondent (length of time in services, job description, comfort level, and training regarding issue of DKS-SSPA, etc.); clients (age, gender identity, sexual orientation, presenting issue, etc.); and, in the final section, clinical knowledge of LGBTQ-IPV, particularly how presentations and experiences of LGBTQ-IPV compare with partner abuse in heterosexual relationships. The second survey was shorter, consisted of twenty-five questions, and was intended to ascertain how agencies responded to LGBTQ-IPV, particularly in terms of policy development and staff training and recruitment. The research data was collected and then analyzed using both qualitative and quantitative methods. For the purpose of this chapter, I am presenting the results of the qualitative analysis for which I was responsible. Priority is given to the findings from the service provider survey. The findings from the agency survey will be directly referenced when they are included, otherwise the research findings refer to the service provider data.

Originally, there had been a plan to develop two additional surveys that would poll members of the Toronto Police Services and legal professional (including duty counsel, lawyers, judges, legal aid staff, probation officers, etc.). Although talks continue with representatives from both of these communities, it is unlikely that the research will come to fruition as it has proven challenging to produce a research instrument that satisfies the interests of the researchers and representatives of both professional organizations.

Incident Rates

There has been a paucity of research undertaken on the issue of abuse in LGBTQ relationships, particularly abuse occurring in bi-sexual and trans relationships. Presumably, this is due to a number of factors, including a lack of research funds, political will and clinical interest in this issue. One of the aspects that I have found particularly challenging about working on the issue of LGBTQ-IPV is the widespread reluctance to explicitly name the homo/trans/biphobia that operates at every level of our experience of this phenomenon. For this reason, in the course of writing this chapter I have availed myself of every opportunity presented to be explicit about the context of homo/trans/biphobia that frames the phenomenon of LGBTQ-IPV. I therefore note that the lack of research funds, political will and interest in the issue of LGBTQ-IPV are just such expressions of homo/trans/biphobia.

There are a few key researchers whose works is cited again and again in relation to the issue of LGBTQ-IPV, chief among them being Cook Daniels (1996), Letellier (1996), Renzetti (1992), and Ristock (2002a). Many of these researchers are known for their work with one particular subgroup of the queer community—lesbians in the case of Renzetti and Ristock, gay men in the case of Letellier and trans folks in the case of Cook-Daniels. Because of the dearth of research in the area, it is difficult to say anything definitive regarding incident rates for LGBTQ-IPV. According to Statistics Canada's Family Violence Survey (2005), 25% of women will experience violence at the hands of an intimate partner. The rates of abuse in LGBTQ relationships seem to correspond closely with rates reported in heterosexual relationships (Balsam and Szymanski 2005; Brown 2008; Burke and Follingstad 1999; Greenwood et al. 2002; Hamberger 1996; McKendry et al 2006; McLaughlin and Rozee 2001; Miller et al. 2000; Poorman 2001; Renzetti 1996; Seelau et al. 2003; Walsh 1996). This fact is born out by experiential knowledge gained from four years of working on this issue with Toronto's LGBTQ community. In addition, it has been my experience that more and more individuals—particularly couples—are presenting with abuse issues. This may indicate increasing rates of LGBTQ-IPV or more willingness to self-identify and access services due to reduced stigmatization and greater public awareness. For the purpose of this project, it was enough to recognize that abuse in intimate relationships was an issue for the LGBTQ community—it happens, it happens at significant rates, and there is an acknowledged lack of published clinical knowledge guiding our efforts to respond to the issue. Our purpose in doing the research was to investigate the knowledge and clinical models that service providers both developed and applied to the cases of SSPA that they were necessarily encountering in their work. My hope was to be able to make a meaningful contribution to the clinical literature regarding this issue.

In total, there were fifty-one respondents to the on-line service provider survey and twenty-seven to the agency survey. The questions were presented in a variety of formats and the survey link was disseminated widely through a number of networks. The majority of respondents identified themselves as social workers, with many others identifying as psychotherapists and counselors. Counseling, case management, and advocacy were the most prevalent types of services provided by respondents. The number of respondents who listed advocacy as a central activity attests to the political nature of domestic violence work,[6] as well as the inadequacy of existing services and the extent of the barriers that individuals experiencing domestic violence face.

Only four out of fifty-one respondents indicated that they work exclusively, or almost exclusively, with the LGBTQ community and three more indicated seeing high number of LGBTQ clients. A sizeable number of providers (25% in total), however, presumably serving in front line non-dedicated agencies, reported a significant number of their clients as being LGBTQ and having experienced IPV (20% of their total case load). This number far exceeded the estimated 10% that is commonly thought to represent the percentage of LGBTQ individuals within the general population. It also does not take into consideration the number of clients who may not identify as LGBTQ out of fear, the inadequacy of existing identifiers or internalized homophobia. This means that either a higher proportion of LGBTQ individuals reported experiencing trauma or a higher proportion of LGBTQ individuals who experienced IPV are requesting service. Regardless, these findings support the claim that LGBTQ-IPV is an issue for the LGBTQ community and service providers. Service providers reported that their LGBTQ clients experienced emotional, physical, and sexual abuse in their intimate relationships, with emotional abuse being the most often reported, followed by physical and sexual abuse. In most cases there were multiple forms of abuse being reported by the client.

Despite the number of service providers who reported serving LGBTQ clients regularly, very few reported having received anti-oppression training that included LGBTQ issues. Fewer service providers had received training specifically for LGBTQ-IPV and of these most had received training only once. This lack of training is particularly worrisome considering the percentage of case loads that were reported as being made up of clients who identified as LGBTQ. This is even more problematic when considering that the majority of respondents stated that they worked differently with LGBTQ identified clients. This later information appears to reflect that among service providers there is an understanding that sexual orientation is a key factor shaping individual and social experience and circumstances. However, it appears that intuitive responses to these circumstances and identity factors are not being reflected in the clinical knowledge that informs practice.

UNSETTLING BINARIES, EMBRACING COMPLEXITY: GENDER, COMPULSORY HETEROSEXUALITY AND MYTHS ABOUT LGBTQ IDENTITIES AND RELATIONSHIPS

Respondents identified many similarities between intimate partner violence in same sex and heterosexual relationships including difficulties associated with leaving these relationships, the effects of abuse on victims, and power and control strategies used by the abuser. The differences, however, were also numerous. Chief among the differences cited was the lack of services for LGBTQ survivors, internalized homophobia, homophobia among service providers, and differences in abusive tactics particularly with regards to threats to "out" one's partner to employers, family and friends.

Interestingly, it is only regarding this question of asking for a comparison between IPV in LGBTQ and heterosexual relationships, that homophobia was explicitly and repeatedly referenced. A reoccurring response to several of the questions involving presentation and practice was that abuse in LGBTQ relationships was extremely complex and defied popular understandings of relationship abuse as it has been derived from research and experience working with heterosexual couples. This representation of LGBTQ identities and relationships as complex, along with the challenge of received understandings of how various identity and social factors operate to structure abusive dynamics in relationships, is also very prevalent in the literature regarding LGBTQ-IPV (Chung and Lee 1999; Gillis and Diamond 2006; Hamberger 1996). The concept of complexity is a central organizing feature of the following discussion.

LGBTQ relationships go a long way in sending up the neat binary categories—man/woman, perpetrator/victim—that society, and the mainstream domestic violence community, relies on to create frameworks for understanding and responding to violence in intimate relationships. It is not that gender is not a factor in LGBTQ relationships but that nothing about gender roles and the resulting power relations can be taken-for-granted, particularly as the knowledge guiding our understanding of how gender operates to structure abuse in intimate relationships has been gleaned from studying heterosexual relationships. Moreover, the heterosexual relationships to which members of the LGTBQ community compare their experiences of abuse, are often of a particular order marked out by specificities of race and class, as well as gender and sexuality.[7] Hence, the comment made repeatedly by many of our research respondents who stated that conventional understandings of domestic violence are inadequate to a whole range of relationships and not just those occurring between LGBTQ individuals.

Gendered roles and behaviors can and do exert an influence in LGBTQ relationships but, as they do not necessarily have the same meanings as they do in heterosexual relationships, power does not accrue to them in the same way. This can be difficult to grasp, as the idea that gender can have multiple, rather than fixed, meanings is not commonly acknowledged. Complex interactions and power differences based on race, class, and ability, as well as the effects of what some researchers refer to as "marginalized stress," the stress related to occupying a marginalized place in society (Balsam and Szymanski 2005; Brooks 1981; Byrne 1996; Murray et al 2001; Waldron 1996), must also be recognized while considering how dynamics of abuse are created and sustained in some LGBTQ relationships.

The strictures concerning appropriate gendered behavior are integral to a system that enforces heterosexuality as the only acceptable mode for being in a relationship. It is a factor that is integral to understanding the kinds of myths that circulate regarding LGBTQ individuals and their relationships, as well as explaining the invisibility of these relationships and the lack of services available to survivors of LGBTQ-IPV.

Further, society's aversion to seeing men as victims of domestic violence means that same-sex partner abuse in gay relationships is often dismissed and/or devalued as "boys will be boys." (Burke and Follingstad 1999; Island and Letellier 1991; Merrill 1996; Walsh 1996). As a result there are very few services available for gay men who experience this type of violence. The services that do exist are underfunded, understaffed, and often run on a volunteer or ad hoc basis. In Toronto, there are spaces available for gay men fleeing violence in a few of the homeless shelters across the city, and gay men's groups have tried to maintain a network of safe houses where individuals are willing to take victims into their homes for short periods in emergency situations.

On the other hand, lesbian "batterers" challenge the myth of women's inherent non-violence. The idea that a woman would abuse another woman, or would actually be feared by her partner, is difficult for many people to understand—including lesbians (Balsam 2001, Burke and Follingstad 1999; McLaughlin and Rozee 2001; Merrill 1996; Walsh 1996). Identifying one's partner as abusive can feel like a betrayal of the feminist sisterhood. Admittedly, this experience of betrayal appears to be more applicable to a white, middle-class lesbian relationship. The turbulent politics that have rocked the feminist community over the last two decades surrounding issues of race and class are indicative of the complex relationship some women have with the concept of feminist sisterhood. Overall, the complicated power dynamics that can exist in lesbian relationships may also render violence in these relationships difficult to address. Few lesbian couples conform to a clearly demarcated butch/femme dyad. If and when they do, power still does not necessarily accrue along traditional gendered lines. Similarly, although factors of race, age, ability, class, etc. can play a part in determining who has power and who does not, they do not always play out as expected.

Considering the ways in which gender roles militate against an acknowledgement of violence in LGBTQ relationships, dismantling, or at least easing, our rigid gender system is the only way that LGBTQ identified individuals will be able to live free of the violence that accompanies marginalization—violence that plays itself out within both the public and the private spheres. The relationship between private and public forms of violence is especially relevant to abuse dynamics within relationships where one or more partner is a member of a marginalized community. For example, a trans woman who has experienced violence in her family of origin as a result of her gender identity, who also faces violence everyday in the public realm for much the same reason, has an interesting dilemma facing her when it comes to partner abuse. She must choose between continuing to endure abuse in her home against exposing herself to increased levels of public violence as she enters the shelter system, is forced to spend more time on the street or return to an abusive family situation.

The complex relationship between LGBTQ identities, gender and power present a particular challenge to the gender-based understandings of IPV that pervade the clinical knowledge that survey respondents accessed to support their work with individual clients. This was apparent when respondents were asked about factors that they felt contributed to abuse in LGBTQ relationships. Many identified a range of factors, aside from gender, that they felt influenced LGBTQ-IPV. The most prominent of these were ability, class, and degree of "outness" (indicating the extent to which an individual identifies as LGBTQ and is therefore connected to the community). Race, age, and spirituality were also cited as significant issues, although to a lesser extent than the ones previously listed. Interestingly, gender identity (i.e., clearly defined butch/femme identities) was also cited as a factor in LGBTQ relationship abuse. Presumably, given the low rate of trans clients reported, gender identity refers to stereotypical gender role expression and reflected either service providers' misinterpretation of the role of gender in LGBTQ relationships, or the belief that abusive relationships exhibit more rigid gender role division than non-abusive relationships. Isolation and a previous history of abuse were also strong factors said to be influencing abuse in same sex relationships. That respondents raised the issue of ability was unexpected and particularly significant given the lack of attention given to this population within the LGBTQ service community in Toronto.

In particular, the relative degree of "outness" between partners was cited as a major source of power imbalances between same sex partners and therefore a significant risk factor for LGBTQ-IPV. This corresponds with the common understanding that individuals in their first LGBTQ relationship are more at risk for LGBQ-IPV (Renzetti 1992). Threatening to out one's partner to friends, family or employers was cited as a frequent tactic used by abusers in same sex relationships. Respondents also reported that abusers would threaten to "out" partners as politically reactionary or homo/trans phobic to the LGBTQ community. The pivotal role that degrees of "outness" was reported to play in conditioning abusive relationship dynamics is indicative of the context of homo/trans/biphobia in which LGBTQ relationships are situated. It also indicates the important role that community plays in LGBTQ lives and the rigid political strictures that pervade some marginalized communities (also indicative of a context of oppression), as well as demonstrating the inadequacy of a gender-based frame for understanding IPV as it cannot account for risk factors such as "outness." However, there is an issue as to whether the focus on degrees of "outness" indicated the extent to which this concept had become the signifier of difference, and therefore operates to occlude a more complex understanding of the uniqueness of relational dynamics between LGBTQ individuals. In other words, degrees of outness or the threat of outing as a tactic in LGBTQ relationships satisfies the need to account for difference while simultaneously foreclosing on the pursuit of further penetrating inquiry. After all, it is difficult to find words to explain or account for what lies outside of existing explanatory paradigms and more difficult still to construct additional explanatory paradigms.

Considering that respondents reported a very high percentage of their clients as coming from ethnically diverse or immigrant communities, few reported race or ethnicity as being a significant influence on power dynamics in LGBTQ relationships. This could be accounted for by the fact that many individuals of color report feeling torn between their racial, gender and sexual identities (Hill Collins 2005; Kanuha 2005), or by the fact that many LGBTQ services are predominantly white and therefore are not the first point of contact for racialized members of the community. The fact that restricting access to children was cited as a frequent threat in same sex relationships speaks to the challenges that LGBTQ parents continue to face in an environment characterized by homophobia but also exemplifies the changing face of the LGBTQ community and partnerships (Epstein 2009).

Several respondents commented that the gender-based model of domestic violence is often inadequate for understanding violence in some heterosexual relationship, as well as LGBTQ relationships. Consider the following comment made by one of the respondents: "Only that I recognize that unlike woman abuse in hetero relationships, talking about and responding to same sex partner abuse is very complex and has many layers that need to be unraveled and explored. We are still learning about abuse in hetero relationships and I feel that we are just at the beginning of understanding the dynamics and complexities within the LBGTQ communities related to abuse issues." LGBTQ relationship dynamics are complex and therefore it is tempting to take respondents repeated comments about this complexity at face value. However, I am convinced that the perception of complexity is often due to discomfort and/or lack of experiential knowledge of these relationships. An additional factor is the inflexibility, and therefore inadequacy, of attempting to understand real-lived experience through the uncritical application of universal models—particular models that reflect dominant relations and subject positions. In other words, I suspect that rather than admitting ignorance, respondents will default to a claim of complexity, a truism concerning LGBTQ relationships that is misapplied in this situation. There is a difference between something being complex and something being unknown or perhaps unknowable.

Comments, such as the one cited previously, tell us much about the limitations of universal models in general, as well as indicate the cultural specificity of the gender- based model of domestic violence. One respondent described the "tunnel vision" associated with gender-based models for understanding domestic violence. Similarly, the following quotation speaks to limitations and effects of the gender based model, as well as the political complexity of working with LGBTQ populations: " . . . when working with heterosexual clients I assume that the woman is the victim. That assumption informs my work until another version of the situation emerges. This default abuse/abused is not so clear with same sex partners. I have found that FTMs in the community who are taking T [Testosterone] are at higher risk of abusing their partners, but I also feel there is something fundamentally transphobic about feeling this way."

Many individuals who have experienced violence and abuse in LGBTQ relationships struggle with a sense of their own culpability because they fought back. The fact that same sex couples are often more evenly matched in terms of strength and physique, as well as the fact that gender expectations do not operate as a deterrent, makes fighting back an option that may not be prevalent in heterosexual relationships. This is in part due to female victims often being much smaller than their partners, and gender role expectations may support a more passive response to abuse when one's abuser is male. Fighting back muddies the water regarding who is the abuser and who is the victim and makes screening for abuse in the context of service provision very difficult (Veinot 2008). This has led to the development of a number of very innovative screening tools for applying to same sex relationships that help to identify the subtleties and nuances of relationship dynamics and the effects of abuse (for example see Anti-Violence Project New York Chapter 14 in this volume). The issue of mutuality has been hotly contested among LGBTQ activists, service providers and community members (Ristock 2002a).

Many of the survey respondents reported being unclear as to who is the abuser and who is the victim in same sex relationships and attributed this lack of clarity to the complexity of relationship dynamics. Said one respondent: "complicated relationship dynamics & context makes assessments difficult." However, this confusion is also easily attributable to the distortion in the conceptual frame used to understand violence, which requires a much different focus for our attention than that of understanding the specificity of LGBTQ relationships.

There was some recognition, although limited, that LGBTQ-IPV shared similarities to violence within relationships involving members from other marginalized communities such as communities of color or seniors.[8] One respondent suggested that the shift to defining abuse as being about power and control made differences such as sexual orientation, gender identity and race irrelevant. Although expressed by only one respondent, a similar sentiment was implicit in several of the other comments wherein respondents appeared to insinuate that attention to power and control indeed elided a detailed understanding of difference as it would be caught by a close attention to relationship dynamics.

The idea of paying close attention to relationship dynamics, although one that as a clinician I would always support, left me with a similar impression as did the focus on degrees of "outness." Did this directive to pay close attention sometimes operate as a default position that made further theorizing, particularly clinical theorizing obsolete? For me it is reminiscent of the "add-on" arguments made by feminists of color regarding race (Hill Collins 2004). Hill Collins argues that feminists have responded to the voices of women of color by adding race as an additional category of oppression, sometimes equal and sometimes secondary to gender. The critique that Hill Collins levels is that such an "add-on" response does not engage with the complex intersectional nature of different aspects of social identity and thus cannot account for the experiences of women of color in a meaningful way. My impression in this regard was supported by the seeming reluctance by respondents to specifically reference the context of homophobia in which LGBTQ relationships are situated. This tendency to individualize and psychologize violence is a somewhat necessary corrective to the exclusive systemic focus of some early work in domestic violence, but one wonders whether things have perhaps swung too far the other way. Respondents were also silent regarding polyamorous relationships and SM (sadomasochism) within the LGBTQ community. The silence on these issues perhaps speaks to the level of self-monitoring carried out by the respondents, as the myth that LGBTQ couples are more apt to engage in "deviant" behaviors such as polyamory or SM and are thus are more unstable and indicative of a perverse or immature sexuality have been debunked in many LGBTQ-IPV educational materials.[9] However, it is also possible that the silence indicates an aversion to engage in a more substantive, and therefore politically sensitive, analysis of the issue of LGBTQ-IPV.

If violence and abuse in lesbian and gay relationships is poorly understood, violence and abuse in trans and bi relationships is even less understood. Although there are a few people and organizations that have begun to do work in this area, there is very little research being conducted, and therefore little knowledge available to support clinical practice. What we do know is that gender, and the intricate politics at the personal, community, and societal level exert an influence on abuse dynamics in these relationships in ways we don't completely understand. As a result, bi and trans individuals are a particularly vulnerable and under serviced segment of the LGBTQ community. Although trans individuals were specifically included in the survey questions, the survey failed to elicit any responses specific to the trans community. This is mostly likely due to the way that questions were framed, in that there were no questions that reflected an informed understanding of trans issues in this area, as well as that respondents reported seeing few trans clients. Again, the inability for trans individuals to identify abuse and then seek help can be linked to the transphobic environment in which they are struggling to forge intimate partnerships.

DEALING WITH DIFFERENCE

A significant challenge associated with the DKS-SSPA project involved staying attuned to the differences that exist within the LGBTQ community. During workshops and presentations I often explained that, with regard to the LGBTQ community, difference ran along multiple axes. One axis pertained to differences based on sexual orientation and gender identity, which mark out LGBTQ individuals as different in relation to the dominant heterosexual culture. Another axis crosscuts the community, dividing members from each other through factors such as race, class, ability, as well as gender identity and sexual orientation. In other words, although difference organizes the relationship between the LGBTQ community and dominant society, the concept of difference is also relevant to the internal structure of the community. The various subcultures that fall under the umbrella term LGBTQ are united in their marginal status and its derivation from the differential expression of gender and/or sexual identities. For many, however, this is the only point of convergence. Race, gender, class, ability, and sexuality—in a broad sense conceptualized as an amalgam of identity, expression and practice—create hierarchies of difference within the LGBTQ community that affect the way that IPV is experienced and to which it is responded. There is no necessary correlation between the relationship dynamics—abusive or otherwise—as experienced by individuals who identify as gay, lesbian, bi, trans and queer. Nor is there a necessary correlation between relationship dynamics as experienced by members who fall within these subgroups.

The conventional framework for understanding abuse is derived from observing white, middle class heterosexual relationships and is therefore not appropriate to accounting for abuse that takes place in relationships in which power operates along additional lines of difference and is conditioned by a particular set of contextual relations that impact partners in particular ways. Similarly, abuse in gay relationships differs from abuse in lesbian relationships as well as from abuse in bi and trans relationships. Thus, abusive dynamics cannot be understood through the application of a universal framework that reflects the perspective of a particular set of experiences. My appreciation of the scope of these differences between members of the LGBTQ community developed across the life of the project. Hence, the survey did not ask respondents to speak to their experiences of internal differences within the LGBTQ community nor did anyone offer up such an observation unbidden. Perhaps this is due to the paucity of research available regarding trans and bi identities and relationships. Perhaps it speaks to the extent to which stereotypes operate to create a universal identity for the LGBTQ community that preserves the privileged status that accrues to white, middle class lesbians and gays.

As there are significant difference between sub groups within the LGBTQ community, individual difference in circumstance and life experience further complicate the picture of abuse in LGBTQ relationships thus requiring more nuanced theoretical and practical models of response. Histories of childhood abuse, homophobic violence or internalized homophobia do not excuse abuse but they do make it harder to identify, respond to and determine the degree of intentionality.[10] Consensual SM in a community that had been highly sexualized adds to this complexity and multiplies the possibilities for misunderstanding or stigmatizing.[11]

In the context of the project, it became a constant battle to attend to the different experiences of particularly bi and trans individuals, as well as the differences that cut across these identities. The project was an opportunity to advocate for all members of the LGBTQ community but not at the expense of consolidating the silences that surrounded the experiences of the most marginalized members. This tension led to the production of a very complicated and detailed analysis that informed the development of project deliverables such as educational materials. Hence the decision to publish a series of pamphlets that retained an internal focus on how queer community members differ in relation to heterosexuals, while also attending to differences in gender identity and sexual orientation among community members. The pamphlets addressed four subgroups within the community—gays, lesbians, bisexuals, and trans. Common to all the pamphlets was reference to the discrimination experienced by LGBTQ community members in general. In addition, effort was made to address the specific forms of discrimination that were unique to each of the four subgroups, as well as those experienced by members of each group where race or class identity increased vulnerability. Attention to various axes of difference led to the development of an educational program that was built around modules that explored the unique presentation of abusive relationship dynamics and effects due to identity and context factors. The diversity reflected in the client populations served by respondents underscores the need for more culturally appropriate services for individuals who identify as LGBTQ and have experienced some form of trauma.

Despite the difference that exists between members of the LGBTQ communities, however, there is still much that is relevant to the community as a whole with regards to the issue of IPV. In particular, there are a number of challenges integral to the experience of LGBTQ individuals who are in abusive relationships that make doing the work that the project entailed difficult. These include barriers to identification and admission at an individual, community, and clinical level, and many stem for the overriding fact that all LGBTQ lives and relationships are conducted within a social context that is marked by homophobia, transphobia, and biphobia.

A common experience is that the fear of betraying the community is often a major barrier to LGBTQ individuals acknowledging the fact that they are being abused. Like many other marginalized communities, LGBTQ lives and relationship have been, and continue to be, pathologized.[12] As a result, many LGBTQ individuals feel protective towards their communities and are therefore willing to withhold information about abuse—consciously or unconsciously—so as not to provide fodder to their critics. The experience of having to choose between cross-cutting allegiance to self and community, or to chose to privilege one identity over another, is familiar to individuals from a range of marginalized communities. The sexualized nature of LGBTQ identities, a major component of homo/trans/biphobia also means that LGBTQ individuals leaving intimate relationships where violence and abuse is a factor confront difficult identity issues that have no corollary in the world of heterosexual partnerships.

HOMO/TRANS/BIPHOBIA AS CONTEXT

The fact that society does not support the rights of LGBTQ individuals means that LGBTQ relationships are not accorded status equal to that of heterosexual relationships. As a result, our study found that service providers fail to screen for violence when dealing with members of the LGBTQ community, or when confronted with it, fail to treat it as seriously as they would evidence of domestic violence in heterosexual relationships. While coordinating the project, I was asked to evaluate a training program being developed for health professional in the area of domestic violence and found there was no mention that LGBTQ individuals could be at risk for violence in their relationships. This is certainly not an isolated occurrence.

Many of my clients frequently reported having their complaints dismissed by police as situations of "mutual aggression" or "cat fights." Many LGBTQ individuals are reluctant to admit the nature of their relationship to police because they do not trust the police to treat them respectfully and fairly. The police services have come a long way in this regard but homophobia is still an issue particularly when homophobia is supported by attitudes such as classism, racism, and sexism. Trans and bi phobia are issues for all service communities, even those who have actively struggled against homophobia. Individuals that have been identified as being particularly vulnerable to LGBTQ-IPV include those individuals diagnosed with HIV/AIDS, living with disabilities, living in rural communities, from ethnic or religious communities where homosexuality is particularly stigmatized, and two-spirited people of the First Nations (Ristock and Timbang 2005). The heightened vulnerability of these communities is due to the extreme lack of appropriate services, disconnection or marginalization within the larger LGBTQ community, a marked history of neglect or persecution by institutions associated with the dominant society and a history of forced dependency (Ristock and Timbang 2005).

The fact that many LGBTQ individuals have formed families and are raising children is also relatively invisible to mainstream society. The result is a lack of services for children who have witnessed violence in same-sex families. A history of poor treatment at the hands of child protection workers has made many LGBTQ individuals reluctant to report abuse because they fear the involvement of these services. Consequently, under-use of the system allows homophobic attitudes and practices to go unchallenged.

Furthermore, homo/trans/biphobia and sexism are not only social attitudes but can be internalized thus making it more difficult for individuals to identify the fact that they are being abused, and therefore hold their abusers accountable. For example, gay men live in a rigidly gendered society that makes it difficult for them to reconcile their masculinity with victimization. In addition, many LGBTQ individuals have experienced public and private violence and abuse throughout their lives, making it difficult for them to draw distinctions between what is acceptable and unacceptable treatment and behavior. Many LGBTQ individuals experience marked degrees of isolation because they have been abandoned by their families of origin, and/ or are closeted for fear of loosing their jobs, children or facing deportation. Isolation renders individuals vulnerable to abuse and violence. The majority of survey respondents recognized the extreme isolation experienced by many LGBTQ clients reporting abuse. There was no overt link made between the degree of social isolation and a context of homo/trans/ bi phobia, however.

Even though a number of respondents cited social devaluing of LGBTQ relationships as a significant difference associated with LGBTQ-IPV, it was surprising that more providers did not identify this as being an issue for both the LGBTQ community and service providers. Equally surprising was that internalized homophobia was never mentioned as a factor influencing LGBTQ-IPV. Considering the degree of negative feelings that were publically aired during the same sex marriage debate in Canada, it seems to defy common sense that these attitudes should not have been internalized to some degree by every Canadian—LGBTQ or heterosexual.[13] The fact that this is not overtly acknowledged as a possibility, or inevitability, could indicate a lack of awareness of the process and prevalence of the internalization of negative messages regarding LGBTQ individuals and relationships. Or perhaps it's indicative of a reluctance to admit to being influenced by these processes. The latter poses a significant challenge to practice and training, as what is not revealed, or existing in consciousness, is difficult to challenge and therefore shift. It also speaks to the highly politicized nature of the work and the community, a characterization that although understandable and necessary, is also a potential impediment to growth and change.

Respondents stressed the isolation and marginalization of LGBTQ individuals as having a myriad of effects on the level of service and experience, as well as marking a major difference between violence experienced by heterosexual and LGBTQ individuals. Respondents identified the biggest barriers to providing service to individuals who have experienced LGBTQ-IPV to be the lack of appropriate services, the lack of safety associated with existing services, a noted resistance of individuals to identify themselves as victims of abuse and the failure of the gender based model to further our understanding of abusive relationship dynamics in LGBTQ relationships. Regarding the issue of service, respondents stressed the need for more education and training within mainstream services, more cooperation between LGBTQ dedicated services and mainstream services, and the need to develop dedicated services especially with regards to currently under serviced populations, namely gay men and trans men and women. There was no mention made of the effects of having experienced homophobic violence—past or present—or the stress associated with homo/trans/biphobic attitudes and its implications for LGBTQ-IPV. First Nations communities were never overtly mentioned by respondents indicating the degree to which two-spirited people are not included in the LGBTQ designation. A clear picture emerged from the research of inadequate or nonexistent services, particular for the most vulnerable members of the LGBTQ community.

RESPONDING TO LGBTQ-IPV

There were several comments made by respondents that raised questions as to whether perceptions regarding the LGBTQ-IPV reflected actual circumstances or were the result of the internalization of negative stereotypes of LGBTQ individuals and their relationships. These included comments regarding the mutual nature of abuse in lesbian relationships, the prevalence of sexual abuse in gay male relationships and the tendency to engage in stalking and lying as tactics in lesbian relationships. Because all of these responses corresponded closely with myths that circulate regarding LGBTQ-IPV and/or LGBTQ relationships and identities in general, the possibility that perceptions are shaped by contextual influences such as wide-spred homophobia, particularly in its heavily cloaked liberal manifestations (i.e., diversity programs, multiculturalism, diversity initiatives that give the principle of tolerance pride of place), make it difficult to engage with comments that are presented as unmediated observations of real events and circumstances. Even the discussion around the mutuality of abuse is subject to the influences of internalized homophobia. The social context of homophobia, and therefore the potential to internalize negative stereotypes, was so infrequently mentioned by respondents it's unsettling, and attests to the need for more work to be done with service providers regarding anti-homophobia training, in addition to training specific to DKS-SSPA, before we can entertain many of these questions with any hope of finding an answer. The issue of mutuality is ever-present in discussions of LGBTQ-IPV but rarely talked about openly due to the reactionary discourse with which it has been embedded. Traditional positivist research does not always allow for queer readings, or readings that attend to the silences or omissions in discourse, therefore the nuances of real lived experiences cannot be explicated. In this regard, it is significant to me that the issue of mutuality was rarely referred to, although at times it appeared to be recoded in the responses as "complexity," particularly the complexity that made it difficult for providers to determine the nature of the abuser. My feeling is that rather than wade into the boggy terrain of debating the appearance of mutuality, which by the way is a salient issue for straight relationships as well, respondents tended to skirt the issues by employing the "complex" defense. Whether mutuality exists or that there is always a primary aggressor in abusive relationships has long been debated within the LGBTQ service delivery, if not in print then around many a conference table. It remains a charged issue because to claim mutuality is to reify some of the most problematic myths that exist concerning LGBTQ. However, to not engage in the discussion is to foreclose on a difficult issue that might yield some surprising and valuable insights.

When asked about screening for abuse and specific indicators for abuse that pertain to LGBTQ relationships the majority of respondents stressed the need for paying close attention to patterns in relationship dynamics and the power relations that these patterns reveal. This is certainly a best practice scenario regardless of the client population but the fact that it was said in relation to a question regarding the difference between screening for abuse in LGBTQ and heterosexual relationships reveals something of the explanatory power that gender holds for domestic violence in mainstream service work. There was also a rather troubling comment made by one respondent that there was no need to inquire about children in LGBTQ relationships. Presumably, this is because LGBTQ individuals are not parents. This indicates an additional stereotype that circulates about LGBTQ relationships, and underscores the need as well as attests to the value of the recent surge in research regarding LGBTQ parenting issues.[14]

SUMMARY OF RESEARCH AND PROJECT LEARNINGS

There are a couple of key findings that resulted from the activities undertaken as part of the DKS-SSPA project, in particular the research done with service providers and community service agencies. There is a wide spread assumption that LGBTQ relationships are characterized by a complexity that appears to exceed that of heterosexual relationships. There is a question, however, as to whether presumptions of complexity reflect a general unfamiliarity on the part of providers regarding these relationships, a lack of clinical data informing work with LGBTQ individuals and relationships, a recoding of negative stereotypes of LGBTQ relationships or the real circumstances surrounding LGBTQ relationships. What is significant is the confusion that service providers struggle with in working with the LGBTQ community around relationship and abuse issues.

Although there is little reference to the social context of homo/trans/biphobia in which LGBTQ-IPV takes place, and to the differences between the manifestations and experiences of these three related but separate forms of oppression, I am convinced that it is this aspect of LGBTQ-IPV that needs to be front and center in our understanding of violence and abuse in these relationships. Our work in this regard is inherently political. In addition, our understanding of context features must also allow for an explicit understanding of oppressions relating to class, race, ability and the colonial relationships that have shaped the communities and identities of First Nations people in Canada.

There is also an understanding among service providers, and it is one that I support, that working with LGBTQ individuals, particularly those who have been abused by their intimate partner, requires an approach that is unique to this population and circumstances, although many ideas and interventions drawn from mainstream domestic violence practice apply. Examples of these would include recent work that addresses models of the self drawn from Self-Psychology, which advocates mindfulness as a practice for affect regulation or investigates the models of attachment that structure abuse dynamics (Courtois and Pearlman 2005; Ogden, Minton and Pain 2006). Many mainstream resources are not applicable to LGBTQ- IPV. In particular, the gender-based model for understanding violence in intimate relationships is inadequate when applied to LGBTQ relationships as it obfuscates or inhibits, rather than promotes, understanding. As a result, there is a need for a more subtle, flexible, and mindful approach when responding to LGBTQ-IPV. Furthermore, there is some discussion as to whether this would not be a best practice regardless of the nature of the gender identity and sexual orientation of the partners involved in the relationship under consideration (Sokoloff 2005).

There are significant similarities between intimate partner violence as it is experienced by LGBTQ individuals and as it is experienced by members of other marginalized communities due to the degree of social isolation and difference from the norm that characterize the life experience, identities and circumstances of members of marginalized social groups in general.

RECOMMENDATIONS FOR RESEARCH AND PRACTICE

In response to the key themes outlined above there are a series of recommendations that emerge as a result of the initiatives that form the DKS-SSPA project. These include recommendations regarding research and knowledge production, training, service provision, and clinical practice.

Regarding training, it is recommended that community service organizations, both mainstream domestic violence and LGBTQ dedicated services, pursue a two-tiered training program, implemented on a regular basis, that provides training for working with LGBTQ individuals using an anti-oppression framework, in order to attend to the diversity that exists within the LGBTQ community, and training for working with survivors of LGBTQ-IPV.

Regarding service provision, more specialized services are required, particularly for members of the LGBTQ community who are most vulnerable and/or underserved. This includes gay men, trans men and women, bi men and women, LGBTQ individuals living with disabilities, LGBTQ seniors and LGBTQ individuals who identify with particular cultural communities. Specialized services include dedicated services, as well as building knowledge and competency within mainstream agencies. It is in the area of service provision that the institutional nature of homophobia is most apparent. The fact that in Toronto, a LGBTQ community that numbers in the hundreds of thousands is served by a handful of specialized service providers is a travesty and a testament to the lack of political will that exists to address the needs of this population. In an era of reduced social expenditure the most vulnerable are often the hardest hit. The politics within the domestic violence sector, represented in the aforementioned debate regarding the terminology of "woman abuse" makes it difficult for service providers to access mainstream funding for LGBTQ-IPV services. Finally, existing domestic violence services offer claims of inclusivity that do not hold up under scrutiny.

There is also a need for more collaboration between mainstream service providers and their LGBTQ colleagues. There are gains to be made on both sides as a result, as well as the obvious benefits that would accrue to clients. Collaboration is particularly important during the period that dedicated services are being developed but it should not end when dedicated services are launched. Collaboration is relevant to a diverse range of activities pertaining to IPV work including service provision, policy development, advocacy, and education. There is a need for culturally appropriate services for survivors of LGBTQ-IPV within both mainstream and dedicated LGBTQ community services. Both mainstream and LGBTQ providers and agencies should do outreach within the community in order to educate community members about LGBTQ-IPV. Given the barriers to admission and access to services, outreach should be sustained and should take multiple forms (i.e., workshops for building relationship skills, as well as more traditional anti-violence work).

More research is required into the dynamics and context of LGBTQ relationships, as well as incidents of abuse within these relationships. In particular, there should be an emphasis placed on research with LGBTQ community members that are most vulnerable, due to conditions of lack of appropriate services or multiple forms of oppression. A major goal of this research should be the development of clinical knowledge and practice models that can support clinicians who work in the area of LGBTQ-IPV.

Regarding public education and advocacy, there is a need to develop more specialized resources in the area of LGBTQ-IPV to support public education campaigns within the LGBTQ community and beyond. It is recommended that literature reflect the diversity of the community rather than perpetuating the stereotype of an essentialized undifferentiated LGBTQ identity. Resources should particularly reflect those identities that are most vulnerable. Mainstream service providers, due to their greater access to policy development and funding sources, have a special responsibility to ensure that LGBTQ-IPV is included on the domestic violence agenda. All individuals concerned about the issue of LGBTQ-IPV should be mindful of the threat that this issue possesses to some individuals who have fought hard for domestic violence to be recognized as "woman abuse" and the need to find ways of emphasizing the benefits of expanding our repertoire with regards to the issue of intimate partner violence.

CONCLUSION

The DKS-SSPA project ended in February of 2007. As the sole source of dedicated LGBTQ-IPV services in the city of Toronto the demise of the project represents a significant loss to the community. The project was born out of years of dedicated activism, however. Presumably, this activism will continue and will give rise to future projects of this kind. In writing this chapter, I outlined some of the major learnings that emerged from the activities that comprised the three year DKS-SSPA project and to capture this learning for future research, activism, advocacy, and practice around the issue of LGBTQ-IPV.

From a personal standpoint the project challenged my thinking in several areas. It reinforced my belief that working as a clinician and researcher requires that I always pay attention to the context of my clients' lives, particularly their experience of multiple forms of oppression. Beyond "paying attention," it is also important to name these oppressions for what they are—homophobia, transphobia, racism, ableism, and so forth—and to attend to the multiple ways that these conditions and relationships structure the ways individuals experience IPV. Similar to violence against women, intimate violence between members of the LGBTQ community occurs within a broader context of social sanctioned public violence against LGBTQ people. The more work I do in this area, the more I have come to believe that what makes LGBTQ-IPV unique is the way that the forces of homo/trans/biphobia and the intersectionality of class, race, gender, ability etc. shape our experiences.

The work has also challenged my thinking around the relationship between gender and violence. In particularly it has fore-grounded the conflict that I feel sometimes arises between my feminist and lesbian selves. As a feminist, I want to honor the work that has been accomplished to recognize domestic violence as a form of gender violence that affects women, and thus connect it to other forms of violence against women both public and private. As a lesbian, however, I am aware that to adopt an exclusively gender based understanding of domestic violence obscures other forms of violence that is organized around other social axes such as race, class and sexuality. This conflict can be projected writ large on the service community that works with survivors of various kinds of violence and it is one that needs to be attended to with respect and compassion. The interests and principles informing feminist and queer theory and politics are not mutually exclusive, nor are the interests and concerns of the mainstream and LGBTQ service community with regards to IPV. Coexistence requires, however, that together we develop a nuanced and flexible approach to our knowledge and practice in the area and find the courage to acknowledge the silences that are inherent to both perspectives.

NOTES

1. Both sets of brochures are available via the Internet. The text for the original set of brochures can be access through Educational Wife Assault (now known as Springtide Resources) at: http://www.womanabuseprevention. com/html/samesex_partner_abuse.ht.ml. An updated set of brochures and the set of posters are available for view on the DKS website at: http://www. fsatoronto.com/programs/dks/res_samesex.html.

2. Sex refers to physical anatomy and gender; the culturally determined response to the sexed body. This distinction has long been central to feminist thought (Beauvoir 1949; Rubin 1984) as it has supported the claim that the category of woman cannot be naturalized through recourse to a theory of biological determinism. Rather, the category of woman is a social construct as are the inequalities that accrue as a result. This distinction is important for the queer community because it allows for a sense of fluidity in gender identity that reflects the lived experience of members of this community, as well as buttressing a similar denaturalizing of heterosexuality. However, recent critiques of the easy demarcation of sex and gender have arisen in the black feminist community (e.g., hooks 1984; Hill Collins 2004), and from the queer community itself (Butler 1986; Califia 1997; Hausman 1995).

3. I was unable to find any literature to support my experience and personal knowledge of this particular conversation regarding the politics of language (i.e., domestic violence vs. intimate partner abuse). My understanding is that the language of IPV was intended to be more inclusive but many feminist activists have criticized the term for its tendency to depoliticize and render less visible the uniqueness of the violence, and therefore the injury, that takes place in marriages and domestic relationships. For more on the politics of language in domestic violence research and writing, see Lamb (1999) and Sokoloff (2005).

4. A discussion of the challenges associated with attempting to merge funded projects with pre-existing coalitions made up of volunteers could be the subject of a whole separate paper, as well as the effects of marginality—material and psychological—on organizing.

5. These can be ordered directly from David Kelley Service or downloaded as pdf files off the website at: http://www.familyservicetoronto.org/programs/ davidkelley.html.

6. Again I find myself running up against the trap that is language. Feminists have fought long and hard for a shift in terminology from the obfuscating terminology of domestic violence to the explicit, political laden terminology of woman abuse. As a feminist I laud their efforts. As a member of the LGBTQ community, however, I also experience this move as exclusionary. This is an example of how different aspects of our identities can be pitted against each other forcing us to make hard decisions that threaten to compromise or dilute our politics. Because this chapter is about LGBTQ-IPV, I have chosen to return to the terminology of domestic violence when talking about the mainstream services available to survivors.

7. See Sokoloff (2005) for a collection of articles critiquing the particularity of much domestic violence discourse. In addition, see Seidman, Meeks and Treaschen (1999) for an excellent discussion of the heterosexual norms that

LGBTQ individuals necessarily need to negotiate in order to gain respectability.

8. The commonality of experience that exists between similarly marginalized and under serviced communities such as communities of color, immigrants, seniors and LGBTQ communities with regard to the issue of IPV arose repeatedly over the life of the project.
9. See the materials produced by DKS or Education Wife Assault as cited earlier.
10. See Ristock and Timbang (2005) for a discussion of the concept of intentionality and partner abuse in lesbian relationships.
11. In fact, it has been argued that SM is no more prevalent in LGBTQ communities than it is among heterosexuals. However, the sexualized nature of LGBTQ individuals and their relationships leads inevitably to the attribution of a myriad of commonly considered "deviant" or "immoral" sexual behaviors and conditions to this community.
12. For a classic article concerning the history of pathologizing discourse as it has been applied to lesbian subjects see Stevens and Hall (1994).
13. For more information concerning the events surrounding the legalization of same sex marriage in Canada, particularly the extent of the right wing and religious opposition to the move, see: Cotler (2006); McCain (2006); Nicol and Smith (2008); Sommerville (2007); Wilkinson (2004); and Wilkinson and Kitzinger (2005).
14. An excellent example of recent work being conducted in this area is Toronto's LGBTQ Parenting Network. (www.familyservicetoronto.org/programs/lgbtparenting.html).

REFERENCES

Balsam, K. F. and D. M. Szymanski. 2005. Relationship quality and domestic violence in women's same-sex relationships: The role of minority stress. *Psychology of Women Quarterly* 29: 258–269.
Beauvoir, S. 1949. *The second sex*. New York: Vintage Books.
Brooks, V. R. 1981. *Minority stress and lesbian women*. Lexington, MA: Lexington Books.
Brown, C. 2008. Gender-role implications on same sex intimate partner abuse. *Journal of Family Violence* 23: 457–462.
Burke, L. K. and D.R. Follingstad. 1999. Violence in lesbian and gay relationships: Theory, prevalence and correlational factors. *Clinical Psychology Review* 19: 487–512.
Butler, J. 1986. *Gender trouble: Feminist and the subversion of identity*. New York: Routledge.
Butler, L. 1999. "African American lesbian women experiencing partner abuse." In *A professional's guide to understanding gay and lesbian domestic violence: Understanding practice interventions,* ed. J. C. McClennen and J. Gunther, 181–206. Lewiston, NY: The Edwin Mellen Press.
Byrne, D. 1996. Clinical models for the treatment of gay male perpetrators of domestic violence. In *Violence in gay and lesbian domestic partnerships*, ed. C. M. Renzetti and C. H. Miley, 107–116. New York: Harrington Park Press.
Califia, P. 1997. *Sex changes: The politics of transgression*. CA: Cleis Press.
Cotler, I. 2006. Marriage in Canada—Evolution or revolution? Special issue: The evolution of marriage, *Family Court Review*, 44(1): 60–73.
Chung, C. and S. Lee. 1999. Raising our voices: Queer Asian women's response to relationship violence. Family Violence Prevention Fund. Available at: www.

endabuse.org/programs/immigrant/files/ RaisingVoices.pdf [accessed November 26, 2010].

Cook-Daniels, L. 1999. Lesbian and gay male elder abuse. In *A professional's guide to understanding gay and lesbian domestic violence: Understanding practice interventions*, ed. J. C. McClennen and J. Gunther, 207–223. Lewiston, NY: The Edwin Mellen Press.

Courtois, C. A. and L. A. Pearlman. 2005. Clinical applications of the attachment framework. *Journal of Traumatic Stress* 18(5) 449–459.

Epstein, R. 2009. *Who's your daddy? And other writings on queer parenting.* Toronto: Sumach Press.

Family Services Toronto. LGBTQ Parenting Network. www.family servicetoronto. org/programs/lgbtparenting.html

Farley, N. 1996. A survey of factors contributing to gay and lesbian domestic violence. In *Violence in gay and lesbian domestic partnerships*, ed. C. Renzetti and C. M. Miley, 35–42. New York: Harrington Park Press.

Gillis, J. R. and S. Diamond. 2006. Same-sex partner abuse: Challenges to the existing paradigms of intimate violence theory. In *Cruel but not unusual: Violence in Canadian families*, ed. R. Alaggia and C. Vine, 127–144. Waterloo, ON: Wilfrid Laurier University Press.

Greenwood, G. L., M. V. Relf, B. Hung, L. M. Pollack, A. Canchola and A. Catania. 2002. Battering victimization among probability-based sample of men who have sex with men. *American Journal of Public Health* 92: 1964–1969.

Hamberger, L.K. 1996. Invention in gay male intimate violence requires coordinated efforts on multiple levels. In *Violence in gay and lesbian domestic partnerships*, ed. C. Renzetti and C. M. Miley, 83–92. New York: Harrington Park Press.

Hausman, B. L. 1995. Changing *sex: Transsexualism, technology and the idea of gender.* Durham: Duke University Press.

Hill Collins, P. 2004. *Black sexual politics: African Americans, gender and the new racism.* New York: Routledge.

———. 2009. *Black feminist thought: Knowledge, consciousness and the politics of consciousness.* New York: Routledge

hooks, b. 1984. *Feminist theory: From margins to centre.* Boston: South End Press.

Island, D. and P. Letellier. 1991. *Men Who Beat the Men Who Love Them.* New York: Harrington Park Press.

Kanuha, V. K. 2005. Compounding the triple jeopardy: Battering in lesbian of color relationships. In *Domestic violence at the margins: Readings on race, class, gender and culture*, ed. N. Sokoloff, 71–82. New Brunswick, NJ: Rutgers University Press.

Lamb, S., ed. 1999. *New version of victims.* New York: New York University Press.

Letellier, P. 1996. Twin epidemics: Domestic violence and HIV infection among gay and bisexual men. In *Violence in gay and lesbian domestic partnerships*, ed. C. Renzetti and C. M. Miley, 69–82. New York: Harrington Park Press.

McClain, L. 2006. The evolution—or end—of marriage ? Reflections on the impasse over same-sex marriage. *Family Court Review* 44(2): 200–208.

Mckenry, P. C., J. Serovich, T. L. Mason and K. Mosack. 2006. Perpetration of gay and lesbian partner violence: A disempowerment perspective. *Journal of Family Violence* 21: 233–243.

McLaughlin, E. M. and P. D. Rozee. 2001. Knowledge about heterosexual versus lesbian battering among lesbians. In *Intimate betrayal: Intimate partner abuse in lesbian relationships*, ed. E. Kaschak, 39–58. New York: Haworth Press.

Merrill, G. S. 1996. Ruling the exceptions: Same-sex battering and domestic violence theory. In *Violence in gay and lesbian domestic partnerships*, ed. C. M. Renzetti and C. H. Miley, 9– 21. New York: Harrington Park Press.

256   *Patricia Durish*

Miller, A. J., R. F. Bobner and J. J. Zarski. 2000. Sexual identity development: A base for work with same-sex couple partner abuse. *Contemporary Family Therapy* 22: 189–201.
Murray, V. M., P. A. Brown, G. H. Brody, C. E. Cutrona and R. L. Simons. 2001. Racial discrimination as a moderator of the links among stress, maternal psychological functioning, and family relationships. *Journal of Marriage and the Family* 63: 915–926.
Nicol, N. and M. Smith. 2008. Legal struggles and political resistance: Same-sex marriage in Canada and the USA. *Sexualities* 2(6): 667–687.
Ogden, P., K. Minton and C. Pain (2006). *Trauma and the body: A sensorimotor approach to psychotherapy.* New York: W.W. Norton & Co.
Poorman, P. B. 2001. Forging community links to address abuse in lesbian relationships. *In Intimate betrayal: Intimate partner abuse in lesbian relationships*, ed. E. Kaschak, 7–24. New York: Haworth Press.
Renzetti, C. 1992. *Violent betrayal: Partner abuse in lesbian relationships.* Thousand Oaks, CA: Sage.
———. 1996. The poverty of services for battered lesbians. In *Violence in gay and lesbian domestic partnerships*, ed. C. Renzetti and C. M. Miley, 61–68. New York: Harrington Park Press.
Renzetti, C. and C. M. Miley, eds. 1996. *Violence in gay and lesbian domestic partnerships.* New York: Harrington Park Press.
Ristock, Janice L. 2002a. *No more secrets: Violence in lesbian relationships.* New York: Routledge.
———. 2002b. Decentering heterosexuality: Response of feminist counselors to abuse in lesbian relationships. In *Intimate betrayal: Intimate partner abuse in lesbian relationships*, ed. E. Kaschak, 59–72. New York: Routledge.
Ristock, Janice L., and Norma Timbang. 2005. Relationship violence in lesbian/gay/bisexual/transgender/queer [LGBTQ] communities: Moving beyond a gender-based framework. Minnesota Centre against Violence and Abuse: Violence against Women Online Resources. Available at: http://www.mincava.umn.edu/documents/lgbtqviolence/lgbtqviolence.html [accessed November 28, 2010].
Rubin, G. 1984. The traffic in women: Notes on the political economy of sex. In *Toward and anthropology of women*, ed. R.R. Reiter, 157–210. New York: Monthly Review Press.
Seelau, E. P., S. M. Seelau and P. B. Poorman. 2003. Gender and role-based perceptions of domestic abuse: Does sexual orientation matter? *Behavioral Sciences and the Law* 21: 199–214.
Seidman, S., C. Meeks and F. Treaschen. 1999. Beyond the closet: The changing social meaning of homosexuality in the United States. *Sexualities* 2(10): 9–43.
Sokoloff, N. 2005. *Domestic Violence on the margins: Readings on race, class, gender and culture.* New Brunswick, NJ: Rutgers University Press.
Somerville, M. 2007. Children's human rights and unlinking child-parent biological bonds with adoption, same-sex marriage and new reproductive technologies. *Journal of Family Studies* 13(2): 179–201.
Statistics Canada. 2005. Family violence in Canada: A statistical profile—2005. http://www.statcan.gc.ca/pub/85–224-x/4064472-eng.htm.
Stevens, P. and J. Hall. 1994. A critical analysis of the medical construction of lesbianism. In *Women's health, politics and power: Essays on sex/gender, medicine and public health*, ed. E. Fee and N. Kreiger, 233–251. New York: Baywood Publishing Co.
Sullivan, J. S. and L. R. Laughlin. 1999. Identification and treatment modalities for victims of same-sex partner abuse. In *A professional's guide to understanding gay and lesbian domestic violence:*

Understanding practice interventions, ed. J. C. McClennen and J. Gunther, 95–106. Lewiston, NY: The Edwin Mellen Press.

Waldron, C. M. 1996. Lesbians of color and the intimate partner abuse movement. In *Violence in gay and lesbian domestic partnerships,* ed. C. M. Renzetti and C. H. Miley, 43–59. New York: Harrington Park Press.

Walsh, F. 1996. Partner abuse. In *Pink therapy: A guide for counselors and therapists working with lesbian, gay, and bisexual clients*, ed. D. Davies and C. Neal, 187–198. Philadelphia: Open University Press.

Wilkinson, S. 2004. Equal marriage/Le Droit Égal au Mariage: A personal view from Canada. *Feminism & Psychology* 14(1): 9–15.

Wilkinson, S. and C. Kitzinger. 2005. Same-sex marriage and equality. *The Psychologist* 18(5): 290–293.

Wise, A. J. and S. L. Bowman. 1997. Comparison of beginning counselors' responses to lesbian vs heterosexual partner abuse. *Violence and Victims* 12(2): 127–137.

Veinot, T. (2008). Who is the abuser? A screening challenge. Education Wife Assault. Available at: www.womanabuseprevention.com/html/screening.html [accessed November 28, 2010].

13 There's No Pride in Domestic Violence

The Same Sex Domestic Violence Interagency, Sydney, Australia

Kate Duffy[1]

INTRODUCTION

This chapter considers an Australian interagency of government and non-government agencies working in partnership to reduce the incidence of domestic violence in same sex relationships. A key strength of the "Same Sex Domestic Violence Interagency" (the interagency) is its longevity due to the commitment by its members and the diversity of agencies that they represent. The interagency has representatives from many fields of expertise working to provide services to respond to domestic violence. From police to health care workers, community organizations to private practitioners, each member is committed to creating awareness of same sex domestic violence (SSDV) in the wider community and working towards the provision of adequate services for people experiencing this violence. The interagency is unfunded and relies on the kind support and volunteer hours supplied by participating individuals and agencies.

The interagency has always based itself in the inner city suburbs of Darlinghurst and Surry Hills in Sydney, and consequently, much of the work has centered on the local area. This area is historically and culturally linked to the gay community. Although much of the work of the interagency is Sydney-focused, it operates across the state of New South Wales. This chapter will examine the work of the interagency between 2001 and 2009.

THE INTERAGENCY

Made up of a variety of representatives from government and non-government agencies in Sydney including members of women's groups and queer advocates, the purpose of the interagency is to monitor and review patterns in SSDV and to advocate for improvement in data collection practices. Other functions of the interagency include collecting and distributing current research and knowledge on SSDV; identifying and applying for sources of funding to support the strategies of the interagency; developing prevention and social support strategies to address the issues identified; increasing the community's awareness of SSDV, the resources available, and encouraging reporting; providing an educative and advisory role to key agencies and services; sharing information by organizing and hosting SSDV Education Forums and encouraging best clinical practice; making recommendations regarding allocation of resources to various strategies; advocating for policy development around SSDV; maintaining and further developing, when required, campaigns on SSDV; and actively engaging with individuals and organizations working in the area of SSDV.

Now in its tenth year, the interagency meets monthly, and with little to no money, has developed and implemented a number of projects and campaigns, promoted awareness and improved the response of service providers dealing with SSDV. Some of these initiatives have included: developing the state wide community awareness campaign *There's No Pride in Domestic Violence*; publishing an informative resource for people experiencing same sex domestic violence titled *Another Closet*; and conducting a data collection exercise which led to the production of a research report titled *Fair's Fair*.

The interagency was born out of a lack of specialist services specifically for gay men experiencing domestic violence. Ten years later there are still no specialist services for gay men. This has been the biggest challenge for the interagency and one that remains unresolved. Other challenges which will be explored in this chapter include: the fear of enhancing homophobic attitudes in the community by creating an awareness of SSDV; defining SSDV as different from heterosexual domestic violence; the ongoing struggle to source funding for various initiatives; the inadequacy of data collection systems and practices; the challenges of reaching the gay and lesbian community—particularly in rural, regional and remote areas; the backlash from the community particularly surrounding the effects of drug use and domestic violence; and the question of mutual abuse and working with perpetrators.

Despite the multiple challenges, the interagency boasts a number of achievements largely due to the strong commitment and diversity of the individuals and agencies involved, which have provided significant support and many volunteer hours. As a result of the strategic relationships formed by the interagency, New South Wales has seen the beginning of funded specialist SSDV services. ACON (formerly the AIDS Council of NSW—a gay and lesbian health promotion organization) received funding for the SSDV Officer role and the Inner City Legal Centre received funding to develop a SSDV court assistance scheme now known as the Safe Relationships Project. A new SSDV interagency—Speak Out Against Relationship Abuse (SOAR) has recently been established to service the greater Sydney area. Finally, perhaps the biggest achievement of the interagency has been the innovative nature of its projects, which have helped to create a dialogue on SSDV within the gay and lesbian community, and beyond. Before exploring the initiatives, challenges and strengths of the interagency in more detail, it is important to place the interagency, and the context of SSDV, in an Australian context.

THE AUSTRALIAN CONTEXT

Gay and Lesbian Inequality in Australia

A major contextual feature of the work of the interagency has been the unequal status of gay men and lesbians under Australian law. In NSW, for example, male homosexual sex was considered a criminal act until 1984, and same sex relationships were only recognized by the law as recently as 1999. The unequal legal status of gay men and lesbians individually, and in same sex relationships, has been a focal point for many gay and lesbian community initiatives, which have been directed at portraying the positive aspects of gay and lesbian lifestyles. As a result, community organizations have been reluctant to engage in initiatives that portray the gay and lesbian community in a negative light.

These fears have, in part, been realized by those critical of gay and lesbian individuals. Relationship violence is often used to lend credence to the notion that same sex relationships are "immoral," "unhealthy" and "deviant." Conservative Christian groups have publicly used *Fair's Fair* data (a report developed by the interagency, which will be discussed further below) to argue against equality for same sex relationships. For example, during the 2009 Australian Senate inquiries into equal marriage and the NSW Government inquiry into making adoption available to same sex couples, *Fair's Fair* was quoted as evidence that lesbian couples were more violent toward each other than heterosexual couples, and therefore should not be allowed to raise children (Salt Shakers n.d.). Consequently, with very little community dialogue about SSDV and only recent legal acknowledgment and recognition of same sex relationships, it has been difficult for some government agencies to acknowledge and identify SSDV. This is the context in which the interagency has had to work.

Changes in Australian Law to Recognize Same Sex Relationships

In 2008, both the NSW and federal governments amended a large number of laws in an attempt to give greater recognition to all relationships. While same sex couples continue to be denied access to adoption, and under federal law, are unable to get married, same sex couples are more recognized and closer to gaining equality than ever before. One area of significant development is that non-biological parents in same sex relationships will now have equal standing to biological parents under family law if any disputes arise about children after separation. While it remains to be seen how these changes to the law will impact the work of the interagency, a move towards legislative equality is an important step in ensuring that SSDV issues are included in future legislative and policy discussions on domestic violence.

Defining SSDV

Same sex domestic violence can be very difficult for the gay and lesbian communities to understand. Often the first challenge is communicating that SSDV really does exist—the concept of a woman hitting another woman or a man being a victim can be very provoking for some people, and can require a significant shift in thinking.

The next challenge has been distinguishing SSDV from heterosexual domestic violence. Although there are similarities, SSDV has unique aspects that require explanation and understanding. Homophobia, both internalized and external, can be particularly important in the experience of SSDV. For some victims of SSDV, homophobia can prevent them from telling their friends and family that they are in an abusive relationship because they may fear an inappropriate response. It may stop them from seeking help from counseling and medical services. There is also the fear of being outed and the fear of discrimination from the police and legal system (Cruz 2003; Merrill and Wolfe 2000).

Compounded by the historical lack of recognition and discrimination experienced by gay men and lesbians, and the gendered language that dominates most work on domestic violence, definitional issues have also exacerbated attempts to educate the wider community about domestic violence in same sex relationships (Ball and Hayes 2010; Letellier 1994). As wider community education is one of the key aims of the interagency, clarifying the definition of SSDV and drawing out its unique aspects have been integral to the work of the interagency. This is the framework in which the interagency has operated.

THE BEGINNINGS

In 2001, domestic violence service providers in the Surry Hills and Darlinghurst area noticed an increase in referrals for counseling and practical assistance for gay men experiencing the effects of domestic violence. In April 2001, a forum was organized at the St Vincent's Community Health Service's Darlinghurst Centre, to discuss this increase as well as the lack of services available for gay men affected by domestic violence. Over forty representatives including a range of government departments (Health, Housing, Police, the Attorney General's department, and Centrelink-Australia's welfare government department), as well as several non-governmental organizations, including gay and lesbian community organizations, legal centers and a homeless brokerage service, attended. A range of issues were canvassed at the forum and, as a direct result, the Same Sex Domestic Violence Interagency was formed to act to address the issue of domestic violence in gay and lesbian relationships.

During these early years the interagency produced comprehensive reading resources and a website, and was also successful in convincing the state's Department of Housing that someone escaping SSDV should be considered eligible for emergency housing. Although this amounted to three nights accommodation in a hotel (clearly not an ideal situation for victims of SSDV), it was a better alternative to what had previously been available.

The interagency also developed a report detailing the findings of an audit of 484 files at ACON counseling, a primary counseling service for gay men and lesbians in Sydney. The report was significant as it was the first substantive document demonstrating the incidence of SSDV. The files were examined for references to abuse and violence in same sex relationships, and it was found that violence was occurring in 11% of the files examined. The interagency also began a trial volunteer court support scheme for victims of SSDV at Waverley Local Court in Sydney. The court support service received some media attention by the local gay press, however it was discontinued shortly after its inception because it was not sustainable without funding.

In 2003, the interagency held a roundtable discussion that targeted service providers and government department representatives beyond the interagency membership. The aim of the roundtable was to ensure that these key services were aware that an SSDV community awareness campaign was being launched and that they were prepared for any increase in calls for service by people experiencing SSDV. This was a significant step on the road to addressing SSDV, as it was attended by about eighty people, representing a wide range of agencies including women's refuges, the police, counseling and support services, gay and lesbian services, health agencies, education services and legal services. Although, the response to the roundtable was mainly positive, there were some concerns from a group of women who objected to gay male inclusion in SSDV. The roundtable also received coverage in the gay and lesbian media, further increasing the awareness of the issue in the community.

INITIATIVES

In February 2004 the interagency launched the *There's No Pride In Domestic Violence Campaign*. This campaign emerged as a result of several years of work by the interagency to raise awareness of domestic violence in gay and lesbian relationships, and has been one of the interagency's most sustained and successful campaigns. As such, it warrants an in-depth discussion.

Campaign Considerations

In 2003 the interagency received $50,000, from the Attorney General's Department (AGD) to produce an SSDV community awareness campaign. Four broad considerations fed into the development process and ultimately shaped the final campaign. First, the interagency was determined not to develop a campaign that portrayed all gay and lesbian relationships in a negative light or that reinforced negative stereotypes. The interagency wanted to acknowledge that most gay and lesbian relationships are based upon love and respect. This would have the effect of reinforcing healthy relationships and encouraging individuals to reflect on the basis of their own relationships.

Second, as specialist services for lesbians were limited and they were practically non-existent for gay men, the interagency sought to strengthen the services available for victims. Without sufficient services to help people wishing to escape domestic violence, it was considered unethical (and possibly damaging) to develop a campaign that specifically encouraged people to escape their abusive relationships.

Third, the interagency sought to increase awareness of SSDV, as those agencies working with victims reported that their clients had a limited understanding of domestic violence. As there had never been a large scale, community wide campaign in the gay and lesbian community, the interagency made the assessment that the overall understanding of domestic violence was low.

Finally, the funding for the campaign specified that it target both gay men and lesbians, so the resources needed to represent both genders. Based on these considerations the aim of the campaign became to "increase community knowledge and understanding of domestic violence as a gay and lesbian issue." The majority of resources targeted the entire gay and lesbian community about the issue of same sex domestic violence rather than solely addressing individuals in abusive relationships.

Messages and Resources

The campaign title *There's No Pride In Domestic Violence* was decided on after extensive focus testing, as it juxtaposed the concept of community "pride" with "domestic violence," and stated that the two were mutually exclusive. The opening line in the main text stated that "most gay and lesbian relationships are based on love and respect. Some are based on abuse and control." This aimed to show that while the majority of relationships were healthy and positive, some were not. To further reinforce this message, the campaign artwork showed one lone black heart among a field of colored hearts. The final line of the poster stated: "Domestic violence exists in our community." This was followed by a number of referral details including the contact information for the NSW Domestic Violence Line.

A range of resources were produced including posters for gay and lesbian venues; as well as materials for mainstream locations like police stations, doctors' offices, counselors' offices, youth centers and so on; print advertisements for the lesbian and gay press media; a pamphlet that described what domestic violence was, how it manifested itself in gay and lesbian relationships, and referral options; stories from six survivors of same sex domestic violence; and a website.

Campaign Launch

The campaign launched in February 2004 at the Sydney Gay and Lesbian Mardi Gras Fair Day, a major gay and lesbian community event with up to 40,000 community members attending, and was a fun, high profile affair. In support of the aim to reinforce positive relationships, 10,000 heart-shaped, red, glitter-covered stickers printed with the phrase "Our Relationships" followed by "Love & Respect," "Long & Strong," "Unique & Equal," "Single & Happy" or "Single & Looking" were produced. The campaign was officially launched to an audience of thousands on the Fair Day main stage by drag performer Mitzi Mackintosh and ACON Board Member, David Buchannan SC. Prominent lesbian performer Shauna Jensen sang "Respect."

Another Closet: Resources for Victims, Friends, and Family

In February 2005, the second phase of the campaign was launched. This phase, entitled *Another Closet,* included a thirty-six page booklet, a business-card-sized information card and an upgraded website (www.anothercloset.com.au). The website was essentially an online version of the booklet, while the information card contained an abridged version of the information with a particular focus on contact details for services, and was designed specifically so it could easily be concealed.

These resources, unlike those for the *There's No Pride in Domestic Violence* campaign, were written for people experiencing domestic violence as well as their friends and family. For someone experiencing domestic violence, the resources included a relationship checklist for identifying abusive behaviors, descriptions of the different forms of abuse, safety planning suggestions, and strategies for recovering from abuse and violence. For friends and family, the resources outlined why a victim might stay in an abusive relationship, and strategies for helping them. Six survivors of SSDV were also asked to write their stories, and extracts from these stories were used to illustrate points throughout the *Another Closet* resources. Feedback from readers often focused on the strength of these extracts in encouraging them to seek help.

As a testament to the success of the campaign in getting the message out into the community, about 2,500 booklets and 10,000 information cards were produced using the original grant, while a further 10,000 booklets and 10,000 z-cards were printed in 2005 with $14,000 from the AGD NSW Victims of Crime Grant.

FAIR'S FAIR REPORT: A SNAPSHOT OF VIOLENCE AND ABUSE IN SYDNEY LGBT RELATIONSHIPS, 2006

Building upon the success of the *There's No Pride in Domestic Violence* campaign, the interagency began developing a two-paged self-completed survey to be conducted at the 2006 Mardi Gras Fair Day. The aim of the survey was to get a snapshot of the experiences of people in Sydney's gay and lesbian community in relation to domestic violence. Although the inter-agency predominantly works with violence in gay and lesbian same-sex relationships, this report also sought responses from transgendered individuals. A convenience or accidental sampling strategy was used to recruit respondents. The survey aimed to gather information about the experience of domestic violence in same sex relationships as well as the help-seeking behaviors of those respondents who reported experiencing abuse or violence within their relationship.

The survey found a range of important issues, providing the first significant picture of SSDV (Farrell and Cerise 2006). In all, the total sample of 308 Australian respondents demonstrated significant levels of violence and abuse in same sex relationships. Overall, it found that similar patterns of violence and abuse occurred across all genders in the sample. For participants of all genders (and referring to both previous and current relationships), it found that the forms of violence included: controlling/jealous behavior (in 48% of relationships); humiliation (45%); physical abuse (34%); social isolation (31%); financial control (18%); sexual abuse (17%); and outing (17%). In particular, young people between the ages of fifteen and twenty-five recorded high levels of some form of abuse, especially humiliation, outing and controlling or jealous behavior. Additionally, those who reported that they experienced abuse in a previous relationship were more likely to have entered into another abusive relationship. Finally, the survey found that children were a factor in violent relationships. A number of respondents (14%) who reported abuse in their current relationship had children under the age of sixteen in their care (this was more common for women (27%) than men (5%)), while 16% of respondents who reported one or more forms of abuse in a previous relationship indicated that they had children in their care during the relationship.

With regard to the help-seeking of victims and other support issues, the survey found that the majority of respondents who reported any abuse in a current or previous relationship (58%) did not seek any support in relation to the abuse. In particular, 67% of male respondents reporting one or more forms of abuse in a current or previous relationship did not seek any support. For those respondents that *did* seek help, the most common form of assistance was informal support from family and friends (33%), and the most common type of formal assistance sought was from counselors, psychologists, or social workers (19%).

OVERCOMING CHALLENGES

Throughout its existence, the interagency has encountered a number of limitations and challenges in achieving the aims of reducing SSDV, increasing awareness, and helping victims. This section will discuss these challenges so that others hoping to establish a campaign against SSDV are aware of some of the potential hurdles they might face.

Funding

The capacity of the interagency to undertake projects to respond to SSDV is in many ways limited by the lack of financial support. Considerable work has gone into writing grant applications and applying for funding. These grant applications, when successful, have enabled the interagency to implement many of the projects described earlier; however, without reliable and ongoing funds, the interagency is continuously redirected to look for financial support.

Support arrangements from members of the interagency are common and directly impact the ability of the interagency to continue to function. For example, ACON has consistently hosted meetings of the interagency and administered any funding received. Without this type of support from member agencies, the interagency would not have the capacity to implement these types of strategies to address SSDV.

Lack of Specialist Services

Lack of funding has been a constant challenge to the work of the interagency, as well as to the delivery of services to gay men who are experiencing domestic violence. The funding available to address domestic violence almost exclusively follows a gendered language and is offered either by organizations that support women or for projects addressing domestic violence in the traditional context—that is with women as victims and men as perpetrators. There are currently no services for gay male victims of domestic violence in NSW. At present, if a gay man is in need of crisis accommodation as a result of escaping a domestic violence situation, he has nowhere to turn to for housing other than homeless shelters, which are often inappropriate and may present a risk for gay men. Gay men frequently resort to asking friends or family for a place to stay, or alternatively pay for a hostel or hotel. The lack of crisis accommodation for gay men was a standing agenda item at the interagency meetings during 2004–2007, and it remains an issue to address in future work plans.

Rural/Regional/Remote Areas

For people in same sex relationships living in rural, regional, or remote (RRR) areas, the distances and isolation further exacerbate the problems they may be facing in their relationships. When both the abuser and the victim live in the same town, their options are often limited when it comes to social and community activities and support services.

The experiences of lesbians and gay men who live in RRR areas are extremely different to the experiences of lesbians and gay men who live in the city. There is certainly a belief that people living outside the metropolitan "melting pots" of larger cities like Sydney are less accepting of difference. The expectation is that people living in RRR areas are more likely to be conservative and homophobic. This is a generalization and is not always the case, but in some instances a "small town mentality" applies, where everyone knows everyone and no one's business is private. Those that are experiencing SSDV are more likely to be closeted for fear of homophobic responses from neighbors and the community. The lack of services in RRR areas also mean that it is harder for people to access the support they need when experiencing domestic violence. The interagency has found it difficult to ensure that the various campaigns reach those people living in RRR areas. Gay newspapers and magazines (in which the interagency campaigns are featured) are not distributed to RRR areas, or if they are, they are not freely available. Additionally, some community members believe that those magazines do not represent the lives of lesbians and gay men living in RRR areas. The distance from the cities and the conservative and homophobic attitudes that occur in RRR areas will continue to be a great challenge for the interagency.

Data Recording

The lack of acknowledgement of SSDV in the community and among service providers suggests that SSDV is under-reported. This is supported by research evidence within Australia and beyond (see Ball and Hayes 2010; Jeffries and Ball 2008). The lack of reliable data on SSDV means a greater reliance on anecdotal reports and personal stories to measure and describe the problem of SSDV within the community. The need for more rigorous data is vital for any funding application. Despite some successful attempts at data collection, such issues continue to pose a challenge for the interagency in its quest to successfully apply for funding from government and other sources.

The issue of under-reporting is compounded by the fear of a negative response from authorities such as police, and a fear of inaccurate recording of the event. A domestic violence incident between two men in a same sex relationship for example, is often viewed as a "fist fight" between two roommates. If it *is* recorded correctly as domestic violence on the Computerized Operational Policing Reports System (COPS)—the database used by the NSW Police Force—the system does not specifically record incidents of "same sex domestic violence." Consequently, to ascertain whether certain incidents are SSDV, one would have to manually examine individual records on the database to determine the gender of parties involved and the nature of the relationship, if known. This process is quite labor intensive and impractical.

In relation to court data, most domestic violence matters, including applications for apprehended violence orders (AVOs) are heard in local courts.

The only way to identify SSDV matters is to examine the court lists—or in other words to read through the facts of the application and look at the names and gender of the "person in need of protection" and the defendant in order to determine if there is an intimate relationship.

COMMUNITY BACKLASH TO FAIR'S FAIR

Lesbian Domestic Violence

There has been some criticism of the results of *Fair's Fair*. In particular, one survey question asked about the experience of abuse in previous relationships. The results of this question showed that approximately 40% of the female respondents said they had been in a previous abusive relationship. However, there was no follow-up question that asked whether this previous abusive relationship was with a woman or a man. It is therefore unknown if the abuse reported in the survey is wholly SSDV, or if it included heterosexual domestic violence. The *Fair's Fair* report thus shows that lesbian domestic violence occurs at a greater rate than heterosexual couples, which may or may not be entirely accurate.

Drug Use and Domestic Violence

Another issue that arose after the release of *Fair's Fair* and the data collected was a backlash from the community about differentiating domestic violence and the impact of violent "come downs" from drug use. One community member, Steven Easy, wrote in an article called "Fighting Fit" in the *Sydney Star Observer* on June 14, 2007:

> My frustration with the Fair's Fair report is the way alarming statistics and statements about gay men are being used in an apparent attempt to secure government funding. If this is a problem that's more prevalent among lesbians than gay men, I think we should say that. And if this is a problem that's actually more about violent drug comedowns and substance abuse issues (particularly ice) than partners hitting each other, I think we should say that, too. (p. XX)

The impact of drugs on SSDV is relatively unknown. The challenge that remains is addressing the issue without taking responsibility away from the perpetrator. The interagency has since resolved to consider violence targeted against the victim, despite drug use, as domestic violence.

In response to the preceding article, Brad Gray from the interagency, in the June 21, 2007 issue of the *Sydney Star Observer wrote* that:

> While it's true that drugs can make some people violent it's also true that in most cases people who are violent towards their partner when

they are on drugs are also emotionally abusive to, and controlling of, their partner when they are not on drugs. This is well understood in the broader health, legal and welfare sectors. By excusing DV as a result of drugs (including alcohol), we, as individuals and a community, allow the perpetrators to abrogate responsibility for their action. (p. XX)

PERPETRATORS AND SERVICE PROVISION

Determining who is the victim and who is the perpetrator of an SSDV incident remains an issue for domestic violence service providers. The interagency, made up of various domestic violence service providers, has to address this question on a daily basis, particularly by deciding who the primary aggressor is and who is deserving of the service. An original goal of the interagency was to serve both perpetrators and victims because at times mutual abuse may be present, or it may be too unclear to recognize one clear victim and one clear perpetrator. However, the group diverted from this focus in favor of assisting victims, largely due to member agencies from health organizations being unable to deal with perpetrators because of their workplace policies and guidelines. The interagency, however, has seen the benefit of including issues of perpetration, holding forums for clinicians on this subject, as well as addressing it in conferences and workshops.

STRENGTHS

Beyond the limitations outlined above, there are a number of important strengths of the interagency. These are outlined further in the following section, and may also be useful for those seeking to establish and maintain a successful collaborative program devoted to addressing the issue of SSDV.

Diversity of Interagency Members and Commitment

Domestic violence is an area that crosses all boundaries, and therefore government and non government agencies acting together in partnership for the community is imperative. The interagency is one of the longest running and most productive interagency meetings in Sydney, and has greatly benefited from the collaborative approach of its members.

Strategic Relationships

Auspiced by ACON

A key element in the success of interagency projects has been its partnership with ACON. The interagency is not a formal organization, and when it was successful in receiving funding from the Attorney General's Department in 2002, one of its member agencies had to auspice the interagency to receive the funding. ACON was chosen and having the support of the nation's largest LGBT health organization in this capacity meant interagency campaigns could become widespread and the resources of ACON were accessible for the interagency to use.

The interagency also paved the way for ACON to integrate SSDV into their heath awareness campaigns. Beginning in 2005, SSDV joined gay and lesbian sexual health, homophobic violence, and drug use as one of the key areas of focus in ACON's health campaigns. The SSDV message was injected into party-theme campaigns and included in press advertisements. In 2006 and 2007 ACON continued to include domestic violence elements in their community campaigns.

NSW Police Force

The partnership with the NSW Police Force has been invaluable in raising awareness of SSDV among police officers and in effectively training police to respond appropriately to SSDV situations. As the police are often the first point of contact for victims of SSDV, particularly when there has been physical assault, the response of police significantly impacts the experience of victims. SSDV has been incorporated into the Gay and Lesbian Liaison Officer training as well as training for specialist police Domestic Violence Liaison Officers, and since 2005, an interagency representative has been included in all SSDV training being conducted for members of the police force.

An ongoing issue in training police officers is to clearly define SSDV by drawing out the similarities and differences to heterosexual domestic violence. Police officers are trained to respond to all incidents of domestic violence in a consistent fashion, as law enforcement officers, in the interests of protecting the victims from harm. However, they are also encouraged to examine each situation and all aspects of diversity to enable an appropriate response. This may appear contradictory at times, reinforcing the need for good quality training and policy direction.

Media

When the interagency first approached the gay press media in Sydney, the media wanted to speak to someone who had personal experience with SSDV. Finding a person who is willing and able to talk about their experiences in a public arena is incredibly difficult on many levels. The *There's No Pride in Domestic Violence* campaign allowed the interagency to form better relationships with the media in outlining a language to discuss the issue of SSDV. There is now a greater understanding in, and more cooperation with, the media in highlighting the issue of SSDV, as it is clear that media exposure is important for a campaign to be successful.

ACON's Anti Violence Project SSDV Officer

After the launch of the *Fair's Fair* Report, ACON applied for funding from the NSW Department of Premier and Cabinet Office for Women's Policy for a full time SSDV Officer for twelve months. ACON was successful with this grant and employed an SSDV Officer in October 2008 to undertake initiatives to build the capacity of mainstream services to respond to SSDV.

The role of the SSDV Officer has been invaluable for the interagency. Allocating a full time position to respond to SSDV gave the interagency a "go to" person for project leads. A central component of the twelve-month project was to conduct an analysis of existing services available for people experiencing SSDV, identify gaps, and make recommendations for improvements. A key recommendation from the gap analysis is the development of a toolkit to assist mainstream service providers to improve services for people experiencing domestic violence in same sex relationships. The project is waiting for further funding to continue in 2010.

Safe Relationships Project

At the start of 2008, the Inner City Legal Centre (ICLC)—a member agency of the interagency—applied to the Public Purpose Fund (a non-government fund that collects interest from law firm trust accounts) for additional funding to establish services that address the legal needs of specific groups of disadvantaged people in NSW. ICLC was successful in its application and received funding for a project for a three-year period. ICLC decided to put the money towards developing what is now the Safe Relationships Project (SRP).

The SRP is a new court assistance scheme for people in same sex relationships, transgender and transsexual people, and intersex people who are experiencing domestic violence. It is the first of its kind in Australia (and quite possibly the world). The aim of the SRP is to assist clients in accessing legal representation and applying for Apprehended Violence Orders as well as to provide support, advocacy, referrals, and information. This is to ensure that a person's right to safety is protected through the legal process, regardless of their sex, gender, or sexual orientation. The SRP can also assist victims of domestic violence in related legal matters, including support during criminal proceedings, family law matters, disputes over children and property, and victims compensation. The SRP was launched in July 2009 and has been assisting clients since that time. The SRP is still working hard to develop its profile in the community and is working very closely with the interagency to respond to and prevent SSDV.

Speak Out Against Relationship Abuse (SOAR) Interagency

SOAR is a Community Education Project initiated in February 2009 by Wimlah, a Blue Mountains Specialist Domestic Violence Service in NSW. SOAR seeks to address specific service barriers for lesbian victims of domestic violence in rural areas including increased isolation, fewer services, more intense experiences of community homophobia, minimization, and silencing attitudes. As a newly formed pilot interagency, SOAR held its first meeting in November 2009. Ten agencies were present who are committed to strengthening the greater Sydney service response to SSDV by promoting inclusive, collaborative, anti-homophobia domestic violence resources, service directories, training, on-going community forums and consultations. SOAR aims to raise awareness about the hidden nature of lesbian domestic violence within our communities. It also seeks to source, research, educate and assist in the creation of best practice SSDV models for government services in this region, which will increase appropriate and safe referral pathways for lesbians accessing mainstream domestic violence and other health, legal or welfare services.

CONCLUSION

The projects led by the interagency have been groundbreaking in bringing SSDV out of the closet and making the community aware that domestic violence does exists in our communities. By no means have these initiatives been able to help all victims, or highlight all forms of domestic violence in the gay community—the continuing invisibility of transgender and intersex people is a clear example of this. However, the interagency has been somewhat effective and will continue to build towards overcoming the unique challenges that SSDV work entails in order to provide an effective response and prevent domestic violence in same sex relationships. The interagency is hopeful that funding for specialized SSDV services and SSDV training, and for mainstream domestic violence services, will become more regular and secure in the future.

NOTES

1. Acknowledgments: Thank you to Vanessa Viaggio, Yasmin Hunter, Brad Gray, Elisabeth Childs, Jackie Braw, Matthew Ball, Celia Hutton and Deb Gavan for their contributions.

REFERENCES

ACON (AIDS Council of NSW) and Same Sex Domestic Violence Interagency (SSDVI). 2006. *Fair's fair: A snapshot of violence and abuse in Sydney LGBT relationships*. Sydney: ACON.

Ball, M. and S. Hayes. 2010. Same-sex intimate partner violence: Exploring the parameters. In *Queering Paradigms*, ed. Burkhard Scherer, 161–177. Oxford: Peter Lang.

Cruz, M. 2003. Why doesn't he just leave? Gay male domestic violence and the reasons victims stay. *Journal of Men's Studies* 11–(3): 309–323.

Easy, Steve. 2007. Fighting Fit. *Sydney Star Observer*, June 14.

Gray, Brad. 2007. *Sydney Star Observer*, June 21.

Inner City Legal Centre. Safe relationships project and inner city legal centre. http://www.iclc.org.au/srp.

Jeffries, S. and M. Ball. 2008. Male same-sex intimate partner violence: A descriptive review and call for further research. *Murdoch University E-Law Journal* 15(1): 134–179. Also available at: https://elaw.murdoch.edu.au/archives/issues/2008/elaw_15_1_Jeffries_Ball.pdf.

Letellier, P. 1994. Gay and bisexual male domestic violence victimization: Challenges to feminist theory and responses to violence. *Violence and Victims* 9(2): 95–106.

Merrill, G. and V. Wolfe. 2000. Battered gay men: An exploration of abuse, help seeking and why they stay. *Journal of Homosexuality* 39(2): 1–30.

Salt Shakers. Salt shakers: Helping Christians make a difference. Available at: http://www.saltshakers.org [accessed November 25, 2010].

SSDVI. Another closet: Domestic violence in gay and lesbian relationships. Available at: http://www.anothercloset.com.au [accessed November 25, 2010].

14 Running Same-Sex Batterer Groups
Critical Reflections on the New York City Gay and Lesbian Anti-Violence Project and the Toronto David Kelley Services' Partner Assault Response Program

Jesmen Mendoza and Diane R. Dolan-Soto

Services for lesbian, gay, bisexual, transgender, queer (LGBTQ) partner abuse are needed and important. However, to successfully address the issue of LGBTQ partner abuse, communities need to take a two-pronged approach to this issue. First and foremost is the provision of services for victims and the families impacted by LGBTQ partner abuse in delivering a coordinated approach to intervening with this societal problem. The second prong of this approach involves addressing the abusive behavior of batterers. Services for LGBTQ partner abuse have been limited and primarily focused on victims. A cursory survey of the literature that we conducted confirms this gap in service. The gap however, is even more pronounced when one considers the lack of research on batterers in LGBTQ partner abuse (Murray, Mobley, Buford, and Seaman-DeJohn 2008; Schwartz and Waldo 2004). Despite the limited research, batterer programs for LGBTQ abusers have developed in some major city centers across North America.

The aim of this chapter is to describe and compare two of these batterer programs for LGBTQ partner abuse and we hope to stimulate a discussion on how such programs should best be delivered. The first part of this chapter describes two programs from two major city centers that have a visible and active queer community presence—New York City and Toronto. Each program's origins are described along with program delivery, curriculum and the populations served. Attention is given to the context and how each of these programs evolved. Distinct differences are outlined with respect to funding, and referral base between the two programs. However, similarities are also noted with respect to curriculum and program delivery.

The second part of this chapter synthesizes critical reflections on both programs. Despite the differences, staffs from both services have come to similar conclusions about facilitating groups for LGBTQ partner abuse offenders, such as the need to offer separate groups for men and women, and that LGBTQ partner abuse or violence is a gendered phenomenon. Such critical reflections will serve as a springboard for recommendations for delivery of service for offenders of LGBTQ partner abuse. Our hope is that our recommendations will be useful, and that they might serve as guidelines for developing, creating and delivering group programs for LGBTQ partner abuse offenders.

NEW YORK CITY GAY AND LESBIAN ANTI-VIOLENCE PROJECT'S SEEKING NON-VIOLENT ALTERNATIVES PROGRAM (SNAP)

Origin

In 1980, a growing awareness of the AIDS epidemic in New York City coincided with a rise in hate crimes targeted at gay men. With no formal support services and ineffectual and biased responses coming from the city's police force at that time, a grassroots community response erupted. Several years of volunteer and community-supported effort coalesced to form the New York City Gay and Lesbian Anti-Violence Project, a non-profit agency dedicated to serving LGBTQ victims of crime.

Amid the incidents of bias and violence there were unexpected reports of intimate partner, rather than stranger violence. Although initially seen as anomalies, by 1983 reports of same sex violence accounted for 30% of the agency's hotline calls. By 1986, a continued rise in calls resulted in the establishment of a formal program to address gay and lesbian domestic violence. By 2000, intimate partner domestic violence, including violence involving transgender and bisexual victims, accounted for about 50% of new incidents reported annually (Dolan-Soto 2002).

The agency sought to raise awareness of domestic violence with an educational subway campaign in the mid 1980s. Responses from the community ranged from disbelief to concern that this "airing of dirty laundry" would provide further fodder for discrimination and marginalization. For LGBTQ individuals affected by partner violence there was a more immediate challenge; both victims and abusers expressed confusion about what constituted abuse in an intimate relationship, and what role they had in the violence. Anti-Violence Project (AVP) services could address victims' needs and could raise awareness through education and outreach to the community. It became apparent through computer tracking of victims' services, however, that reported batterers moved on to abuse new victims. Without services to address batterers it was clear that domestic violence would continue.

Responding to this gap in services in 1991, a collaborative effort between AVP and a team of clinical professionals donating their time and expertise resulted in the development of Seeking Non-Violent Alternatives Program, better known as SNAP, New York's first same sex batterers' program.[1] The program involved a five-person team comprised of a clinical supervisor and two male and two female facilitators. Two groups were offered, one for gay men and another for lesbian batterers.

The program ran for one year. Groups had an average of six participants ranging in age from their mid thirties to forties. All participants had engaged in a range of controlling and abusive behaviors. Physical abuse included hitting, pushing, slapping and punching to threats and intimidation, destruction of personal property, choking and use of weapons. Commission of physical abuse was not a marker required for entering the program, although all participants had been physically abusive at some point with their partners. About half of all participants reported some level of police involvement (reported by a neighbor, friend, family, or the victim; an arrest etc.). All batterers expressed a concern that without help they would hurt their partner again, or would be arrested for their behavior. The need for services and the structure were formulated based on the precepts that: (1) gay male abusers would likely be at risk of bias and violence if they attended heterosexual male batterers' groups; (2) there were no services to address female batterers; and (3) issues specific to gender identity and sexual orientation would probably not be able to be effectively addressed in a mixed group of gay male and lesbian batterers, as power imbalances, primarily based on gender, would more likely surface. The last precept anticipated that gendered dynamics would emerge between participants that would disrupt the group work and distract from the focus on participant accountability. The groups were effective and ran for a full year. It was not possible to continue this as a volunteer-only effort and with no funding available the program was unable to be maintained.

In 1999, SNAP was re-launched. AVP was able to generate limited funding through community donation and foundation funding for facilitators, intake assessments, supervision, and curriculum development. The second run of the program offered the opportunity to review the founding ideology and program structure. The experience of SNAP in 1991 had supported and reinforced the need to maintain separate groups for lesbian and gay male batterers. Consideration of gender and sexual orientation also led to the extension of service to abusers of transgender victims, regardless of sexual orientation, or to transgender identified batterers. Heterosexually identified batterers of transgender victims were considered unlikely to be served in traditional batterers' programs, as they were apt to be targeted by other participants. The program was designed to include transgender identified individuals or partners who abused transgender partners according to their self-identified gender.

Delivery

SNAP originally involved a fourteen-week format based on the Duluth model (as is the case for Toronto). This model conceived in 1981 was formulated on coordinated community response that "hold[s] perpetrators and intervening practitioners accountable for victim safety, offer[s] offenders an opportunity to change (including punishment if it enhances victim safety) and ensure[s] due process for offenders through the intervention process" (Domestic Abuse Intervention Programs n.d.). Among other philosophical approaches, the Duluth Model asserts that "[i]nterventions must account for the economic, cultural, and personal histories of the individuals who become abuse cases in the system," and that "[b]oth victims and offenders are members of the community; while they must each act to change the conditions of their lives the community must treat both with respect and dignity recognizing the social causes of their personal circumstances" (Domestic Abuse Intervention Programs n.d.). For the LGBTQ community this model is limited in that it generally posits intimate partner violence between male abusers and female victims and interventions address male perpetrators' abuse of power and privilege inherent in a patriarchal society. SNAP developed a curriculum using similar assertions of abuse perpetrated in a context of power and privilege but expanded the understanding of power imbalances within LGTBQ relationships to include such additional hierarchical issues as heterosexism, socioeconomic status, age, gender, and other factors.[2]

Implemented over a two-year period, observations of the program, referral sources and impact of wait times, and curricula refinement led to the development of a new structure. The program evolved from fourteen consecutive sessions to a revolving twenty-three session, two-tiered structure. The expanded format allowed for several extended sessions to focus on topics that posed greater difficulty for participants (sexual and economic abuse, internalized homophobia, etc.) Rather than groups with a fixed start and end period, the revolving format was conceived to lessen wait-list times. Participants could enter the initial round of twelve sessions (Tier I) within the first six weeks. In order to move to the remaining sessions (Tier II) participants had to complete all Tier I sessions which required that they understood, regardless of their own past experiences or perceptions of victimization, their sole responsibility and accountability for their actions. Threaded throughout Tier I was a focus on making participants aware of their attitudes and behaviors, which were abusive to their partners. Tier II sessions built on these lessons of responsibility and accountability in some of the more subtle challenging material handled in extended sessions.

SNAP was funded as a community initiative and worked with primarily self-referred (as opposed to court-mandated) clients. Rather than a criminal justice driven program, SNAP was driven by community need and therefore had a public health focused contextual mandate with services geared to reduce or prevent intimate partner violence and improve lives at the individual/couple level and for the community at large.

Although some participants were referred by the criminal court system, the program itself was not structured to provide a court-mandated evaluation. Court-referred participants were informed that the program would not provide regular reports or confirmation of program completion.

Participants who chose to pursue participation fell roughly into two categories: those who expected the courts would lessen or drop charges because
of their participation; and those who felt the program was necessary to
prevent things from getting worse, generally for themselves and secondarily
for their partner. The first category of batterers often did not complete
the program, as it did not serve their primary intention to avoid criminal
charges. A letter to indicate a participant had attended program sessions
was provided if requested by the participant, but again no formal report of
participation or compliance was made available. Courts found the program
refreshing for its emphasis on personal accountability and SNAP quickly
gained respect within the criminal justice system. Over the course of the
program, however, referrals from the courts accounted for little more than
2% of participants. Overwhelmingly, referrals for the program came from
victimized partners, and the LGBTQ batterers themselves.

Potential participants were required to initiate a screening appoint-
ment. Co-facilitators conducted psychosocial assessments of the appli-
cant's history of violence, noting the presence or absence of remorse and
accountability—those who clearly exhibited a strong feeling of guilt and
regret for their actions and who were receptive to owning responsibility
for the impact of their actions on their partner or others. This of course
had to be backed up behaviorally (e.g., arriving on time for appointments, being actively engaged in understanding and owning the impact
of their actions, being willing to reflect on or question their own behavior
and attitudes). These qualities proved to be key indicators of a potential
participant's ability to utilize the program effectively. Absence of these
qualities could be considered indicators significant for denial of entry to
the program.

Intakes were reviewed in a group supervisory format to determine appro-
priateness for participation. This enabled the team to recognize problematic
presentations and identify trends. Group review prevented facilitators from
missing key gaps, or being inadvertently swayed by interviewees' emotional
manipulations to gain entry into the program.

Written information provided to participants outlined the program's
emphasis on behavior change and personal accountability to effect change,
including responsibility to pay for participation in the program. Applicants
were required to sign forms acknowledging receipt of program information, agreement to the rules of the program and to notification of the appli-
cant's current partner/victim. Partner notification offered information on
the program, the limits of what could be expected, and information about
where the victimized partner could access supports and services. Under the
auspices of AVP's victims' services, the focus of SNAP maintained a clear
emphasis on victim safety.

SNAP groups started when six or more participants completed intake.
Participants fell broadly in two groups; those that successfully completed
the program and those that did not. Nearly all successful participants

expressed the need for on-going services to maintain behavior changes. A number of successful participants requested the opportunity to repeat the entire program to reinforce learning and behavior change. One lesbian batterers' group expressed the need for "an after-care" program and unanimously decided to repeat the program due to their own concerns about maintaining behavior change without further reinforcement. Among participants who completed SNAP there were no reported recidivism by participants, their partners, or from police or the criminal justice system.

Curriculum

The curriculum explored not only the social context within which domination and abusive behaviors were learned, related belief systems, and forms of oppression such as racism and sexism, but more specifically looked at the impact of homophobia, transphobia and biphobia, power dynamics specific to same-sex couples, and the means by which conceptualizations and expressions of sexual orientation and gender identity can be used as a means of control.

LGBTQ batterers recognized the relevant contextual understanding of power and oppression. Facilitators used this heightened awareness to clarify personal choice and responsibility for acting in ways that coerce, dominate, or isolate victims. Many of these topics generated reports by participants of their own abuse histories and experiences. It was critical that facilitators remained focused on the impact of participants' abusive behaviors and beliefs on their partners/victims. The curriculum maintained an emphasis on skill-building, highlighting communication, and management of co-factors (anxiety, stress, etc.) with the overall goal of establishing and maintaining changed behaviors.

The expanded format enabled facilitators to address areas that presented greater challenge to behavior modification. Forms of abuse detailed in the Power and Control In Lesbian, Gay, Transgender & Bisexual Relationships Wheel developed by the New York City Gay and Lesbian Anti-Violence Project (2000) were presented in full session units; these included "psychological and emotional abuse, threats, physical abuse, entitlement, using children, economic, sexual and HIV-related abuse, intimidation, isolation: restricting freedom, heterosexism homophobia, biphobia, and transphobia. Several forms of abuse, which posed significant challenges for batterers, were extended into two session units each to identify and challenge participant's beliefs and clearly delineate personal responsibility for abusive behaviors. For example, batterers were confronted with their behaviors in great detail, looking at underlying tactics of psychological and emotional abuse (constant criticizing, verbal abuse, insults and ridicule; undermining a victimized partner's self-esteem, humiliating or degrading in private or public; manipulating with lies and false promises; denying their partner's reality) and similar tactics in economic abuse (controlling economic resources and how they are used; stealing money, credit cards or checks; running up the victimized partner's debt; fostering total economic dependence; using economic status to determine relationship roles/norms, including controlling purchase of clothes, food, etc.) as well as sexual abuse (forcing sex and/or specific sex acts, sex with others; physical assaults to "sexual" body areas; refusing to practice safe sex; refusing to negotiate or not respecting contract/scene limits or safe words for those who engage in S&M). Expanded sessions were also used to address managing conflict, developing mutual communication skills, and maintenance of changed behaviors and beliefs.

Populations Served (Referral Base)

The population of SNAP participants reflected the gender ratio of victims seen by AVP's Intimate Partner Domestic Violence Program; on average more women than men sought services. Whites comprised more than half of participants among male and female participants, African Americans accounted for about a third with the remaining participants of Latino, mixed or other race/ethnicity. Participants ranged in socioeconomic standing from unemployed to professional, with education for the majority of participants at college level or higher.[3] Participants ranged in age from thirties to mid-forties with some limited representation before and beyond this age range.

The majority of participants either viewed themselves as having "lost control," or as in need of couple's services in order to save their relationship. A small number of self-referred participants sought services for fear that incidents of violence would result in police involvement. As noted earlier, only a limited number of participants at the start of the program had interaction with the police or criminal justice system. Even of these participants, most were self-referred. As mentioned, 2% of participants were court-referred. This appeared to be a reflection of the low rate of participant follow-through and not the actual number of referrals made by court personnel. A slightly larger percentage of referrals came from victims, or family or friends of the abuser. The largest segment of participants who engaged and successfully completed the program were those who had demonstrated a sense of remorse and personal accountability for their actions, had sought services of their own accord, and who demonstrated no known recidivism or physical violence toward their partner over the course of the program.

TORONTO'S DAVID KELLEY SERVICES' LGBTQ PARTNER ASSAULT RESPONSE PROGRAM

Origin

Prior to the spring of 2001 in the city of Toronto, there were no formal services for perpetrators of same-sex partner abuse. Those that self-identified as being abusive to one's partner did not have any resources that they could access. Those court-ordered or needing to meet the conditions of their probation orders were typically sent to community counseling programs where staff were not necessarily trained in engaging offenders, working with LGBTQ issues or delivering a service that met their needs. The majority of those that were mandated for counseling were typically sent to the David Kelley Services of the Family Service Toronto. David Kelley Services (DKS) is a community counseling program that offers short to medium-term counseling to lesbian, gay, bi, transgender, and queer adults. This program has run a number of community initiatives and has been involved in many community development projects for the queer community. DKS had slowly started to see an increase in referrals and the counselors within the community counseling program had not been equipped to assist those referred to the program. The increase in referrals led to the hiring of a part-time counselor dedicated to seeing LGBTQ partner abuse perpetrators; the Ministry of the Attorney General funded the position.

The hiring of a part-time staff member, who was familiar with same sex partner abuse issues, versed in helping clients navigate the criminal justice system, and liaising with the criminal justice system itself, had been pivotal in the growth of the program. A knowledgeable and skilled staff member was charged with promoting awareness of the program to key stakeholders in the criminal justice system. This then allowed probation officers in the community and crown attorneys from the court to send referrals to the David Kelley Services without reservation. Emphasis for promotion of this program was focused on the criminal justice system because it provided the funding for the position of the part-time counselor; thus court or probation-referred clients took precedence in being invited to group. Little promotion occurred with respect to inviting people in the broader LGBTQ community to attend because it was not the primary focus based on the funding of the counselor position. As a result, the DKS Partner Assault Response (PAR) program was born and began seeing court or probation referred clients on an individual basis. In the first year alone, five gay men, and one lesbian were ordered by court and probation to be seen by the program. Over the next year the referrals doubled as probation and parole, along with the courts, gained confidence in the program. Such referrals led to pressure on the DKS PAR program. Clients needed to be seen in a timely fashion in order to meet the time limits imposed by one's probation or court order. Hence, groups evolved as the logical next step in service delivery.

As the DKS PAR group program developed, debate arose in the community as to where to house such a program. The struggle that emerged was whether such a program should be located in a queer social service agency or housed at a treatment agency for batterers. A treatment agency that specialized in delivering battering programs had delivered two PAR group programs for gay men with two gay male co-facilitators in the city of Toronto. There were not, however, enough referrals in the city to sustain both programs. Treatment agencies in the city of Toronto that specialized in the provision of service for male batterers could not ensure that they could always hire queer staff. Ultimately, DKS reasoned that such a program would best be served if it were housed at a queer-specific agency thereby ensuring that queer staff would always deliver the PAR program.

Delivery

In delivering a government funded PAR program in the province of Ontario and in the city of Toronto, PAR programs are required to meet certain standards and address certain themes as set out by the Ministry of the Attorney General and the Woman Abuse Council of Toronto (WACT), which coordinate the organization and the delivery of service to batterers. Two part-time co-facilitators and a part-time partner contract counselor are required to staff one PAR group. The challenge that DKS faced was delivering a PAR service with three staff members to a diverse group of individuals that would be referred for same-sex partner abuse. Having a separate men's and women's program for same-sex partner abuse would have been the ideal model of service delivery because they could have addressed specific dynamics relevant to each community. Funding was not available, however, for such a model and instead the program had to use a mixed group format where gay men, and lesbians would sit together to explore issues of perpetrating partner abuse. Such a format ultimately meant utilizing a co-gendered program and co-facilitation staffing configuration. This program was piloted and ran for four cycles; each cycle consisted of a sixteen-week period addressing the themes required by the Ministry of the Attorney General and WACT.

The best practice guidelines of WACT and the Ministry recognize that the primary goal of this work is the safety of the partners and children exposed to the violence of the perpetrator. Although the program directly worked with perpetrators, this program was ultimately in the service of keeping their partners and families safe. Unless partners had declined from participating, a counselor separate from the co-facilitation team made contact with partners to address their safety.

Partners/victims were invited to participate in the partner contact program of the batterer intervention service. Those that chose to participate in partner contact would be contacted at quarterly intervals during the program and informed of and given the option to access resources with a partner contact worker who did not work with the batterers directly. Partners were informed of batterers progress in the program, and partners/victims were also given the opportunity to have their batterer challenged on a particular issue/behavior in group provided that the partner/victim felt safe and did not fear reprisal. Partner contact proved useful in that it allowed DKS to offer services to victims or refer them to other community resources. Partner contact workers would constantly assist partners/victims with their safety plans and partners were informed about the nature of the program as well as the realistic gains that their batterer could make.

Members of the batterers program were told upfront that their participation and membership in the program would be contingent on them giving the program the explicit consent to contact their partners/victims to inform them of the member's enrollment, their participation in the group as well as a member's early termination from group. Batterers were also informed that any interference with the services to their partners would result in their termination from the program. Further, batterers were informed that the program would not serve as a means by which those who were estranged or separated from their partners could communicate with them. Such precautions were taken in order to prevent any batterer using the system to further abuse his/her partner. Participants' initial reactions to these features of the program were reluctance if not resistance. Facilitators, however, were trained to work with participants to help them to understand that the rules were to reduce the risk of violence to their current partner or to a future partner.

CURRICULUM

As mentioned earlier, the DKS PAR program itself was and is required to meet certain curriculum requirements drawn from best practice guidelines developed by WACT, the coordinating body in the city of Toronto that organizes the referrals and delivery of service to offenders and the Ministry of the Attorney General which provides governmental monies towards funding community programs for offenders. The themes that are required and addressed include the following: Defining partner abuse; exploring attitudes and beliefs related to partner abuse; investigating the impact of one's abusive actions; accountability; responsibility; and safety planning/developing healthy behaviors.

The program itself is sixteen weeks long and participants are required to attend all sixteen sessions. The specifics of how the above themes were delivered and the approach taken were at the discretion of the agency and the facilitators, provided that such approaches and specifics did not circle blame on the victim. The DKS PAR program took a primarily cognitive-behavioral approach to explore the previously mentioned themes, but also employed expressive exercises (e.g., collages, art depictions).

Specifically, the curriculum originally borrowed from the Duluth model of intervention for batterers, which challenges batterers on their patriarchal attitudes that provide rationalizations for their use of controlling, abusive and/or assaultive behaviors, so as to be consistent with other programs in the city of Toronto that were based on this model of intervention. The Power and Control Wheel for Gay, Lesbian, Bisexual and Trans Domestic Violence, as developed by the Texas Council on Family Violence (2009), was used as a discussion tool to help participants define partner abuse. Attitudes and beliefs related to partner abuse were explored using the Duluth control logs (Domestic Abuse Intervention Programs n.d.) which helped participants explore aspects of their battering (e.g., beliefs, impact, use of minimization, denial, and blame) and ways of challenging their abusive behaviors. The impact of one's abusive actions focused on the impact on oneself, one's partner and others (e.g., family, friends). Making accountability statements were required of participants and participants were encouraged to give each other feedback on how accountable their statements were, on how they abused their partners, and the incident of assault that led to their referral to the program. Safety-planning not only focused on taking responsible time-outs but also on rebuilding trust after one's use of abuse and communication skills.

The curriculum was later amended to include themes that are relevant to the gay, lesbian, bisexual, and transgender community. For example, forms of abuse like HIV-control and heterosexism/internalized homophobia were explored in these groups. Groups also took time to explore the community's perception of same-sex partner abuse, the shame that one feels regarding their perpetration of abuse and, most recently, how minority stress contributes to one's perpetration of partner abuse. These topics were included because the curriculum suggested by WACT and the Ministry did not fully address all of the contextual issues specifically relevant to examining partner abuse in LGBTQ relationships. To map curricula developed for the heterosexual community onto LGBTQ relationships would have reinforced the idea that a gendered analysis is the correct lens through which to view LGBTQ relationships. Hence, it became important to look at prompts and contextual factors specific to the LGBTQ community. Not only did this make the curricula more relevant, it acknowledged that distinct differences exist between LGBTQ and heterosexual partner abuse.

Populations Served (Referral Base)

The city of Toronto is exceptionally diverse. Hence, a diversity of clients attended the DKS PAR program with different racial, educational, class, and language backgrounds. Prospective clients needed to be able to acknowledge responsibility and agree to expectations about their participation, such as being constructive within group discussion and being receptive to challenges from facilitators as well as other group members. The majority of participants that attended these programs were mandated and were typically charged with assault, assault causing bodily harm, assault with a weapon and/or uttering death threats towards their partners/ex-partners. Participants ranged in age from eighteen to sixty-four. As mentioned previously, referred clients came from one of two referral streams. The first and original stream of clients came from probation and parole. Completing an accredited PAR program was a condition of their probation order and clients were required to complete this program before their probation expired.

The second set of referrals came from criminal courts that specialized in domestic violence. If a prospective accused participant met certain conditions (e.g., no history of assault, the assault towards the partner did not involve a weapon or cause bodily harm), then the PAR group may have been offered as an option to them as a pre-trial diversion initiative, provided batterers could take responsibility for the charge for which they were accused. The hope of this diversion program was that clients would be diverted away from attending trial and redirected to sentencing, and that if clients were indeed successful then they might also be eligible for reduced sentencing. This diversion from trial and redirection to a PAR program would save time and money for the court system in general, the accused, and society; the average time an accused would otherwise spend in the criminal court proceedings would be up to and possibly over a year with at least an additional year to be served while under probation. If clients were not successful, or not able to take responsibility for the charge that they were accused of, clients would be redirected back to the court and given the option of going forward with a trial.

Occasionally, some participants who came to the group attended because they were "socially mandated" to come at the request of one's partner, friends, family members, or other attending professionals. Only a handful of members came to the DKS PAR program under these conditions, however, and all had left the program before it was completed. Socially mandated clients were not specifically recruited for this group because the funding that was provided for the program reserved spots for those involved with the criminal justice system.

CRITICAL REFLECTIONS

We have described two differing approaches to batterer programs. We have been intrigued that these programs from two different countries, and initiated from what appeared to be opposite ideological and programmatic vantages, resulted in nearly identical theoretical orientations as well as curriculum development. Over the course of our discussions three themes emerged for us and seemed important to highlight for others, especially for those considering developing their own services for LGBTQ batterers. These include: the need to re-conceptualize LGBTQ batterers' intervention services as a matter of public health as well as a component of the criminal justice system; the need for clarity of purpose about who these programs are meant to serve; and lastly the need for service providers to understand what motivates LGBTQ participants to enter batterers' intervention programs.

Before addressing these themes, however, there is an overarching a priori framework derived from mainstream batterers' intervention programs that requires some discussion to help situate our reflections. Batterers' intervention programs have been formulated to serve as a component of the criminal justice system either as the end result after an offender is sentenced or as a diversion from the court process (Dalton 2007; Saunders 2008). In a recent survey, more than half of the programs aimed at heterosexual batterers in the United States have identified themselves as being based on the Duluth model of intervention where consciousness-raising of male privilege and the vigorous challenging of participants to take responsibility is the key to their interventions with heterosexual batterers (Saunders 2008). This dominant paradigm used to understand abuse within intimate relationships in heterosexual batterers' intervention programs is formulated through a patriarchal gendered lens (Dalton 2007). The heterosexual gender paradigm, however, does not encompass the range of expressions of gender identity and sexual orientation in LGBTQ intimate relationships. Adopting this binary way of understanding abuse in intimate relationships, as recounted in our historical sections of both the New York City and Toronto programs, could not fully explain the use of abuse in LGBTQ intimate relationships accurately. The theoretical climate of using this patriarchal gendered lens initially dictated that we use this paradigm in our respective programs. To date, literature and program outcome research has been non-existent on services for batterers in LGBTQ relationships (Murray, Mobley, Buford and Seaman-DeJohn 2008). To our knowledge, no discussion on the literature has occurred with respect to what theoretical perspective needs to be taken to understand batterers' use of violence in LGBTQ intimate relationships.

To make the Toronto and New York LGBTQ batterers' programs relevant and effective in confronting attitudes and abuses of power we felt it was essential that the programs encompass the fullness of participants' gender identities by employing an analysis that goes beyond a gendered analysis of power and control, and abuse. That women and men can be batterers within same-sex relationships means that a heterosexual paradigm of power and control has a limited amount of relevance to same-sex couples. The majority of same-sex relationships that we have encountered do not utilize a heterosexual gender-role construct. From our experience in working with the community, LGBTQ intimate relationships involve a constellation of gender identity expressions and sexual orientations. The relationship of the LGBTQ individual with the society at large becomes clearer by broadening power and oppressions to include not only gender, but also heteronormativity (the view that heterosexuality is the standard or norm), and socially-imposed perceptions as well as internalized negative self-perceptions (e.g., discomfort with others, or with their own, gender expression and/or sexual orientation) in the form of homophobia, biphobia, and transphobia. By further including a spectrum of oppressions expressed in economic, racial and other terms, LGBTQ batterers' were confronted with all aspects of their attitudes and behaviors. Controlling behaviors towards a partner are a vehicle for all types of oppressions, given an expanded understanding of the concept of oppression, which allow and are contingent upon one individual exerting power and control over another. With this expanded context in mind let us look at the three themes that emerged from our discussions.

Re-Conceptualizing the Framework for LGBTQ Batterers' Intervention Services

It became clear to us that batterers' services were not just a matter of expanded criminal justice efforts generally aimed to reduce the burden at the court level and to limit or avoid the need for incarceration as the literature puts forward (Saunders 2008). Rather, batterers' services needed to be conceived of as a public health intervention which recognizes that conflict in an intimate relationship can exist on a spectrum from healthy, to high conflict, to abusive.

By intervening in abusive relationships, and especially by placing the onus on the batterer (the coercive partner) rather than on the victim, a clear message is sent. The one who took power over the other needs to take responsibility and be aware of the impact of their misuse of power. In an intimate relationship based on mutuality and trust, abuse of power is a betrayal. Abuse in intimate relationships becomes a public matter because community norms are violated. Such norms typically dictate that when one member of a partnership is betrayed by another through an abuse of power, the community is no longer in equilibrium. A community that does not try to achieve equilibrium by addressing power imbalances ultimately teaches some members that they are of less value and less deserving of respect and protection. This is antithetical to a fully thriving community.

In our discussions we realized that we approach work based on a premise of healthy LGBTQ relationships and communities. Healthy LGBTQ relationships, as with any intimate relationship, involve mutuality, communication and respect, and flourish when they are valued and respected by the larger society. When some people, a gender, or some relationships are accorded less value, there is an opening—and for some an invitation—to undermine, invalidate, or in the extreme to annihilate that which would seek equal value. Although both the Toronto- and New York City-based programs came at batterers' intervention from different contextual prompts and funding sources, it became clear to us that to work toward healthy LGBTQ relationships it was essential to re-conceptualize the framework of programs. Services to LGBTQ batterers intended to interrupt the cycle of violence within a single intimate relationship not only targeted the cessation of abuse but the promotion of healthy relations. Batterers' services can and ultimately should be understood as geared to reduce intimate partner violence and work towards healthy LGBTQ relationships within the public at large. With this extrapolation, batterers' services are a matter of public health.

Recognizing that batterers' intervention services are a matter of public health does not exclude the idea that criminal actions occur in LGBTQ relationships. This too is also important to recognize. Empirically, the experiences of the New York and Toronto programs validated that it is more helpful to understand LGBTQ batterers' intervention services as both a public health issue *and* a matter of criminal justice. Such a re-conceptualization has implications for how we see conflict in intimate relationships, changes the meaning of who uses aggressive behaviors, and encourages us to re-think what other interventions are needed and how they need to be coordinated.

First, conflict between partners is a natural part of any intimate relationship. However, as the ability to deal with conflict effectively decreases, and the use of forceful behaviors increases, intimate aggression, regardless of form, begins where its primary effect is to systematically control the other *instead* of the resolution of the conflict. Once the intent to control the other person is determined, there is no benefit in distinguishing the severity among the types of controlling behaviors that a partner might use, whether the behavior ranges from verbal and emotional abuse to physical violence. As the victim seeks to avoid or reduce a partner's anger, the impact of any type of abuse results in the narrowing of the victim's autonomy and life experience (e.g., a victim stops making phone calls to family and friends because of the arguments that inevitably follow, eliminating familial and social support). We conceptualize conflict on a spectrum where it can include healthy conflict (discussion of disagreements, negotiation, mutually beneficial compromise), high conflict (arguments, difficulty discussing or reaching mutually beneficial outcomes), to abusive behaviors regardless of severity (there is no mutually beneficial discussion, negotiation or resolution of disagreements.) At the abusive end of the spectrum the controlling partner's needs are served while the other partner's needs are minimized or disregarded. Control is exerted through coercion, isolation and varying forms of abusive behaviors. (e.g., emotional economic, threats, outing, physical, sexual, and other forms).

Second, distinguishing controlling behaviors from the problematic means of handling conflict, as well as who is using abuse as a means of control, is initially complex. On the surface, it might seem that conflict is mutual and not appear that there is a clear aggressor (abusive partner). Careful clinical probing and expertise can delineate when the impact of one partner's behaviors serve to consistently narrow the scope of life experience and autonomy of the other. As the inability to deal with conflict and the use of severe aggressive behaviors increases, the identification of the abusive partner may become more distinct. Both programs have learned through their experience that victims may vary in their use of physical aggression and may initially complicate the picture in determining who the aggressor is in the relationship. However, it is important to consider that some victims who use aggressive behaviors may do so because it is a way of protecting themselves, pre-empting other attacks by the abusive partner, or a way of lessening the impact of the violence that they or their children experience. Their use of violence has a different context and does not establish a systematic pattern of controlling their partner. To clarify, context here refers to power distribution. The victim does not have the power to coerce, dominate, or isolate the abusing partner; the victim does not have the means—physical, emotional, or otherwise—to enforce control. The physical actions are taken out of fear, usually to diffuse building anger in the abusive partner (starting an argument when tension is beginning, for example, might result in yelling or objects being thrown rather than the victim being punched or choked), or to avoid or protect from harm (pushing the abusive partner into a doorframe while trying to get away from a physical blow).

Third, addressing the continuum of conflict in intimate relationships from a public health perspective has the primary purpose of raising the community's consciousness where the use of any controlling and abusive behavior as a means of resolving conflict is not justifiable. Instead, healthy conflict is encouraged. These interventions may take such forms as community forums on healthy relationships or couples counseling for those in conflict but with no intimate aggression present. For those using aggression in their intimate relationships moving to a criminal justice approach with batterer intervention programs is needed, along with incorporating monitoring and judicial consequences into anti-violence programming and intervention services for those who use extreme forms of violence in an attempt to control their partners. For abusers who have become physical and have required police involvement, coordinating batterer's intervention programs with criminal court procedures offers a means for abusers to learn different behaviors. Alternately if the abuser is unable to do so, the criminal justice system can clearly and possibly more effectively intervene with more intense and regular programming.

Thus, we not only wish to reconceptualize the framework for batterers' intervention programs for LGBTQ relationships as both a public health and a criminal justice matter, but also wish to recognize that conflict can range across a variety of situations, which has profound program implications. We instead need to re-conceptualize the question of which program is right for batterers to which program is right for which situation. This helps to clarify that service delivery needs to be comprehensive, coordinated, and that funding sources must come from a variety of places and allow programs to address the breadth of intimate relationship issues to effectively deliver the services that we suggest.

As a case in point, funding sources in both the New York and Toronto programs came from two different parts of the community (i.e., community donation / private foundations and the criminal justice system). These two funding sources influenced the framework adopted and how each program was delivered. Within the Toronto program, primary funding came from the criminal justice sector and was based on the "seats for participants" model. Essentially, it contracted the DKS program to run a program specifically for those charged or on probation for assault charges towards one's same-sex partner. The program was discouraged from promoting the program to prospective participants without criminal justice system involvement and hence, promotion to the general LGBTQ community at large was not pursued, also eliminating a means of serving the community before violence reached criminal justice involvement. In contrast, the New York program was supported through community and foundation funds to raise awareness and promote services to aid the general community and received referrals accordingly. The New York program was not formulated to serve a mandated population, limiting its capacity to address abusers already involved in the criminal justice system. Reporting to the criminal courts on participant participation, although standard procedure for mainstream batterers' intervention programs, presented possible administrative complications for AVP's (victim) client-service funding. Interaction with the criminal justice system was limited to acknowledging a participant's involvement in the program. Such limited interactions led New York's program to become responsive to community expressed need, which in the end cultivated a structure and funding targeted to serve the general community, drawing socially mandated, rather than court mandated referrals.

Ideally, LGBTQ batterers' intervention programs would be a mixture of these two approaches—community driven and criminal justice supported or reinforced. Either approach slants who is given services and who benefits. The one concern about a criminal justice primary approach is that intimate partner violence necessarily has to reach the level of physical violence and criminal offense before intervention is activated. Starting from a public health perspective, preferably in collaboration with the criminal justice system, meanwhile, offers the possibility of early intervention thus reducing the extent of harm endured by victims. Collaboration with the criminal justice system enables abusers the clarity that their actions are heading toward criminal behavior with consequences. Further, for initial offenders who might otherwise blow off their behavior because of receiving nothing more significant than a parking ticket or a slap on the wrist, the batterers' intervention programs offer education and new ways of managing themselves in relationship.

Clarity of Purpose

Batterers' intervention programs provide services to abusers, however it is the victims of abuse that these programs are meant to benefit. Services to LGBTQ batterers are intended to reduce, and hopefully to prevent, the violence experienced by their intimate partners. The New York program recognized a gap in services *to victims* and sought to lessen the risk of further violence for them through development of a batterers' intervention program. Documentation of services led to the further realization that unaddressed batterers moved on to new victims. For the Toronto program, working under the auspices of WACT made it clear from the outset that the intended beneficiaries of batterers' program are the victims. Services of both programs were developed with the intent to not only reduce risk for current partners but to intervene in the *batterers'* cycle of committing violence in an attempt to reduce/eliminate risk for future partners. In actuality, it is the victims/survivors that are the "clients" of batterers' intervention programs.

Toronto-based services explicitly addressed the issue of "victims as clients" by defining its goal as increasing the safety of the victims and their children by working with batterers as secondary clients. This goal was implemented in three ways: (1) partner/victim notification that the batterer was attending the program; (2) batterer understanding of the program's primary goal; and (3) interventions that kept partners/victims at the forefront, which will be discussed in more detail below. Such support and guidelines provided by the coordinating entities of WACT and the Ministry of the Attorney General enabled the program to actualize service development with the victim as primary client and to better integrate social service and criminal justice efforts.

Without a comparable integrated social service and criminal justice effort, the New York program could not directly integrate services to victims like the Toronto program. However, similar emphasis on reaching victims was addressed by means of notification to victims of their partner's participation in a batterers' program as a requirement of program compliance. Outreach offered information about victims, services and expressed what realistic expectations batterer's participation in such a program could offer. As the Toronto programs demonstrates, coordinated approach from all levels of the community and government that holds the victims, the children and their safety as the true clients of batterers program can create a comprehensive effort to reduce LGBTQ partner violence.

Shifting the goal of batterers' intervention programs to serve victims results in objectives with greater immediacy and emphasis on interrupting abusive behaviors and raising personal responsibility and accountability. Reconsidering who the primary client is becomes an important shift because it not only holds batterers accountable but also holds programs to be accountable to the current or potential future partner/victim. Thus, every programmatic feature, including curricula and administration, must be reflective of this idea that the program exists to serve, increase safety and reduce risk for current or future partners/victims. An illustrative case in point lies in the Toronto program, where facilitators continuously worked to amplify specific victims' voices in the group. Victims were regularly consulted and asked if there were behaviors by their abusive partner that they wanted the facilitators to address in group. Their comments therefore were not just generally useful, but addressed specific and current abusive behaviors. As one facilitator described, "I imagine that the partner is constantly whispering in my ear, letting me know what he wants said in the group." This was a way of the program holding its participants accountable, and also encouraged facilitators not to collude with the batterers. Facilitators would routinely give voice to the perspective of batterers' actual partners/ victims throughout the program, and challenged members to reconcile their understanding with the partner's/victim's perspective that was presented.

It follows then that any theoretical approaches to working with batterers have to pay attention to the idea that curricula is more than about centering responsibility on batterers' use of abuse toward the partner/victim. In the early development of both the Toronto and New York programs, the Duluth Model of intervention for batterers was employed because it theorized that batterers were responsible for their use of violence under a patriarchal lens, and because it was a dominant analysis used in understanding abuse in intimate relationships, as discussed at the beginning of this second half of this chapter. Although initially useful, the focus had to be broadened beyond a gender-power based paradigm because it did not encompass socially constructed oppressions related to sexual orientation, gender identity, race, socioeconomic status, and other relevant factors. To address the intersection of layered oppressions, integrating feminist theory into the curriculum proved useful. Curricula in both of these programs reflected this by consistently relating contextual factors such as sexism, heterosexism, and homophobia, and contrasting these with personal choices made by batterers.

For example, in the Toronto program, regular discussions were threaded throughout the course of the group on how social privilege and social difference (e.g., differences in HIV-status, class differences, educational differences) were used as a way of leveraging control over one's partner. Further, if facilitators could be immediate within the program, they would highlight how oppression occurred during the course of group (e.g., white gay men abruptly and intentionally interrupting gay men of color), ask participants to take responsibility for that behavior, and ask participants to reflect and share with other members on how social oppressions are reaffirmed in their intimate relationships. Their use of any social privilege as a rationale to use abusive and controlling behaviors was framed as a choice and the emphasis was on how to make more respectful choices.

Another example of how social privilege and oppressions played out and were addressed in the Toronto program lies in why separate programs for men and women where ultimately decided upon with respect to service delivery. Again, four sixteen-week cycles of the Toronto program ran where both men and women participated in a mixed gender group. Facilitators noticed that a common dynamic occurred. Misogyny and sissyphobia was constantly being addressed throughout the group and across all four cycles. Some gay men would make sexist remarks towards female members. Alternatively, some gay men would use the gender stereotype of all women being nurturing as a way of minimizing or denying fellow female members as being abusive or controlling in their intimate relationships. Similarly, some lesbians would discuss the effeminate nature of some the male participants as a way of downplaying the severity of the abuse that the male participants perpetrated. Facilitators were immediate and challenged members on these other forms of oppressions. However, the discussion was constant and diverted discussion from abuse in LGBTQ relationships. Ultimately, the constant redirection only led to a superficial discussion on LGBTQ partner abuse. To have a deeper understanding of why one perpetrates abuse, separate men's and women's programs were offered so as to address specific issues relevant to the men's and women's community respectively and not be overly distracted with discussion of the greater LGBTQ community's misogyny and sissyphobia. Expanded understanding of the social context in which battering occurs and a directed and focused approach to addressing behaviors meant that these programs increased the personal relevance to LGBTQ batterers. Such an approach avoids the heteronormativity of the gender-based power paradigm.

Feminist theory was not the only approach employed in raising consciousness with LGBTQ batterers. A cognitive behavioral approach informed the means to address the personal accountability of batterers' behaviors. The term cognitive-behavioral therapy or CBT as it is commonly referred to is not a distinct therapeutic technique but classifies therapies that address connections between, thought, emotion, and behavior (National Association of Cognitive-Behavioral Therapists n.d.). This technique enables facilitators to examine how batterers made personal choices based on beliefs that promoted the use of violence within their intimate relationships. The focus on choice promotes personal responsibility. This technique further lent itself to explore how controlling beliefs were formed and led to topics like family of origin (how family beliefs may relate to batterers' perceptions) and alcohol/substance use and abuse. Exploring such topics is useful so long as victims/partners are not blamed for the abuse and that the thrust of any exploration is the batterers' use of violence in their intimate relationships.

Service providers of LGBTQ intervention programs for batterers need to be clear for whom these programs are designed. Inasmuch as they are intended to reduce the controlling and abusive behaviors of its participants, such participants are actually the secondary clients of the program. Participants of such a program receive direct service but it is the victims/partners and their children that are the primary clients. With the victims/partners and their children being the primary client group of LGBTQ intervention programs for batterers, programmatic features of the service must incorporate this re-conceptualization of the purpose of who benefits from such a program. Therapeutic techniques and theoretical analysis can be used in such programs, insofar as it encourages the discussion towards healthy conflict and that the therapeutic discussions do not circle the blame back on the victims/partners and their families. Incorporating such a re-conceptualization not only benefits this primary client group, but also encourages accountability to them as well.

Understanding Participant Motivation

Factors that motivate participant interest in a batterers' intervention program are instrumental for a service provider to understand; they offer a means of distinguishing appropriate fit with the program and who may be likely to be able to effect attitude and behavior change. Abusers may be motivated to enter a batterers' intervention program for many reasons: to affect the outcome of their criminal justice proceedings, to demonstrate that they are taking action (not necessarily changing): to convince their partner to stay: they feel remorse and personal accountability for having caused harm: or the intent to make real changes in their behavior. For each of these reasons it is possible to draw some conclusions about a potential participant's likely interest and openness to the material they will encounter. A person who presents with the intent of affecting the outcome of their criminal proceedings is likely seeking to avoid or reduce penalty for their actions. If the charges are dropped and there is no sense of personal remorse and accountability for his/her actions, there is no longer pressure or motivation to pursue participation until the violence again results in criminal justice involvement. In our experiences as service providers working with LGBTQ batterers, this pattern became all too familiar. Similarly, intent to enter a batterers' intervention program based on the next two reasons—demonstrating that the abusers are taking action and/or convincing partners to stay—rest on goals outside the program which include coercing, convincing (themselves and) the victim that change is happening and that the victim should therefore stay. When the tension that led to the abuser seeking services is reduced and there is no immediate threat of the victim leaving, it is likely the participant will be unmotivated to continue. In such cases it is interesting to watch all the issues that get in the way of attending sessions. Over a third of participants' relationships ended in the course of attending the New York program. Review of these relationships indicated that partners/victims might have found leaving to be safest while their batterer was in the program. The providers for New York's victims' services and the batterers' intervention program monitored these relationships through regular case conferencing, and exchanged notification when there appeared to be potential for risk to partners/victims.

For both the Toronto and New York program, remorse and personal responsibility were observed to be high indicators of participants who were able to effect attitude and behavioral change. Those that seemed more reluctant to take responsibility and express remorse were more likely not to complete the program or to re-offend. For the New York program, lack of remorse and personal sense of accountability/responsibility became flags indicating that the program was not likely to be useful. The facilitators in the Toronto program used these flags to indicate the need for an intervention crafted with the help of the criminal justice system (e.g., probation officers) where the participants were encouraged to take responsibility for their behavior and entry into the program was delayed until this could be demonstrated. For example, prospective participants in the intake session that proved to be overly resistant to the program's expectation, as outlined in the program's agreement form to participate, were typically encouraged to discuss their reservations with their probation officer. Facilitators worked with probation officers to discuss what reservations a prospective participant had and probation officers would intervene with prospective participants on reframing such reservations.

It has been our observation that participants who present an awareness of the impact of their behaviors, have a fear or concern that their behavior will escalate without help and a sense of remorse for their actions as well as a belief in personal responsibility and accountability, are all good candidates for participation in an LGBTQ batterers' intervention program. These motivations seem to be essential to successfully make it through a program, in effecting attitude and behavioral change, and also appeared to be consistent among the participants who invested themselves in the program because of what it offered for their own lives. Individuals who demonstrated such capacity in other areas of their lives and were receptive to being challenged to rethink their attitudes and behaviors were also likely to be viable participants.

Service providers can learn a lot about possible motivations with the use of a thorough assessment that requires participants to talk in *detail* about episodes of violence (emotional, physical, etc.), *their* role, the *impact on their partner*, police involvement and what brought them to consider entering such a program. Recognizing multiple motivations is critical to the ability of group facilitators to successfully contract and engage with participants. Outside events that will occur during the course of the program may also influence whether participants are motivated to continue the program. The New York and Toronto programs both stressed to participants that they could not control others or outside events, but could control their own responses. Whatever a participant's motivation, program facilitators must emphasize behavioral change for the improvement of the participant's life, and for all those with whom s/he interacts.

Recommendations

As we discussed and reflected on the experiences of the New York and Toronto programs, there seemed to be several areas of recommendations to offer providers considering developing LGBTQ batterers' intervention programs. Primary among considerations for any program serving LGBTQ individuals is the need for LGBTQ staff along with other staff who are educated about how multilevel oppressions intersect with and impact LGBTQ clients' lives. It has been our experience that mainstream programs will often seek to be inclusive by hiring usually one self-identified member of the LGBTQ community and then direct all LGBTQ clients and programming to that point person. This ironically creates a separatist, rather than inclusive approach. A separatist approach can leave this staff member pre-disposed to being isolated, and ultimately perpetuates the ostracizing of the Other at an institutional level.

The second and alternate approach for some mainstream programs is to participate in cultural diversity training and then to develop their own LGBTQ programming without including LGBTQ personnel or collaboration with an agency with LGBTQ expertise. Although this is well intentioned, normal staff turnover and lack of direct LGBTQ experience result in loss of the knowledge gained. Often the learning and programming has not become an integrated piece of the agency's mission and service goals. When the staff and administrators who were dedicated to these issues leave, so usually does the institutional knowledge and commitment to LGBTQ programming.

A third, often problematic, approach by existing batterers' intervention programs is to believe that providing mainstream services to a separate class of usually gay male clients is appropriate and inclusive. This approach fails to address the heteronormativity in which mainstream programs are entrenched, and also fails to effectively identify and challenge the many other forms of power and oppressions that shape LGBTQ batterers' attitudes and beliefs. It is in such programs where providers will misguidedly think that if there is only one gay male batterer waiting for a program it is okay to include him with heterosexual male batterers, often leaving the gay man open to homophobic bias, ridicule and even physical assault from other participants. For these reasons we recommend that mainstream organizations interested in doing this work should consider collaborating with a local LGBTQ organization to serve LGBTQ batterers.

Beyond the question of staffing, primary for LGBTQ batterers' services is the need to maintain focus on the safety of partners/victims and children as the program's actual clients. This can be effective when made formal through program structure such as the Toronto program did in its collaboration with WACT. Along with this is the need to integrate a comprehensive partner contact component that serves the partners/victims and their children fully. This means having dedicated staff/tasks that involve outreach to victims/partners, offering victims services and information about realistic expectations of participation in batterers' intervention. What the Toronto program further offers in its unique collaboration is for facilitators to be aware not just of the participants' views, but as important, the victims' experiences with their batterers. Often victims avoid expressing their feelings or concerns because of fear of how their batterers will respond. For victims who participate in this collaborative program there is the knowledge that they are valued, that they have options and that both victim and batterer are well aware that "people are watching"—group facilitators, victims' service providers and the criminal justice system. This reinforces what behaviors are acceptable and that violation of these will involve a lot of witnesses and consequences, to the batterer.

The next set of recommendations address service provision. The New York program anticipated what the Toronto program in fact experienced, that participants would use differences among them as distractions to avoid dealing with the material addressing attitude and behavior change. Groups need to be separated by gender to effectively maintain participants' focus on the impact they've had on their victims/partners, and the role of choice in establishing new patterns.

Along with a need for a well-structured curriculum, we also agree that a range of techniques and theories could be applied to work with LGBTQ batterers with two caveats: (1) they promote behavior change toward healthy conflict; and (2) they *do not* circle the responsibility for violence back on the partner/victim. For the New York program extending more challenging topics to two session units lengthened the time batterers' were brought to contend with these issues (sexual and economic abuse, use of internalized homo/bi/transphobia within the relationship, etc.) and the impact of their attitudes and behaviors on their partner/victim and others. For the Toronto program, use of creative techniques (e.g., asking participants to draw and depict roadmaps of the choices that led to them being referred to the group as well as a roadmap leading away from the program when they have successfully completed all the sessions) allowed participants to explore with facilitators their possible reluctance to join the group, their current level of remorse and responsibility-taking, and which healthy behaviors participants think they need to learn.

As a last point on services, despite their attitudes and behaviors, participants still have the right to be treated in a respectful and dignified manner. Programs should be free to use techniques and theories that engage participants provided that they recognize the participant's dignity. For example, exploring a participant's reluctance in a program may lead to more authentic engagement and hopefully encourages positive change.

In terms of funding, support for LGBTQ batterers' programs, must come from sources that understand that conflict occurs on a continuum and that its expression may range from a public health issue to a criminal justice matter. In our experience, the programs were limited to what directives the funding set or did not set. In Toronto, criminal justice funding enabled solid on-going programming, but dissuaded addressing public health through promoting and extending services to the local LGBTQ community. The limited funding also promoted the ill-advised gender combined batterers' groups with differences of gender and power that detracted from focusing batterers on their own sources and misuse of power within same-sex relationships. For the New York program, victims' services funding prevented a direct linkage with criminal justice that could prospectively have reinforced the program's efforts to address victims' safety and to reach same-sex batterers already engaged in the criminal justice system.

We view same-sex partner abuse as a societal issue, as such coordination among all stakeholders is important. Flow of information is necessary among those providing services, those suggesting or mandating treatment, and the direct recipients of services. Such flow of information prevents batterers from leveraging the system to their advantage, promotes accountability to the partners/victims, and allows transparency to be a guiding principle in all service delivery provisions.

Lastly, we recommend providers recognize that LGTBTQ batterers' intervention programs are only one spoke in the hub of interventions needed to address the issue of same-sex partner abuse for the LGBTQ community as a whole. Communities must explore other avenues such as counseling, education and advocacy to address this issue including consideration of such formats as awareness campaigns, community forums, and healthy relationships workshops.

SUMMARY

Historically, LGBTQ individuals and their relationships have been portrayed as sexually deviant. Socially dictated expectations, positive and negative, can often serve to be self-reinforcing. As a result, many LGBTQ individuals, as in other denigrated minorities, experience a sense of devalued worth, which is manifested in substance abuse, depression and a basically lowered expectation of what can come of their lives and relationships (Meyer 2003).

The provision of services to batterers for intimate relationships involving imbalances of power, indicate that the reverse must be equally valid, that there are LGBTQ relationships that involve a balance of power, the ability for compromise, mutuality and communication, in other words, healthy LGBTQ relationships. To assert this has been and will likely be for some time experienced systemically as a radical act.

Establishing healthy conceptualizations of LGBTQ relationships fundamentally challenges a societally institutionalized deprecation of sexual orientation and gender identity. If the true goal of batterer intervention services, however, is to reduce violence in society generally and the involvement in the criminal justice system specifically by aiming for improved functioning versus symptom reduction, then reframing the issue as a matter of both public health and criminal justice shows the potential for greater long-term benefit for both system and individual. Too often, the primary conceptualization of dealing with partner abuse has been solely a matter of criminal justice. Partner abuse must be seen as part of the continuum for LGBTQ relationships, and intervention and emphasis must be paid and expanded to all facets of this continuum, including recognition and support for healthy LGBTQ relationships.

LGBTQ batterer intervention programs also must not lose sight that their primary clients are the partners/victims, children, and their families. This reconceptualization of the primary client is not only a shift in thinking about what batterers' intervention programs deliver to their participants but is a means of keeping such programs accountable to victims and their children. This should be a first principle for developers of new LGBTQ batterers' intervention programs.

Support and reinforcement of the value of healthy LGBTQ relationships requires service providers to rethink all aspects of their services, from using clinical approaches that do not center the blame on victims and partners, including falsely attributing abuse to occurring because of an "alternative" lifestyle, to creating integrated victim support systems that interface respectfully with batterer intervention programs structured to address the societal context and oppressions faced by LGBTQ individuals. This is in effect the challenge of how to address LGBTQ batterers with dignity and respect.

Social context and oppressions also have relevance for identifying and addressing participant motivation. Motivations of participants lie on a continuum from being socially influenced to being court ordered. This includes making room in programming for those individuals who can recognize and want help to stop the violence before it reaches criminal levels. Taking the time to understand and address participant motivations is crucial to aiding authentic engagement. Without such engagement, intervention programs may have minimal impact on the change process for batterers.

In summary, the provision of services for same-sex batterers requires the recognition of the existence of healthy LGBTQ relationships, and the need for services that span the continuum of conflict from public health to criminal justice while reinforcing and protecting the wellbeing of LGBTQ individuals and their families.

NOTES

1. In the early 1990s an all-volunteer effort facilitated by Stephen McFadden, LCSW, in collaboration with AVP developed New York's first same sex batterers' program. The program was conducted and under the leadership of Executive Director Matt Foreman and the Director of Client Services, Bea Hanson, MSW. In 1999 McFadden approached AVP and the program was relaunched under the leadership of Executive Director, Richard Haymes and the Director of Client Services, Diane R. Dolan-Soto, CSW.
2. The SNAP curriculum of 1999–2002 was developed by Stephen McFadden with the financial support of the New York City Gay and Lesbian Anti-Violence Project.
3. Based on comparison of internal program reporting and annual intimate partner domestic violence program activities.

REFERENCES

Dalton, B. 2007. What's going on out there? A survey of batterer intervention programs. *Journal of Aggression, Maltreatment and Trauma* 15(1): 59–74.

Dolan-Soto, D.R. 2002. *Lesbian, gay, transgender and bisexual domestic violence in New York, 2001: A report of the New York City gay and lesbian anti-violence project*. New York: New York City Gay and Lesbian Anti-Violence Project.

Domestic Abuse Intervention Programs (DAIP). Duluth model on public intervention. Available at: http://www.theduluthmodel.org/duluthmodel.php [accessed October 1, 2009].

Meyer, I. H. 2003. Prejudice, social stress, and mental health in lesbian, gay, and bisexual populations: Conceptual issues and research evidence. *Psychological Bulletin* 129(5): 647–697.

Murray, C. E., A. K. Mobley, A. P. Buford, and M. M. Seaman-DeJohn. 2008. Same-sex intimate partner violence: Dynamics, social context, and counseling implications. *Journal of LGBT Issues in Counseling* 1(4): 7–30.

National Association of Cognitive-Behavioral Therapists. NACBT online headquarters: Cognitive behavioral therapy. Available at: http://www.nacbt.org/whatiscbt.htm [accessed October 1, 2009].

New York City Gay and Lesbian Anti-Violence Project. 2000. *Power and control in lesbian, gay, transgender and bisexual relationships*. New York: New York City Gay and Lesbian Anti-Violence Project.

Saunders, D.G. 2008. Group interventions for men who batter: A summary of program descriptions and research. *Violence and Victims* 23(2): 156–172.

Schwartz, J. and M. Waldo. 2004. Group work with men who have committed abuse. In *Handbook of group counseling and psychotherapy*, ed. J. L. DeLucia-Waack, D. A. Gerrity, C. R. Kalodner, and M. T. Riva, 576–592. Thousand Oaks, CA: Sage.

Texas Council on Family Violence. (2009). Available at: www.tcfv.org [accessed October 1, 2009].

15 "We Are All Treaty People"

An Anti-Oppressive Research Ethics of Solidarity with Indigenous LGBTQ People Living with Partner Violence

Catherine G. Taylor and Janice L. Ristock

In addressing the topic of partner violence in the lives of LGBTQ Indigenous people, we are working as white lesbian allies who have served as researchers engaged in community-based work on issues facing Canadian Aboriginal, Two Spirit and transgender communities (Ristock, Zoccole, Passante 2010; Taylor 2006, 2009). It is obvious that LGBTQ Indigenous people, not white settler people, should be controlling the terms of analysis and response to partner violence in their lives. It should also be obvious, given the extreme marginalization of LGBTQ Indigenous people in Canada both demographically and culturally, that outsider allies are important to social change struggles in this regard. The limited number of LGBTQ Indigenous people with access to research infrastructure should not be expected to conduct all the research that needs to be done on issues affecting members of their identity group. As an Aboriginal colleague said in answer to our question, "Should two white people really be conducting this research?": "If not you, then who? I'm already involved in ten projects."

However, the history of well-intended white people professing to act in Aboriginal people's best interests is an ugly one in Canada, as it has been internationally, with missionary, church, school, and state interventions from first contact onwards having proved extremely damaging. Indigenous people worldwide including in Canada have been extensively studied by settler anthropologists, sociologists, and historians, often with negative effects ranging from misrepresentation to appropriation of sacred items, stories, knowledge, and rituals as anthropological artifacts and data (Kovach 2005). The result has been that "research" has become a "dirty word" to many Indigenous people (Denzin and Lincoln 2008) and dominant-culture researchers are often regarded with suspicion. Bridges (2001) summarizes the concern: "outsiders cannot properly understand and represent [participants'] experience and are exploitative and disrespectful, and . . . having outsiders articulate your views for you is intrinsically disempowering" (abstract), whatever the intentions or use made of the research.

Two critical approaches to decolonizing the research process have been developing through community-based research (CBR). While Indigenous methodologies incorporate Indigenous teachings and traditions into a research process that is by, for, and with Indigenous people (Kovach 2005, Wilson 2008), an "OCAP" approach advocates for allies to work with Aboriginal communities through an anti-oppression framework that is committed to producing meaningful knowledge that respects the integrity and rights of Indigenous peoples and communities to Ownership of the project, Control of the process, Access to the data, and Possession of the findings (First Nations Centre 2007; Schnarch 2004). In this chapter we argue that an anti-oppression framework for a research ethics of solidarity with LGBTQ Aboriginal people experiencing interpersonal violence logically compels academic researchers not only to respect OCAP principles but to engage in direct political action to oppose state violence. In so doing, we support Andrea Smith (2005) who declares, "our strategies to combat violence within communities (sexual/domestic violence) must be informed by approaches that also combat violence against communities, including state violence—police brutality, prisons, militarism, racism, colonialism, and economic exploitation" (151).

We believe this is the conclusion that researchers arrive at if we commit fully to the CBR principle of taking direction from the experiences and perspectives of research participants that critical theorist Roger Simon calls "an attentiveness to an otherness that resists being reduced to a version of our own stories" (Simon, Di Paolantonio and Clamen 2005: 135). This stance of specificity is epistemologically necessary if outsider researchers hope to bridge the gap between the material and discursive realities of their own lives and the realities of research participants' lives. This principle is consistent with Wahab and Olson's (2004) recommendation against aggregating research data on partner violence across groups because of the large number of culturally different American tribes, but instead exploring it contextually (360). A growing body of research on same-sex partner violence takes this context-specific approach as well (Ristock and Timbang 2005). Similarly Ann Russo and Melissa Spatz (2007) argue for the need for strategies to end violence to be grounded in communities rather than in "one size fits all" approaches often used by agencies responding to domestic violence.

While research concerning many people's experiences inevitably involves processes of generalization, striving for specificity guards against obscuring the facts in those processes, in part by reminding us to be as specific as the level of generalization allows (e.g., "Cree" rather than "Aboriginal," "Aboriginal" rather than "Indigenous"), and also by reminding us that even the most careful generalizations inevitably obscure differences. The broad strokes of extreme marginalization may be generalizable—poverty, violence, drug and alcohol addiction—but the specific factors that intersect to lock people into the uninhabitable zones of a society where these constitute everyday experience are unique. If we are trying to surface the realities of LGBTQ Aboriginal people living with partner violence, it is therefore methodologically vital to center the analysis in their experiences, rather than adding them onto existing understandings that have been normed around dominant narratives of partner violence as it is experienced by other people living in nonidentical intersections of gender, sexuality, and race discourses.

Andrea Smith (2005) writes in Conquest,

> An alternative approach to "inclusion" is to place women of color at the center of the organizing and analysis of domestic violence. What if we do not make any assumptions about what a domestic violence program [or program of research] should look like, but instead ask, what would it take to end violence against women of color? What would this movement look like? . . . Beth Richie suggests we need to go beyond just centering our analysis on women of color. Rather, she asks, what if we centered our attention on those abused women most marginalized within the category of "women of color"? (153)

We believe that Indigenous LGBTQ people are so imperiled within categories of "Aboriginal," "women" and "men," and "healthy sexuality" that it is crucial for researcher allies to follow Smith and Richie's lead by putting these "most marginalized" people at the center instead of just adding them to existing understandings of partner violence.

In this chapter we provide background information on Aboriginal people in Canada and what is known about their experiences of interpersonal and state violence. We then discuss the ethical stance that proceeds from centering our analysis in the realities of Aboriginal LGBTQ people experiencing partner violence.

TERMINOLOGY

In this chapter, "LGBTQ" refers to lesbian, gay, bisexual, trans, Two Spirit, and queer people. "Two Spirit" refers to sexual and gender variation among people of Indigenous North American descent. The term "Two Spirit" was chosen as an empowering (and strategic) reminder that lesbian, gay, bisexual, and trans people existed in traditional Indigenous societies, often with honored roles (Wilson 1996). Walters et al. (2006) explain that the term is used to reconnect with traditions in some First Nations related to sexual and gender identity; to move beyond Eurocentric binary categories of sex and gender; to signal the fluid, non-linear nature of identity processes; and to contradict heterosexism in Aboriginal communities and racism in LGBTQ communities. We use "LGBTQ" rather than "Two Spirit" because many LGBTQ Indigenous people in Canada do not identify as Two Spirit and see the term as highlighting trans identities but obscuring others. The variety of identities specified in "LGBTQ" also signals the importance of not over-generalizing about diversely situated people's experiences.

"Aboriginal" in Canadian usage denotes all Canadian Indigenous people including First Nations people with membership in hundreds of culturally and historically diverse bands across the country, Inuit people of northern Canada, and Métis people with First Nations and European ancestry (as in the Canadian Constitution Act [1982]). This definition includes all Status, Non-Status, and blended people that choose to self-identify as Aboriginal (Guimond 2003).

BACKGROUND

As Battiste (2008) notes, academics are aware that the legacy of colonization of Indigenous people has been extreme poverty and violence across the world. But the specific histories and current conditions of life for geographically and culturally diverse Indigenous peoples differ and cannot be accurately generalized (in keeping with Wahab and Johnson). For example, some form of mandatory boarding-school system for Indigenous children was implemented by British colonial governments to destroy Indigenous culture in Australia, the United States, and Canada, but not in Africa, where Indigenous people were not considered educable. In Australia, it was mainly Indigenous children with some level of white ancestry who were required to attend boarding school because only they were considered educable (Buti 2002), while in Canada and the United States, all First Nations children were forced to attend residential schools as boarders from approximately age six (Smith 2005), as were some Métis children. We therefore begin by offering background on the situation of LGBTQ Aboriginal Canadians in order to establish the need for specificity in research, in preparation for our argument that such an approach leads to logically and in an ethical sense, necessarily, to political action.

CANADIAN CONTEXT

In the last Canadian Census, more than one million people, or 3.8% of the country's total population, identified themselves as Aboriginal: Indigenous Canadians who are First Nations, Inuit, or Métis people. Over 80% of Aboriginal people live in the province of Ontario and the four western provinces. Less than half of Aboriginal people (46%) live in reserves or other rural communities, and over half (54%) in urban areas (Statistics Canada 2009). Although many Aboriginal people have moved from reserves to urban centers, there is great diversity in the community, with eleven major language groups, fifty-eight dialects, five hundred and ninety-six bands, and 2,282 reserves (Kirmayer, Simpson and Cargo 2003).

STATE VIOLENCE IN ABORIGINAL LIVES

The violence characterizing life for many Aboriginal people in Canada is above all the legacy of the residential school system, a social engineering effort beginning in 1879 and continuing until 1976 that placed Aboriginal children in Church-run residential schools where they were taught to value British culture and be ashamed of their own (Sinclair and Hamilton 1991). These were "total institutions" in Goffman's (1961) sense of all-encompassing environments where every aspect of life is under the direct control of the organization, in this case, one aggressively dedicated to "solving the Indian problem" by "killing the Indian in the child" (Milloy 1999). As the residential school system was being phased out, the "Sixties Scoop" began, a second wave of state violence against Aboriginal families that continued into the 1980s, this time in the form of the forcible transfer of an estimated 15,000 Aboriginal children from their parents to white middle-class families in Canada and the United States (Dickason 2006). Other contributing factors exacerbated the fracture of social structure and family bonds that resulted, such as dishonored treaties that resulted in First Nations bands being relocated to economically non-viable remote reserves with an extremely high cost of living. This was coupled with high unemployment, chronic underfunding of reserve infrastructure and reserve schools (which replaced the residential schools), extremely overcrowded living conditions, substandard healthcare, crowded housing, and toxic water supplies; outlawing traditional language, cultural traditions, and beliefs; and forced adoption of ill-fitting governance structures that devalued the status of women (Armitage 1995). However, the residential school system alone was such a perfect recipe for undermining Aboriginal societies, and so effective in achieving its goal, that it alone would have been sufficient to account for the high rates in many Aboriginal people's lives of poverty, homelessness, substance abuse, interventions by child welfare authorities, incarceration, suicide, partner violence, and other violence. Some historians argue that violence was a feature of pre-contact Indigenous societies (Bamforth 1994), but there is no indication in the historical record that there was anywhere near the level of interpersonal violence found in contemporary times, and much evidence that children in particular were well treated. In other words, the violence in LGBTQ Aboriginal people's lives in Canada today can be traced to state violence. (Sinclair and Hamilton 1991; McGillivray and Comaskey 1999)

Five centuries of state interference have disrupted cultural continuity and made it difficult to know what pre-contact approaches to sexual orientation and gender were among Aboriginal people. As Byrne Fone (2000) has documented and Andrea Smith (2005) points out, "the first people targeted for destruction in Native communities were those who did not neatly fit into Western gender categories" (178): men and women who had same-sex relationships and were sometimes transgender. Ironically, the best source of information now available is sometimes the distorted, culturally-biased accounts of early missionaries and colonizers who had encountered people who did not fit European social categories, such as a man married to the chief or a woman living as a warrior (Napoleon 2002). Spanish conquistadors, for example, encountered gender variant Indigenous people who had honored places in their society, but called them *berdache*, a derogatory name meaning a male prostitute or submissive male (Fone 2000). While sexism and homophobia probably existed in some pre-contact cultures, Val Napoleon (2002) concludes that most Aboriginal nations were highly flexible and open to gender and sexual diversity before the "pathologically sexphobic settler regime" took hold (Justice 2010: 208). It has often been observed that one outcome of residential school education was homophobic attitudes resulting from exposure to Christian moral doctrine concerning sexual conduct (Meyer Cook and Labelle 2004), lessons which continue today in many reserve churches:

Another devastating result of the residential school experience was the denigration of women and Two-spirit people in Aboriginal communities. The dominant religion did not make room for women to have roles equal to those of men, or for there to be alternate genders or sexual preferences than that of heterosexuals. As a direct result of the residential school experience, homophobia is now rampant in most Aboriginal communities, even more so than in mainstream society. The religious dogma of the Residential Schools have erased a proud and rich history of Two-spirit people in most Aboriginal communities. (Urban Native Youth Association 2004).

In addition, it seems highly likely that homophobia would have resulted from survivors' experiences of sexual abuse by priests and nuns in the residential schools whose primary access was to children of the same sex, leading to the traumatized survivors' enduring identification of child sexual abuse with homosexuality, and consequent negative reactions to learning of LGBTQ identity in their own children. Efforts have been made to recover the lost gender and sexuality traditions of Indigenous people, in books such as Will Roscoe's (1988) *Living the Spirit* and Sabine Lang's (1998) *Men as Women, Women as Men: Changing Gender in Native American Cultures*, and in cultural moves such as claiming the identity term "Two Spirit" to reclaim the authentic place of gender and sexual diversity in traditional Aboriginal cultures (Wilson 1996). In contemporary Canada, however, Indigenous communities seem to be as likely to be homophobic as other parts of the country, leading many LGBTQ Aboriginal youth to leave their sometimes violence-plagued reserves for larger urban centers (where they may encounter less homophobia but more racism; O'Brien-Teengs and Travers 2006).

IPV IN ABORIGINAL LIVES

Statistics Canada (2006) reported that Aboriginal women were 3.5 times more likely than non-Aboriginal women to have experienced spousal assault (24% compared to 7%) and Aboriginal men were three times more likely to have experienced spousal assault than non-Aboriginal men (18% versus 6%). Aboriginal women were also much more likely to have been seriously injured by a partner, to have feared for their lives, and to have experienced multiple assaults from the same partner. Rates of spousal homicide were also high, with Aboriginal women being eight times more likely than non-Aboriginal women to have been killed by a spouse, and Aboriginal men twenty-eight times more likely than non-Aboriginal men. Aboriginal women in Canada are more likely than other women to live in poverty and to be involved in survival sex work, putting them at high risk of violence. In addition to the many cases of assault and murder of Aboriginal women that we know of, over five hundred Aboriginal women in Canada are currently listed as missing and suspected to have been murdered (Amnesty International 2009).

Given the high rates of violence known to be experienced by Aboriginal people generally, it is concerning that there have been no published studies on partner violence in the Canadian Aboriginal LGBTQ population. Agencies providing services for Aboriginal LGBTQ people have recognized the problem and attempted to provide appropriate resources and services. One example is Two Spirit People of the First Nations in Toronto, Ontario, which has produced a set of fact sheets on domestic violence for people experiencing violence (www.2spirits.com). Some studies do refer to partner violence in Aboriginal LGBTQ relationships as part of a larger focus, as in this collection and other work (Ristock 2005; Morris and Balsam 2003).

There is more information on the multiple forms and sources of violence in Indigenous LGBTQ people's lives internationally. For example, Balsam et al. (2004) compared the experiences of one hundred and fifty-four heterosexual and twenty-five LGBT people, all of them urban American Indian and Alaska Native (AIAN) adults, with respect to trauma, physical and mental health, and substance use. Compared with their heterosexual counterparts, LGBT participants reported higher rates of childhood physical abuse and more historical trauma in their families. More recently, Lehavot, Walters and Simoni (2009) interviewed one hundred and fifty-two sexual minority AIAN women as part of an investigation addressing the health concerns of Two Spirit persons. Women in their study reported disturbingly high prevalence of both sexual (85%) and physical (78%) assault, both of which were associated with worse overall mental and physical health.

Additionally, studies of other issues in Canadian Aboriginal life have reported some findings on partner violence, and suggest that it is only one of many forms and sources of violence experienced in their lives. For example, Taylor's (2009) needs assessment of trans and Two Spirit people in Manitoba reported high incidence of multiple forms of violence. The Winnipeg study involving seventy-eight participants found that there was a continuum of violence from all sources in the everyday lives of the participants from childhood through adulthood (Taylor 2006), and that the situation of the twenty-eight Aboriginal participants was especially dire (Taylor 2009). Participants were asked to identify how often they had experienced various forms of hostility or assault which they reasonably believe were related to their sexuality or gender identity, ranging from being refused service and verbal insults to sexual assault or attempted murder. All of these rates of experience of insult, threat, and violence were high among Aboriginal participants, but several stand out, especially when compared to non-Aboriginal participants' experience: Over a third (34.6%) of Aboriginal respondents had been assaulted with a weapon (7% of non-Aboriginal). Over half (53.8%) had had objects thrown at them at least once (compared to 18.6% of non-Aboriginal). Over half (57.6%) reported that a friend had been killed or assaulted (28.6% of non-Aboriginal). Further, almost half (48.1%) of Aboriginal participants had pre-tax incomes under $10,000, and 70% under $25,000. Aboriginal participants were less likely to know if they or their friends had been threatened or assaulted in various ways because of their sex/gender identity, presumably because being Aboriginal and living in poverty also elevate the risk of assault. One person asterisked her "often" response to the last item, adding "A lot of sex trade workers were killed (my friends)" (Taylor, 2009: 79).

The Winnipeg study adapted scales used to measure symptoms of post-traumatic stress disorder (PTSD) arising from the experiences of bullying, harassment and discrimination, including depression, loneliness, anxiety, guilt, impaired memory, low self-esteem, and physical numbness. The vast majority of Aboriginal participants reported having experienced all of the specified symptoms of mental distress at some point, with the rates of physical numbness and sudden anger being slightly lower. The study asked participants to indicate how safe they felt in various places in their everyday lives. Over a third of Aboriginal participants indicated they had felt "completely unsafe" in school, social services, and places of worship. On the other end of the scale, a full 85% indicated that they now feel quite safe or very safe in LGBTQ spaces, compared to 46% earlier, which could reflect a combination of increased integration of trans Aboriginal people into the larger LGBTQ community, and simply the increased acceptance of the LGBTQ community. A strong indication of possible partner violence is that only half (54.2%) of Aboriginal participants indicated that they now felt "very safe" at home, and only a quarter (26.3%) had felt very safe at home in the past. Most (83.4%) felt at least "quite safe" at home, compared to less than half (47.4%) earlier, which could reflect the difference between their current living situation and either an earlier situation with a previous partner or their situation in childhood when trans people are first confronting hostile family reactions.

Further, two studies on migration reveal information about partner violence. In Doris O'Brien-Teengs and Rob Travers' (2006) interview research with Two Spirit youth who migrated to Toronto, participants often reported leaving home communities because of experiences of "gay bashing" and other forms of homophobia. While moving to the city often had a positive effect on identity formation, other issues emerged such as homelessness, increased vulnerability to HIV, and dating/relationship violence. Ristock et al's (2010) mobility and migration study of the impact of moving on health and well-being on Aboriginal LGBTQ people found high levels of reports of domestic violence. Forty-two of the forty-nine people interviewed in Vancouver and Winnipeg reported experiences of domestic violence and many cited relationship violence as a reason for moving. For example, one participant stated: "I had to get out of this abusive relationship that I was in and I chose Vancouver because my sister, my older sister lives here, and if I went back to Edmonton, my ex would have found me and it would have been really horrible."

In Ristock's 2002 study of violence in lesbian relationships a few women who were Aboriginal spoke about partner violence and the larger impact of violence across their lifespan. A recurrent feature of other women's accounts was the context of a lifetime of violence that occurred on many levels and that had a normalizing effect. One woman had been sexually abused as a child, worked as a prostitute, was beaten by johns, used drugs and alcohol, got involved in an abusive relationship with a woman and then she became abusive in another relationship with a woman:

> As I look back my mom's physically abusive to me and my brother, I was sexually abused by my grandfather and that was huge for me . . . plus I'm from Alberta and there is a lot of racism towards Natives. People running people over and not caring. What I seen is what I thought was acceptable. (Esme)

She spoke without offering excuses, identifying herself as an abuser although her account reflects a context of violence in which the neat categories of victim and abuser no longer seem to hold. Her story also exposes the limits of focusing too narrowly on domestic violence. She has experienced a lifetime of violence that is linked to—and supported by—larger social structures that create and sustain inequalities and disadvantages. Racism, sexism, and homophobia intersect to shape the context in which sexual abuse, child abuse, stranger violence, and partner violence are initiated and thus continue.

Another woman spoke about her abuse in the context of colonization. She identified as Metis and her partner as First Nations. Each had experienced sexual violence and racial violence, as had their families:

> My mother is Cree and her parents were really devastated by residential schools and my mother grew up in an extremely violent, abusive,

alcoholic home. And I remember thinking that I was living out that legacy. I recall thinking . . . it was like two opposites. At one hand it was like this is the legacy that we carry. It is to be expected, I mean what do you expect from an Indian? Right? Just because we are so inundated with violence, we become normalized to it. And on the other hand, I also knew this is not normal, this is not acceptable. (Ruth)

Both Esme and Ruth's comments encapsulate the multiple sources and intersections of personal and state violence that are experienced by many Aboriginal LGBTQ people living in the wake of Canada's colonization efforts, and that saturate the lives of some, like Esme and Ruth, completely. Limited by meager material resources and threatened by violence wherever she goes, staying with an abusive partner may well seem like her best available option.

DISCOURSES OF COLONIZATION AND HOMOPHOBIA

It is often reported in the media that many Canadians feel that the residential school system and the Sixties Scoop are behind us now as a nation, and that Aboriginal people need to leave the past behind and develop a positive attitude to education, employment, and assimilation. This is stated even though the multi-generational impacts of past state violence persist into the present, including high levels of violence, removal of children from troubled families, and incarceration of Aboriginal people who were the children and grandchildren of residential school students. As bad as it is, the situation of Aboriginal LGBTQ people experiencing partner violence is made worse by the ongoing legacy of colonization in the form of homophobic and racist discourses that structure Aboriginal LGBTQ people's relationships with their families, home communities, service providers, and non-Aboriginal LGBTQ communities. (The term "discourses" is used here in the sense of systems of thought reinforced by social and institutional practices [Foucault 1972].)

As argued previously, the violence in Aboriginal LGBTQ people's lives in twenty-first century Canada can be understood in significant part as an outcome of systematic state assaults on Aboriginal culture that were designed to solve "the Indian problem" beginning in the nineteenth century. These actions were in turn made possible by the context of racist, heteropatriarchal discourses that were in evidence from the first Indigenous-colonizer encounters five centuries ago and persist today.

The past persists in multiple generations of mainstream non-Aboriginal Canadians who have been exposed to racist discourses of British supremacy that justified the residential school system, reserve system, and other examples of state violence enacted against Aboriginal people for purposes of colonization as "for their own good." These discourses have dominated representations of Aboriginal people in the public school system, every-day experience, and media coverage. Daniel Francis (1997), for example, writes of the construction of the "textbook Indian" in Canadian school textbooks until the 1960s that routinely demonized Aboriginal people as "sinister, vicious figures without history or culture" who threatened settlers and needed to be brought under control. Contemporary textbooks are less racist in their depictions and students are more likely to hear respectful descriptions of Aboriginal history and current issues such as poverty, but there is little critical discussion of impact of colonization in school curricula, leaving it open to an interpretation that poverty among Aboriginal people is their own fault. In addition, media coverage of land claims and financial settlements tends to pit the interests of Aboriginal people against the interests of Canada.

The persistence of racist attitudes can only make Aboriginal people hesitate to seek help from mainstream social service agencies. Aboriginal LGBTQ people may also hesitate to approach other potential sources of support, both mainstream and Aboriginal, because of the expectation of homophobia.

Discourses that stress restoration of traditions have proved valuable to community efforts to heal from the impacts of colonization, but these often exclude LGBTQ people. Justice (2010), writing about hostile American Indian community responses to same-sex desire and same-sex relationships, explains that such hostility is often grounded in false claims that homosexuality is contrary to tradition. According to Justice, traditionalist discourse reveals "a transparent fear of the perception of male effeminacy and, as a result, the fear that the Nation as a whole will be judged by other Native peoples to be diminished or degenerate if same-sex relationships are affirmed" (213–214). He also advocates using the Mississippian concept of anomaly as a way "to move beyond the trap of the 'traditional' in exclusivist and reactionary ideologies in Indian Country" (209). In Canada, Aboriginal communities across the country trying to help members recover from the impact of sexual abuse by residential school priests and nuns often invoke a traditionalist discourse in which survivors of residential schools and their descendents are encouraged to recover a healthy appreciation of the sacred sexual bond between man and woman. The Two Spirit movement which has attempted to intervene in traditionalist discourse by asserting the honored place of LGBTQ people in Aboriginal traditions, has been a very important source of strength for many LGBTQ Aboriginal individuals, but it has met with mixed reactions from Aboriginal communities, including the response that calling LGBTQ Aboriginals "Two Spirit" is an inappropriate use of a sacred concept (Meyer-Cook and Labelle, 2004). There have been successes as well, such as the feast hosted by Squamish First Nation in 2009 where trans Two Spirit people were formally danced into the community with an apology for past exclusion, and many reserves are described by their members as quite accepting of gender and sexuality diversity. However, homophobic or heteronormative healing discourses dominate in the home reserves and urban community organizations available to many Aboriginal LGBTQ people who are experiencing partner violence.

Andrea Smith (2005) describes the impact of discourses of Aboriginal tradition in mainstream agencies that offer in-service diversity training in the form of quick thirty-minute cultural competence workshops that rely on a simplified version of traditionalist teachings. If LGBTQ Indigenous people are not represented in these workshops, non-Aboriginal participants are left with a very heterosexualized view of Aboriginal culture. However, problems of exclusivist discourse tendencies are not unique to heteronormative spaces. LGBTQ Aboriginal people can encounter other examples in training that is officially "LGBTQ" but ignores the specific realities of trans people, in gay bars and LGBTQ community organizations that are open to everyone but more welcoming to non-Aboriginal clientele, and in LGBTQ activist groups that do not integrate a race critique into their political work (Lamble 2008).

What these add up to for Aboriginal LGBTQ people in Canada is a life lived in a kind of "perfect storm" of oppressive discourses that leaves individuals dealing with partner violence squeezed out of many parts of Canadian, Aboriginal, and LGBTQ society. Even within activist communities and progressive services, LGBTQ Indigenous people encounter vested interests in downplaying key aspects of their identities and key factors in the realities of their lives including LGBTQ activist discourses that whitewash racism, traditionalist Aboriginal healing discourses that pathologize homosexuality as source or outcome of sexual abuse and valorize traditional heterosexual gender roles, homonormative discourses in the LGBTQ community and in services that include "trans" in the acronym but often nowhere else, settler culture discourses that persist in seeing cultural genocide1 as an isolated error by well-intended authorities. LGBTQ Indigenous people are further marginalized in all of these "inclusive" encounters.

DISCUSSION

We have argued that understanding the realities of Aboriginal LGBTQ people's experiences of partner abuse and of racism and homophobia leads logically to a commitment to opposing state violence. Outsider researchers need to commit to understanding the discourses structuring our own consciousness if our commitment to understanding the realities of participants' lives is to move from the kind of old-style anthropology described by Smith, towards simple human response to others' distress. To do this, we need to become aware of our attachments to oppressive discourses. For example, John Lowman (2000) described how a "discourse of disposal" that had developed in media coverage of efforts to rid Vancouver residential areas of prostitution made people think of prostitutes as disposable and thus contributed to a sharp increase in murders of street prostitutes in

British Columbia after 1980. It seems possible that current media coverage of Aboriginal involvement in a wide range of issues from urban gangs to expensive land claims might be reproducing the colonial discourse of the "Indian problem" that made "killing the Indian in the child" seem sensible for a hundred years. It was a racist discourse that upheld Aboriginal people themselves were the problem that needed to be gotten rid of, rather than the social issues they were caught up in. The system of thought in which Aboriginal people are "the problem" exerts pressure on them through institutional practices such as police hostility and social practices such as widespread apparent indifference to their distress.

Whatever the specifics of mainstream Canadians' attitudes to Aboriginal people, few people seem to have taken to heart the discourse intervention attempted in the current slogan, "We are all treaty people" (Office of the Treaty Commissioner 2010). Realizing that we are all treaty people who are honor-bound to treat each other respectfully would require allies to examine our own conscience about Aboriginal people in order to understand how we became so tolerant of their suffering and so resistant to doing something about it. To do this we must work at understanding the discourses that structure our responses to realizing that their experiences of personal violence are historically and currently linked to and exacerbated by state violence.

Foucault made it clear that it is impossible to encounter each other in a pure discourse-free zone outside history (1972), but, given the difficulties of seeing through the fog of oppressive discourses that structure our misrecognitions of LGBTQ Aboriginal people, it is important for allies who hope to see what is actually happening in participants' lives to work at coming to the encounter with the least discursive interference possible. This work can be grounded in what the great Brazilian critical educator Paulo Freire (2007) called "conscientization": in this case, a process of soul-searching by IPV researchers to become conscious of the ways in which we are implicated in the oppression of LGBTQ Aboriginal people by virtue of our unexamined indoctrination into pessimistic views of Aboriginal people through white supremacist discourses in which Aboriginal people are "always, already" (to use Louis Althusser's [1971 p. 172] phrase) "the problem" and assimilation into mainstream society is the solution.

This seems so ethically obvious that we must ask, what makes it so hard for dominant culture researchers to move marginalized people, in their specificity, from the margins to the centre of our analysis? Further, why does well-intentioned attentiveness not always lead to the activist imperative in practice?

Conscientization is difficult not only because the oppressive logic of discourses seems like common sense, but because dominant discourses have built in logics that serve the interests of current power arrangements. Murdocca (2009) argues that Canada as a "nation remains fundamentally committed to an understanding of colonial history in which it is not guilty of wrongdoing and hence arrives at an official stance that suggests that the Canadian state is not responsible for the continued ramifications of colonialism" (23). To move beyond this impasse, Murdocca argues that we need to recognize "the ways in which histories of colonial violence, genocide and systemic racism, along with global and economic relations of labour and production, interweave with government policies in criminal justice at the local and national level" (41). In the present context, this would involve becoming aware of our own impulses to deflect our responsibilities in order to recognize how colonization is at work in LGBTQ Aboriginal people's experience of partner violence.

This situation is not unique to Canadian outsider researchers or to topics involving Aboriginal people. Morgensen (2010) argues that to ally with Indigenous feminists working towards the end of the heteropatriarchal nation-state, non-Native allies have to deconstruct their own attachments to oppressive settler discourses:

> Non-Natives who seek accountable alliance with Native people may align themselves with these stakes if they wish to commit to denaturalizing settler colonialism. . . . [T]heir more frequent effort to stabilize their identities follows less from a belief that settlement is natural than from a compulsion to foreclose the Pandora's box of contradictions they know will open by calling it into question. In U.S. queer politics, this includes the implications of my essay: queers will invoke and repeat the terrorizing histories of settler colonialism if these remain obscured behind normatively white and national desires for Native roots and settler citizenship. A first step for non-Native queers thus can be to examine critically and challenge how settler colonialism conditions their lives, as a step toward imagining new and decolonial sexual subjectivities, cultures, and politics. (123–124)

Specifically, we need to challenge mainstream settler discourses of white supremacy and gender normativity that continue to structure the experience of partner violence in the lives of LGBTQ Aboriginal people. In so doing, outsider researchers need to take our direction from LGBTQ Aboriginal people to avoid the mistakes of the past, not just have Indigenous people on our research teams or advisor groups:

> White queers challenging racism and colonialism can join queers of color to create new queer politics marked explicitly as non-Native, in that they will form by answering Native queer critiques. As part of that work, non-Native queers can study the colonial histories they differently yet mutually inherit, and can trouble the colonial institutions in which they have sought their freedom, as steps toward shifting non-Native queer. (Morgensen 2010: 124)

As Marie Battiste (2008) observes, "[m]ost academics are not lost to the fact that Indigenous peoples have been colonized and marginalized and suffer from the effects" (500). However, most academics have not fully integrated this knowledge into research practice. The extreme paucity of research on LGBTQ Aboriginal people's experiences of IPV to date is a sign that allies are needed, and the extreme levels of marginalization being endured by LGBTQ Aboriginal people experiencing partner violence should be understood as calling for direct opposition to all forms of state violence against them and the larger Aboriginal community. Everyone needs to contribute to the effort to take responsibility for the damage done by colonization— academics, researchers, service providers, and other members of dominant culture. As Smith (2005) says, instead of asking, "What should a domestic violence program look like," we need to ask "What would it take to end violence" against these people? (153). Part of the answer might be to work for large scale education about the residential school system and other programs of colonization and its social and family effects on Indigenous people in order to counter lingering colonization discourses of Aboriginal disposability. This link has to be made evident not only to providers and responders who want to be "culturally competent" but also to a Canadian public who need to get serious about demanding an end to continuing genocidal injustices committed in our names.

A CALL TO ACTION

Fieland, Walters and Simoni (2007) explain that the one universal in Indigenous LGBTQ people's lives may well be the experience of colonization. It therefore remains imperative that we keep our efforts at responding to relationship violence aligned with the broader struggles against oppressive discourses that sustain and rationalize state violence in its many forms. In advocating for an emphasis on social transformation, we are at the same time arguing for continued attention to the specifics of IPV in people's lives. In the case of Indigenous LGBTQ people experiencing violence, we are persuaded that attentiveness to specific contexts of violence coupled with conscientization leads logically to the conclusion that researchers who see our work as opposing personal violence need to actively oppose state violence through our research and in our public lives. As allies, we need to continue to think critically, consciously and reflexively about how to engage in transformative work that centers the experiences of marginalized people, recognizes the implication of state violence in personal violence, and integrates both these principles into our research, service, and community actions.

NOTES

1. The United Nations (2010a) Convention on the Prevention and Punishment of the Crime of Genocide was drafted soon after the Nazi genocide of World War II and entered into force in 1951. Article 2(e) of the Convention defines genocide to include "forcibly transferring children of the group to another

group." Although the United States did not ratify the convention until 1988, Canada was an early ratifier in 1952 (United Nations 2010b), while Aboriginal children were still being forcibly transferred to white Canadians through the residential school system. The convention was thus technically in force in Canada when the residential school system was replaced by the "Sixties Scoop." The UN Declaration of Indigenous Rights that denounces "the removal of Indigenous children from their families and communities under any pretext" was not adopted until 2007, and has yet to be endorsed by two countries: Canada and the United States (United Nations 2007).

REFERENCES

Althusser, L. 1971. Ideology and ideological state apparatuses: Notes toward an investigation. In *Lenin and philosophy and other essays*, ed. Louis Althusser. London: New Left Books.

Amnesty International. 2009. *No more stolen sisters: The need for a comprehensive response to discrimination and violence against indigenous women in Canada*. London: Amnesty International. Available at: www.amnesty.ca/amnestynews/upload/AMR200122009.pdf [accessed December 10, 2010].

Armitage, A. 1995. *Comparing the policy of Aboriginal assimilation: Australia, Canada, and New Zealand*. Vancouver: University of British Columbia Press.

Balsam, K. F., B. U. Huang, Karen C. Fieland, Jane M. Simoni and Karina L. Walters. 2004. Culture, trauma, and wellness: A comparison of heterosexual and lesbian, gay, bisexual, and two-spirit Native Americans. *Cultural Diversity & Ethnic Minority Psychology* 10: 287–301.

Bamforth, D. 1994. Indigenous people, Indigenous violence: Pre-contact warfare on the North American great plains. *Man, New Series* 29(1): 95–115.

Battiste, M. 2008. Research ethics for protecting Indigenous knowledge and heritage: Institutional and researcher responsibilities. In *Handbook of critical and Indigenous methodologies*, ed. Norman K. Denzin, Yvonna S. Lincoln and Linda Tuhiwai Smith, 487–500. Thousand Oaks CA: Sage.

Bridges, D. 2001. The ethics of outsider research. *Journal of Philosophy of Education* 35(3): 371–86.

Buti, A. 2002. The removal of Aboriginal children: Canada and Australia compared. *University of Western Sydney Law Review* 2: 26–38. Available at: http://www.austlii.edu.au/au/journals/UWSLRev/2002/2.html [accessed December 10, 2010].

Canadian Constitution Act. 1982. Available at: http://laws.justice.gc.ca/en/const/Const_index.html [accessed December 10, 2010].

Castellano, M. 2004. Ethics of Aboriginal research. *Journal of Aboriginal Health* 1(1): 98–114.

Denzin, N. K. and Y. S. Lincoln. 2008. Introduction: Critical methodologies and indigenous inquiry. In *Handbook of critical and indigenous methodologies*, ed. N. K. Denzin, Y. S. Lincoln and L. Tuhiwai Smith, 1–19. Los Angeles, CA: Sage.

Dickason, O. P. 2006. *A concise history of Canada's First Nations*. Toronto: Oxford.

Fieland, K. C., K. L. Walters and J. M. Simoni. 2007. Determinants of health among Two-Spirit American Indians and Alaska Natives. In *The health of sexual minorities: Public health perspectives on lesbian, gay, bisexual and transgender populations*, ed. Ilan H. Meyer and M. E. Northridge, 268–300. New York: Springer.

First Nations Centre. 2007. OCAP: Ownership, control, access and possession. Sanctioned by the First Nations Information Governance Committee, Assembly of First Nations. Ottawa: National Aboriginal Health Organization.

Fone, B. 2000. *Homophobia: A history.* New York: St. Martin's Press.

Foucault, M. 1972. *The archaeology of knowledge and the discourse on language.* Trans. A. M. Sheridan-Smith. New York: Pantheon.

Francis, D. 1997. *National dreams: Myth, memory and Canadian history.* Vancouver: Pulp Press.

Freire, P. 2007. *Pedagogy of the oppressed.* New York: Continuum.

Goffman, E. 1961. *Asylums: Essays on the social situation of mental patients and other inmates.* New York: Doubleday.

Guimond, E. 2003. Fuzzy definitions and population explosion: Changing identities of Aboriginal groups in Canada. In *Not strangers in these parts, urban Aboriginal peoples,* ed. D. Newhouse and E. Peters, 35–49. Available at: Government of Canada Policy Research Initiative ISBN 0–662–67604–1. http://policyresearch.gc.ca/doclib/AboriginalBook_e.pdf [accessed October 1, 2007].

Justice, Daniel Heath (Cherokee Nation). 2010. Notes toward a theory of anomaly. *GLQ: A Journal of Lesbian and Gay Studies* 16(1/2): 207–242.

Kirmayer, L., C. Simpson and M. Cargo. 2003. Healing traditions: Culture, community and mental health promotion with Canadian Aboriginal peoples. *Australasian Psychiatry* 11(Supplement): 15–23.

Kovach, M. 2005. Emerging from the margins: Indigenous methodologies. In *Research as resistance: Critical, Indigenous, and anti-oppressive approaches,* ed. L. Brown and S. Strega, 19–36. Toronto: Canadian Scholars' Press.

Lamble, S. 2008. Retelling racialized violence, remaking white innocence: The politics of interlocking oppressions in Transgender Day of Remembrance. *Sexuality Research & Social Policy* 5(1): 24–42.

Lang, S. 1998. *Men as women, women as men: Changing gender in Native American cultures.* Trans. John L. Vantine. Austin: University of Texas Press.

Lehavot, K., K. Walters and J. Simoni. 2009. Abuse, mastery, and health among lesbian, bisexual, and two-spirit American Indian and Alaska Native women. *Cultural Diversity & Ethnic Minority Psychology* 15(3): 275–284.

Lowman, J. 2000. Violence and the outlaw status of (street) prostitution in Canada. *Violence Against Women* 6(9): 987–1011.

McGillivray, A. and B. Comaskey. 1999. *Black eyes all of the time: Intimate violence, Aboriginal women, and the justice system.* Toronto: University of Toronto Press.

Meyer-Cook, F. and D. Labelle. 2004. Namaji: Two-Spirit organizing in Montreal, Canada. *Journal of Gay and Lesbian Social Services* 16–(1): 29–51.

Milloy, J. 1999. *A national crime: The Canadian government and the residential school system.* Winnipeg: University of Manitoba Press.

Morgensen, S. L. 2010. Settler homonationalism: Theorizing settler colonialism within queer modernities. *GLQ: A Journal of Lesbian and Gay Studies* 16(1/2): 105–131.

Morris, J. and K. Balsam. 2003. Lesbian and bisexual women's experiences of victimization: Mental health, revictimization, and sexual identity development. *Journal of Lesbian Studies* 7(4): 67–85.

Murdocca, Carmela. 2009. From incarceration to restoration: National responsibility, gender and the production of cultural difference. *Social & Legal Studies* 18(1): 23–45.

Napoleon, V. 2002. Raven's garden: A discussion about Aboriginal sexual orientation and transgender issues. *Canadian Journal of Law and Society* 17(2): 149–171.

O'Brien-Teengs, D. and R. Travers. 2006. "River of life, rapids of change": Understanding HIV vulnerability among Two-Spirit youth who migrate to Toronto. *Canadian Aboriginal Journal of Community-based HIV/AIDS* Research 1(Summer): 17–28.

Office of the Treaty Commissioner. 2010. We are all treaty people. Available at: http://www.otc.ca/ABOUT_TREATIES/We_Are_All_Treaty_People/ [accessed December 10, 2010].

Ristock, J. L., and N. Timbang. 2005. Relationship violence in lesbian/gay/bisexual/transgender/queer [LGBTQ] communities: Moving beyond a gender-based framework. Minnesota Centre against Violence and Abuse: Violence against Women Online Resources. Available at: http://www.mincava.umn.edu/documents/lgbtqviolence/lgbtqviolence.html [[accessed June 20, 2010].

Ristock, J., A. Zoccole and L. Passante. 2010. Aboriginal Two Spirit and LGBTQ migration, mobility, and health research project. Final report. Unpublished.

Roscoe, W. 1988. *Living the spirit: A gay American Indian anthology.* New York: St. Martin's Press.

Russo, A. and M. Spatz. 2007. *Communities engaged in resisting violence.* Chicago: Women and Girls Collective Action Network. Available at: www.womenandgirlscan.org/communities_engaged.pdf [accessed April 20, 2010]

Schnarch, B. 2004. Ownership, Control, Access, and Possession (OCAP) or self-determination applied to research: A critical analysis of contemporary First Nations research and some options for First Nations Communities. *Journal of Aboriginal Health* 1(1): 80–95.

Simon, R., M. Di Paolantonio, and M. Clamen. 2005. Remembrance as praxis and the ethics of the inter-human. In *The touch of the past: Remembrance, learning and ethics,* ed. Roger Simon, 132–155. New York: Palgrave Macmillan.

Sinclair, M., and A. C. Hamilton. 1991. *The ustice system and Aboriginal people: Report of the Aboriginal justice enquiry of Manitoba,* Vol. 1. Winnipeg MB Canada: Queen's Printer. Available at: http://www.ajic.mb.ca/volume.html [accessed December 20, 2010].

Smith, A. 2005. Anticolonial responses to domestic violence. In *Conquest: Sexual violence and American Indian genocide,* 137–175. Cambridge, MA: South End Press.

Statistics Canada. 2006. Measuring violence against women: Statistical trends 2006. Prepared by H. Johnson. Ottawa: Statistics Canada. Available at: http://www.statcan.ca/english/research/85–570-XIE/85–570-XIE2006001.pdf [accessed December 10, 2010].

Statistics Canada. 2009. 2006 Census: Aboriginal Peoples in Canada in 2006: Inuit, Métis and First Nations. 2006 Census: Findings. Available at: http://www12.statcan.gc.ca/census-recensement/2006/as-sa/97–558/p1-eng.cfm [accessed December 10, 2010].

Taylor, C. 2006b. *Nowhere near enough: A needs assessment of health and safety services for transgender and Two Spirit people in Manitoba and Northwestern Ontario.* Final Report to the Crime Prevention Branch of Public Safety and Emergency Preparedness Canada, 2006.

Taylor, C. 2009. Health needs of Aboriginal transgender/Two Spirit people in Manitoba. *Canadian Aboriginal Journal of Community-based HIV/AIDS Research* 2(Winter): 65–84. Available at: http://www.caan.ca/english/grfx/resources/publications/Winter%202009%20-%20EN.pdf [accessed December 10, 2010].

United Nations. 2007. United Nations Declaration on the Rights of Indigenous Peoples. UN Permanent Forum on Indigenous Issues. United Nations. Available at: http://www.un.org/esa/socdev/unpfii/en/drip.html [accessed]. Available at: http://www.un.org/esa/socdev/unpfii/en/declaration.html [accessed December 10, 2010].

United Nations. 2010a. Convention on the Prevention and Punishment of the Crime of Genocide [text]. Human Rights Web. Available at: http://www.hrweb.org/legal/genocide.html [accessed December 10, 2010].

United Nations. 2010b. Convention on the Prevention and Punishment of the Crime of Genocide [Signatories and objectors]. Chapter IV, Human Rights. Multilaterial Treaties Deposited with the Secretary General. Paris, November 9, 1948. United Nations Treaty Collection. Available at: http://treaties.un.org/Pages/ViewDetails.aspx?src=UNTSONLINE&tabid=2&mtdsg_no=IV-1-&chapter=4&lang=en#Participants [accessed December 10, 2010].

Urban Native Youth Association. 2004. Two-Spirit youth speak out! Analysis of the needs assessment tool. Vancouver. Available at: www.unya.bc.ca [accessed December 10, 2010].

Wahab, S. and L. Olson. 2004. Intimate partner violence and sexual assault in Native American communities. *Trauma, Violence, & Abuse* 5(4): 353–366.

Walters, K. L., T. Evans-Campbell, J. M. Simoni, T. Ronquillo and R. Bhuyan. 2006. "My spirit in my heart": Identity experiences and challenges among American Indian Two-Spirit women. *Journal of Lesbian Studies* 10(1/2): 125–149.

Wilson, A. 1996. *How we find ourselves: Identity development and Two-Spirit people. Harvard Educational Review* 66(2): 303–317.

Wilson, S. 2008. Research is ceremony: Indigenous research methods. Winnipeg, MB: Fernwood Publishing.

Contributors

Janice L. Ristock is Associate Vice-President (Research) and Professor of Women's and Gender Studies at the University of Manitoba. Her research interests include violence in LGBTQ relationships, feminist community-based research, health, and mental health issues facing gender and sexual minorities. She received a book award for *No More Secrets: Violence in Lesbian Relationships* from Division 44 (Society for the Psychological Study of Lesbian, Gay, and Bisexual issues) of the American Psychological Association for making a distinguished contribution to LGBT psychology.

Nicola Brown is the Program Coordinator for the Research and Training division of Pride & Prejudice at the Central Toronto Youth Services in Canada. Her dissertation examined the topic of sexual-minority women partners of female-to-male transsexuals.

Douglas A. Brownridge is Professor in the Department of Family Sciences, Faculty of Human Ecology at the University of Manitoba. He has published over thirty refereed journal articles in some of the most prestigious journals in the field of family violence namely, *the Journal of Interpersonal Violence, Violence Against Women, Violence and Victims, and the Journal of Family Violence.*

Kierrynn Davis is Senior Lecturer in the School of Health and Human Sciences at Southern Cross University, Australia. Her main research interests are violence against women and children survivng relatonship trauma. Her co-authored articles have been published in several journals.

Diane R. Dolan-Soto is the Director of Clinical Programs at the New York City Gay and Lesbian Anti-Violence Project. She is a clinical therapist who has worked in the area of trauma and crisis intervention for over ten years. She specializes in work with victims/survivors of domestic violence, rape, and incest. She is recognized in direct service circles as being a prolific speaker and trainer both locally and nationally on the unique aspects of lesbian, gay, transgender, and bisexual domestic violence and trauma related issues.

Catherine Donovan is Senior Lecturer in Sociology in the School of Health, Natural and Social Sciences at the University of Sunderland. Her research interests are in the sociology of the family, gender, and sexuality; and the sociology of health and assisted conception techniques, particularly in so far as they facilitate the creation of new kinds of families. She is the co-author (with J. Weeks and B. Heaphy) of *Same Sex Intimacies. Families of Choice and Other Life Experiments,* London: Routledge. 2001.

Kate Duffy is a solicitor at the Inner City Legal Centre and is the Chairperson for the Same Sex Domestic Violence Interagency in Sydney, Australia.

Patricia Durish was the Co-coordinator of the David Kelley Same-Sex Partner Abuse Project for the LGBTQ community in Toronto, Canada. Dr. Durish is also a sessional instructor and research associate at the University of Toronto.

Nel Glass is a Research Professor of Nursing at Australian Catholic University, Melborne, Australia. Her main research interests are healing, hope, resilience, optimism and her research findings have been disseminated in books, journals and art exhibits.

Joshua Mira Goldberg has been involved with anti-violence work as a client of anti-violence services, a street outreach worker, a war tax resister, a prison justice advocate, and a supporter of Indigenous people protecting their communities from colonial violence. Joshua was the Coordinator of Vancouver Coastal Health's Transgender Health Program. Joshua is the author of numerous publications relating to transgender issues and has been invited to speak at several universities and colleges about transgender health issues.

Marianne Hester is Professor of Gender, Violence and International Policy, in the School for Policy Studies at the University of Bristol. She is the author of over seventy publications in the field of family violence including the recent co-authored book with Lorraine Radford, *Mothering Through Domestic Violence*, London, UK: Jessica Kingsley Press. 2006.

Diane Hiebert-Murphy is Associate Professor in the Faculty of Social Work at the University of Manitoba. She is also the Director of the Couples Project, a therapy program that works with couples who have experienced abuse in their relationships and who now wish to work toward an abuse-free relationship.

Cindy Holmes is a doctoral candidate and SSHRC Doctoral Fellow in Interdisciplinary Studies (Women's Studies, Sociology, Human Geography) at the University of British Columbia. Her research draws on critical race, feminist, queer, and spatial analyses to theorize the links between different forms of violence, with a focus on queer anti-violence discourses in Canada. She teaches in the Department of Sociology and Anthropology at Simon Fraser University. Alongside her academic work, she has worked with community groups for over twenty years in the areas of anti-violence, health and anti-oppression education, and organizing.

Maurice Kwong-Lai Poon is Assistant Professor in the School of Social Work at York University in Canada, and Chair of the advisory research committee at Asian Community AIDS Services. His work has appeared in *The Canadian Journal of Human Sexuality*, *Ethnicity & Health*, *Journal of Gay & Lesbian Social Services*, *Sexuality & Culture*, and *Sexualities*.

Keren Lehavot is a Doctoral Candidate in Clinical Psychology at the University of Washington, Seattle. Her CDC-funded research concerns extension of Meyer's minority stress model to the physical and mental health of sexual minority women. She has received a host of awards and honors, including the prestigious Student Ethics Award from the APA Office on Ethics and an international fellowship to study the experiences of Indigenous people at the University of Auckland in New Zealand.

Jesmen Mendoza recently completed his dissertation in Counseling Psychology at the University of Toronto on the topic of explanatory factors for gay men's relationship violence. He is currently a counselor at the David Kelley Services Partner Assault Response Program in Toronto, Canada.

David W. Pantalone is a Clinical Psychologist and Assistant Professor of Psychology at Suffolk University in Boston, MA. His clinical and research interests include HIV/AIDS prevention and treatment, interpersonal violence, substance use, LGBT health, and the dissemination of evidence-based psychological treatments. He completed his doctoral training at the University of Washington where he conducted the NIMH-funded, mixed-methods study from which the data for this chapter were drawn.

Jane M. Simoni is Professor of Psychology and Women's Studies at the University of Washington, Seattle. A clinical health psychologist by training, Dr. Simoni has been continuously funded for more than ten years by NIMH on projects related to the health behaviors of people living with HIV/AIDS, and has emerged as an international expert in interventions to increase medication adherence in this population domestically as well as on the U.S.–Mexico border and in China.

Carrol Smith is a Clinical Assistant Professor in the College of Nursing at the University of Illinois and Chicago. Her primary areas of interest are women's health, lesbian health, and lesbian intimate partner violence. She recently received funding from the Lesbian Health fund to develop a prevention program for lesbian abusers.

Catherine G. Taylor is Associate Professor cross-appointed to the Faculty of Education and the Department of Rhetoric, Writing, and Communications at the University of Winnipeg in Canada. Her recent work on research ethics, LGBTQ wellbeing and LGBTQ-inclusive education, and confrontations between LGBTQ and heteronormative discourses has been published widely in scholarly books and in journals such as *Canadian Aboriginal Journal of Community-based HIV/AIDS Research, Feminism and Psychology, Journal of Gay and Lesbian Social Services,* and *Journal of LGBT Youth.* Dr. Taylor is P.I. in partnership with Egale Canada for the First National Climate Survey of Homophobia and Transphobia in Canadian Schools.

Karina L. Walters is Professor in the School of Social Work at William P. and Ruth Gerberding University, and founding Director of the Indigenous Wellness Research Institute at the University of Washington. Dr. Walters has been the recipient of a Senior Fulbright Scholarship to New Zealand as well as numerous grants from NIH. She is a world-renowned scholar on American Indian and Alaskan Native health, HIV prevention, mental health, and substance abuse.

Caroline White is Acting Program Director for the Child, Family & Community Safety Division Justice Institute, British Columbia, Canada. She is a trans ally who in 1994 initiated trans-related policy and training at the sexual assault centre where she worked. Since then, she has worked with trans, anti-violence and other organizations to produce policy, educational materials, and curriculum, as well as to deliver trans-specific anti-violence training. Caroline is also a member of several LGBT anti-violence education and training initiatives.

Index

Page numbers followed by 'n' refer to notes.

A

Aboriginal LGBTQ people living with partner violence 301–18; background to 304; in Canadian context 304; discourses of colonization and homophobia 306, 310–12; in history textbooks 311; homophobia within communities of 306, 308, 309, 311–12; inclusion strategies in anti-violence workshops 218, 220; IPV in lives of 246, 248, 307–10; mandatory boarding-school system 304, 305, 306, 309, 310, 311; and researchers' ethics of solidarity to challenge state violence 312–16; spousal homicide rates 307; state violence in lives of 305–6, 310–11; terminology 303–4; and traditional honored position for LGBTQ people 311

Abuse Assessment Screen (AAS) 185–6

abusers: see perpetrators of abuse

ACON 259, 262, 266, 269–70; anti-violence project SSDV officer 271

activism: anti-violence 56–7, 61, 63–4, 209, 211; trans 57, 58, 155

addictive behaviors 107, 114, 136

age as a risk factor for IPV 38, 40, 149, 265

Ahmed, S. 219, 226

AIDS: see HIV/AIDS

alcohol: to cope with stress 184, 196, 197; use in adolescence 136, 145, 148, 196; and violence 41, 169; see also substance abuse

Alexander, C. 112

anger management 116, 120, 141

Another Closet 259, 264

anti-oppression: feminist philosophy of 215–18; masking other motivations 219, 220; service-provider training 287; training in justice system 164

anti-oppressive research: see Aboriginal LGBTQ people living with partner violence

anti-racism 72, 216, 219; black feminists critique of 'add on' responses regarding women of colour 132, 216, 218–19, 220, 242–3, 303

anti-violence activism 56–7, 61, 63–4, 209

anti-violence education: alliance with neo-liberalism 211–12; conflation of gender and sexual orientation in LGBT 217; feminist approach to 56–7, 61, 63–4, 209; focus on LGBT 'healthy relationships' 211; see also anti-violence education, trans; Safe Choices Support and Education Program, Canada

anti-violence education, trans: LGBT vs. trans-specific approaches in 65; limitations of conventional frameworks, practices and tools 61–7; personal context 59–61; political context 57–9; problems of conventional gender in trans anti-violence work 61–5, 70; problems with a trans-specific approach 67–9; recommendations for 70–2; regional context

328 *Index*

David Kelley Services – Same Sex
Partner Abuse (DKS-SSPA)
Project 232–57; in context of
homophobia 246–8; dealing
with difference 243–6; differences in experience between
victims of same sex and heterosexual IPV 237–43; funding
234, 252; incidence of abuse in
LGBTQ relationships 235–7;
methodology 235; pamphlets
245; recommendations 250–2;
responding to LGBTQ-IPV
248–9; similarities in experience
between victims of same sex and
heterosexual IPV 237; surveys
235, 236, 240, 242, 243, 244,
247; terminology 233
Davis. K. 14, 20, 25, 26
de Vidas, M. 110
Denzin, N.K. 132, 133, 148, 301
depression: in abusers 119, 135, 141–2,
191, 192, 193, 194; in HIV-
positive men 184; as a result
of childhood abuse 141–2,
194; and risk of PV 184, 203;
substance abuse to alleviate 196;
treatment for 203; of victims 51,
107, 109, 208
Diagnostic Manual for Mental Disorders (DSM) 117
disability 48, 51–2
'disclosing intimacy' 84, 85, 93
discourse: biologically based 161–2,
163–4; of colonization and
homophobia in Canada 306,
310–12; of community connection 224–5; of disposal 312–13;
feminist 29–30, 31–2, 216;
health promotion and psychology 220–4; heteronormative
domestic violence 5, 16–18,
211; of minority stress 160–1;
need to challenge oppressive
discourses towards Aboriginal
people 312–16; of neo-liberalism
211–12; perpetrators' responsibility 120–1; structuring knowledge through 102–3, 122–3; of
victimization 164; of victims and
perpetrators in gay male partner
abuse 118–22; of whiteness 219
discrimination: a barrier to seeking help
156, 261; a factor of minority

stress 170–1, 175, 177, 178,
179; from police and legal
system 139, 155, 246, 261; as
reported in Statistics Canada
survey 1; Same Sex Partner
Abuse (DKS-SSPA) Project and
efforts to address 245
Dixon, C. 111
Dolan-Soto, D. 104, 108, 109, 114,
275, 299n
domestic violence: court records of 267;
critique of feminist approach to
82–3, 96; drug use and 268–9;
gendered patterns of experience
87–9; heteronormative discourse
of 16–18, 211; neo-liberal
responses to 221, 223; and
resistance to police help for 25;
Statistics Canada survey report
on 1–2; terminology 4–5, 15;
U.S. National Violence Against
Women Survey 2; see also
emotion work in domestically
abusive relationships
Domestic Violence in Gay and Lesbian
Relationships 15
Donovan, C. 3, 85, 88, 92, 93, 98
Douglas, E.M. 83, 147, 173, 174
drug use: in perpetrators of domestic
violence 268–9; in sexual minority men with HIV 191, 195, 196,
197, 198, 199, 200; see also
substance abuse
Duluth Model 16–17, 26, 276–7, 283,
284, 286, 292
Dunbar, H. 122
Duncombe, J. 85, 86, 88, 91

E
Easy, S. 268
Eaton, L.M. 13, 15, 18, 20, 39
education: see anti-violence education;
anti-violence education, trans
Elliott, P. 17, 82, 98, 110
emotion work in domestically abusive
relationships 81–101; appeals
to sympathy and/or loyalty
94–5; declarations of love
91–3; emotional disclosures
93–6; exploiting vulnerabilities
95–6; and gendered approach
to love 85–6, 97, 99; love and
intimacy 83–7; methodology
for research on 87–9; and

poverty 22–3, 46, 47–8, 49; of sexuality 42, 45, 219, 303; in studies of violent intimate lesbian relationships 26–33, 142–50; in a study of non-intimate lesbian violence 22–6; and understanding women's risk for abuse 41–3, 47–52, 53–4; in women's identities 219–20

interviews: in Australian case study of lesbian partner violence 21; in exploring emotion work in domestically abusive relationships 87; for study of partner violence in sexual minority men with HIV 186; in study of women who abuse their female intimate partners 133–4

Island, D. 81, 82, 98, 102, 104, 106, 107, 108, 109, 110, 113, 114, 116–17, 131, 239

J

Jamieson, L. 84, 85, 86
jealousy 114, 139, 265
John, L. 116

K

Kalpagam, U. 116
Kaminsky, N. 116
Kavanagh v. Attorney General of Canada 2001 164
Kiely, E. 215, 223, 224
Klinger, R. 109, 110, 114
knowledge structuring through discourse 102–3, 122–3
Koyama, E. 58, 68, 72
Krippendorf, K. 186, 187

L

Lamb, S. 115–16, 117, 118, 121, 122
Lancombe, D. 18, 19
Lang, S. 306
Laughlin, L. 105, 107, 108, 113, 114, 119
learned helplessness 108–9, 115–16
Lee, S. 211, 238
legal assistance scheme 271–2
lesbian abusers of female intimate partners study 131–52; adult intimate relationships 137–40, 144–5; alcohol and drugs use 32, 139, 140, 141, 142, 145–6, 148, 149, 309; coming out 137,

144, 147–8; findings 135–42; forms of abuse 138, 145; future research 149; intersectionality in 142–50; lives after the abuse 140–2, 146; methodology 132–3; preventative programs for 149–50; reasons for abuse 139–40; research design 133–4; sociodemographics of participants 134–5; troubled childhoods 135–6, 141, 143–4

Lesbian Partner Abuse Scale 39

lesbians: anti-violence education program see Safe Choices Support and Education Program, Canada'bar culture' 140; ' batterers' challenging myth of women's non-violence 239; black 42–3, 87, 132, 137, 147–8, 180; butch/femme dyad 97, 132, 239, 240; community responses to talk of violence among 24–5, 27, 28–9, 33, 98; emotion work in domestically abusive relationships 89–90, 91–2, 94, 95; and experiences in RRR areas 266–7; first relationships vulnerability 40, 158; heteronormative discourses of IPV to explain 16–18; heterosexual community views on 148; internalized homophobia 17, 28, 83, 98, 138; intersectionality and women's experiences of IPV 19–21, 22–6, 26–33, 40, 41–3, 47–52, 142–50; as pioneers of pure relationships of confluent love 84; power and control dynamics in abusive relationships 20, 22–3, 26, 28–9, 32–3; prevalence of intimate partner violence among 2, 15–16, 268; problems accessing abuse support groups for 211; social oppression of 17–18, 42, 142, 148; Speak Out Against Relationship Abuse (SOAR) 259, 272; support from non-lesbian friends 29; terminology of violence among 15; violent intimate lesbian relationship study 26–33, 142–50; violent non-intimate lesbian relationship study 22–6; see

marginalized communities 164;
emotional disclosures 96, 98;
fighting back 23–4, 28, 242,
288–9; and focus on individual
pathology 115–17; gendered
patterns of experience 87–8;
heterosexual male 131; homophobia reinforcing social isolation of
83, 98, 247; innocence 105–6;
learned helplessness 108–9,
115–16; leaving relationships
a catalyst for further abuse 92;
low self-esteem 107–8; loyalty
to abuser 94–5; moving on from
victimization 122; vs. perpetrators of abuse 118–22; personality
characteristics 106–7; portrayals
of, in violent gay relationships
105–9; as responsible for abuse
106; and revictimization 202; Statistics Canada survey 1–2; trans
people as 154–7, 160; vulnerabilities exploited by abusers 95–6
violence: blurring of private and public
forms in marginalized communities 239, 247, 309; community
191; as learned behavior 110,
115; as normative or acceptable 191, 201, 203, 309; state
violence in lives of Aboriginal
people 305–6, 310–11

violence against women 3, 17, 52, 61,
118, 121–2, 303; dominant
discourse of 4, 13, 56, 60, 182;
neo-liberal approach to 212,
223
Violence Against Women Survey
(VAWS) 43

W
Wahab, S. 302, 304
Walber, E. 104, 105–6, 113
Walker, G. 116, 119
Walker, L. 108, 109, 119
Walsh, F. 106, 108, 112, 113, 236,
239
Walters, K.L. 184, 188, 198, 199, 200,
203, 303, 307, 315
web-based research questionnaires
172–3
Weeks, J. 85, 88, 97
Wellford, C. 115
When It's Time to Leave Your Lover
116
White, C. 60, 61, 217
whiteness 124, 213, 218–19, 223
Wolfe, V. 83, 102, 106, 261
Woman Abuse Council of Toronto
(WACT) 282, 283, 284,
291
Women/Trans Dialogue Planning Com-
mittee (W/TDPC) 59